TOURISM MANAGEMENT

TOURISM MANAGEMENT

Managing for change

Stephen J. Page

AMSTERDAM BOSTON HEIDELBERG LONDON NEW YORK OXFORD
PARIS SAN DIEGO SAN FRANCISCO SINGAPORE SYDNEY TOKYO

Butterworth-Heinemann
An imprint of Elsevier
Linacre House, Jordan Hill, Oxford OX2 8DP
200 Wheeler Road, Burlington MA 01803

First published 2003

British Library Cataloguing in Publication Data
A catalogue record for this book is available from the British Library

Library of Congress Cataloguing in Publication Data
A catalogue record for this book is available from the Library of Congress

ISBN 0 7506 5752 9

For information on all Butterworth-Heinemann publications, visit our
website at www.bh.com

Composition by Genesis Typesetting, Rochester, Kent
Printed and bound in Italy

Contents

Figures

Plates

Tables

Preface

This book is written as a simple, plain language introduction to tourism and assumes no prior knowledge of what tourism is and how it affects our everyday lives. To read it, you need to ask one question: why is there so much interest in tourism? If you are inquisitive about tourism and how it has developed as a business, then read on. This is a book that looks at what the tourism industry is and does, and why it is such an important global business. In simple terms, it shows how it is organized, run and managed – and how our desire to take holidays and use our leisure time creates an industry that is expanding and is sometimes seen as being out of control. This book does not pull any punches: it is not full of jargon, buzzwords and academic goobledegook – there are far too many books like that which fail to convey the excitement that tourism engenders: it tells a story chapter by chapter about how tourism has developed, what tourism is, and how specialist businesses meet the insatiable demand for holidays and travel. Where terminology *is* used, it is explained in lay terms for the general reader. The book offers many insights into a fascinating business that is changing so fast that even commentators find it hard to keep abreast of it.

The book takes a global look at what tourism is, with examples from various countries and places, and asks: *If tourism is so important to our economies and society, what can we do to manage it? Whose responsibility is it? Is it too late to control it?* Such questions can only be answered after explaining how the tourism industry exists as a large unwieldy set of interests that are united by one key principle: making money from the visitor and their pursuit of pleasure or travel. The book is comprehensive in the way it treats the different elements of the tourism sector, and questions what the challenges of managing tourism are.

This will be essential reading for anyone interested in tourism – even just as tourists – to understand how the business works, how it makes profits, and the effects of its activities on destinations. The book examines all the key trends now affecting the tourism industry, from the impact of technology to the way in which low-cost airlines have transformed the market for leisure travel.

We are all living in an age of major social and economic transformation, and tourism is part of that transformation. Reading this book will at least help you to understand what is driving these changes in tourism, and what is likely to stimulate future changes. For the tourism manager, the book will undoubtedly spell out a few home truths. For the general reader, it will show how difficult it actually is to be a manager in tourism, and the problems that we the travelling public – *the tourists* – actually pose for businesses, both as an opportunity and as a challenge.

I hope you enjoy reading this book – it is certainly not the largest book ever written on tourism, but it provides a clear and frank assessment that is easy to follow and above all shows how everything fits together – since tourism is not a simple business, all about holidays – or is it? Why not read on and find out?! Happy reading.

Stephen J. Page is Scottish Enterprise Forth Valley Professor of Tourism at the University of Stirling, Scotland, UK

Acknowledgements

A number of people have helped with this book in one way or another. They include Neil McLaren, Sheila Sim, Sharon Martin and the staff in Marketing at the University of Stirling. A number of organizations and individuals have granted copyright permission to use illustrations, plates and tables. For permission to reproduce figures, Elsevier for 2.1, 2.2 and 9.5; Taylor and Francis for 3.1 and 9.3; John Wiley and Sons for 3.4; Mintel for 5.4; Boeing Commercial Airplane Group for 6.2 and 6.3; Eric Laws for 8.4; Jo Connell for 9.5 and the Scottish Executive for 11.3. For Plate 6.1, permission was kindly granted by South West Airlines. For permission to reproduce tables, the following consented to the reproduction of: 4.1 and 12.5 Elsevier; 5.1 SUSTRANS; 5.3 and 7.2 MINTEL; 6.2 Prentice Hall; 8.7 Eric Laws; 8.3, 8.4 and 8.5 the Civil Aviation Authority, UK; 9.6 Jo Connell; 12.2, 12.3 and 12.4 The Stationery Office, Norwich.

I am grateful for the encouragement of Sally North at Butterworth-Heinemann, who commissioned this book, and for her interest in developing something that is more accessible to the wide range of readers.

A number of people have kindly provided material, advice or direct input or data for the book including: James Fraser, CEO, Argyll, the Islands, Loch Lomond, Stirling and the Trossachs Area Tourist Board; Brian Hay, Visit Scotland; Julie Franchetti, Scottish Enterprise; Michael Hall, University of Otago, New Zealand; Craig Jones, Visitor Solutions, New Zealand; Bill Kerr, Scotland; Eric Laws; and Holly Bennett for sorting out the remaining copyright permissions and general help at the manuscript stage. Thanks also to Linda Walker for preparing the index. If an unknowing use of copyright material has been made please contact the author via the publisher, as every effort was made to trace the owners of material.

Last but not least, Jo and Rosie made a big difference – especially with all the hours of fun and enjoyment when not writing. No book would be complete without a mention of someone special who always encouraged me in writing – my mum, whose memory will always be with me. This book is dedicated to her memory.

Chapter **1**

Tourism today: why is it a global phenomenon?

Learning objectives

This chapter provides an overview of tourism as a subject of study. After reading it you should be able to understand:

- why tourism has emerged as a major leisure activity;
- how tourism can be defined as a human activity;
- how to distinguish between domestic and international tourism;
- why tourism has to be measured, and the importance of tourism statistics;
- the scale and importance of tourism at a global scale, and some of the reasons for its growth;
- why tourism is a difficult activity to manage.

Introduction

The late twentieth century and the new millennium have witnessed the continued growth of interest in how people spend their leisure and non-work time. There is also a growing interest in what people 'consume' in these non-work periods, particularly those times that are dedicated to travel and holidays. At a global scale this interest is becoming an international phenomenon known as tourism, which is based on the use of leisure time to visit different places, destinations and localities that often (but not exclusively) feature in the holidays and trips people take in their leisure time. For example, in 2002 the World Travel and Tourism Council (WTTC) estimated that travel and tourism as economic activities generated US$4421.1 billion, which is expected to grow to US$8613.8 billion by 2012. This is a 4.5 per cent increase in the demand for travel and tourism per annum, which is far in excess of the scale and pace of growth in the economies of most countries. At a global scale, the economic effects of travel and tourism are estimated by WTTC to be responsible for 198098000 jobs, which is equivalent to 7.8 per cent of world employment (or 1 in every 12.8 jobs). This number is expected to grow to 249486000 jobs by 2012.

Therefore the growing international significance of tourism can be explained in many ways, and in an introductory context such as this it is important to stress the following factors and processes at the outset to illustrate the reasons why it assumes an important role not only in our lives but also globally:

- Tourism is a discretionary activity (i.e. people do not need to do it to survive, as with consuming food and water).
- Tourism is of growing economic significance at a global scale – in excess of the rate of growth for many economies.
- Many governments see tourism as offering new employment opportunities in a growing sector of the economy, which may assist in developing and modernizing the economy, focused on service industries.
- Tourism is increasingly becoming associated with quality-of-life issues because it offers the opportunity to take a break from the complexities and stresses of everyday life and work – it provides the context for rest, relaxation and an opportunity to do something different in a new environment.
- Tourism is becoming seen as a basic right in the developed, westernized industrialized countries, and it is enshrined in legislation regarding holiday

entitlement – the result is that many people associate holiday entitlement with the propensity to generate tourism.

- Holidays are a defining feature of non-work for many workers.
- Global travel is becoming more accessible in the developed world for all classes of people with the rise of budget airlines and cut-price travel, fuelling a new wave of demand for tourism in the new millennium and potentially replicating the demand in the 1960s and 1970s. Then, growth was fuelled by access to transport (i.e. the car and air travel), which provided new leisure opportunities.
- Discretionary items such as travel and tourism are being perceived as less costly items in household budgets, and are also much easier to finance with the rapid rise in credit card spending in developed countries
- Technology such as the Internet has made booking travel-related products easy for the new generation of computer-literate consumers, who are willing to organize their own annual holidays.

From this brief list of reasons as to why tourism is now assuming a major role in the lives of people, it is evident that it is also becoming a powerful process that affects all parts of the globe. It is not only embraced by various people as a new trend or characteristic, and a defining feature of people's lives, but is also an activity in which the masses can now take part (subject to access to discretionary forms of spending). This form of discretionary activity mirrors the post-war changes in western society, with the rise in disposable income and spending on consumer goods and services. The first major wave of growth concerned home ownership, the second car ownership, and now, finally, access to tourism and international travel. In fact international and domestic travel is a defining feature of the modern-day lifestyle that characterizes the consumer society. Whilst the car has given more people access to tourism and leisure opportunities within their own country, access to air travel has made international travel and tourism products and services more widely available to the populace.

Tourism is thus a phenomenon that is constantly evolving, developing and reformulating itself as a consumer activity. Tourism is constantly being developed by the tourism industry and individual businesses to appeal to the consumer, as marketing is used to develop new ideas, products, services and destinations. For example, there is an international interest in developing niches, which are specific interests and activities that people might find interesting as an activity focus for their holiday. Recent developments that characterize this include the rise of nature-based or ecotourism products, such as nature watching in the Galapagos Islands. Similarly, the rise of wine- and food-based tourism, following on people's interests and hobbies, provides an example of a successful development of niche products. Tourism appeals to the human imagination and as an activity it knows no bounds – it is global, and it affects the environment it occurs in, the people who host it, the economies it seeks to benefit and the tourist who consumes it as an experience, product and a life element. With this all-embracing role it is no surprise that many commentators, researchers and governments have agreed on the need to manage tourism as a process and activity, but above all as a phenomenon that has the potential to snowball and grow out of proportion if it is not managed. Therein lies the basic proposition of this book – tourism needs managing if it is to be successful and beneficial, and not a modern-day scourge.

Yet one of the fundamental problems in seeking to manage tourism is in trying to understand what it is, how it occurs, why it occurs where it does, its affect on people and environments, and why it is a very volatile activity that can cease as quick as it can start. These types of questions are what this book seeks to address, along with why tourism as a consumer activity is built on dreams, images and what people like to do. This is notoriously difficult to understand, as it enters the realms of psychology and trying to read the mind of the individual tourist. Furthermore, these psycho-logical elements are bound up in notions of enjoyment, in feelings, emotions, and seemingly intangible and unseen characteristics. These are complicated further when taking into consideration the fact that these notions change throughout the life of an individual as a tourist consumer. In other words, being a tourist is based on the principle of non-work and enjoyment of free time in a different locality, and results in an experience, a treasured memory and something personal. As a result, under-standing what tourism is, how it operates, what it means to people and how to manage it are key challenges for any locality, with the global growth of tourism activity. So why study tourism?

Why study tourism?

Tourism and its analysis has become a relatively recent field of study among academics, researchers and commentators. Some of the very early textbooks on tourism can be dated to the early 1970s, with a second wave being produced in the 1980s and then a massive explosion in the late 1980s and 1990s as tourism education and training expanded worldwide. There are a range of commonly recognized problems in studying tourism, some of which are important to our understanding of whether it is just about enjoyment and taking holidays.

Tourism is a multidisciplinary subject, which means that a wide range of other subjects examine it – psychology, geography and economics to name but a few – and bring to it various ideas and methods of study. This means that there is no overarching academic agreement on how to approach the study of tourism; it really depends on how you are looking at tourism, and the perspective you adopt.

This has led to a lack of clarity and definition regarding how to study tourism. It is often defined by what some researchers call *reductionism*. What this means is that tourism is normally defined by reducing it to a simple range of activities or transactions (e.g. What types of holidays do people choose? How do people purchase those holidays?) rather than focusing on the framework needed to give a wider perspective or overview of tourism as a dynamic and important subject.

These problems often compound the way people view tourism as a subject, emphasizing the holiday or enjoyment aspects of travelling (either in spare time or on business) as the defining features or reference points of tourism. To the general public tourism is something everyone knows about – it is something many have engaged in, and thus have an opinion on regarding what it is, its effects and its widespread development.

Those involved in the study of tourism face similar situations within the institutions and organizations where they work, since many academics and researchers have a broad awareness of tourism and so have prejudices and opinions about it as a subject. Therein lies one of the continual problems facing the student of tourism: anyone that is charged with the study of pleasure, enjoyment and the use of leisure time cannot be engaged in serious academic study, can they? Other researchers in science, the arts and humanities work in long established disciplines and have generations of literature and knowledge behind them, along with the tradition of studying serious problems in society, such as disease control, societal problems (such as homelessness, poverty) and the negative aspects of life and their improvement. So tourism is not perceived a serious subject, as it does not address societal problems. In reality, these prejudices and attitudes are fundamentally flawed, outdated and ill informed in a society where leisure and pleasure are now key elements in the quality of life of the population. Admittedly tourism is about pleasure and enjoyment, but its global growth and expansion are now creating serious societal problems and issues that require a fundamental understanding of tourism so that the impacts and problems it can cause can be managed and controlled. One way of beginning to understand that tourism is more than holidays and enjoyment is to consider why tourism is so important in modern society (i.e. its social, cultural and economic significance) by looking at an important process that has led to the demand for it – the rise of the leisure society.

The leisure society

Tourism is now widely acknowledged to be a social phenomenon, as the nature of society in most advanced developed countries has now changed from one that has traditionally had an economy based on manufacturing and production to one where the dominant form of employment is in the services and consumer industries. At the same time, many countries have seen the amount of leisure time and paid holiday entitlement for their workers increase in the post-war period, so that workers now have the opportunity to engage in the new forms of consumption such as tourism. These changes have been described as being part of what has been termed as the leisure society, a term coined in the 1970s by sociologists. They were examining the future of work and the way in which society was changing as traditional forms of employment were disappearing and new service-related employment, increased leisure time and new working habits (such as flexitime and part-time work) emerged. Some commentators described a 'leisure shock' in the 1980s, as many workers were still not prepared for the rise in leisure time and how to use it.

As society has passed from the stage of industrialization to one now described as post-industrial, where new technologies and ways of communicating and working have evolved, sociologists such as Bauldrillard (1998) argue that we have moved from a society where work and production predominated to one where leisure and consumption are now dominant. This has been reflected in social changes, such as the worldwide rise in the new middle class in many developed and developing countries, with a defining feature – the concern with leisure lifestyles and consumption. The new-found wealth of the growing middle class has been reflected in increased spending on leisure items and tourism. The international growth in taking holidays is directly related to this new and larger middle class. If the UK is fairly representative of changes in other countries, then recent changes in consumer expenditure illustrate the growth of this leisure society.

- In 1998–1999, The Family Expenditure Survey (undertaken by the Office for National Statistics) recorded that households in the UK spent over £18 a week on holiday expenses – four-and-a-half times the amount spent in real terms in 1968.

- In 1998–1999, for the first time in weekly patterns of expenditure, the largest element of household expenditure was leisure goods and services (of which tourism is an item). Growing levels of disposable income have allowed many more people to spend money on non-essential items such as holidays.
- These patterns of spending also have a social and economic dimension, as those in employment and self-employment spent 17 per cent of household expenditure on leisure, compared to 14 per cent for the unemployed and 19 per cent for the retired.
- Interestingly, few geographical variations existed in the spending on leisure goods and services, despite variations in wealth, prosperity and income.
- In terms of spending on holidays, 211 735 000 nights were spent abroad on holiday by UK residents in 1999, who spent £12 370 000 million.

This snapshot of the UK shows that tourism is a major element of the leisure spending of households, reflected in what researchers have described as 'leisure lifestyles', of which tourism is a significant element. With these issues in mind, our attention now turns to what is meant by the terms *tourism*, *tourist* and *travel*.

Concepts – tourism, the tourist and travel

There have been numerous attempts to define tourism, and very often the terms travel and tourism are used interchangeably. According to the international organization responsible for tourism, the World Tourism Organization (WTO):

> Tourism is defined as the activities of persons travelling to and staying in places outside their usual environment for not more than one consecutive year for leisure, business and other purposes not related to the exercise of an activity remunerated from within the place visited. The use of this broad concept makes it possible to identify tourism between countries as well as tourism within a country. 'Tourism' refers to all activities of visitors, including both 'tourists' (overnight visitors) and 'same-day visitors'. Source: www.world-tourism.org

This seemingly straightforward definition has created a great deal of debate, which is not a recent issue. Controversy has surrounded the development of acceptable definitions since the League of Nations attempt to define a tourist in 1937, including subsequent attempts by the United Nations Conference in 1963, which considered definitions proposed by the then IUOTO (now the WTO). There have also been subsequent attempts to clarify what is meant by the term 'visitor' as opposed to 'tourist', and the distinction between tourists who travel within their own country (domestic tourists) and those who travel to other countries (international tourists). What these debates on the technical definition of tourism show is that it is far from an easy task in agreeing what constitutes a 'tourist'. For example, should we include visitors who are staying in their second home? Similarly, how far away from their home area do people have to travel, and do they have to include an overnight stay before it is deemed tourism? A further problem is associated with the category of cruise ship passengers docking at a port and visiting briefly but not staying overnight, or cross-Channel excursionists who may cross an international boundary but return within the day and do not stay overnight. To try and encompass many of these anomalies and problems the WTO produced guidelines for classifying of tourists (see Figure 1.1). What is increasingly obvious is that new forms of research are needed to

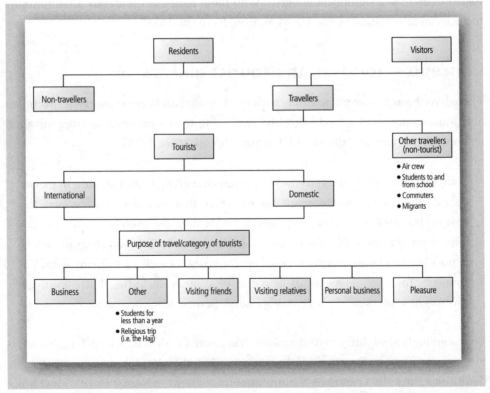

Figure 1.1 The classification of tourists (developed and modified from Chadwick, 1994)

understand how the phenomenon loosely defined as tourism is evolving, as it is far from static. For example, research on tourism has identified the short-term migration of the elderly who winter in warmer climates (such as the UK pensioners who overwinter in the Mediterranean) as a new type of tourism. This includes second-home owners, tourists and seasonal visitors who spend two to six months overseas in locations such as Tuscany, Malta and Spain. This pattern of tourism and migration also generates flows of people who are visiting friends and relatives, which is somewhat different to the conventional images of package holidaymakers destined for these locations.

Therefore, the following definition of tourism might be useful (Chadwick, 1994: 65):

... the field of research on human and business activities associated with one or more aspects of the temporary movement of persons away from their immediate home communities and daily work environments for business, pleasure and personal reasons.

In the USA there is a tendency still to use the term 'travel' when in fact tourism is intended. What is clear is that tourism is associated with three specific issues:

- the movement of people;
- a sector of the economy or an industry;
- a broad system of interacting relationships of people, their needs [sic] to travel outside their communities and services that attempt to respond to these needs by supplying products.

From this starting point we can begin to explore some of the complex issues in arriving at a working definition of the term's 'tourism' and 'tourist'.

Probably the most useful work to provide an introduction to tourism as a concept, and its relationship with travel, is Burkart and Medlik's (1981) seminal study *Tourism: Past, Present and Future*. This identified five characteristics associated with tourism (p. 42):

- Tourism arises from the movement of people to, and their stay in, various destinations;
- There are two elements in all tourism; the journey to the destination and the stay including activities at the destination;

- The journey and the stay take place outside the normal place of residence and work, so that tourism gives rise to activities which are distinct from those of the resident and working populations of the places through which tourists travel and in which they stay;
- The movement to destinations is of a temporary, short-term character, with intention to return within a few days, weeks or months; and
- Destinations are visited for purposes other than taking up permanent residence or employment remunerated from within the places visited.

All tourism includes some travel but not all travel is tourism, while the temporary and short-term nature of most tourist trips distinguishes it from migration. But how does tourism fit together – in other words how can we understand the disparate elements? One approach is to look at tourism as an integrated system, which means asking how tourism is organized and what its defining features are.

An organizing framework for the analysis of tourism

The most widely used framework is that developed by Leiper (1990), who identified the tourism system as comprising: a tourist; a traveller-generating region; tourism destination regions; transit routes for tourists travelling between generating and destination areas, and the travel and tourism industry (e.g. accommodation, transport, and the firms and organizations supplying services and products to tourists). This is illustrated in Figure 1.2, which shows that transport forms an integral part of the tourism system, connecting the tourist-generating and destination regions together. Thus a 'tourism system' is a framework that enables us to understand the overall process of tourist travel from both the supplier's and purchaser's perspective (known respectively as supply and demand) while identifying the organizations that influence and regulate tourism. The system also allows us to understand where the links exist between different elements of tourism – where the tourist interacts with the travel organizer (travel agent or retailer), the travel provider (airline, or mode of transport), the destination area, and the tourism sector within the destination. This approach is also helpful in understanding how many elements are assembled by the tourism sector to create an experience of tourism. One major element in this experience of tourism is the tour, which is a feature of holidays and the use of leisure time.

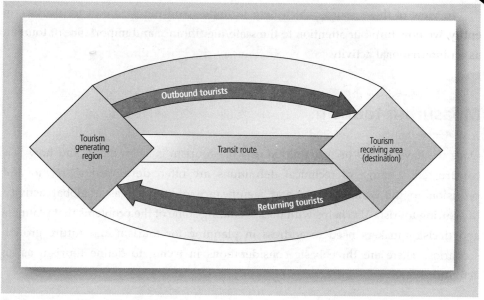

Figure 1.2   Leiper's tourism system (redrawn from Page, 1995; based on and modified from Leiper, 1990)

The tour, holidays and leisure time

What is evident from Leiper's model of the tourism system is that the tour (a trip that involves travel anywhere for pleasure or leisure) is a vital element in the system. It is an underpinning feature of tourism that touring is a prerequisite for tourism to occur, as the consumer has to be brought to the product or experience. This requires travel, and is a reciprocal event – the traveller travels out and back again. Transport is therefore necessary, with the journey involving travel to a single or multiple destinations. The conventional definition of a tour inevitably implies travel to one or more places, called destinations. There are various forms of tours, including excursions by road or rail (where the travel may have a scenic element, known as a touring route) and those incorporated in a cruise, where the ship tours a range of destinations or ports of call. Conversely, the excursion element may be something that the tourist undertakes at the destination as a day trip or a more sustained trip, with a planned or unplanned itinerary. Whilst the holiday is something that encompasses the entire experience or use of leisure time, the tour is a distinct element of the holiday and has distinct patterns and travel patterns.

iese issues, which help to understand the nature of tourism as an
irn our attention to the scale, significance and importance of tourism
ial activity.

Measuring tourism

Once we have agreed on a definition of what tourism is as an entity and how it is
constructed, a range of technical definitions are often developed to try to add
precision to the scale, volume and significance of tourism as a global activity.
Measuring tourism also helps with understanding some of the problems that planners
and decision-makers need to address in planning for tourism and future growth
scenarios. There are three basic considerations in trying to define tourism as an
activity:

1 What is the purpose of the travel (e.g. business travel, holiday, visits to friends and
relatives, other reasons)?
2 What time dimension is involved in the tourism visit? (In most cases, tourism
would involve a minimum of 24 hours and a maximum of a year away from
home.)
3 What situations exist where some countries may or may not choose to include
travellers as tourists (e.g. cruise passengers, tourists in transit, excursionists who
stay less than 24 hours at a destination)?

There are five main reasons why measuring tourism is important:

1 To understand why it is significant and to what degree for certain destinations,
countries and regions, in terms of the scale and value of the visitors
2 To understand how important it is for countries in terms of their balance of
payments, as it is an invisible export that generates foreign currency and income
3 To assist the tourism industry and governments in planning for and in anticipating
the type of infrastructure that is required for tourism to grow and prosper
4 To assist in understanding what type of marketing is needed to reach tourists as
consumers, and what factors will influence them to visit a country or destination
5 To help the tourism industry in making decisions regarding the type of action
needed for further development in this area.

At a general level, measuring tourism through the collection, analysis and interpretation of statistics is essential for the assessment of the volume, scale, impact and value of tourism at different geographical scales, from global to country level and down to individual destinations.

Figure 1.3 demonstrates the trends in global tourism since 1950. Using the WTO arrival statistics for each year, it shows that international tourist arrivals have not simply grown annually. A number of downturns have occurred in tourist arrivals, most recently owing to the impact of foot and mouth disease in the UK, the terrorist attacks in the USA on 11 September 2001 and in Bali in September 2002, other terrorist events, and factors such as the economic crisis in Argentina, the strength of the US dollar and conflict in the Middle East. In other words, a range of factors impact upon visitor arrivals at an international level, because tourism is a very fickle activity (i.e. it is vulnerable to the external factors mentioned above, which act as deterrents to travel; these adverse events can act as shock waves that send ripples across the world and impact upon people's willingness to travel for pleasure reasons). At the same time, major religious events such as the Hajj, a trip to Mecca that most Muslims are expected to take once in their lifetime, is one of the largest tourism events in the world every year and is also an enduring event that is less susceptible to shock waves than other forms of tourism. Table 1.1 shows the recent patterns of arrivals by WTO region and some of the local trends in international tourism.

The findings can be summarized as follows:

- International tourism is dominated by Western European destinations
- New areas for tourism activity, such as East Asia Pacific (including the growing economies of Singapore, Thailand, South Korea, Taiwan and China) are expected to overtake the traditional dominance of Western Europe
- The dominant destinations worldwide in terms of arrivals in 2001 were France, Spain, the USA, Italy, and then China. Of these destinations, arrivals increased by 6.2 per cent in 2000–2001 and decreased by 12.6 per cent in the USA owing to the impact of 11 September 2001 and other factors. These five destinations accounted for 35.3 per cent of all international arrivals, illustrating the dominance of certain countries in global patterns of tourism.

However, one of the enduring problems (which is not evident from Table 1.1) is that, far from being a comprehensive source of information, tourism statistics are often only an estimate of the total pattern of tourism. In addition, such statistics are often dated

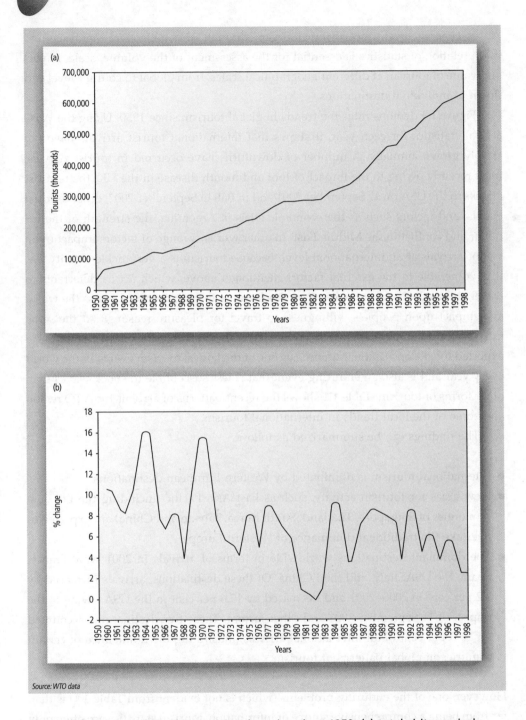

Source: WTO data

Figure 1.3   The growth of international tourism since 1950: (a) total visitor arrivals; (b) percentage change year on year

Table 1.1 International tourist arrivals by region in 2001 (modified from WTO). Source: www.world-tourism.org, press releases

Region	Arrivals (millions)
Africa	28.5
Americas:	
• North America	83.7
• Caribbean	16.7
• South America	14.4
• Central America	4.5
East Asia Pacific	114.9
Europe:	
• Northern Europe	42.2
• Western Europe	140.2
• Central/Eastern Europe	76.3
• Southern Europe	127.1
• East Mediterranean	14.7
South Asia	6.0
World	688.5

when they are published because there is a significant time lag in their generation, analysis, presentation and dissemination. This is because many published tourism statistics are derived from sample surveys, with the results being weighted or statistically manipulated to derive a measure that is supposedly representative of the real-world situation. Hence many tourism statistics at a country or regional level are acknowledged as being estimates for this reason. In reality, this means that tourism statistics are often subject to significant errors, depending on the size of the sample.

The typical problems associated with measuring tourism include the following as Latham (1989) found:

• Tourists are a transient and highly mobile population, making statistical sampling procedures difficult when trying to ensure statistical accuracy and rigour in methodological terms

- Interviewing of mobile populations such as tourists is often undertaken in strange environments, typically at ports or points of departure or arrival where there is background noise that may influence responses
- Other variables, such as the weather, may affect the responses.

Even where sampling and survey-related problems can be minimized, such tourism statistics have to be treated carefully because it is important to be aware of what constituted a tourist and the type of approach used. The main ways of measuring tourists through surveys include:

- Pre-travel studies of tourists' intended travel habits and likely choice of destination (intentional studies)
- Studies of tourists in transit, to provide information regarding their actual behaviour and plans for the remainder of their holiday or journey (actual and intended studies)
- Studies of tourists at the destination or at specific tourist attractions and sites, to provide information regarding their actual behaviour, levels of satisfaction, impacts and future intentions (actual and intended studies)
- Post-travel studies of tourists on their return journey from their destination or on-site experience, or once they have returned to their place of residence (post-travel measures).

Such studies can also be used to examine different facets of the tourist, as the following three approaches suggest:

1 Measurement of tourist volume, enumerating arrivals, departures and the number of visits and stays
2 Expenditure-based surveys, which quantify the value of tourist spending at the destination and during the journey
3 Investigation of the characteristics and features of tourists, to construct a profile of the different markets and segments visiting a destination.

In the commercial world, tourism data are also collated by organizations that specialize in its collection and analysis – including marker research companies such as Mintel, in London. Tourism consultants may also be commissioned specifically to collect data for feasibility studies of tourism developments or new business opportunities, and much of the information gained remains confidential to the client due to its commercial sensitivity. However, in most cases national governments collate tourism statistics through studies of domestic and international tourism. International tourism is more widely studied, and results are normally passed to the World Tourism Organization (WTO) and the Organization for Economic Co-operation and Development (OECD), which collate and publish international travel statistics from member nations.

Once there is an understanding of how tourism is measured and collated, then we can begin to think about what the patterns and trends in tourism mean at a global level and what the implications are – particularly the more critical issues of what forces are affecting tourism as a global activity.

New forces affecting tourism

When looking at the patterns of tourism, and those areas that are growing in terms of international tourism, it is evident the majority of outbound travellers are from the developed countries of Europe, North America and Australasia, and the new middle class in many developing countries. In some cases tourists are travelling to developing countries where the majority of the population live at subsistence levels or at a much lower standards than the visitors. The contrast in wealth between visitor and host is often very large, and highlights a clear inequality between those who have the disposable income to enjoy the luxury of international and domestic travel and those who work in the industry for low wages and in low-paid unskilled jobs. This situation is made worse by the growing impact of globalization. Globalization is a process associated with the growth of large international companies and corporations, which control various forms of economic development and production from their host country by using low production costs in developing countries to make goods and deliver services at a lower cost using cheap labour. Tourism is no exception to this, where large multinational hotel chains and tour operators use developing countries and destinations as the basis for their tourist product. In these situations the economic linkages with the local community are limited, so that unskilled jobs and low economic benefits are traded off against the profits and economic benefits of tourism development that are expropriated to the country of origin of the multinational firm. In many cases the weakly developed nature of local economic linkages in developing countries' tourism economies means that they are trapped in such exploitative relationships because they do not have the indigenous capital or entrepreneurs to set up tourism businesses themselves. A lack of education and know-how and the inability to negotiate with multinationals to maximize the benefits for local people means that tourism can be a form of exploitation for such communities.

Developing local products to nurture linkages with the local economy, rather than importing foodstuffs to meet the tastes of tourists and the demand for internationally recognizable brands, may counter this. Although tourists export their leisure lifestyles with them on holiday, and can be seen to be increasingly consumptive and conspicuous by the spending power they exercise; this could be harnessed for the benefit of the local economy. This is not just the case in the less developed world, but is also a growing problem in many tourism destinations worldwide where the growth of tourism and expropriation of the profits from developing tourism means that the environmental resource base that is used to attract tourists (e.g. attractive beaches, wildlife and the cultural and built environment) is endangered. There is growing interest in the extent to which tourism is a sustainable economic, social and environmentally based activity. The use of the environment without conserving it for future generations and for posterity is one of the central points in the debate on the inequalities that tourism poses for different localities. International agencies, governments and local people have a responsibility to lobby and take action to ensure that the tourism development that occurs in different countries and locations is not only sustainable but also seeks to minimize negative impacts as far as possible. Vulnerable groups such as children and the workforce should not be marginalized, bearing in mind that the International Labour Organization (ILO) has estimated that between 10 and 15 per cent of the tourism workforce worldwide is comprised of children who do not enjoy appropriate standards of labour and employment conditions.

Tourism needs to be developed in an ethical manner so that exploitation is not its hallmark. This is a theme that we will return to later in the book, but at this point it is clear that tourism development and activity needs not only to be socially and environmentally responsible but also to be sustainable in the long term rather than short term and exploitative; the tourism industry needs to work with communities, local bodies and people to ensure that tourism is a win–win activity for everyone and is integrated into the local community rather than just exploiting its local assets. This may require a significant change in emphasis in the way in which tourism is developed and managed, and is an enduring theme that is highlighted at different points in the book. Tourists and tourism businesses have a greater responsibility to ensure that tourism is promoted as an activity that will not only enhance global understanding and interaction between people of different cultures and societies, but is also able to promote dialogue, benefits and opportunities for the tourist, the host and the environment. Hence in some situations tourism may be a way of providing the stimulus and means for preserving and conserving endangered species and environments, as well as providing benefits beyond those that that normally accrue to the tourism industry.

Tourism has to operate as a profitable activity but, for its long-term future, mutually beneficial relationships and links between the industry, people and the environment can bring financial and sustainable benefits for all and enhance the reputation and image of tourism as a global phenomenon. The benefits of tourism to tourists can also be extended to the host population and help to address many of the global inequalities that exist as multinational enterprises seek to exercise greater control of the choice and nature of tourism offered to consumers. Although this book cannot address all of these issues, it is hoped that they will remain at the forefront of readers' minds so that they are aware of the implications of the tourism industry and its activities at a global, national and local level.

A framework for the book

As the title of this book is *Tourism Management*, it is useful to present an organizing framework for the book and to identify what is the tourism management means. By this stage it is evident that the focus of the book and subject matter is tourism; however, the term 'management' is often used ambiguously. Therefore we will examine here the relationship of tourism with management, and its meaning in the context of this book.

Tourism and management

At a very general level, in this context the word 'management' could be taken to mean how tourism needs to be managed as a growing activity at global, national and local levels so that its often contradictory forces (i.e. the pursuit of profit as a private sector activity and its impact on the resource base it uses, such as a beautiful coastline on a Pacific island) are reconciled and balanced so that tourism develops and is pursued in a sustainable and balanced manner. Whilst this is an overriding concern for readers of this book, there is also a need to examine the basic principles associated with the term management and how these elements of management can be integrated with the study of tourism as an activity. The basic principles concern:

- *Planning,* so that goals are set out and the means of achieving the goals are recognized
- *Organizing,* whereby the work functions are broken down into a series of tasks and are linked to some form of structure before these tasks are assigned to individuals
- *Leading,* which is the method of motivating and influencing staff so that they perform their tasks effectively; this is essential if organizational goals are to be achieved
- *Controlling,* which is the method by which information is gathered about what has to be done.

Each of these functions involves decision-making by managers, businesses, tourist destinations or organizations so that the tasks can be harnessed to achieve the objectives associated with managing tourism. The word 'organization' is often used as an all-embracing term to refer to the type of tourism entity that is involved with tourism as a business. These businesses are motivated by their involvement in tourism to make a profit, and therefore the efficient organization and management of their activities is essential to ensure that company or organizational objectives are met. There is a school of management thought that argues that management only occurs when chaos occurs, and that the function of management is to impose order and structure to that chaos so that managerial skills are then harnessed. Within organizations dealing in the tourism sector (e.g. travel agents, airlines, tour operators and associated businesses) they harness resources such as employees, finance, capital, technology, equipment and knowledge to provide an output, which in the case of tourism is normally a product or service. This output is achieved through management of the resources.

There is also a debate among tourism researchers, who argue that tourism is a unique sector in that it displays characteristics of partial industrialization (Leiper, 1989: 25) where:

> . . . only certain organizations providing goods and services directly to tourists are in the tourism industry. The proportion of (a) goods and services stemming from that industry to (b) total goods and services used by tourists can be termed

the index of industrialization, theoretically ranging from 100% (wholly industrialized) to zero (tourists present and spending money, but no tourism industry).

What Leiper's approach to the tourism sector shows is that the management of the broad phenomenon called 'tourism' is complex for a number of reasons:

1 The tourism industry is not a homogenous sector or segment of the economy: it is made up of various organizations that are directly involved in tourism (i.e. those that directly service tourist needs) and those that are indirectly involved and hence may be described as allied industries (e.g. food suppliers, retailers and other service providers)
2 Some of the organizations directly involved in tourism are responsible for encouraging and promoting tourism development and marketing
3 The allied industries do not always see themselves as tourism-related enterprises
4 The destination or area that the tourists visit is not usually the sole responsibility of one business or group of businesses; the public sector intervenes to ensure that business objectives (i.e. profit and increasing tourism numbers and revenue) are balanced with local needs and business interests (known as stakeholder interests) in relation to the resource base that tourism utilizes (i.e. beaches, attractions, the infrastructure and overall environment)
5 The public sector is responsible for trying to liaise, plan and manage the diverse group of interests that are associated with tourism, as well as having an underlying responsibility in many cases for the marketing and promotion of the destination.

We can see from this how complex the management of tourism is when the interests and the variety of organizations involved in tourism are considered, and the concept of partial industrialization is then introduced.

From this discussion, it is clear that we identify who is responsible for tourism management at a number of levels:

● At the individual business level, it is the manager(s) involved with the functioning and running of the enterprise.
● At the destination level, it is often a public sector led agency such as the tourism department (either as a stand-alone body or as part of a local authority department). In extreme situations where a destination is deluged with tourists due

to its popularity, the public sector may lead, with a public–private sector partnership involving business interests to manage the visitors on the ground.

- At the country level, National Tourism Organizations (funded by the public sector through taxes) with, sometimes, private sector members promote and market the country as a place to visit and attempt to manage the diverse interests involved in tourism.
- At every level, there is a complex web of interactions and interrelationships that need to be taken into account in the decisions, interests and actions taken to manage tourism.

This is not an exclusive list, but rather a range of illustrations. In each of these illustrations the functions of management are harnessed, and what makes tourism management more complex is that there is great debate regarding what tourism is, what needs to be managed, and who should be responsible. The fact that tourism can be seen as an experience and is based on the pursuit of pleasure and profit involves many complex issues, including whether the tourist is consuming a product, experience or service, and leads to many debates on what to manage and how far management controls should be exercised by both the tourism industry and the public sector.

So how does this book address these questions?

One way is by viewing the managerial process of tourism as being a multi-layered process, where the various organizations and stakeholders involved in tourism engage in at different levels through time. Figure 1.4 demonstrates this principle, where the focus begins with the individual business and the management processes (controlling, planning, leading and organizing) are continuous throughout the interconnected stakeholder groups. These interests and connections between management at different levels and between groups mean that in reality these groups also have to be aware of external factors that will impact upon management, such as the visitor, the business environment, consumer trends, the growth of the leisure society, and political processes affecting tourism at government level. The book is organized in such a way that these issues are explained in a manner whereby the links between different elements of the tourism sector are addressed through examples and case studies. As a result, each chapter builds upon the preceding one to develop the knowledge and understanding of what the tourism industry is, the management challenges facing each sector, and the importance of the process of change. Accommodating, anticipating and responding to that level of change provides one of the major challenges for tourism management in the new millennium.

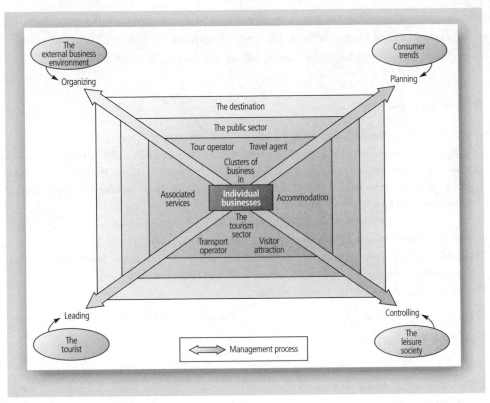

Figure 1.4 A framework for tourism management

This chapter seeks to examine how the tourism phenomenon has emerged as a part of modern-day society, as a prelude to discussing tourism as a business activity in Chapter 2. Chapter 3 provides a review of why people engage in tourism, focusing on the demand for tourism experiences by people. In Chapter 4, the discussion focuses on how the demand for tourism is met by the tourism industry, and this provides an organizing framework for Chapters 5 to 8, which examine various facets of the tourism industry, namely air transportation, land-based transport, the provision of accommodation and hospitality services, and tour operations and retailing. Chapter 9 discusses the significance of visitor attractions, which provide a context for visitor activity and spending in destinations. Chapter 10 returns to the theme of tourism management as a context for understanding how tourism is organized, managed and developed in specific environments. This theme is pursued in the public sector context in Chapter 11. Both Chapters 10 and 11 provide the underpinning for Chapter 12, which discusses some of the practical issues and problems associated with managing visitors and sites of tourist activity. Chapter 13 reviews the future of tourism activity in a global context, highlighting future issues and trends in its development.

References

Baudrillard, J. (1998) *The Consumer Society: Myth and Structure*. London: Sage.

Burkart, A. and Medlik, S. (1981) *Tourism, Past Present and Future*, 2nd edn. London: Heinemann.

Chadwick, R. (1994) Concepts, definitions and measures used in travel and tourism research. *In*: J. R. Brent Ritchie and C. Goeldner (eds), *Travel, Tourism and Hospitality Research: A Handbook for Managers and Researchers*, 2nd edn. New York: Wiley.

Latham, J. (1989) The statistical measurement of tourism. *In*: C. P. Cooper (ed.), *Progress in Tourism, Recreation and Hospitality Management, Vol. 1*. London: Belhaven, pp. 57–76.

Leiper, N. (1990) *Tourism Systems: An Interdisciplinary Perspective*. Palmerston North, New Zealand: Department of Management Systems Occasional Paper 2, Massey University.

Page, S. J. (1995) *Urban Tourism*. London: Routledge.

Further reading

Lickorish, L. and Jenkins, C. (1997) *An Introduction to Tourism*. Oxford: Butterworth-Heinemann.

Page, S. J., Brunt, P., Busby, G. and Connell, J. (2001) *Tourism: A Modern Synthesis*. London: Thomson Learning.

Questions

1 Why is tourism such an important activity in the twenty-first century?

2 How would you classify tourists?

3 Why is tourism management important for a business operating in the tourism sector?

4 How stable is tourism as an economic activity?

Chapter **2**

Tourism: its origins, growth and future

Learning objectives

This chapter provides an historical perspective of the evolution of tourism as a business activity through the ages, and some of the management challenges it has faced. After reading it you should be able to understand:

- the underlying processes affecting tourism: continuity and change;
- the importance of the resort lifecycle;
- the role of coastal resorts in leisure and tourism during the nineteenth and twentieth centuries;
- the role of historical sources such as diaries in reconstructing past patterns of tourism activity;
- the evolution of tourism in the post-war period;
- the factors associated with the future trends in tourism development, such as space tourism.

Introduction

Tourism is not a recent phenomenon. Whilst it was argued in the last chapter that tourism has become a widely accessible product in the consumer-led leisure society, its historical roots can be traced back almost to the origins of civilization. The historical study of tourism does, however, indicate that the nature of what tourists do in their leisure time may have changed as technology has expanded the opportunities for travel. Tourism has also evolved from being an activity that was the preserve of the 'leisured classes' (i.e. the aristocracy, who had both the leisure time and means to engage in travel), to a mass phenomenon. This chapter will show that tourism has varied in terms of accessibility to different groups in society throughout history as the development of a leisure ethic and increased prosperity have created new tourism opportunities. In any historical overview of tourism, two underlying themes are important: continuity and change. *Continuity* means that tourism has continued to be an important process, remaining influential in the leisure lifestyles of certain social classes. *Change*, on the other hand, characterizes the evolution of tourism through the ages, since tourism is a dynamic phenomenon. Much of the change is based upon the interaction between the demand for and supply of tourism opportunities through time. In simple terms, destinations developed for tourists and tourists visited them, thus creating an interaction; this is implicit in all forms of tourism – the movement from origin area to destination and *vice versa*. The discovery and development of these destinations also exhibits elements of continuity and change through time.

The history of tourism

There are comparatively few studies that document the history of tourism through time, with many being focused on specific eras or epochs in time. Much of the attention by historians has focused on the evolution of mass tourism in both a domestic setting (i.e. the rise and demise of the English seaside resort) and an international setting (i.e. the post-war growth and development of the package holiday). However, equally important is the historical evolution of tourism from classical times, since this established many of the principles of the use of leisure time for holidays and travel.

Tourism in classical times

The ancient civilization of Greece was not so much important for its major development of tourism, but more so for the Greek philosopher's recognition, endorsement and promotion of the concept of leisure upon which tourism is based. Aristotle considered leisure to be a key element of the Greek lifestyle, where slaves and other people should do the work required while the Greek freemen should put their leisure time to good use.

This positive leisure doctrine may well have been the original 'leisure lifestyle', where the pursuit of music, philosophy, non-work and measures of self-development were elements of Greek society. The development of the Olympic Games in 776 BC also provided a vital stimulus for tourism. Greeks travelled to the site of the Olympic Games and were housed in tented encampments. However, international travel in Greek times was limited due to the Greek wars.

By contrast, the rise of Rome and the Roman Empire was based upon the twin elements of military conquest and administration. The state and private individuals created leisure facilities (such as spas, baths and resorts) and enjoyed similar leisure lifestyles to the Greeks. Tourism-related facilities were created by the construction of colosseums for events and spectator sports. The affluent also began to move from the town to the country, building rural villas for recreational purposes.

Two elements of tourism can be discerned in Roman society: first, domestic tourism focused on urban places where the resorts and facilities/events existed, so that the middle classes in Roman society had opportunity to spend their 200 holidays a year; secondly, the conquest of overseas territories and their administration created a demand for business-related travel connected with the territorial management and control of these peoples. The middle classes also had expanded opportunities to travel, afforded by new territories, trade, and the provision of roads linking the Roman origin area to seaside resorts, summer villas and historical sites, for health, pleasure and spiritual reasons.

Rome, with its function as a capital city, also emerged as an important urban tourism destination. To service tourist needs, inns, bars, tour guides and souvenir sellers developed. Thus many elements of modern-day tourism were established in Roman times, made possible mainly due to political stability and the provision of infrastructure and facilities, and were stimulated by prosperity among the middle classes – who enjoyed travel for leisure and business.

The Middle Ages

The years following the demise of the Roman Empire, from AD 500 through to the end of feudalism and the Black Death in 1381, are known as the Middle Ages. The early part of this period has also been described as the Dark Ages – a time when the civilization and progress of the Roman era declined. In place of the pleasure-seeking society of the Roman era, the rise of Christianity and the development of monastic orders saw the evolution of a society based on landed estates and a feudal system of peasants and nobility. Yet even in these seemingly dark times tourism can be discerned, with the emergence of festival- and event-based tourism stimulated by the activities of the nobility and knights. Jousting tournaments and spectatorship saw a demand emerge for temporary accommodation and travel to these events.

In the latter part of the Middle Ages, pilgrims travelled to the Holy Land. Travel was difficult owing to the poor quality of access, although this difficult access created a demand for accommodation and hospitality services *en route*. Business travel to centres of commerce across Europe and farther afield was limited.

The Renaissance and Reformation

The Renaissance originated in Italy after 1350, and reached its zenith in England during Elizabethan times. The earlier trends of festivals and fairs continued, again forming a nucleus of domestic tourism activity. The rise of travelling theatres and patronage of the arts created opportunities for travel and a more enlightened era. The affluent continued to build villas in the country, for both long- and short-term use (in Italy, this process of withdrawing to a country villa was called villeggiatura during the Renaissance). After 1500 the Reformation emerged with the ideas of Luther and Calvin, whose religious zeal created what has been termed the Protestant work ethic. This was a notable turning point in the history of leisure (and thereby tourism), as Lutheran and Calvinistic ideas questioned the value of leisure, portraying it as idleness. These ideas can be seen more clearly in the rise of the industrial society, where leisure was denigrated by the needs of capitalists and entrepreneurs in order to create a more profitable economy.

In Europe, the leisure and tourism activities of different social classes began to be separated. In one of the most influential studies of the history of tourism, Towner (1996) explains how the upper classes withdrew from popular culture. In England the sale of Church lands after the dissolution of the Monasteries by Henry VIII created vast areas of land, which provided the basis for country estates as places for recreation and tourism. The wealthy built country residences throughout the eighteenth and nineteenth centuries.

The European Grand Tour

In the sixteenth century, another important development emerged as an aristocratic form of tourism – the Grand Tour. This was a traveller's circuit of key destinations and places to visit in pursuit of culture and education, and was restricted mainly to the wealthy, aristocratic and privileged classes. Such tours did not of course originate in the Middle Ages; some elements of Roman society travelled to Greece in pursuit of culture and education. However, it reached its peak in the eighteenth century as a highly developed form of tourism. Some commentators have suggested that this was the forerunner of the modern-day overseas holiday.

Within Western Europe, the Grand Tour has been recounted in the diaries, letters and memoirs of travellers, as well as being documented in guidebooks and historical records associated with tourism. According to the most detailed research on the subject, by Towner (1985, 1996), typical tourists were young aristocrats who were accompanied by tutors – although this may be an oversimplification of travel in the sixteenth century. By the eighteenth century, the emerging middle classes were forming a growing element of Grand Tourists. Towner (1985) estimated that in the mid-eighteenth century between 15 000 and 20 000 Britons toured continental Europe – around 0.2–0.7 per cent of the population.

Much of the interest in the Grand Tour can be related to the Renaissance and the emergence of interest in classical antiques, promoted by learning and developments in philosophy that encouraged travel to expand the human mind. This emerging travel culture, which was destined to mainland Europe, saw a growing link with the knowledge of and interest in the classics, art, the appreciation of architecture and intellectual thought prior to the expansion of mass forms of education and learning. The Grand Tour was far from a static entity, as ideas from Europe were brought back to England and changing fashions and tastes in the interests of Grand Tourists can also be discerned between the 1550s and early 1800s. For example, the emergence of interest in landscape and scenery viewing from the 1760s and a wider range of pursuits characterized such tours. Figures 2.1 and 2.2 illustrate some of the typical Grand Tour routes taken in Europe, and the dominance of certain centres (e.g. Paris, Turin, Florence, Naples and Rome). The rise of Switzerland as a destination and the pursuit of scenic tourism were also notable, as new modes of transport on land, inland waterways and rivers created opportunities for this (one example is the appearance of steamers on Swiss lakes in the 1820s). In the UK travellers such as Celia Fiennes during the 1680s and Daniel Defoe in the 1720s reflected the traits of the European

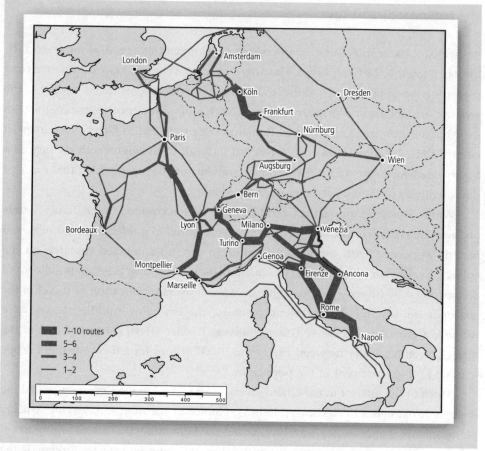

Figure 2.1 Grand Tour routes in Europe, 1661–1700 (© Elsevier). Reprinted from *Annals of Tourism Research*, vol. 12, J. Towner, The Grand Tour: A key phase in the history of tourism: 297–333 © 1985 with permission from Elsevier

Grand Tour in their changing attitudes to landscapes and scenery as elements of tourism, and England's Lake District became popular in the 1740s following images presented by writers and artists.

Box 2.1 describes spa development, an enduring theme from Elizabethan times to the early nineteenth century that reflects both the continuity and the change in the history of tourism.

Some researchers have attempted to explain the growth, stagnation and decline of tourist resorts such as spas in terms of a resort life cycle. Butler (1980) suggests that resorts follow a specific cycle of growth following the initial exploration by tourists. This is followed by a period of involvement, often with patronage or popularization,

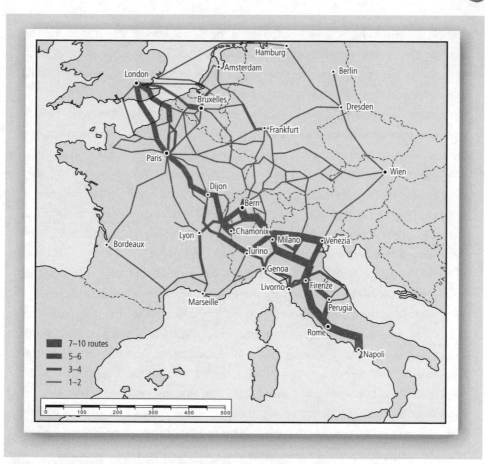

Figure 2.2 Grand Tour routes in Europe, 1814–1820 (© Elsevier). Reprinted from *Annals of Tourism Research*, vol. 12, J. Towner, The Grand Tour: A key phase in the history of tourism: 297–333 © 1985 with permission from Elsevier

Box 2.1   Case study: changing patterns of spa development in England, 1558–1815

There is a long historical tradition in western society of taking mineral waters for health and pleasure, and this can be dated back to Roman times. These *aquae*, as they were known, were distributed throughout the Roman territories. What is notable in terms of the continuity and change in the history of tourism is that they declined after Roman times (i.e. *change*) but formed the basis for the future growth of spa resorts in later times (i.e. *continuity*). Examples include Bath in the UK, Aquae Calidae in Vichy, Aquae

Mattiacae in Germany, and the hot springs in the Bay of Naples. Whilst many Roman spas were less exclusive than those for designed for later users, in some countries (such as Hungary) spas continued in use from Roman times to the Middle Ages. But why did spas develop as sites for tourist consumption?

Certain factors were a prerequisite for development, such as the existence of a spring site to provide the waters, individuals or agents promoting their development, and favourable conditions relating to accessibility and positive trends in spa visiting. There was also the associated development of accommodation, hospitality and ancillary services, which often coalesced to comprise a distinct spa resort. In fact, in colonial America, Philadelphia had spas at Abington, Bristol and Yellow Springs; these urban centres supported nearby springs, and access to the outlying springs led to the development of resorts and facilities in the urban centres.

In many spas that developed in England between 1660 and 1815, patronage by royalty, the nobility and the growing affluent classes stimulated demand. Entrepreneurs, public authorities or a partnership of both led to the growth of spas, with individual landowners amongst the gentry or aristocracy providing the land and thus the basis for tourism-based speculative development. In Harrogate in Yorkshire public sector promotion by the Corporation in the 1720s provided the basis for development, as did the Federal Parks Department in Canada at Radium Hot Springs in the 1920s. In some cases, such as Rotorua in New Zealand, the advances in spa-based health treatments (e.g. hydropathy) saw the New Zealand Tourism and Publicity Department manage and promote the major facilities as a basis to stimulate tourism development. In Scotland, late Victorian and Edwardian entrepreneurs created a range of successful (and unsuccessful) hydro hotels, providing focal points for spa and health tourism at locations such as Dunblane and Crieff.

These examples illustrate the fact that spa development has a longevity in historical terms. Factors promoting the growth of some resorts (e.g. the advent of the railway age) led to the continued prosperity of some resorts such as Buxton, Harrogate and Llandrindod Wells, whilst others declined due to difficult access, changing tastes and oversupply.

which sets the stage and creates tourism tastes and fashions emulated by the visitors. This contributes to development, followed by consolidation and then stagnation. At this point the resort can either decline or action might be taken by agents of

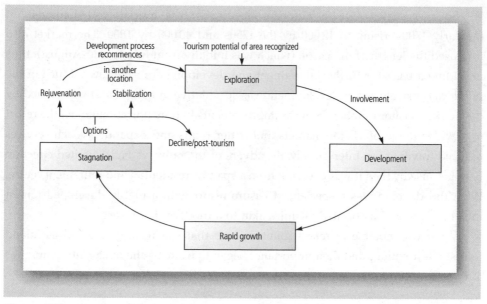

Figure 2.3   The resort life cycle (developed and modified from R. Butler (1980)

development (such as an entrepreneur, the public sector or a combination of both) to rejuvenate the resort, this being the last stage of the model (see Figure 2.3).

Although such models are highly generalized and simplify the reality of resort development, they provide a starting point for the analysis of resorts such as spas through history. For example, many of the 173 rural spas that were created in England between 1558 and 1815 had a short-existence compared to their urban counterparts. Figure 2.3 illustrates this pattern through time, and is a combination of the creation (i.e. birth) and decline (i.e. death) of resorts. Whilst certain spas (such as Buxton and Bath) had an enduring history, others (such as Wellingborough, which was in existence in the late 1600s but had disappeared by 1711) were less long-lived.

Probably the most well known example of spa development is Bath in England. It emerged from its Roman origins with an enduring pattern of visitation during the Middle Ages owing to the medicinal value of its waters. Its rapid expansion is illustrated by its rise in population from under 2000 in the 1660s to 13 000 in the 1760s and 33 000 in 1801, mainly as a result of the spa-based growth of the town. The increase in tourists illustrates patronage by visitors from London and Southern England initially, in the sixteenth century. This gradually expanded to a national market, to include courtiers, the aristocracy, gentry, clergy and professional classes (both the infirm seeking cures and those of good health looking for preventative medication).

Some estimates of visitor numbers suggest that 8000 tourists visited annually in the early 1700s, rising to 12 000 by the 1750s and 40 000 by 1800. The market also increased the length of its season (which was initially from July to mid-August), thus providing a basis for further investment and development in the town. Much of the public and private sector development was speculative in nature, and was fuelled by the market. Visitor numbers grew as improvements in transportation linked the resort to a wider range of visitor markets and better roads and expanded coach services reduced travel times. Interestingly, the advent of the railways had a limited effect on Bath because by then it was evolving from a spa to a residential and retirement centre. What did develop was a specialized leisure resort with a highly developed tourist infrastructure and associated facilities akin to a modern-day resort.

What was notable in many countries was that spa resorts emerged as inland tourism destinations and their importance began to wane by the nineteenth century as a new genre of tourism emerged – the seaside resort.

Tourism and the coast: the seaside resort

In the late eighteenth century, coastal areas emerged in many European countries as the new form of tourism destination for the leisured classes. This was at a time when spas and other inland resorts were still expanding. Up to the eighteenth century the coast had been a revered landscape, where religious ideals, cultural attitudes and tastes had not encouraged visiting – in fact the coast was considered an environment to avoid due to the forces of nature and evil. However, during the eighteenth century the impact of poets, artists (such as Constable) and romanticists led to the beach and coastline being discovered as a site for pleasure – a place for spiritual fulfilment and a site for tourism as bathing slowly developed as a social and leisure activity between 1750 and 1840.

A number of key landmarks in the early history of coastal tourism can be recognized, including:

- Dr Russell's (1752) treatise on the use of seawater for health reasons as well as bathing
- The popularization of sea-bathing by Royal patronage (e.g. George III bathed at Weymouth in the late eighteenth century)
- Royal patronage of resorts such as Brighton by the Prince Regent
- The combining of health reasons for visiting with pleasure and fashion

- The search by Europe's social elite for more exclusive and undiscovered destinations
- The rise of resorts with a wide range of social and ancillary services to meet the needs of visitors (e.g. reading rooms, accommodation, assembly rooms, promenades, excursions and entertainment).

The early patronage by the upper classes soon encouraged growing access to coastal recreation and tourism as transport technology made resorts accessible – for example, with the provision of paddle steamers in the 1820s between London and the Kent coastal resorts. The railway era, from the 1840s onwards, also connected many coastal resorts to the main source of demand – the urban industrial heartland of the UK. It was not until the 1871 and 1875 Bank Holiday Acts in the UK, when four statutory holidays days were provided, that workers had an opportunity to engage in coastal tourism more fully. These Acts made the coastal resorts in the UK more accessible to the working classes; middle-class workers had already begun to take more extensive holidays from the 1850s.

A social differentiation in coastal resorts also existed, where developers, municipal authorities and businesses positively attracted certain types of visitor. For example, in northwest England Blackpool developed as a working-class resort, meeting the needs of the Lancashire textile towns, where cheap rail travel and savings schemes promoted holidays. The different timings of industrial holidays in different towns in northwest England also enabled resorts to extend the traditional summer season, so that accommodation and hospitality services had a wider range of business opportunities and resorts such as Blackpool developed a highly specialized tourism industry.

In terms of the supply of coastal resorts in England and Wales, no major population centre was more than 70–80 miles from a coastal area. In the eighteenth century a number of early resorts such as Scarborough combined spa and coastal tourism trades, although the majority of resorts were in southern England owing due to the proximity of London. During the industrialization and urbanization of England in the late eighteenth and early nineteenth centuries, a number of other regional markets developed in southwest England and in a limited number of northern and Welsh locations. By 1851 there was a continuous increase in the number of resorts from Devon to Kent in southern England, complemented by the rising popularity of the Isle of Wight, Wales, northwest and eastern England. By 1881 growing access to the coast led to more specialized resorts, with specific markets emerging, the growing social divide of visitors to certain resorts (i.e. the middle classes visited Bournemouth while the working classes went to Southend, Margate and Blackpool). By 1911 the current-day pattern of resorts was well established, although over-supply and seasonality was common in the holiday trade in these resorts. In Scotland, resort development in western areas dependent upon the urban population of Glasgow provided a wide range of opportunities, and the integration of rail and steamers provided a complex system of destinations by the 1880s.

Running parallel to the mass tourism phenomenon of the coastal resorts were the origins of the modern-day tourism industry, with the emergence of commercially organized tourism by Thomas Cook. Cook organized the first package tours, initially utilizing the Victorian railway system (Leicester to Loughborough in 1841), with railway tours to Scotland in 1848 and overseas tours in the 1850s. In 1866 Cook organized his first tours to America, and passenger cruises on the River Nile followed in the 1880s. Other entrepreneurs, including Henry Lunn, also organized overseas packages for skiing in Switzerland in the 1880s, and the upper and middle classes engaged in new overseas tours as well as domestic tourism to coastal resorts.

Tourism during the Edwardian and inter-war years

By the 1900s, coastal tourism, overseas travel by passenger liners and the rise of socially segregated travel offered a wider range of international holiday options to the elite in western society. The imperial trade of many European powers also created a demand for business travel and limited volumes of recreational travel. For example, by 1914 up to 150 000 American visitors were entering the UK each year. The Edwardian years saw the continued expenditure of the middle classes on overseas travel and a growing fascination with rural and scenic areas, popularized by the pursuit of outdoor activities such as shooting and hunting in the Highlands of Scotland, and cycling. Almost 10 per cent of *Black's Shilling Guide to Scotland* (1906) was devoted to cycling, using hotels and other accommodation establishments. The railway also extended access to mountain climbing activities in the Highlands, and the Ladies Scottish Climbing Club was founded in 1908, reflecting the growing emancipation of women and their role as travellers in Edwardian society. Hiking also emerged as a popular activity, with the rise of the Scottish Youth Hostels Association in 1931. The emergence of sleeper services on long-distance rail journeys also encouraged middle classes to travel further afield.

Guidebooks provide one of the historical sources that enable us to understand how and where the Edwardians travelled. An interesting example is the *Queens Newspaper Book of Travel* (1910), which had been published annually since 1903 and was compiled by a travel editor who was a geographer. This provided descriptions of places that visitors from the UK might visit both domestically and overseas, or where they might be stationed in the British Empire. It had candid insights, as this extract on visiting Rangoon, in Imperial Burma, shows:

A damp place; and the first feeling on arrival is generally one of prostration, followed by slight ague and fever; but this in robust people soon passes away, and although Rangoon is not regarded as a healthy station, yet of late years sanitary improvements have somewhat bettered its climate ... All clothing should be packed in airtight cases. One requires an abundant supply of Indian gauze underclothing (not less than three changes a day, even to corsets).

It is also useful in providing detailed itineraries published from actual tours taken by guidebook users. For example, Box 2.1, entitled 'A Tour of Scotland', is a diary of a trip and places visited. It highlights a diversity of transport modes used and was clearly an extensive tour by someone from the leisured classes, as it lasted for more than two weeks – a luxury that many of the working classes could not afford in Edwardian Britain. The diary entry also highlights the wide range of private railway companies and transport companies in existence, a feature also evident in Figure 2.4, which records the large number of Edwardian ferry crossings from Great Britain to mainland Europe, many with boat–train connections.

Such itineraries were encouraged by the railway companies, who published illustrated guides such as the *Through Scotland* (priced 3d and produced by the Caledonian Railway Company), which was 170 pages long, as well as free hotel and furnished lodgings guides. Advertisers in the *Queens Newspaper Book of Travel* also promoted hotels and accommodation as well as travel products.

The First World War obviously curtailed the growth of international tourism, although domestic tourism continued in a number of countries, as the R&R (rest and recuperation) function following the ravages of war provided a renewed boost for many resorts. The depression of the 1920s and early 1930s suppressed the demand for international and domestic tourism, although recreational pursuits replaced some of the demand for travel and new forms of low-cost tourism emerged among poorer

Box 2.1 Tour of Scotland

Departs London *August 14th*, heading to Glasgow *August 15th*, visited Glasgow Cathedral, parks and the Art Gallery.

August 16th, made a trip by rail from Glasgow Central Station and then by steamer from Weymss Bay to Ardishaig; lunch and tea on board.

August 17th, left Glasgow Central by rail for Loch Lomond, steamer to the Inversnaid Hotel; many fishermen staying in the hotel; sport fair in the loch.

August 18th, drove to Stronachlacher, thence by steamer and coach to the Trossachs Hotel; lunched there, and thence to Callander by coach – a most enjoyable trip. Took train via St Fillians to Crieff (Drummond Arms Hotel), and stayed one night there.

August 19th, by early train to Loch Awe (via Loch Earn Side – an enchanting journey). We then took the steamer from Loch Awe Station and Hotel; thence a short journey by train to Oban.

August 20th, spent Sunday in Oban.

August 21st, by early steamer to Fort William (Prince Charlie's country), and thence through the Caledonian Canal to Inverness; Palace Hotel (good bedrooms).

August 22nd, left for train to Aberdeen. In Aberdeen, the Grand Hotel is at present time looked upon as the best.

August 23rd, by train to Ballater (lunch), and thence by motor omnibus to Braemar (Invercauld Arms), where we met with every attention; good food, pleasant rooms.

August 24th, by coach across Spital of Glenshee to Blairgowrie, and on to Dunkeld. The Birman Hotel is excellent.

August 25th, in Dunkeld.

August 26th, by rail to Aberfeldy, coach to Kenmore, thence by steamer down Loch Tay to Killin, where we again took the train for Callander (Dreadnought Hotel).

August 27th, in Callander (Sunday).

August 28th, by rail from Callander to Edinburgh (Princes Street) (Caledonian Railway Company's Station Hotel).

August 29th, left Edinburgh (Princes Street section) for London by West Coast Mail Route.

(Source: *Queens Newspaper Book of Travel*, 1910: 106)

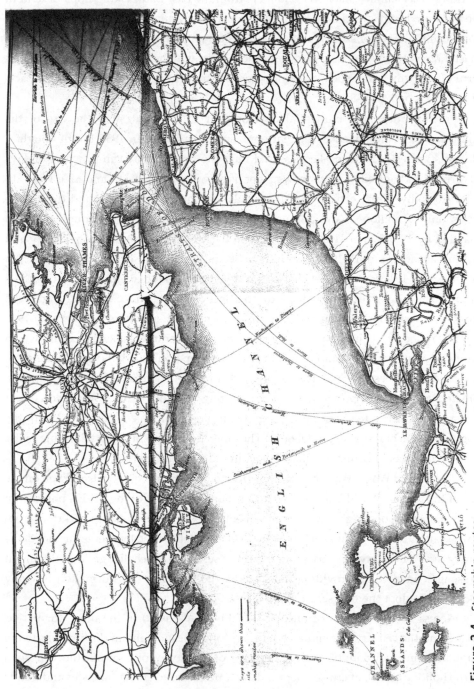

Figure 2.4 Steamship routes

working-class families, such as Londoners from the East End picking hops in Kent in the autumn. Mechanization in the post-war period gradually removed these tourism opportunities. The construction of second homes on plots of land in the green belt or coastal areas by the working classes in the 1930s saw a new, chaotic and unplanned form of tourism. Many such dwellings were subsequently removed by planning acts in the 1930s and 1940s.

Probably the most influential development in the 1930s was the rise of the holiday camp, epitomized by the entrepreneur Billy Butlin. In 1936 Butlin bought a plot of 40 acres of land in Skegness and built the first holiday camp, with holidays advertised in the *Daily Express* newspaper at between 35 shillings and £3 a week. In the 1920s only 17 per cent of the UK population had paid holidays and during the 1930s only 3 million of the population had holiday with pay, although this had changed by 1939, when 11 million people in the UK received holidays with pay and Butlin's attracted almost 100 000 visitors to Skegness and to a second camp at Clacton in Essex. By 1948 it estimated that one in twenty holidaymakers stayed at Butlin's camps. The origins of the holiday camp concept can be traced to the organized workers associations' cycling and tent camps earlier in the twentieth century. By 1939 a wide range of such camps emerged as planned commercialized resorts, which provided a fantasy world and offered relatively cheap domestic holidays. At the same time, second homes developed as a more widespread phenomenon in many countries. Greater advertising, promotion and marketing by tour operators, resorts and transport providers (e.g. the railways and shipping companies), combined with the popularization of travel in guidebooks. Thus inter-war tourism begin to acquire many of the hallmarks of commercialized travel in the post-war period.

The Second World War impeded the growth of international tourism. Even on the eve of the Second World War in 1939, fewer than 50 per cent of the British population spent more than one night away from home. However, car ownership had risen from 200 000 in 1920 to 2 million in 1939, and other notable developments included the emergence of embryonic passenger airline services to challenge the dominant passenger liners, thus providing the seeds of the post-war transformation of many societies to adopt the overseas travel bug.

Access to new forms of transport (notably road-based) in the inter-war period opened up the countryside and a wider range of domestic tourism destinations to the population in many countries. The emergence of new forms of domestic tourism (such as the holiday camp), of cruise liners and of air travel led to changing tastes and trends in holiday taking. Whilst many resorts and transport providers responded to a widening range of opportunities for travel and holidaying with the use of marketing and promotion, the real rise of mass tourism was a post-war phenomenon.

Post-war tourism: towards international mass tourism

In Chapter 1 the trend in international tourism, dating back to the 1950s, illustrated the phenomenal growth in international travel, which was punctuated by drops and troughs in demand. Many of the current-day trends in tourism can be dated to the post-war period – particularly the rise in demand for holidays. This period saw a growth in income, leisure time and opportunities for international travel. In the immediate post-war period, surplus military aircraft were converted to passenger services and the 1950s saw the introduction of jet airliners. As airlines bought new jets, older aircraft became available for charter holiday companies to operate services to holiday destinations. In the UK Vladimir Raitz is credited with offering the first package holiday, subsequently developing Horizon Holidays (now part of Thomson Holidays), and he was soon followed by a number of other tour operators. By 1959,

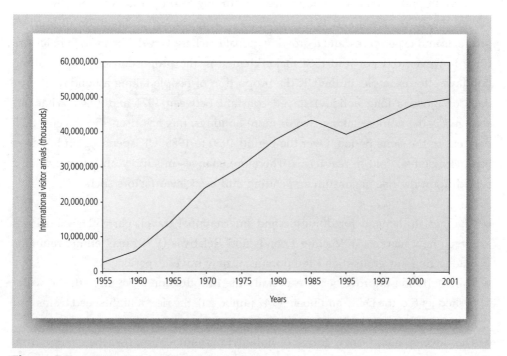

Figure 2.5   The growth of tourism in Spain

2.25 million Britons took foreign trips, 76 769 of which were to Spain. Yet during the 1960s the numbers taking foreign holidays was set to rise by 230 per cent, and by 1967 there were 5 million British holidaymakers going abroad. Regarding Spain, Figure 2.5 shows how the rise of the package holiday led to the growth of Mediterranean resorts. By 1965 Spain had become Europe's leading tourism destination, with 14 million visitors a year (this has grown to nearly 48 million in 2001). Spain saw its share of the UK holiday market rise from 6 per cent in 1951 to 30 per cent in 1968. In the late 1960s package holidays to Mallorca cost £30, which was equivalent to a week's salary. The ill-fated Clarkson's tour operator saw its number of clients grow from 16 000 in 1966 to 90 000 in 1967 – a sign of the massive growth in package holidays. Consumer spending on domestic holidays rose by 80 per cent between 1951 and 1968, and on overseas holidays by 400 per cent. In 1951 a UK holiday cost an average of £11, a foreign holiday £41. By 1968 the prices were £20 and £62 respectively. By 1968 Clarkson's clients had risen to 175 000; however, the oil crisis in the 1970s, the Arab–Israeli war and the oil embargo of 1973 saw increased fuel prices and a drop in package holidays, which led to a massive reduction in tourist travel. In 1974 Clarkson's collapsed, with tourists stranded in 75 resorts in 26 coastal areas. This resulted, in part, from a sustained price war among tour operators in the UK.

In the 1970s, 1980s and 1990s, there was an increasing proliferation of tourism products and experiences, and a growing global reach for travel. The growth in leisure time, however, did not lead to a major change in the proportion of people taking holidays – for example, in the UK the proportion of people taking a holiday of four days or more (a long holiday) stayed constant between 1971 and 1998. What has changed is the number taking two or more holidays; this has risen 15 per cent to 25 per cent in the same period. Over the period 1950 to 1988, UK spending on holidays has increased six-fold in real terms. Therefore changes in supply and demand have seized upon the rise in consumer spending and associated factors such as:

- Changes in demand for domestic and international travel, particularly business travel, new markets in Visiting Friends and Relatives (VFR) (e.g. ethnic reunions among migrant groups) and the pursuit of new travel experiences
- Transportation improvements, especially the introduction of jet aircraft, the wide-bodied jet (i.e. the DC10 and Boeing 747 jumbo jet), the rise of high-speed trains and larger aircraft such as the planned Airbus 3XX
- The development of new forms of holiday accommodation (i.e. the change from holiday camps to timeshare, self-catering and second homes)

- Innovations by tour operators, including the rise of the holiday brochure, new forms of retailing such as direct selling, buying via the Internet, more competitive pricing and the evolution of one-stop shop retailing (i.e. the package, insurance, holiday currency, airport transfers and pre-flight accommodation and car parking)
- Greater availability of information on destinations to visit from the media, brochures, guidebooks, the Internet and travel programmes
- Increased promotion of destinations by governments, growing consumer protection to ensure greater regulation, and resort promotion in the media and via the Internet.

Many of these factors combine to enable a destination to develop its tourism industry, and the case study in Box 2.2 provides a profile of inbound tourism to the USA in the new millennium, highlighting the importance of forecast changes in its development as a destination.

Box 2.2   Case study: inbound tourism to the USA in the new millennium

Tourism has emerged as a key element of the US economy since the 1980s, increasing from US$26 billion in 1986 to US$90 billion in 1996. This figure is expanded if the impact of direct and indirect revenue is considered, in that tourism supports over 18 million jobs in the USA and creates US$92 billion in taxes. This is supported by domestic and international tourism, the latter of which grew by 5 per cent in 1999–2000 to 50.9 million arrivals. International visitors comprise two distinct groups. Almost half of the arrivals are border crossings from Mexico and Canada, with the remaining 26 million coming from Western Europe (11 million), Asia (7.5 million), South America (nearly 3 million), the Caribbean (1.3 million), Central America (nearly 822 000), Oceania (Australia and New Zealand, 731 000), the Middle East (702 000), Eastern Europe (500 000 million) and Africa (295 000). In 2000, almost two-thirds of the arrivals from Asia were Japanese and 660 000 came from South Korea. British arrivals have been experiencing a boom in the new millennium, at 4.7 million. These figures confirm the position of the USA in 2001 as the second-ranked inbound destination at a global level, with 18% of world travel receipts. Indeed, despite a healthy outbound travel market, in 2000 the USA generated a travel surplus US$14 billion (i.e. international visitors spent this much more in the USA than US residents spent when travelling abroad).

Tourism remains the fourth most important export for the US economy, and the top states visited in 2000 were:

- California (5.7 million visits)
- Florida (5.3 million visits)
- New York (5.9 million visits)
- Hawaii (2.7 million visits)
- Nevada (2.4 million visits)
- Massachusetts (1.4 million visits)
- Illinois (1.4 million visits)
- The American territory in the North Pacific, Guam (1.3 million visits)
- Texas (1.2 million visits)
- New Jersey (909 000 visits).

The most popular destinations were New York City, Los Angeles, Orlando, Miami, San Francisco, Las Vegas, Washington DC and Boston.

The top activities for international visitors were:

- Shopping (87 per cent)
- Dining in restaurants (84 per cent)
- Sightseeing in cities (43 per cent)
- Amusement/theme park visits (31 per cent)
- Visiting historical places (31 per cent).

Many visitors visited two destinations during their trip. A high usage of taxis (41 per cent), rental cars (31 per cent), domestic flights (29 per cent), buses between cities (10 per cent) and rail (7 per cent) illustrates this trend towards inter-destination travel. Over 81 per cent of visitors preferred to use hotels, and 78 per cent were repeat travellers with 22 per cent first-time visitors.

The predicted future growth of overseas arrivals to the USA (excluding revisions for the effects of 11 September 2001) is shown in Table 2.2. This shows that arrivals are forecast to rise to 57 million up to the year 2005, assuming annual rates of growth of 4.3–7.9 per cent to achieve these targets. For individual markets such as Europe strong performance is expected, but much of this will depend upon:

- The degree of political stability at a global level and within the USA
- The impact of currency valuations (i.e. the strength of the US dollar)
- The impact of inflation, disposable income and holiday prices in origin and destination areas
- The competition for visitors from alternative destinations outside of the USA.

Table 2.1 Forecasts for international tourism arrivals in the USA (in thousands) 2000–2005 (modified from the US Department of Commerce)

Source area	2000	2001	2002	2003	2004	2005
Mexico*	10 322	9 558	9 996	10 718	11 647	12 607
Canada*	14 594	13 384	14 038	15 074	16 057	17 088
Overseas	25 975	21 526	22 362	24 222	25 923	27 490
Europe	11 597	9 148	9 633	10 622	11 374	12 054
Asia	7 554	6 061	6 313	6 684	7 131	7 536
South America	2 941	2 618	2 688	2 866	3 094	3 317
Caribbean	1 331	1 181	1 206	1 311	1 365	1 414
Central America	822	759	783	848	913	970
Oceania	731	569	597	672	730	775
Middle East	702	576	504	531	575	647
Africa	295	253	269	293	314	328
Total	50 891	44 467	46 366	50 014	53 627	57 185

*Canada and Mexico are not counted as international arrivals.

Space tourism

Whilst the forecasts of future tourism arrivals illustrate the importance of looking ahead in trying to anticipate changes, one new trend that is likely to emerge in the next 50 years and is therefore worthy of discussion is space tourism.

Since a member of the public recently joined a Russian space flight, there has been increasing interest in the future growth of space tourism. However, interest in space tourism is not new, with NASA publishing various reports on the subject in the 1990s – particularly its 1998 Report *General Public Space Travel and Tourism*. In the USA,

12 million people per year visit NASA's Air and Space Museum in Washington, the Kennedy Space Center in Florida and the Johnson Space Center in Texas, while 2 million a year visit Space World, in Japan.

In research studies, the market for space travel in the USA alone is estimated to be worth US$40 billion a year. Much of the future potential market is dependent upon reusable launch vehicles that can carry commercial passengers. Research indicates that once ticket prices can be generated at US$10 000, the market will be expanded. However, this is some way off – the Russian launch vehicle cost US$10 million. Some commentators consider that it will be possible to achieve space tourism, based on short sub-orbital flights, within the next 50 years, although in the longer term other possibilities may include:

- Short earth orbital flights using reusable spacecraft
- Tourism in space hotels located around the earth's orbit
- Moon and Mars tourism.

For the tourist, seeing the earth from 100 km above its surface will provide a lifetime memory. There will also be leisure space for activities such as weddings, sports and games. Yet engineers recognize that, for technology to advance, major developments in propulsion systems are required. For the tourist, certain medical and physical preparation will be necessary, including familiarization with short sub-orbital flights, learning how to perform emergency procedures, and coping strategies to deal with claustrophobia, isolation and personal hygiene. Policy changes may also be necessary to modify the Liability Convention (1971) of the UN, which makes the launching country liable for compensation for losses or damage. However, the existing investment by governments in the USA, Europe and Japan of US$20 billion in space agencies indicates that state funding has already underwritten an element of the investment costs in space tourism, and it has a potential to generate an economic return.

The future demand for space tourism could grow from a conservative estimate of 150 000 trips a year on 1500 flights at a ticket price of US$72 000 (generating revenue of US$10.8 billion), to 950 000 trips on 9500 flights at a ticket price of US$12 000. The flights would rendezvous with a space hotel, unload the incoming passengers and transport the returning passengers to Earth. What is evident is that in the early years of space tourism the demand will be low and price will be high. This will change as the activity becomes more acceptable – similar to a product life cycle.

Summary

The history of tourism can be characterized by continuity and change in the form, nature and extent of tourism activity. The growing globalization and global extent of tourism activity can be explained by wider social access to travel, enabled by a range of factors promoting travel (i.e. income and leisure time). The emergence of mass tourism in the period since the 1960s is a dominant feature of the international expansion of world travel. There has also been a fundamental shift in tourism since the 1960s, as the 1990s saw a move from industry-based standardized packages towards a greater individuality and flexible itineraries, a difference in the nature of experiences sought, and concern with issues such as the environment and sustainability. A greater range of niche products has been developed and marketed to fulfil the demand for increasingly sophisticated travel tastes. At the same time, with ageing populations in many countries, earlier retirement and increasing longevity, longer holidays have seen a resurgence (in the 1930s these were the preserve of the wealthy and upper classes).

With the prospect of space travel now a reality, along with more exploratory forms of marine tourism to the ocean's depths, tourism continues to push the bounds of man's endurance and quest for discovery and something new. What is clear is that tourism has continued to develop and evolve through time, and many current trends will wane as new ones emerge, although these may use existing resources, places and experiences. In some cases new environments, places and experiences will also continue to be developed. Tourism is always changing, and the challenge for the tourism manager and entrepreneur is to anticipate new trends and tastes and to meet them.

References

Butler, R. (1980) The concept of the tourist area cycle of evolution: implications for the evolution of resources, *Canadian Geographer*, **24**(1), 5–12.

Towner, J. (1985) The Grand Tour: a key phase in the history of tourism. *Annals of Tourism Research*, **12**(3), 297–333.

Towner, J. (1996) *An Historical Geography of Recreation and Tourism in the Western World 1540–1940*. Chichester: Wiley.

Further reading

Walton, J. (1983) *The English Seaside Resort: A Social History 1750–1914*. Leicester: Leicester University Press.

Walton, J. (2000) The hospitality trades: a social history. In: C. Lashley and A. Morrison (eds), *In Search of Hospitality: Theoretical Perspectives and Debates*. Oxford: Butterworth-Heinemann, pp. 56–76.

Walton, J. and Smith, J. (1996) The first century of beach tourism in Spain: San Sebastian and the Playas del Norte from the 1830s to the 1930s. *In*: M. Barke, J. Towner and M. Newton (eds), *Tourism in Spain: Critical Issues*. Wallingford: CAB International, pp. 189–212.

Ward, C. and Hardy, D. (1986) *Goodnight Campers: The History of the British Holiday Camp*. London: Mansell.

Questions

1 Why is the historical study of tourism useful in understanding the management problems that many destinations face in the new millennium?

2 How can you explain the continuity and change in the historical development of tourism?

3 What is the value of the resort life-cycle model in explaining tourism growth and development?

4 What are the future prospects for space tourism?

3

Demand: why do people engage in tourism?

Learning objectives

This chapter examines the reasons why people go on holiday and the explanations developed to understand the motivating factors associated with leisure travel. After reading it, you should be able to understand:

- the concept of tourism demand and the ways it may be defined;
- the role of motivation studies in explaining why people go on holiday;
- the different motives used to develop classifications of tourism;
- the role of consumer behaviour in explaining why people select certain holiday products.

Introduction

Understanding why people choose to travel and to become tourists seems at first sight to be a very simple issue. In fact it is a very complex area, and whilst we can all think of simple reasons why people choose to go on holiday, the area has also been extensively studied by psychologists. Theoretical research has sought to classify travellers into groups in order to generalize the reasons for being involved in tourism. As the tourism industry relies upon travellers, understanding what motivates them to go to specific places and resorts has major economic consequences. Yet the explanation of why people travel for pleasure, business and other reasons has become clouded by a fundamental problem: psychologists (who study how humans behave, interact and react to external and internal stimuli) attempt to develop theories, and these theories are detached from the way in which the tourism industry uses very practical marketing-based approaches to understand why consumers choose to travel. This chapter explores the way in which the academic study and practical application of principles associated with tourism demand have been applied in trying to understand what motivates tourists as consumers.

Attempts to classify and group tourists into categories or to develop a model of tourist motivators are fraught with problems, as motivation is a highly individualized element of human behaviour. It affects and conditions how people react and behave, and their attitudes to tourism as something they consume. In other words, while a range of motivating factors can be promoting travel, a range of highly personal and individualized elements still exists. There is no universal agreement on how to approach the tourist demand for travel products and services, although this chapter explores a number of approaches and possible reasons why human beings engage in tourism as a recreational activity. If we understand what prompts people to leave their home area and to travel to other places, then we may be able to develop approaches that will help us to manage these visitors and their impacts. It may be possible to plan for a more enjoyable experience at the place(s) they visit. More fundamentally, understanding tourist motivation may help to explain why certain places developed as successful tourism destinations and then continued to grow, stagnated or declined as tastes, fashions and perceptions of tourism as an activity changed. However, our starting point has to be what is meant by tourism demand, as it drives the growth, development and change in tourism businesses and resorts.

What is tourism demand?

Tourism demand has been defined in numerous ways, including 'the total number of persons who travel, or wish to travel, to use tourist facilities and services at places away from their places of work and residence' (Mathieson and Wall, 1982: 1). Other studies have defined it as '... the relationship between individuals' motivation [to travel] and their ability to do so' (Pearce, 1995: 18). In contrast, more economic-focused definitions of demand are concerned primarily with 'the schedule of the amount of any product or service which people are willing and able to buy at each specific price in a set of possible prices during a specified period of time' (Cooper *et al.*, 1993: 15).

There are three principal elements to tourism demand:

1 *Effective* or *actual demand*, which is the number of people participating in tourism, commonly expressed as the number of travellers. It is normally measured by tourism statistics – typically, departures from countries and arrivals at destinations.
2 *Suppressed demand*, which consists of the population that cannot travel because of circumstances (e.g. lack of purchasing power or limited holiday entitlement). It is sometimes referred to as potential demand. Potential demand can be converted to effective demand if the circumstances change. There is also deferred demand, where constraints (e.g. lack of tourism supply such as a shortage of bedspaces) can also be converted to effective demand if a destination or locality can accommodate the demand.
3 *No demand*, which is a distinct category for the population who have no desire to travel, and those who are unable to travel due to family commitments or illness.

An interesting study by Uysal (1998) summarized the main determinants of demand – economic, social-psychological and exogenous (i.e. the business elements). The useful overview shown in Figure 3.1 is not intended to provide an exhaustive list of factors, but rather to give examples of factors that are likely to affect demand. It provides a general context for tourism demand, but does not adequately explain how and why people decide to select and participate in specific forms of tourism. This is associated with the area of consumer behaviour and motivation.

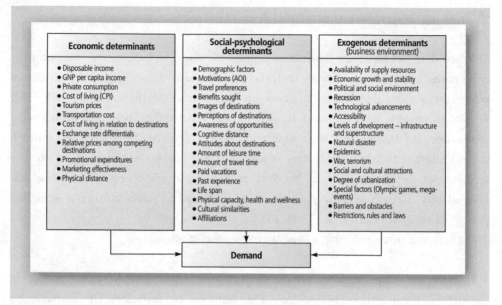

Figure 3.1   Determinants of tourism demand (source: Uysal, 1998 © Routledge). Reproduced from D. Ioannides and K. Debbage (eds), *The Economic Geography of the Tourist Industry*, p. 87, Fig. 5.2, Routledge, 1988

The motivation dichotomy: why do people go on holiday?

In a very comprehensive assessment of tourism motivation, Mountinho (1987: 16) defined motivation as a 'state of need, a condition that exerts a push on the individual towards certain types of action that are seen as likely to bring satisfaction'. Thus demand is about using tourism as a form of consumption to achieve a level of satisfaction for an individual, and involves understanding their behaviour and actions and what shapes these human characteristics. It is important to know what the tourist desires, needs and looks for from the process of consuming a tourism experience that involves an investment of time and money. The expectations a tourist has as a consumer in purchasing and consuming a tourism product or experience are ultimately shaped by a wide range of social and economic factors dependent upon the individual's attitudes and perception of tourism.

Yet tourist motivation is a complex area dominated by the social psychologists, with their concern for the behaviour, attitudes and thoughts of people as consumers of tourism. A very influential motivational study published in 1993 by Phillip Pearce suggested that in any attempt to understand tourist motivation we must consider how to develop a concept of motivation in tourism, how to communicate this to students and researchers who do not understand social psychology, and what practical measures need to be developed to measure people's motivation for travel – particularly the existence of multi-motivation situations (i.e. more than one factor influencing the desire to engage in tourism). Pearce (1993) also discussed the need to distinguish between intrinsic and extrinsic forces shaping the motivation to become a tourist.

Intrinsic and extrinsic motivation

There is no all-embracing theory of tourist motivation due to the problem of simplifying complex psychological factors and behaviour into a universally acceptable theory that can be tested and proved in various tourism contexts. This was discussed by Cooper *et al.* (1993: 20), who pointed at the individual as being a central component of tourism demand:

> . . . no two individuals are alike, and differences in attitudes, perceptions and motivation have an important influence on travel decisions {where} attitudes depend on an individual's perception of the world. Perceptions are mental impressions of . . . a place or travel company and are determined by many factors, which include childhood, family and work experiences. However, attitudes and perceptions in themselves do not explain why people want to travel. The inner urges which initiate travel demand are called travel motivators.

What this illustrates is that the individual and the forces affecting the individual's need to be a tourist are important. These forces can be broken down into intrinsic and extrinsic approaches to motivation.

The *intrinsic motivation approach* recognizes that individuals have unique personal needs that stimulate or arouse them to pursue tourism. Some of these needs are associated with the desire to satisfy individual or internal needs – for example, becoming a tourist for self-improvement or what is termed self-realization, so as to achieve a state of happiness. It may also help to boost an individual's ego (a feature termed ego-enhancement) because of the personal confidence building that travel can encourage. In contrast, the *extrinsic motivational approach* examines the broader conditioning factors that shape the individual's attitudes, preferences and perceptions but are more externally determined – for example, society and culture affect how tourism is viewed. In the former Soviet Union tourism was a functional relationship that was conditioned by the state, which sent workers for rest and re-creation so they could return refreshed to improve output and productivity. In contrast, in a free market economy individuals are much freer to choose how and where they wish to travel, within certain constraints (e.g. time, income and awareness of opportunities).

At a general level, tourism may allow individuals to escape the mundane, thereby achieving their goals of physical re-creation and spiritual refreshment as well as enjoying social goals such as being with family or friends. In this respect, extrinsic influences on the tourist may include family, society with its standards and norms of behaviour, the peer pressure from social groups, and the culture. For example, in the case study examined later in this chapter (see Box 3.1), one of the cultural motivators of outbound travel from New Zealand among youth travellers (those under 30 years of age) is the desire for the 'Overseas Experience' (the 'big OE'). This often gives travellers a chance to engage in a cultural form of tourism to visit Europe and see relatives and friends, and thus achieves a number of social goals. It also has an intrinsic function, as a long-haul trip and a sustained time away from the home environment encourages independence, self-reliance, and greater self-confidence regarding ability and judgment, and contributes to ego enhancement. In the UK there has also been a trend towards a similar experience before commencing study at university, known as the *gap year*, where a similar style of travel, working holiday, voluntary activity or round-the-world trip takes place.

While analysis of tourist motivation is about the underlying psychological value and features of being a tourist, actual tourism demand at a practical level is derived through a consumer decision-making process. From this process it is possible to describe three elements that condition demand:

1 *Energizers of demand*, which are factors that promote an individual to decide on a holiday
2 *Filterers of demand*, which are constraints on demand that can exist in economic, sociological or psychological terms despite the desire to go on holiday or travel
3 *Affecters*, which are a range of factors that may heighten or suppress the energizers that promote consumer interest or choice in tourism.

These factors directly condition and affect the tourist's process of travel decision-making, although they do not explain why people choose to travel. For this reason, it is useful to understand how individual's desires and need for tourism fit into their wider life. This partly reflects upon the intrinsic motivations, and one useful framework devised to understand this is Maslow's hierarchy of human needs.

Maslow's hierarchy model and tourist motivation

Maslow's (1954) hierarchy of needs (Figure 3.2) remains one of the most widely discussed ideas on motivation. It is based on the premise that self-actualization is a level to which people should aspire. Maslow argued that if the lower needs in the hierarchy were not fulfilled, then these would dominate human behaviour. Once these were satisfied, the individual would be motivated by the needs of the next level of the hierarchy. In the motivation sequence, Maslow identified 'deficiency or tension-reducing motives' and 'inductive or arousal-seeking motives' (Cooper *et al.*, 1993: 21), arguing that the model could be applied to work and non-work contexts, such as tourism and leisure. Yet how and why Maslow selected five

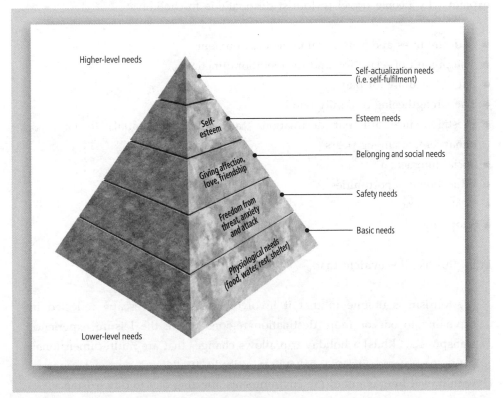

Figure 3.2 Maslow's hierarchy of individual need

basic needs remains unclear, although its appears to have a relevance in understanding how human action is related to understandable and predictable aspects of action – compared to research, which argues that human behaviour is essentially irrational and unpredictable.

Maslow's model is not necessarily ideal, since needs are not in reality hierarchical because some needs may occur simultaneously. However, such a model does emphasize the development needs of humans, with individuals striving towards personal growth, and these can be understood in a tourism context.

Maslow's work has also been developed since the 1950s, with work on specific motivations beyond the concept of needing 'to get away from it all'. For example, 'push' factors that motivate individuals to seek a holiday have been researched and compared with 'pull' factors (e.g. promotion by tourist resorts), which act as attractors. Ryan's (1991: 25–9) analysis of tourist travel motivators (excluding business travel) identified the following range of reasons commonly cited to explain why people travel to tourist destinations for holidays:

- A desire to escape from a mundane environment
- The pursuit of relaxation and recuperation functions
- An opportunity for play
- The strengthening of family bonds
- Prestige, since different destinations can enable individuals to gain social enhancement among peers
- Social interaction
- Educational opportunities
- Wish fulfilment
- Shopping.

From this list, it is evident that:

> ... tourism is unique in that it involves real physical escape reflected in travelling to one or more destination regions where the leisure experience transpires ... [thus] a holiday trip allows changes that are multi-dimensional: place, pace, faces, lifestyle, behaviour, attitude. It allows a person temporary withdrawal from many of the environments affecting day to day existence. (Leiper, 1984, cited in Pearce, 1995: 19).

The tourism tradition of motivation studies: classifying and understanding tourist motives

There are many studies of tourist motivation, dating back to the 1970s, which took many of Maslow's ideas forward and then applied more socio-psychological ideas in a tourism context. In most of the studies of tourist motivation, a common range of factors tends to emerge. For example, Crompton (1979) emphasized that socio-psychological motives can be located along a continuum that explains why certain tourists undertake certain types of travel. In contrast, Dann's (1981) conceptualization is one of the most useful attempts to simplify the principal elements of tourist motivation into a series of propositions (i.e. general statements that characterize tourists), including:

- Travel is a response to what is lacking yet desired
- Destination pull is in response to motivational push
- Motivation may have a classified purpose (this was the focus of many of the earlier studies)

Which leads researchers to focus on two key elements: motivation typologies and motivation and the experiences of tourists.

The elements were simplified a stage further by McIntosh and Goeldner (1990) to:

- Physical motivators
- Cultural motivators
- Interpersonal motivators
- Status and prestige motivators.

On the basis of motivation and using the type of experiences tourists seek, Cohen (1974) distinguished between four types of travellers:

1 *Organized mass tourists* are on a highly organized package holiday, and their contact with the host community in a destination is minimal
2 *Individual mass tourists* use similar facilities to the organized mass tourist, but also desire to visit other sights not covered on organized tours in the destination
3 *Explorers* arrange their travel independently and wish to experience the social and cultural lifestyle of the destination

4 *Drifters* do not seek any contact with other tourists or their accommodation, and
wish to live with the host community.

Clearly such a classification is fraught with problems, since it does not take into
account the increasing diversity of holidays undertaken or the inconsistencies in
tourist behaviour. Other researchers suggest that one way of overcoming this
difficulty is to consider the different destinations tourists choose to visit, and then to
establish a sliding scale that is similar to Cohen's (1972) typology but does not have
such an absolute classification.

One such attempt was by Plog (1974), who devised a classification of the US
population into psychographic types, with travellers distributed along a continuum
from psychocentrism to allocentrism (see Figure 3.3). The psychocentrics are the
anxious, inhibited and less adventurous travellers, while at the other extreme the
allocentrics are adventurous, outgoing, and seek out new experiences due to their
inquisitive personalities and interest in travel and adventure. This means that,
through time, some tourists may seek out new destinations, while others will follow
the more adventurous as the destinations develop and appear safe and secure.
However, criticisms of Plog's model include the fact that it is difficult to use because

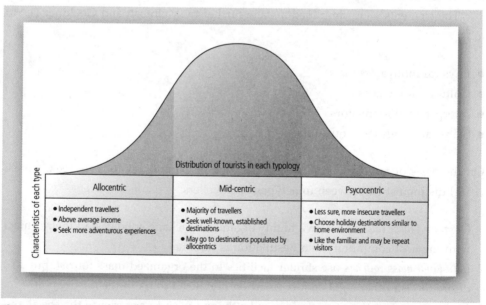

Figure 3.3 Plog's psychographic traveller types (developed and modified from Plog,
1974)

it fails to distinguish between extrinsic and intrinsic motivations. It also fails to include a dynamic element to encompass the changing nature of individual tourists. Pearce (1993: 125) suggested that individuals have a 'career' in their travel behaviour, where people:

... start at different levels, they are likely to change levels during their life-cycle and they can be prevented from moving by money, health and other people. They may also retire from their travel career or not take holidays at all and therefore not be part of the system.

Pearce's model was built on Maslow's hierarchial system, where there are five motivational levels:

1 Physiological needs
2 Safety and security needs
3 Relationship development and extension needs
4 Special interest and self-development needs
5 Fulfilment or self-actualization needs.

From the discussion of motivation, it is apparent that:

● Tourism is a combination of products and experiences that meet a diverse range of needs
● Tourists are not always conscious of their deep psychological needs and ideas, and even when they do know what they are they may not reveal them to researchers, family and friends
● Tourism motives may be multiple and contradictory, with some working in harmony and others working in direct opposition (i.e. push and pull factors)
● Motives may change over time and be inextricably linked together (e.g. perception, learning, personality and culture are often separated out, but they are all bound up together)
● Dynamic models of tourist motivation such as Pearce's (1993) leisure ladder are crucial to understanding not only the role of motivation but also the way that such motives will evolve, change and be conditioned by changes in lifestyle, life cycle and personal growth and development.

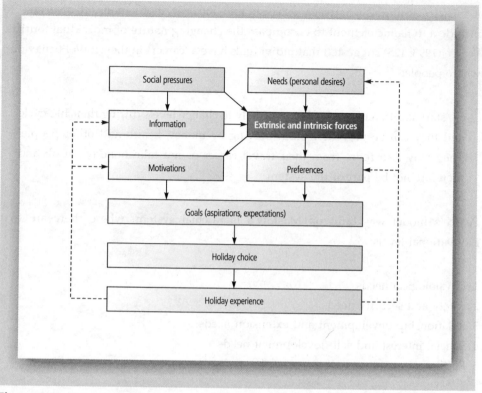

Figure 3.4   The relationship between needs, motivations, preferences and goals in individual holiday choice (source: 'Understanding holiday choice', B. Goodall in C. Cooper (ed.) *Progress in Tourism, Recreation and Hospitality Management*, vol. 3, 1991. © John Wiley & Sons Limited. Reproduced with permission

The important point here is that motivation is about how a general need/want (in this case the desire to travel) is translated in a context where it can be fulfilled. This is often simplified to push and pull factors, but it does raise issues about the ways in which tourists as consumers respond to specific stimuli that encourage them to engage in tourism. Goodall (1991) identified the relationship between needs, preferences and goals amongst travellers, where push and pull factors existed as shown in Figure 3.4. Much of Figure 3.4 is focused on consumer behaviour and the role of marketing in providing the stimuli that lead people to choose specific motivations for going on holiday. For this reason, the role of consumer behaviour in tourism is important in understanding the practical ways consumers choose to become tourists.

Consumer behaviour and tourism

Consumer behaviour concerns the way in which tourists, as purchasers of products and services, behave in terms of spending, and their attitudes and values towards what they buy. Their age, sex, marital status, educational background, amount of disposable income, where they live and other factors such as their interest in travel directly affect this. For marketers who sell and promote tourism products and services, these factors are crucial to how they divide tourists into groups as consumers so that they can provide specific products that appeal to each group. One frequent approach used by tourism marketers to achieve this goal is market segmentation (i.e. the way in which all the above factors can be used to describe different groups of consumers).

There are a range of approaches that can be used in market segmentation, though the most commonly used is *demographic or socio-economic segmentation*, which occurs where statistical data such as those provided by the census are used together with other statistical information to identify the scale and volume of potential tourists likely to visit a destination. Key factors such as age and income are significant determinants of the demand – for example, the amount of paid holiday and an individual's or family's income both have an important bearing on demand. One powerful factor shaping demand in a demographic context is social class, which is related to income, social standing, and the way status evolves from these factors. Social class is widely used by marketers as a way of identifying the spending potential of tourists. In the UK the Institute of Practitioners in Advertising uses the following socio-economic grouping of the population, with six groups:

A   Higher managerial, administrative or professional
B   Middle managerial, administrative or professional
C1   Supervisory, clerical or managerial
C2   Skilled manual workers
D   Semi- and unskilled manual workers
E   Pensioners, the unemployed, casual or lowest grade workers
(After Holloway and Plant 1988.)

The Travel Industry Association (TIA) in the USA recently identified one example of segmentation in relation to domestic tourism beach holidays. In 2001, the TIA study found that US residents made 1018 million domestic trips, with 109.9 million person nights spent on beach holidays that were located 50 miles or more from the home area. The average spend per trip was US$850 per trip (including transportation), which was considerably higher than on other forms of holidays, since use of rental cars and accommodation increased the spend. These trips were making a significant contribution to the US tourism industry, especially post-11 September 2001, with the switch towards domestic travel at a more local scale. The average number of nights spent away at beaches was 5.9 nights, with 35 per cent being for more than 7 nights. A diverse range of other activities were undertaken, including shopping and outdoor activities. The favourite destinations were located in California, where many of the most popular beaches are located. The visits to the top three beaches in 2001 were:

Santa Monica	7.8 million visits
Lighthouse Field State Beach	7.3 million visits
Dockweiler State Beach	3.8 million visits

The scale of these visits are reflected in the Californian economy for the year, with travel and tourism expenditure contributing US$75.4 million to the economy, supporting over 1 million jobs, and generating a further US$4.8 million in tax revenue.

A more sophisticated approach to segmentation (which was discussed in the motivation study by Plog, 1974) is *psychographic segmentation*, which is often introduced to complement more simplistic approaches based on socio-economic or geographic data. It involves using socio-economic and life-cycle data to predict a range of consumer behaviours or purchasing patterns associated with each stage. Examining the psychological profile of consumers to establish their traits or characteristics in relation to different market segments further develops this. The VALS (Value and Lifestyles) research conducted by the Stanford Research Institute in North America used socio-economic data, the aspirations, self-images, values and consumption patterns of Americans to establish nine lifestyles that people could move through. This has been followed by other forms of lifestyle segmentation in consumer behaviour research to reduce the complex reality of the market for products and services into a series of identifiable groupings. It uses variables related to consumers' lifestyles (e.g. their interests, hobbies and spending patterns) as well as more personalized ones such as attitudes, opinions and feelings towards travel and tourism. In other words, by combining the behaviour of tourists and their value systems, comprising their beliefs and how these affect their decision to purchase, the marketers can communicate more effectively with potential consumers by understanding what motivates their decision to purchase certain types of products and services. One example of psychographic segmentation is a specialized product such as ecotourism (travelling to engage in wildlife viewing, visiting natural areas, and a concern with the natural environment); here, segmentation is possible using a range of variables such as age profile of the ecotourists, how they choose to travel, how they book their holidays, what type of budget they have and the motivation for being an ecotourist.

Once the supplier of the services or products has considered these issues, the next stage is to examine how tourists decide to purchase certain products – particularly the most frequent purchase, which is the holiday.

Purchasing a holiday

In a recent study undertaken in Canada in 2002, TripAdvisor found that consumers often take as long as a month to purchase quite complex holiday products online, illustrating how important it is for businesses to understand how the consumer select products both online and from more traditional distribution channels such as travel agents. It also highlights the importance of marketing efforts by tourism businesses to tempt the consumer to book a product. In one study Goodall (1991) constructed a simple model of how consumers select a holiday, which involved a number of stages and answers to questions on what they want from the holiday. This concluded that consumers have a range of holiday options available at specific points in time, based on individual, family and other group preferences. In the case of purchasing tourism products and services, the following factors exert a powerful influence on the decision to purchase:

- Personality of the purchaser
- The point of purchase
- The role of the sales person
- Whether the individual is a frequent or infrequent purchaser of holiday products
- Prior experience.

Any explanation of consumer behaviour in tourism also needs to be aware of the motivations, desires, needs, expectations, personal and social factors affecting travel behaviour. These are in turn affected by stimuli that promote travel (e.g. marketing and promotion), images of the places being visited, previous travel experiences, and time and cost constraints. What this type of debate on tourists as consumers shows is that marketing and promotion are fundamental in a business that seeks to create a four-step process that takes consumers from a stage of unawareness of a product or service through to a point where they want to consume it. Within marketing, much of the attention focuses on using well-known brands or household names in travel (e.g. Thomson Holidays in the UK) to promote the awareness. Marketers describe this process as the AIDA model (Awareness, Interest, Desire and Action).

The AIDA process has recently been used by the Mayor in the Maipo River region, an area just outside the Chilean capital Santiago, to create a unique tourism destination – a UFO tourism zone. Awareness has been created by UFO sightings over two decades, while interest has resulted from increased publicity. To stimulate and satisfy the desire to visit, the action is based on plans to erect two observation centres, signposts of sightings, and to provide workshops. A similar scheme was proposed in Bonnybridge, Stirlingshire (Scotland), where a number of UFO sightings have created an interest in developing a visitors' centre to promote visits.

Much of the efforts in marketing are focused on consumer behaviour, seeking to understand how individuals perceive things and digest the information and messages that advertising and promotion use to develop a tourism image. These images not only impact upon the holiday selection process and the decision to go on holiday, but also, and more importantly, the destinations – the specific places tourists will visit.

The tourist image of products and places

It is generally acknowledged that many consumers will select a range of destinations (often three to five) when considering where to go on holiday. A major element in the decision to select a specific destination is the image of the place. The tourist selects the destination through a process of elimination, but it is not a straight linear process from A to B to C. Often people will look at options, re-evaluate them, and reconsider specific places based on their knowledge, the images portrayed in the media and the opinions of individual(s) and group members. This can make travel decisions lengthy and complex processes based on compromise. For example, the 11 September 2001 terrorist attacks on the USA created widespread negative images of international travel, and one immediate beneficiary of this was the growth of domestic tourism in many countries. This required government and tourism agencies not only to promote 'business as usual' in New York to encourage people to travel again, but also to restore negative images portrayed by the media. It led to temporary changes in inbound and outbound tourism across the world (see Box 3.1), with destinations perceived as safe (such as Australia and New Zealand) recording a short-term boost to arrivals.

Image can be powerful where destinations have memorable elements in the landscape that feature as icons to promote awareness and travel to the destination (e.g. The Eiffel Tower in Paris), leading to tourists associating positive reasons to travel with well-known icons that are safe and popular. In some cases over-popular images of destinations or specific attractions may mean that a degree of caution has to be used to downplay the destination in peak season; this is sometimes called de-marketing. In addition, destinations have to create images of their tourism offerings and locality that help to differentiate them from the competition. In Australia the rise of wine and food tourism based on local products and specialist food products in areas such as Margaret River in Western Australia, have emerged as newly created and re-imaged tourist regions due to emphasizing the uniqueness of the place and thereby creating a desire to visit, even if it has an extraordinary appeal. Another example is in a desolate area of Northern China on the Tibet-Qinghai plateau, where attempts by local government in 2002 have begun to turn a former nuclear weapons research centre (No 221 Plant, owned by the China Nuclear Industry Corporation) into a tourist attraction. Established in 1958, the site was used to test nuclear bombs and nuclear waste is buried there. Some sixteen nuclear tests were carried out over a 30-year period. Here, negative images and publicity present a major challenge in creating positive images of the region for visitors, which the Qinghai Provincial Tourism Association are basing on the region's cultural heritage (Tibetan culture and architecture) and the natural environment (varying from snow-capped mountains to desert-style sand dunes). A number of festivals have been staged to attract visitors, based on horse racing and Buddhist rituals.

Yet much of the image itself is not just about the tangible elements, since tourism is a combination of tangible perceptions of place and emotional feelings about locations. For example, even when rational feelings question the logic of visiting somewhere, the desire to see something may override these concerns. This is related to risk behaviour in holiday purchases. Risk is a complex topic, not least because it is very personal to individuals and may create certain types of behaviour in tourism. For example, the low-risk tourist will book early, reducing the perceived barriers to travel, and may return to the same resort or country due to the apparent feelings of safety and security. In contrast, risk-takers will be less worried about the impact of tourist-related crime, less concerned about the stability and certainty offered by booking a package holiday, and may choose to be independent travellers, organizing their travel and itinerary themselves. Tourists seeking to minimize risks will seek out well-known brands that guarantee quality experiences, often preferring the reassurance of booking at travel agents where the face-to-face contact and positive reinforcement of what the experience will offer encourages the purchaser to go ahead.

Bearing these issues in mind, let us now consider the case study in Box 3.1.

Box 3.1 Case study: outbound tourism from New Zealand

Despite its distance from many of the tourism generating and receiving regions across the world, New Zealand is a relatively mature outbound market. This case study illustrates the significance of consumer spending, the demographic profile of travellers and the factors affecting the demand for outbound travel, as well as some of the recent trends in outbound travel from New Zealand, as an illustration of tourism demand.

Prior to the development of jet services in the 1960s, demand for outbound travel was constrained by the price of travel and the time involved in using long-haul flights and passenger liners. The development of jet services in the 1960s provided cheaper and more frequent access to both short- and long-haul destinations, and the number of outbound trips quadrupled from 112 082 in 1970 to 426 805 in 1980. The trend in outbound travel from 1980 to 1990 has been described as erratic, rising to 451 300 in 1980–1981 and dropping to 361 662 in 1983–1984 before rising again to 778 956 in 1991. In 1992 arrivals dropped to 750 883, but thereafter continue to rise 1 123 000 for 1998. As Table 3.1 shows, there has been little growth since 1998, with only marginal fluctuations between 1998 and 2002. Some commentators have even described this market as having plateaued and as being fairly static. These statistics are collated by the government statistics agency, Statistics New Zealand, based on the departure card that all outbound travellers have to fill in.

Whilst this chapter has shown that a complex array of factors affect the demand for travel, in the case of outbound travel from a relatively isolated country such as New Zealand (which is a three-hour flight from Australia and a twelve-hour flight from the USA) trends in outbound travel can be accounted for in terms of the impact of exchange rates, the price of air fares, and the performance of the New Zealand economy (which

Table 3.1 Number of outbound tourists from New Zealand, 1997–2002 (modified from Statistics New Zealand; all statistics refer to the year ended April)

Major destinations	1997	1998	1999	2000	2001	2002
Australia	597 733	585 679	626 043	644 831	684 338	658 773
Fiji	61 543	64 759	68 251	69 332	43 791	63 256
Asia	147 338	151 310	153 714	152 784	163 874	165 617
Europe	90 792	98 954	103 629	103 395	111 514	101 175
UK	60 571	66 526	68 817	71 504	68 983	60 319
North America	95 042	97 235	92 315	95 741	96 538	81 879
USA	83 361	85 237	79 169	77 442	76 325	64 617
Other countries	55 810	61 091	76 472	83 431	113 724	125 761
Total	1 109 301	1 123 229	1 180 665	1 222 442	1 286 485	1 268 070

affects consumer confidence in discretionary spending on overseas travel). Despite the fluctuations in outbound travel statistics, the gross propensity to travel (the total number of departures as a percentage of the total population) has also increased from 13.4 per cent in 1979–1980 to 32.6 per cent for the year ended October 1998. At the same time, the proportion of net household expenditure spent on overseas travel has increased from 2 per cent in the 1980s to 4 per cent in the 1990s. With a relatively small resident population (estimated at 3 792 000) the New Zealand outbound market is significant compared to that of Australia.

Data on New Zealand outbound travel are extremely hard to compile, as the government agency that collates outbound statistics places a great deal of emphasis on inbound tourism, which is the major driver of the tourism economy. Despite this, the balance of tourism in 2002 was 1 268 000 outbound trips and 1 945 500 inbound trips.

A number of other factors also shape outbound travel, including the geographical distribution and age structure of the population, the relative strength of the New Zealand economy, the amount of holiday entitlement, the cost of airfares, and how the New Zealand dollar performs relative to other currencies.

In terms of population distribution, 69.8 per cent of the population live in fifteen main urban areas: Auckland, Christchurch, Dunedin, Gisborne, Hamilton, Invercargill, Napier-Hastings, Nelson, New Plymouth, Palmerston North, Rotorua, Tauranga, Wanganui, Wellington and Whangarei. A further 7.2 per cent live in secondary urban centres, and the remainder live in rural areas. In fact, 28 per cent reside in the Greater Auckland region, followed by 9.2 per cent in the Greater Wellington region and 7 per cent in the Christchurch region. Each of these regions have outbound airline services, although Auckland is by far the most important source area for outbound travel, with the widest range of direct services and connections to 21 countries.

Some 69 per cent of the economically active population who might be likely to travel are aged 15–65 years. Two age groups that have a strong propensity towards outbound travel are the 15–29-year-olds, who comprise 21 per cent of the population, and the mature market (50–70-year-olds), who comprise 17 per cent of the population. The former group often pursue the traditional New Zealand 'overseas experience' (OE) prior to or after tertiary education, which combines a personal growth experience with temporary work and VFR travel in Australia, North America and Europe. However, these youth travellers spend relatively less per week than the mature market. The weekly expenditure on overseas travel is shown in Table 3.2.

Above all, it is the level of consumer expenditure on outbound travel that highlights its importance as a budgeted item. The average expenditure for all households surveyed in the government-sponsored Consumer Expenditure Survey in 2001 indicated that:

● Of the net household weekly expenditure (including mortgages and savings) of NZ$747.80, an average NZ$26.20 was spent on outbound holidays – equivalent to

Table 3.2 Purpose of trip abroad for outbound New Zealanders, 2000–2002 (modified from Statistics New Zealand; all statistics refer to the year ended April)

Purpose	2000	2001	2002	Change (%)
Holiday	559 084	540 675	529 891	−2.0
Visit friends/relatives	345 365	376 765	371 151	−1.5
Business	251 062	253 826	216 998	−14.5

almost 3.5 per cent. Other spending of NZ$17.70 on leisure services and NZ$11.60 on leisure and recreational goods highlights the significance of outbound travel to the resident population within leisure spending.

- The weekly household expenditure on outbound travel varied from NZ$10.80 for the lowest income households (including lone parents/single households), which earn less than NZ$14 000 *per annum*, through to NZ$81.20 for households that earn over NZ$101 000 *per annum*.

One of the explanations of the propensity for outbound travel among New Zealanders was made evident in a report in October 1998 by the Tourism Council of Australia on tourism competitiveness. This noted that that it was considerably more cost-effective for New Zealanders to take a holiday in Australia than to take a domestic holiday in New Zealand. The report examined an index of competitiveness, based on a package of accommodation, food, beverages, transport and local tours. Using the example of a New Zealander from Auckland selecting a package holiday on the Gold Coast or the cheapest urban short break in Christchurch, the Gold Coast proved to offer a cheaper all-inclusive product.

But where do New Zealanders travel overseas, and what are the main motivations for travel to these destinations? Much of the travel is short haul in nature (i.e. to Australia), and the remainder is either medium haul (e.g. to North Asia) or long haul (e.g. to Europe). Table 3.3 shows that of outbound travel in the year ending April 2002:

- 52 per cent was to Australia
- 5 per cent was to Fiji
- 13 per cent was to Asia, reflecting the growing ethnicity of the New Zealand population and family ties with North Asia (especially China and the Hong Kong area)
- 8 per cent was to Europe, of which nearly 5 per cent was to the UK – reflecting historical ties with the Commonwealth and the history of immigration to New Zealand from Europe in the years since 1840
- 6.5 per cent was to North America.

The motivation to travel varies significantly by market, with considerably more holiday and business travel to Australia and a greater proportion of VFR traffic to the USA, UK and some Asian destinations. The majority of these trips are for less than two weeks in duration. What is apparent from Table 3.3 is that the events of 11 September 2001 had a limited effect on outbound travel from New Zealand, with just a small decline in the USA and European destinations.

Table 3.3 Consumer expenditure on outbound travel by New Zealanders, 2001, by age group (modified from Statistics New Zealand)

Age group	Weekly expenditure on outbound travel ($NZ)
15–24	13.20
25–34	22.40
35–44	25.70
45–54	30.60
55–64	31.00
65+	26.10
All age groups	26.20

What the case study illustrates is that the demand for tourism is variable, and although it may perform in a constant manner (as the outbound trends from New Zealand infer), overall demand factors are constantly under review by consumers and some fluctuations will inevitably occur.

Summary

The reasons why people choose to engage in tourism are diverse and multi-faceted, and no single simple explanation can be advanced to attribute motivations for tourism. Explaining this requires a process of understanding the psychology of tourist decision-making based upon the reasons why tourists wish to travel and take holidays. To simplify some of the reasons, researchers have developed lists of factors and typologies of tourists to try to suggest how humans can be grouped into common types of tourism consumers. However, even this is difficult when the ultimate arbiter of motivation, especially of human needs and wants that can be fulfilled through tourism experiences, is the individual. Understanding the individual is a time-consuming process that is not easily reduced to questionnaire surveys or face-to-face interviews on the beach asking tourists why they are there. Understanding tourists is like peeling an onion – a number of layers need to be peeled away to uncover the extrinsic and intrinsic motivational forces. To continue the analogy, over-analysis may mean removing all the layers so there is nothing left to be eaten and digested; and while slicing the onion in half may reveal the complex thinking and factors shaping human behaviour associated with tourism, predictable and rational behaviour is not necessarily revealed. Consequently, a range of motivational approaches may provide conflicting information. However, what is certain is that taking a holiday and travelling are firmly embedded in modern society, and although fashions, tastes and changes in travel habits may change outward motivation, deep down the intrinsic motivation is a highly personal process for each and every tourist.

References

Cohen, E. (1974) Who is a tourist? A conceptual clarification. *Sociological Review*, **22**, 527–55.

Cooper, C. P., Fletcher, J., Gilbert, D. G. and Wanhill, S. (1993) *Tourism: Principles and Practice*. London: Pitman.

Crompton, J. (1979) An assessment of the image of Mexico as a vacation destination. *Journal of Travel Research* **17** (Fall), 18–23.

Dann, G. (1981) Tourist motivation: an appraisal. *Annals of Tourism Research*, **8**(2), 187–219.

Goodall, B. (1991) Understanding holiday choice. *In*: C. Cooper (ed.), *Progress in Tourism, Recreation and Hospitality Management, Volume 3*. London: Belhaven, pp. 58–77.

Holloway, J. C. and Plant, R. (1988) *Marketing for Tourism*. London: Pitman.

Maslow, A. (1954) *Motivation and Personality*. New York: Harper and Row.

Mathieson, A. and Wall, G. (1982) *Tourism: Economic, Physical and Social Impacts*. Harlow: Longman.

McIntosh, R. W. and Goeldner, C. (1990) *Tourism: Principles, Practices and Philosophies*. New York: Wiley.

Mountinho, L. (1987) Consumer behaviour in tourism. *European Journal of Marketing*, **21**(10), 3–44.

Pearce, D. G. (1995) *Tourism Today: A Geographical Analysis*, 2nd edn. Harlow: Longman.

Pearce, P. (1993) The fundamentals of tourist motivation. *In*: D. Pearce and R. Butler (eds), *Tourism Research: Critique and Challenges*. London: Routledge.

Plog, S. (1974) Why destination areas rise and fall in popularity. *The Cornell Hotel and Restaurant Administration Quarterly*, **15**, 13–16.

Ryan, C. (1991) *Recreational Tourism: A Social Science Perspective*. London: Routledge.

Statistics New Zealand, http://www.stats.govt.nz

Uysal, M. (1998) The determinants of tourism demand: a theoretical perspective. *In*: D. Ioannides and K. Debbage (eds), *The Economic Geography of the Tourist Industry: A Supply-side Analysis*. London: Routledge, pp. 79–95.

Further reading

Argyle, M. (1996) *The Social Psychology of Leisure*. Harmondsworth: Penguin.

Pearce, P. (1982) *The Social Psychology of Tourist Behaviour*. Oxford: Pergamon.

Pearce, P. (1993) The fundamentals of tourist motivation. *In*: D. Pearce and R. Butler (eds), *Tourism Research: Critique and Challenges*. London: Routledge.

Questions

1 Why is it important for tourism managers to understand tourist motivation?

2 What is the role of consumer behaviour in understanding what tourists want to purchase? Do consumers always follow rational decision-making approaches when purchasing products such as holidays?

3 Should the consumer be the starting point for the analysis of tourism demand?

4 How useful is Maslow's model in understanding tourist motivation? Is it redundant and superseded by specific social psychology studies of tourism, or is it still the basis for all analyses of tourist motivation?

4

The supply of tourism

Learning objectives

This chapter examines the way in which tourism supply is assembled by the tourism industry. After reading it, you should be able to understand:

- how individual businesses approach supply;
- how supply issues are affected by macro-economic issues;
- the significance of the tourism supply chain in conceptualizing how tourism businesses meet demand;
- the inter-connections between different elements of tourism (i.e. accommodation, transport, attractions and tourism agencies/services/facilities).

Introduction

Chapter 3 discussed some of the reasons why people choose to go on holiday, and explained the diverse motivations associated with the demand for tourism services and products. However, in any tourism purchasing decision there has to be the provision of a service or product by a business or organization to meet the visitors' needs or demands. This provision is known as tourism supply or, as was explained in Chapter 1, as a form of production. In any analysis of supply there are five basic questions that tourism businesses have to consider, all of which are related to economics:

1 What should we produce as a business to meet a certain form of tourism demand? (i.e. Should we produce an upmarket high-cost holiday package for ecotourists using tailor-made packages, or aim for mass-market, low-cost package holidays?)
2 How should it be produced? (i.e. Should we contract in supplies to provide each element of the package product to reduce costs, or should we produce each element to ensure quality control and consistency in product delivery?)
3 When, where and how should we produce the tourism product? (i.e. Do we produce an all-year round or seasonal tourism product?)
4 What destinations/places should be featured in the tourism experience?
5 What form of business or businesses do we need to produce the tourism services and products in order to meet demand?

These are all real questions that which tourism businesses need to address, as their long-term viability and success or failure will depend upon the management of their organizations' resources to meet demand in an efficient and profitable manner. To many people the concept of tourism supply and the day-to-day operation and management of tourism businesses supplying tourists' needs may seem distant, unconnected and rather unreal. Yet it is the concept of supply that helps us to understand how the wide range of tourism businesses and organizations in the tourism sector (and quite often businesses that do not see themselves as servicing tourists' needs, such as taxi companies) combine to link the tourist with the services, experiences and products they seek in a destination.

This chapter seeks to provide an overview of tourism supply issues by explaining how to view the concept of supply, and in particular the idea of a supply chain and the wide range of industry elements that characterize what is termed the tourism industry. There is one underlying characteristic of tourism supply that distinguishes it from other services, and this is the way in which tourism is consumed by a mobile population who visit destination areas to consume a product, service or experience, while in contrast the supply elements are often fixed geographically at certain places (e.g. hotels, restaurants or visitor attractions). This means that businesses are required to sink considerable capital costs into different forms of tourism services and centres of production, on the basis of an expectation that the destination will appeal to visitors and assist in the promotion of their individual products and services. Therein lies the complexity of tourism supply – the appeal of the product and its influence on the consumption of specific elements of supply is a more complicated proposition than buying other consumer goods or services. Sessa (1983) categorized the elements of supply of tourism services by businesses as follows:

- *Tourism resources*, which comprise both the natural and human resources of an area
- *General and tourism infrastructure*, which includes the transport and telecommunications infrastructure
- *Receptive facilities*, which receive visitors, including accommodation, food and beverage establishments and apartments/condominiums
- *Entertainment and sports facilities*, which provide a focus for tourists activities
- *Tourism reception services*, including travel agencies, tourist offices, car hire companies, guides, interpreters and visitor managers.

These 'elements of tourism' highlight the scope of tourism supply, but a number of less tangible elements of supply (i.e. image) also need to be considered.

As explained in Chapter 3, images of places have a powerful influence in the tourists' search process for a holiday destination, and businesses need to be aware of this when entering the tourist market for the first time, or when introducing new products and goods. What this means is that the wider tourism industry and the agencies responsible for tourism in a destination (e.g. tourist boards) need to pull in the same direction, work towards common goals and promote the attributes of the destination in a positive manner so that the images of the area, place or destination are enhanced or maintained. For example, Iceland's appeal is marketed in terms of its attributes as a clean, green and environmentally responsible destination, with its beautiful lava landscapes, wilderness and views, its Viking heritage, and a diversity of activities for visitors, from winter sports to health-based tourism (thermal resorts).

Influences on tourism supply issues: the business environment

Aside from issues of image, the business environment in which organizations operate can also have a major bearing on tourism supply. For example, in most countries tourism operates within a free market economy and individual businesses operate in open competition. However, in some countries certain sectors of the tourism industry receive assistance from the government through the provision of infrastructure, and through marketing and promotional support from tourist boards and other agencies. It is also apparent that when governments decide to promote inbound tourism to destinations such as Bali, supply needs to be able to meet demand. In many cases demand creates severe pressure on destinations where supply is often a step behind – for example, in the 1930s around 3000 visitors a year visited Bali; by 1970 this had grown to 23 000, rising sharply to 158 000 in 1981 and to over 1 246 000 in 1998. This massive expansion in demand requires supply in all sectors of the industry to keep pace, especially as the beach-resort nature of the destination was actively promoted in the 1980s and 1990s. This also raises the importance of marketing and promotion in developing a demand to fill the available supply. For example, in 2002–2003 the National Tourism Organization for Scotland, VisitScotland, had a budget of £28 million to assist in promoting Destination Scotland domestically and internationally; this budget is due to rise to £31 million in 2003–2004.

There are few industries that gain this degree of leverage from government taxes to promote their activities. Hence tourism does not operate in many countries in conditions of perfect competition, given the level of state support and assistance. Yet as Chapter 11 shows, intervention is justified to develop a tourism destination image and promote the attributes of tourism supply in the form of holidays, although supply is more complex than simply holidays. What does concern individual businesses is the competition they face on a day-to-day basis and the degree of government regulation and intervention, which impacts upon their business activities. For example, in the UK there has been a significant growth in low-cost or budget airlines, which have been licensed to operate from regional and London bases. In each case setting up a new airline operation involves high capital costs (even where aircraft are leased rather than purchased), so the number of companies able to enter this market is limited by the entry costs and government regulations. In the case of low-cost airlines, they have challenged existing market conditions where individual operators had a monopoly on certain routes and could charge a premium (high) price. The effect has been to reduce fares, generate new forms of demand (i.e. leisure travellers) and severely reduce the monopoly operator's ability to charge premium prices and maintain route profitability. In the USA, deregulation of the airline business in the late 1970s saw monopolies (and duopolies, where two companies controlled routes) challenged, new market conditions emerge, and a major reorganization, restructuring and new environment for air travel. A similar example is that of the railways in the UK in the late 1990s, following the privatization of British Rail and the end of its monopoly on rail travel. It is clear from these examples that the competitive environment that affects tourism businesses and their operation needs to be considered in relation to a number of underlying economic issues:

- What competitive market conditions exist for a specific sector of tourism (e.g. the airline sector, hotel sector or attraction sector)? Do conditions of monopoly, oligopoly (i.e. where a limited number of suppliers control supply) or other market conditions exist?
- How many businesses are involved in these markets, and what size are they? Are they able to respond quickly to new competitive pressures, or are they characterized by complacency and an inability to redefine their operations in the light of aggressive competition?
- Do the businesses involved in tourism display patterns of market concentration, where a limited number of businesses dominate all aspects of production (e.g. from retailing through to supply of services and products in the destination such as in the UK tour operator market)?
- What are the capital costs of entering a tourism market? Are there high entry and exit barriers? For example, starting an airline has high entry and exit costs and requires a high level of technical know-how and large capital investment and ongoing finance to service the business; on the other hand, buying a guest house has low entry costs and no barriers to entry in terms of technical competencies required to run, manage and host visitors.
- What types of products already exist in the market, and is there scope for innovation (see Chapter 10) to develop new products without the risk of 'ambush marketing' by competitors who copy the idea and/or undercut the competition by loss-leaders to regain market share? Aggressive marketing and a limited number of loss-leaders have characterized the low-cost airlines and privatized railways in the UK, in an attempt to capture price-sensitive leisure travellers. In other words, is there scope for price discrimination in the market to differentiate a whole range of products?

What these factors indicate is that the market conditions and business environment in which tourism operates are far from static. They are constantly changing, requiring businesses to adapt and to develop strategies to retain their market presence. Unlike many other goods and services, fashions, tastes, preferences and evolving consumer trends quickly translate into opportunities or problems in tourism supply. For example, in early 2002 UK tour operators were reporting low levels of advance overseas summer holiday bookings owing to security concerns after the terrorist attacks of 11 September 2001, fears over interest rate rises, and general angst about long-haul travel. Within four months these fears had been somewhat reduced and normal patterns of consumer behaviour returned.

Managing tourism supply issues

For tourism businesses, recognizing these evolving patterns, new trends and the need for innovation to address market conditions re-emphasizes the importance of managerial skills in the supply of tourism products and services. This also highlights what Mintzberg (1973) identified as the nature of managerial work in organizations – short-term coping, disparate activities and being more concerned with brevity, variety and increasing fragmentation. Tourism managers and businesses are no exception to this, and his research has an important bearing on how managers performed certain roles labelled as interpersonal, informational and decisional (see Table 4.1). The ten managerial work roles that Mintzberg identified illustrate the scope of activities involved in managing a tourism business, as well as some of the complexities of how the individual business interacts with the wider body of interests conveniently labelled the tourism industry. It also suggests how important prevailing market conditions are when they impact upon how a business operates, and manages and responds to opportunities, threats and shortcomings in its own organization. Yet to do this a business needs to also understand its relationship to other tourism businesses. A convenient way to explain this is by using the tourism supply chain concept.

The tourism supply chain

Throughout earlier chapters, the role of tourism as an amalgam of different interests, activities, stakeholders and businesses has been discussed. This section examines how these different interests are functionally linked together to form a distinct supply chain. The supply chain concept originates in economics, and has been used to explain

Table 4.1 Mintzberg's ten managerial roles (source: reproduced from *Tourism Management*, vol. 25, S. Charaupunsirikul and R. Wood, Mintzberg, managers and methodology, 551–6, © 2002, with permission from Elsevier

Interpersonal roles:	
Figurehead	Symbolic head: obliged to perform a number of routine duties of legal and social nature
Leader	Responsible for the motivation of subordinates; responsible for staffing and training
Liaison	Maintains self-developed network of outside contacts/informers who provide information and favours
Information roles:	
Monitor	Through seeking and receiving a variety of special information, develops through understanding of organization and environment
Disseminator	Transmits information received from outsiders and subordinates to members of the organization
Spokesperson	Transmits information to outsiders on organization's plans, serves as expert on organization's industry
Decisional roles:	
Entrepreneurial	Searches organization and its environment for opportunities to bring about change
Resource allocater	Responsible for the allocation of organizational resources of all kinds
Negotiator	Responsible for representing the organization at major negotiations

how different businesses enter into contractual relationships to supply services, products and goods, and how these goods are assembled into products at different points in the supply chain. Tourism is well suited to the concept of the supply chain because the product, service or experience that is consumed is assembled, and comprises a wide range of suppliers. A schematic diagram of a typical tourism supply chain is illustrated in Figure 4.1. This shows that once the consumer has chosen a destination and product, the decision to purchase involves contacting a tourism retailer (e.g. a retail agent, a direct selling company or an Internet-based seller such as

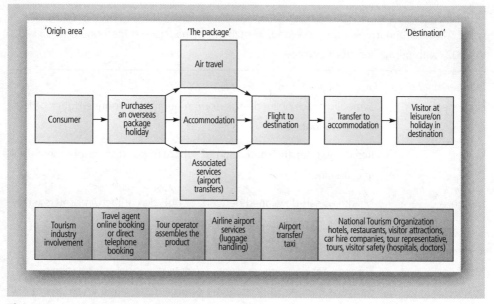

Figure 4.1 A typical tourism supply chain

www.expedia.co.uk). Having chosen a booking medium and selecting a package, the package is then assembled.

The tour operator enters into contractual relationships with tourism suppliers such as airlines (although larger tour operators may also own their own charter or schedule airlines), hotel operators, and suppliers of associated services such as airport transfers. These suppliers in turn contract suppliers who service their business needs, such as in-flight caterers, airline leasing companies, airport terminal services (e.g. check-in services, baggage handling, flight controllers, and customer service agents for visitors and those with special needs). Services in the destination are also contracted – for example, tour representatives are employed to meet guests at the airport, welcome them into their accommodation and utilize the opportunities for retail sales of additional services such as tours and events. This not only yields additional revenue for the tour operator, with representatives paid a commission based on sales targets, but also trades on the visitors' naiveté regarding the destination and the cost of services. In some hotels, similar kick-backs and commissions are paid to the concierge for each sale of a particular company's product, and the display of leaflets and brochures in some hotels in destinations such as Los Angeles are contingent upon the company's commission rate. Typically this will range from below

5 per cent to 10 per cent, thereby artificially inflating the price paid by visitors compared to the local population. Such practices may be culturally acceptable for tourism businesses in the locality, along with blatant and aggressive/intimidatory behaviour by tour guides/drivers demanding gratuities, with expressions such as 'it is customary to give me 10 per cent of your ticket price for being your guide today' or the threat of abuse when the visitor leaves the tour. This can have very negative images for visitors from countries where tipping is not a cultural practice, and certainly promotes the image of tourists as targets to be ripped off by unscrupulous operators – hence some destinations have instigated customer care hotlines to address such issues. What these examples also show is that where tourism services are provided, there are not only formal contracts and relationships but also informal alliances between recommenders (e.g. tour representatives and hotel concierges) and providers at each stage. This shows that a business opportunity is presented, with each agent in the process taking a percentage of the proceeds or using the opportunity to generate additional revenue through indirect means (e.g. goods or service) or by blatant, aggressive and intimidatory behaviour. Whilst thankfully the latter behaviour is not widespread, it does illustrate the value of tourism spending in the destination (or in the home area, where services and tours are pre-paid to the tour operator who also takes a commission).

With so many organizations involved in the tourist supply chain, it is clear that there are critical break or pressure points where the service provision could potentially fall down. What this also suggests is that failings with the destination may be attributed to the tour operator, who is liable under EU law for the well-being and experience of the holidaymaker. This returns to the theme of Chapter 3, and indicates the requirement for the tourism industry to be organized and managed in the destination so the visitor's experience is not adversely affected by the actions or activities of service providers in the destination. For this reason, we now turn our attention to the principal elements of the tourism industry: accommodation, attractions and activities, transport, public and private sector tourism organizations, and associated services.

Accommodation

Accommodation performs a vital role in the tourism sector because it provides the basic infrastructure to accommodate visitors as tourists and business travellers, and a focus for meetings, conferences and entertainment. For many resort areas accommodation comprises the key element in attracting the visitor for a holiday for a week or longer. Accommodation is also the focal point of short-break holidays, often packaged as part of an experience of a place. Accommodation ranges in type from upmarket, luxury five-star establishments with hundreds of bed spaces that charge a premium price to their guests through to the small bed-and-breakfast operator who may have just six bed spaces and open only during the tourist season. This wide range of accommodation types is examined in more detail in Chapter 7, but it is important to recognize here that it is a capital-intensive sector of the tourism industry.

It is not just the size or scale of the accommodation sector that is significant; it is the importance of hotels in the rise of resorts that may be planned leisure environments that become the containing context for the holiday. For example, on many Pacific Islands hotel chains and individual companies have built resort complexes, with the hotel/accommodation complex as the key element around which a beach, leisure facilities, restaurants/hospitality services, activities and events are structured. The result is that visitors can visit the resort and never leave it or experience other areas on the island. Such developments can dominate the tourism industry on small islands. Conversely, accommodation in towns and cities is a significant sector of the tourism industry due to the employment it generates and its ability to host large number of visitors.

Table 4.2 illustrates the scale of rooms in the hotel sector on a global scale in 1998 – estimated to be 15.4 million worldwide, growing at nearly 3 per cent a year. This led to the prediction that by 2002 there would be in excess of 17 million rooms. Independent operators own the majority of these rooms, which are in small,

Table 4.2 Rooms in hotels worldwide in 1998 (based on WTO)

Region	Number of hotel rooms
Africa	425 000
Asia-Pacific	3 487 000
Europe	5 935 000
Middle East	221 000
The Americas	5 641 000

owner-managed units. At the same time, a number of trends have affected accommodation in Europe and many other countries globally, including:

● Increasing change and competition among accommodation businesses
● Growth in the financial power of major hotel chains and multinational companies
● More discerning customers
● New trends, such as the rise of budget hotel chains and their brands.

On a global scale, Europe and North America still dominate the distribution of hotel capacity, although in the period 1994–1998 Asia-Pacific hotel capacity expanded at

Table 4.3 The number of hotels and accommodation establishments in Europe in 1999 (based on Eurostat; ©European Commission)

Country	Number of establishments
Austria	15 378
Belgium	2 015
Denmark	464
Finland	1 004
France	19 379
Germany	38 914
Greece	7 946
Iceland	253
Ireland	5 460
Italy	33 379
Luxembourg	325
Netherlands	2 826
Norway	1 176
Portugal	1 754
Spain	16 229
Sweden	1 898
Switzerland	5 890
UK	51 300

over 6 per cent per annum as it continued to grew as a region of tourism activity. In North America 70 per cent of hotel stock is a recognizable brand (e.g. Radisson, Holiday Inn and Marriott), although (with the exception of Nordic countries) chain domination is only around 20 per cent in the rest of Europe. The pattern of European accommodation is shown in Table 4.3, which illustrates the variations between the principal destination areas (the UK, Germany, Italy, France, Spain, Austria and Greece). Within each country there are also great variations in the location of accommodation, which is located in the gateway cities (e.g. London, Paris, Berlin, Amsterdam and Dublin), business capitals (e.g. Frankfurt, Brussels and Geneva) and resort areas in coastal and other locations (e.g. ski resorts).

Therefore the accommodation sector is a vital element in the supply of services and products for visitors – a feature that is as old as tourism itself. However, what has transformed the accommodation sector through history is the demise of staging-post accommodation on tourist transit routes as transport technology has removed the need for inns and hotels to be located along routes. Whilst tourists still use accommodation when touring, as in the USA and Canada when using recreational vehicles (motor homes) or cars, accommodation has tended to cluster at principal destinations such as cities and resort areas. Yet not all tourists use accommodation, as VFR traffic may stay with family or friends and not be visible in the accommodation sector. This is the case in Auckland, New Zealand, where up to 50 per cent of visitors may seek this type of holiday. However, regardless of where visitors stay, they are in all probability likely to use the attractions of the area they are visiting.

Visitor attractions and activities

During any visit to a destination, tourists engage in activities and events that provide a focal point for the use of their leisure time. Attractions and activities are a fundamental element of any tourist's itinerary, and in some cases the attraction, event or activity may be the *raison d'être* for the visit. Attractions have been divided into numerous categories or listings by tourism researchers to try to understand how they impact upon, interact with and shape the tourists' activities. The conventional ways in which attractions are viewed are in terms of:

● Natural resources, which are naturally occurring and are used by visitors for tourism (i.e. a beach environment) or as a resource during a visit to a destination (e.g. a scenic area). The history of tourism is based on the discovery, recognition of the potential and exploitation of natural resources as tourist attractions, most notably the exploitation of spa waters. In a similar vein, development in the nineteenth century was based on the recognition of the attraction of a landscape and resource (the sea and coastline) as an attraction. Yet even in these areas, these resources saw the tourism industry develop the other category – man-made resources as attractions.

● Man-made resources as attractions, which have emerged as a response to the likely opportunities of a developing tourism market in a locality, often building upon the natural attractions. However, in the post-war period the rise of mass tourism and the rising demand for leisure environments saw the development of purpose-built resources to exploit the opportunity of rising visitor spending. The development of environments by entrepreneurs (such as Walt Disney in California at Annaheim, in creating Disneyland) and the subsequent growth of theme parks highlighted the leisure potential of man-made environments. At the same time, visitors utilize man-made resources that were not specifically designed for a tourism audience – for example, cathedrals, churches, castles, historic gardens and archaeological sites. The diverse range of attractions available to the tourist is continually evolving as the attraction industry seeks to appeal to specific niche markets (consider for example the educational potential of developing science centres such as Living Earth in Edinburgh and the Glasgow Science Centre) by exploiting the educational and entertainment motivations (the so called 'edutainment' market).

Events

Aside from attractions *per se*, visitors are also attracted to destinations and areas by the potential of special events, such as festivals or sporting events (e.g. the soccer World Cup, the America's Cup sailing regatta, the Olympic games). Indeed, sports tourism, which can be defined as spectators travelling to destinations to watch a team compete in a game or competition, is beginning to be recognized as a major growth area of the tourism industry. Complementing the sports spectator are the smaller number of sporting participants such as amateur or professional sports people (e.g. golfers) who travel to destinations to compete in sporting events such as the Ryder Cup or Scottish Open (see Box 4.1).

In each case, the motivation for travel is the attraction of the activity, festival or special event, which is sport-related. Structured around the sporting dimension is a wider range of tourism functions, which might include an extended holiday after the

Box 4.1   Case study: golf tourism in Scotland

The game of golf has developed as a major attraction for hosting events, not least the Scottish Open at St Andrews. Golf has a long history in Scotland and can be dated to 1457, although there is a gap in the evidence available to document its growth and development until the seventeenth century. Some of the earlier golf clubs in Scotland can be dated to the sixteenth century – for example Perth (1502), Aberdeen (1528), St Andrews (1552) and Leith and Edinburgh (1554). Many golfing societies were elite in their initial composition, and the first trophy in golf was offered at St Andrews in 1771. This stimulated the growth of golf as a competitive sport and a focus for sport-related tourism as spectators developed an interest in this sporting activity.

The relationship between sport and tourism is increasingly being viewed as synergistic – that is, each complements the other. Two types of tourists who travel to participate in sporting activities can be identified:

1 *Activity participants*, who pursue sport as a form of leisure for the development and expression of skills and knowledge and for personal enrichment
2 *Hobbyists*, who are competitive and who may be described as players.

The number of people travelling to participate in sporting events, although significant for some smaller urban destinations, is much smaller than the number travelling to observe them. Therefore sport plays an important role in motivating and attracting tourist activity, particularly among domestic travellers. In New Zealand researchers have coined the term 'sport devotees' to describe travellers who are motivated by watching or participating in sports at any level. This segment of the travel market comprises 20.7 per cent of New Zealand's domestic travel activity. Therefore, sport and tourism can generate a significant stimulus to destinations.

Sport and golf tourism in Scotland

It is widely recognized that Scotland is the home of golf, with over 500 courses. The golf course provides a powerful stimulus to tourism development, since it enables many repeat visitors the opportunity to explore and discover new areas. The open championship at St Andrews is one of the most well known events in the golf calendar, with many other courses (such as Gleneagles, Carnoustie and Muirfield) known internationally among the golfing fraternity. This enables Scotland to develop a powerful brand image based around this element of the country's sporting history. In economic terms, golf tourism is estimated to contribute £100 million to the Scottish economy, with 70 per cent from UK visitors. Spending by overseas golfers is cautiously estimated to be £28 million per year, and tourists come from the USA, Sweden, UK, Germany, Norway and Finland. The economic benefits of such visitors are clear from the higher spending per person than other holidaymakers – often three times as much among overseas visitors – which in turn reflects the higher socio-economic groups from which golfers are derived, many with high disposable incomes.

Of the 200 000 golf tourists from the UK (3 per cent of all the UK holidays taken in Scotland), over half count golf as the main reason for taking a holiday while the balance play golf whilst on holiday. However, VisitScotland has recognized that since the 1990s golf tourism has been in decline in Scotland, given major competition from Ireland, where up to 214 000 visitors can be classed as golf tourists and spend £95 million a year. Yet golf tourism also has to be viewed in a wider European context, where the European golf tour has developed. In 1946 there were 13 tournaments in the UK and Europe, but by 1972 this had grown to 27 events and led to the formation of a European tour. By 1997 the tour comprised 34 events, with £29 million in prize money and a substantial economic impact on the destinations hosting the events. Television coverage and sponsorship have increased the impact and effect of such events on both the sporting public and visitors, with substantial place-marketing opportunities for golf tourism destinations to derive positive marketing opportunities during the exposure the media provides at each event.

event. In each case, such events or activities have profound economic impacts on the locality or area in which they are hosted owing to the demand for accommodation, food and beverages, attendance at the event and other ancillary services, as well as associated tourism activities such as sightseeing or touring.

Adventure tourism

Another recent area of growth that links together activities and tourism is adventure travel. Adventure tourism has been defined as a leisure activity that is undertaken in unusual, exotic, remote or unconventional destinations. The defining characteristic of adventure tourism is the heavy emphasis on outdoor pursuits, usually encompassing high levels of risk, adrenaline rushes, excitement and personal

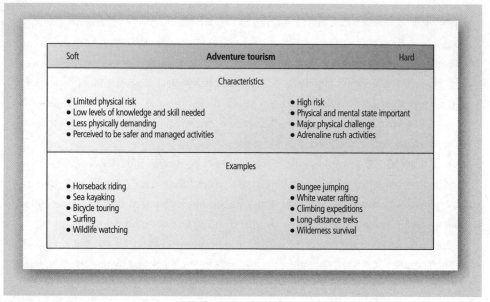

Figure 4.2 The characteristics of adventure tourism

challenge. Adventure tourism is normally viewed as a continuum that ranges from 'soft' experiences such as snorkelling to hard experiences such as climbing Mount Everest (see Figure 4.2).

The size of the adventure tourism market, comprising travellers who have booked a package from an adventure tour operator, is estimated to be 4 to 5 million trips a year, or 1 per cent of the international outbound tourism market. The major generating market is North America, with 2 to 3 million trips a year, with 1 million from Europe and 1 million from other parts of the world. The potential market for such travel experiences is probably ten times that size, offering major growth prospects based on WTO estimates. In the USA alone, in 1997 a Travel Industry Association of America survey indicated that half of the US population (98 million) had participated in adventure activities in the period 1992–1997. The market for adventure travel has also evolved in recent years with the growth of 'charity challenges', where travellers gain sponsorship for a trip. They typically pay the costs of the airfare and undertake to raise a minimum amount for the charity that has devised the trip. Research indicates that these travellers are ethically inclined, and may have participated in Raleigh International community and environmental expeditions for young travellers aged 17–25 years.

Another market that has been developed by the tourism sector is the prestige adventure market, where the participants want to see something unusual, unique and exclusive to them (e.g. an individual ascent of Mount Everest) that offers an adrenaline rush.

The typical profile among the travellers who participate in adventure tourism is of a person aged 40–45 years, very well educated and computer-literate, earning over US$75 000, with large amounts of disposable income and a long holiday entitlement. Women are more likely than men to be participants. In the USA, the fastest growing segment is the middle classes with disposable income. To assist in the promotion of this evolving market segment, the tourism industry in the UK and USA organize travel shows to illustrate the products and destinations available. For example, in the UK the Adventure Travel and Sports Show and in the USA the International Adventure and Outdoor Travel Show provide opportunities for the operators to meet potential clients and showcase their products. This segment of the market was the fastest growing sector of the tourism industry in New Zealand in the 1990s, as it established a number of adventure tourism destinations such as Queenstown with its Awesome Threesome (jetboating, bungee jumping and white-water rafting experiences). These patterns of growth are seeing more tour operators seek to expand their product offering to meet demand, although the recent collapse of HIH Insurance in Australia in 2002 saw some adventure activities suspended due to the absence of insurance cover for participants while new insurers and underwriters examined the risk of covering such operators. Despite such events, and the negative publicity associated with adventure tourism accidents, the demand for such products and experiences continues to grow. Indeed, some operators have established adventure-themed hotels, emphasizing the activities rather than natural attractions (i.e. scenery and location) and destination as the major attractor.

Critics of adventure tourism have pointed to the environmental costs of increasing numbers of travellers seeking remote locations to experience and undertake their activities, especially in National Parks and wilderness areas. Furthermore, relatively affluent visitors travelling to less developed countries to be adventure tourists has increased the potential for crime, abductions and attacks. Nevertheless, with growing accessibility to tourist destinations, the number of undeveloped, remote and unknown locations is fast running out. To reach these destinations, the tourism industry is dependent upon another critical element of supply – transport.

Transport

Transport is the most critical element that has promoted the growth of domestic and international tourism. At a simple level, transport links the tourist from the origin area with the destination area. It enables the traveller to consume the products and experiences they have purchased, because it links the supply chain together. Figure 4.3 illustrates the all-embracing role of transport in *facilitating* the tourist trip to the destination and *enabling* tourist travel within the destination.

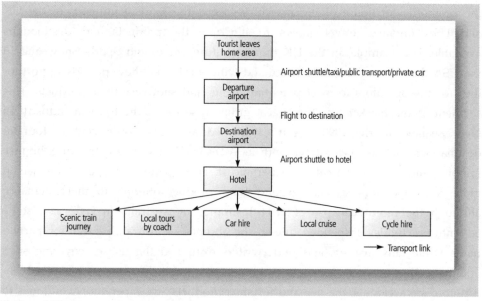

Figure 4.3   The role of transport in tourist travel

In addition, transport may be an attraction in its own right (for example, a cruise ship or a trip on the Orient Express). Tourists who 'tour' by road may use public transport or private transport (e.g. the car) to experience a variety of destinations. Increasingly the transport sector is entering into strategic alliances (i.e. formal business partnerships) where different operators seek to offer seamless transport experiences for travellers, recognizing the selling opportunity. For example, if the tour operator can sell a holiday and also airport transfers, car hire and tours from approved partners with whom they have entered into a strategic alliance, it increases their profitability through commissions. This illustrates the increasing integration within the tourism sector, with different business interests linking together in the supply chain. The tourism industry and its growing complexity has seen the growth of agencies that have been developed to manage the supply of tourism.

Tourism organizations and agencies and the supply of tourism

Within the tourism industry, a number of 'institutional elements' have sought to manage the growing complexity of tourism supply in relation to services and business operations. At one level, the public sector has sought to plan and manage supply issues within countries and destinations to establish an orderly and logical direction for the tourism sector. This is often described as a strategic direction, expressed as a tourism strategy, so that the different business interests work towards the wider development of the tourism sector. In the UK there are a number of national tourist boards, supplemented by regional or area-based tourist boards and the work of local councils in the public sector. These agencies not only promote the region they are responsible for, but also attempt to foster the continued economic development of tourism as well as encouraging members the tourism sector to work together to enhance the quality of provision (see Chapter 11 for more detail).

This has led to a growing number of partnerships between tourism industry partners (stakeholders), the local industry and the destination area. For example, in Western Australia the growth in wine-based tourism has led to the formation of public and private sector partnerships, whereby tourism industry associations have been created. These partnerships not only market the local products, but also, through collaboration and partnership working, seek to raise the area' profile and the number of visitors to it. These lobby groups receive a grant from the public sector and raise additional finance from membership subscriptions. Trade associations also operate at a national level, such as specialist industry sector groups (e.g. the Association of Scottish Visitor Attractions based in Stirling, Scotland). There are also much higher-profile industry lobby groups, such as the Association of British Travel Agents (ABTA), which represents travel agents and tour operators and is a corporate trade association.

Tourist services and facilities

Whilst the public sector can facilitate tourism, it also has a direct role in developing the tourism infrastructure in destinations. This is usually vested in the local authority, which is responsible for managing/overseeing the appropriate provision of water, sewerage, roads and facilities that will be used by residents and tourists alike. At a national level, governments become involved in the strategic decision-making for the provision of infrastructure for tourism. For example, the recent outcome of the government's public inquiry into Terminal 5 at Heathrow Airport in the UK has been the authorization of the expansion of the country's leading tourist gateway and of the infrastructure to support its development. In this instance, the state is approving the development, which a private sector company (i.e. the British Airports Authority) will implement in the long-term public interest. In other cases the state directly invests in infrastructure provision, as in the development of the Channel Tunnel high-speed rail-link project to encourage private sector investment to pump-prime development. In some countries the state has also been directly involved in the provision of tourism services and facilities, such as the state-owned Tourist Hotel Corporation in New Zealand up until the 1990s. In Albania, the state controlled all aspects of tourism supply – airlines, hotel provision, tour guides and transport in the destination – although this is much less common in countries in the new millennium. For this reason, it is useful to consider changes in the supply of tourism, and the business and management implications.

Managing the supply of tourism in the new millennium

Within the European tourism sector a number of important economic changes have impacted upon the structure and organization of tourism. This has been described as consolidation, meaning that a large number of nationally-based private firms have been sold, acquired and merged to create fewer, larger transnational tourism businesses (a transnational business operates across country boundaries). However, the EU and national government monopoly authorities are the main obstacles to continued consolidation. Many businesses are *vertically integrated*, meaning that tour operator A has taken over hotel or transport operator B to make its business larger and to expand its range and market share of the available business through a diversified product base. In Europe a steel and engineering firm, Preussag, now owns the leading travel companies in Germany (TUI) and the UK (Thomson). The consolidation strategy has enabled many travel companies to emerge as large national companies. For example, in Germany the third largest travel retailer, Rewe, built its position by:

- Acquiring a mass-market tour operator, ITS, in the 1990s
- Purchasing the DER Group from the Deutsche Bahn Group in 1999
- The purchase of the LTU tour operator in 2000.

By purchasing stakes in different parts of the businesses, Rewe has acquired three long-haul and short-haul operations. The majority of travel retailing is still dominated by travel agents (between 80 and 90 per cent for many markets), but direct sales both by telephone and on the Internet are beginning to increase.

Therefore it is not surprising that many of the acquisitions and mergers of larger travel businesses have led to investment in expanding the channels for distributing products and services. Yet such activities require large sums of capital investment. Preussag paid £1.8 billion for Thomson, and has continued to invest in the hotels and airlines it owns as part of a vertically integrated tourism business. Similarly, Thomson is expected to invest £100 million in information technology systems and e-commerce.

Consolidation trends have seen some operators, such as Preussag, wanting to have a presence in most major outbound markets, making it the leading operator in the UK, Germany, the Netherlands and Austria. It is the second largest in Scandinavia and Belgium, and is ranked third in Switzerland. In contrast, Airtours was ranked second in the UK, first in Scandinavia, and fifth in Germany.

These trends in the travel industry reflect the highly competitive nature of this business. For many businesses operating in slow-growth or stagnating markets, such as the UK and Germany, cost control is vital. One of the reasons for the collapse of Clarksons in the UK in the 1970s was spiralling costs. Such concerns led Thomson to seek cost reductions in the late 1990s, following poor financial results, seeking to save £50 million in costs in 2000–2002. In fact large travel firms can achieve cost savings after mergers and takeovers by streamlining internal business processes through the use of new technology to avoid duplication of business activities.

The business strategies that travel companies can pursue to develop their supply of tourism services and products include:

- Focusing on a core business (e.g. a holiday company focusing on selling holidays rather than becoming vertically integrated and operating its own airline and hotels). One company pursuing this strategy is Alltours (Germany), which focuses on budget- and normal-priced packaged holiday products.
- Seeking to diversify products. The leading French holiday company Club Méditerranée (Club Med), which traditionally sold packages to its 120 holiday

resorts, has used this strategy. Since 1999, its acquisition of Jet Tours (France's fourth ranked tour operator, which operated to 113 summer and 81 winter locations) it has diversified its operations to sell non-Club Med packages. Rewe in Germany has pursued a similar diversification strategy with its acquisition of a wider range of tour operating businesses in the long- and short-haul markets.

● Choosing to operate in all segments of the tourism market. Preussag has adopted this tactic, and others such as Kuoni are moving towards the same goal.

To implement these business strategies, companies in the tourism industry have adopted marketing-related concepts such as branding to differentiate their products in an increasingly competitive marketplace. For example, Club Med has recently relaunched its worldwide image to re-emphasize its famous name and association with consumers, and particularly its dominant position in the French market. Thomas Cook, now owned by a German company, C&N Touriste, has used its global image and historic association with pioneering tourism to continue its expansion throughout Europe. In 1999, Thomas Cook narrowed its product range from fifteen identifiable brands to its new core brand JMC, with only three specialist brands. Tour operators have to consider the potential for retaining different brands for different markets in the various countries they operate in, or move towards pan-European brands.

For the consumer, changes in the supply of tourism products through a vertically integrated distribution chain has begun to limit choice amongst some of the larger conglomerates. For example, in 1998 Thomson's retail chain Lunn Poly sold 31 per cent of the company's holiday capacity. This translated into 47 per cent of Lunn Poly's sales as Thomson products reflected in other countries, where similar trends exist. Many of the larger travel companies are also investing heavily in direct selling by phone or on the World Wide Web. For example, in 2000 Airtours acquired a US Internet company, Travel Services International, which is the vehicle for its £100 million investment in e-commerce under the brand mytravelco. This mirrored trends by other tour operators such as Thomson.

Many travel suppliers are recognizing that the growth in e-commerce is necessary in order to respond the changes in demand over the next five years, which will include:

● A gradual reduction in the length of main holidays
● A rise in the number of additional (second and third) holidays

- An increasing demand for activity holidays
- Greater flexibility among consumers willing to book last minute holidays, seat-only sales and more short breaks.

These trends in consumer demand illustrate that the supply of tourism products and services requires highly refined management tools among the tourism sector to respond to changes and opportunities.

Summary

Within the larger travel companies pressures for cost reduction and acquisitions and mergers have caused a considerable degree of change in the operating environment, which reinforces the need for leadership and many of the skills observed by Mintzberg. Tourism supply must be customer-focused, and therefore many tourism businesses not only have to think, work and act strategically (i.e. look to the future and the best way to operate), but also have to be be cognisant of immediate operational and management issues so that profitability (the bottom line) is maintained. Being able to respond to the market increasingly requires sophisticated use of information technology, innovative advertising and recognizable brands so that consumers will buy what is on offer. In the supply of tourism products and services, the culmination of transport, accommodation, attractions, associated services and the institutional elements need to co-exist so that destinations continue to attract the visitor. Managing the supply chain to ensure that tourism services are delivered in a coherent manner according to the specification sold to the visitor requires a great many managerial skills on a day-to-day basis. It also requires a fluid business strategy in order to be able to respond to changes in the operating environment. These management skills also require a global understanding of tourism trends, of innovation in product development, and of how to adapt to adverse elements in the marketplace as well as opportunities that arise.

References

Charaupunsirikul, S. and Wood, R. (2002) Mintzberg, managers and methodology: some observations from a study of hotel general managers. *Tourism Management*, **23**(5), 551–56.

Mintzberg, H. (1973) *The Nature of Managerial Work*. New York: Harper and Row.

Sessa, A. (1983) *Elements of Tourism*. Rome: Catal.

Further reading

Ioannides, D. and K. Debbage (eds) (1998) *The Economic Geography of the Tourist Industry: A Supply-side Analysis*. London: Routledge.

Witt, S., Brooke, M. and Buckley, P. (1991) *The Management of International Tourism*. London: Routledge.

Questions

1 Why tourism supply important to the production of the tourist experience?
2 How do economic market conditions affect the competitive environment for tourism businesses?
3 Why does the supply chain concept help to explain the way tourism products are assembled?
4 What future factors will impact upon the management of supply issues for the tourism industry?

Chapter **5**

Transporting the tourist: I Surface transport

Learning objectives

This chapter discusses transport, which forms the vital link between tourists and destinations and also provides the focus for many tourist activities such as sightseeing and cruising. After reading it you should be able to understand:

- the relationship between transport and tourism;
- the significance of different modes of surface transport and their contribution to tourism;
- the role of operational issues in developing competitive modes of tourist transport.

Introduction

The pursuit of tourism through the ages has seen a steady growth in the range of destinations visited, and is characterized by a growing impact upon different countries and places. This is directly related to changes in transport technology and its affordability, or diffusion from a travelling elite initially to a wider mass market. In the nineteenth century the building of railways and cheap fares, combined with increased leisure time, permitted a mass-market development of seaside trips in many European countries, initially as day trips and later as holidays. This is illustrated in Figure 5.1, which shows how the innovation of rail travel and its decreasing cost led to growing numbers of people travelling as tourists as previous modes of transport (e.g. the paddle steamer) were replaced by mass forms of transport. This example also shows that transport is a vital *facilitator* of tourism – i.e. transport enables the tourists travel from their home area (origin) to their destination and return. This tourist trip has a reciprocal element (i.e. a two-way element): the tourist travels out on a mode of transport and then returns at a set period of time later. These simple principles of

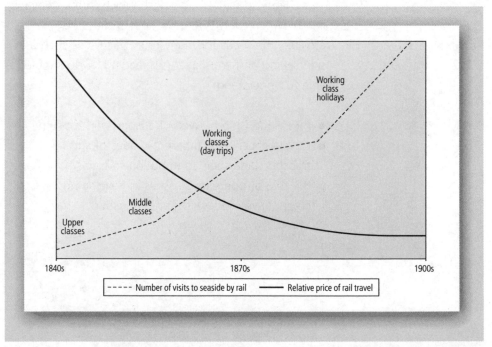

Figure 5.1 Hypothetical example of the impact of railway technology on the growth of coastal tourism in Victorian and Edwardian England

tourist travel were introduced in Chapter 4, and are reiterated here so that they can be used as a basis to differentiate different forms of tourist travel.

In the example shown in Figure 5.2, the tourist travels on a number of different forms of transport from the origin to the destination area. Each element of travel is typically viewed as a passive element, as a means to an end (to travel from the origin to destination area). However, this conventional idea that transport is in itself a passive element in the tourist experience of a holiday or trip is now very outdated. In the case of package holidays, service interruptions (e.g. flight delays) can severely impact upon tourists' enjoyment of their holiday and so, like accommodation, transport is an integral element upon which the experience is built. For example, the major complaints made by clients to a coach operator were about how their holiday had been ruined or affected by being left behind at a pick-up point, by a service breakdown, or by delays that caused inconvenience and stress and tarnished their holiday experience. It was not just the holiday but also the transport that impacted upon the customers' satisfaction. In fact travellers often have unrealistic expectations of transport providers – especially budget travellers, who expect the standards of provision and customer care offered by well known airline brands when delays or operational problems occur. The importance of transport is emphasized in the following extract from Lamb and Davidson (1996: 264–65):

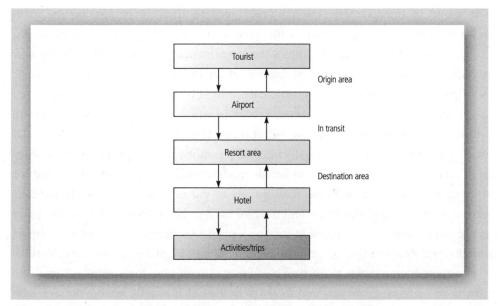

Figure 5.2   Tourist travel from origin to destination area and return

. . . the purchaser of the tourism product (*the tourist*) must experience the trip to access the product, the quality of the transportation experience becomes an important aspect of the tourist experience and, therefore a key criterion that enters into destination choice. Poor service, scheduling problems, and/or long delays associated with a transportation service, for example, can seriously affect a traveller's perceptions and levels of enjoyment with respect to a trip. Tourists require safe, comfortable, affordable, and efficient intermodal transportation networks that enable precious vacation periods to be enjoyed to their maximum potential.

This illustrates the interrelationships between transport and tourism, where four main elements exist:

1 The tourist
2 The relationship between transport and the tourist experience
3 The effect of transport problems on the travellers' perceptions
4 The tourists' requirement for safe, reliable and efficient modes of transport.

Transport, tourism and the tour

The mode of transport by which tourists seek to travel may also be the main motivation for a holiday or the containing context of a holiday, as is the case with a cruise or coach tour. In these examples the fundamental element of tourism, the tour (which takes in a number of destinations on an itinerary), is followed. The basic principle of a tour is shown in Figure 5.3; the tourist travels to the point of departure, then boards the mode of transport (e.g. a coach or cruise ship) and engages in the tour, which follows a set route over a period of time. At each point of call (Areas A to D) an overnight stay may be required, either on the mode of transport (the cruise ship) or in serviced accommodation, and time is made available to visit attractions and for sightseeing. The coach or cruise then travels to the next area. Eventually the tour returns to the point of departure and the tour is completed. However, in recent years cruise companies have introduced the concept of fly-cruises to offer more compact and time-efficient cruises, where passengers fly to a point of departure and undertake a cruise or part of a cruise and return by ship or aircraft. At a less organized level, the principles of touring are inherent in the activities of domestic holidaymakers who undertake driving holidays, or amongst holidaymakers who undertake tours in the

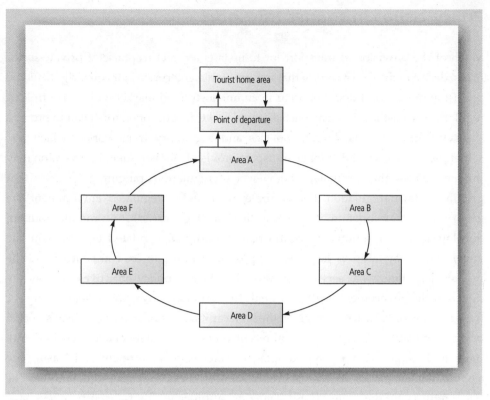

Figure 5.3 A tour with an itinerary, visiting different areas

destination area. Therefore, transporting the tourist, the tour, and travel in general are fundamental elements of the dynamic phenomenon known as tourism.

The movement of people, often in large volumes, requires specific managerial skills and an understanding of logistics – particularly of how the transport system and its different elements are managed. For the transport sector, managing the supply of transport so it meets demand and operates in an efficient, timely and convenient manner is an underlying feature for transporting tourists. For this reason Chapters 5 and 6 examine the transport sector, examining the principal modes of transport by land, water and air. In each case the management issues involving tourists are highlighted along with key concepts associated with each mode of transport. However, prior to discussing land-based transport it is useful to examine a number of concepts that are used in understanding how tourist transport is shaped by government.

Policy issues in tourist transport

Much of the provision of transport for tourists is a direct response of private-sector firms' desire to provide a service that is a profitable enterprise in its own right. Yet the provision of transport does not occur in an unconstrained market with no controls or regulation. Whilst tourists may wish to travel and transport operators want to provide a service, governments develop policies and regulatory frameworks to facilitate, sometimes constrain, and manage transport provision. Government intervention may pursue policies that promote a high level of regulation, ranging to policies that promote total deregulation. For example, in a highly regulated environment the government may operate its own airline (a flag carrier) to promote tourism development in a country. In contrast, in a highly deregulated environment the government may adopt a 'hands-off' approach, wanting to see competition and the market determine what services are provided. Whilst policy objectives may set the direction the government wants to pursue, governments also have responsibility for the provision of infrastructure, given the high capital costs of airports, railways, roads, bridges and waterways. However, in recent years governments have tried to defray these high capital costs by encouraging private-sector investment and leasing the asset to a developer for 20–25 years so they recoup the cost plus a profit, and then the asset returns to the state. These changing approaches to transport policy have followed distinct phases in countries such as the UK, where Button and Gillingwater (1983) identified four eras, each of which had had a clear impact on tourism development and provision:

1 *The Railway Age*, from the 1840s onwards, where private sector investment was employed to develop land-based transport (except during the First World War, when state control was exercised).
2 *The Age of Protection*, which dominated the 1920s and 1930s when road transport emerged and unplanned car and coach travel developed. Governments intervened to prevent excessive competition, which in the USA led to the 1935 Motor Carriage Act. This protected the Greyhound Bus Operators and gave one operator a monopoly on inter-urban bus travel.
3 *The Age of Administrative Planning*, which followed the Second World War, when the weaknesses exposed in railway companies led to nationalization in pursuit of a national passenger network to ensure national efficiency. The financial costs of large-scale nationalization led to major subsidies, which were restructured in the

1960s with the Beeching Report (this cut the network back considerably). In 1968 The Transport Act in the UK also led to further reorganization of public transport, with the creation of the National Bus Company.

4 *The Age of Contestability*, characterized the USA in the 1970s and the UK in the 1980s, was based on the principles of deregulation to achieve greater efficiency and to reduce public subsidies. In the UK, it led to the sale of state-owned assets and the establishment of private transport providers such as British Airways, Stena and, in the early 1990s, to the privatization of British Rail.

A fifth era, *The Age of Public–Private Partnerships*, has emerged in the UK and other EU countries since the Labour government entered power in the late 1990s. It has seen continuity with previous policies of privatization, with a greater emphasis on private sector expertise to manage the transport infrastructure. Concerns for efficiency and renewed investment in infrastructure have led to complex plans to harness public–private partnerships to redevelop aged infrastructures like the London Underground. Where the private sector assesses the risk of investment that is not justified in terms of likely returns, the state has had to reinvest using stage funds. Where competition is seen as beneficial it is promoted – particularly in air travel.

One additional level of policy measure that is important in Europe is the role of the European Union and its attempt to develop pan-European policies towards transport provision. EU states have been slow to engage in rail competition following the EU 91/440 Directive (1991), which sought to separate infrastructure from operations. Sweden was the first to act in separating its operations from the infrastructure, followed by the UK and Germany in 1994 (see Figure 5.4 of the UK railway industry post-privatization). In 1997 France established the RRF infrastructure authority (although most of its responsibilities are delegated to SNCF), and others are following suit.

To compete with air-based traffic and address European air congestion, the EU proposed plans for a trans-European network (TENS) of high-speed road and rail links in Europe. The EU identified nine rail projects totalling 35 000 km of high-speed lines after 1994 (15 000 km of existing railway to be upgraded and 20 000 km of new routes), with a target completion date of 2005. A 1994 study by the EC/Union of International Railway Companies (UIC) forecast that with a TENS network in operation, rail may account for 23.5 per cent of the estimated 1.5 billion passenger kilometres that will be travelled in Western Europe by 2010. However, this would require passengers to switch their mode of travel so that the car accounts for 60 per cent of traffic flows, rail 23.5 per cent and air 16.5 per cent. Whilst the EU has pointed

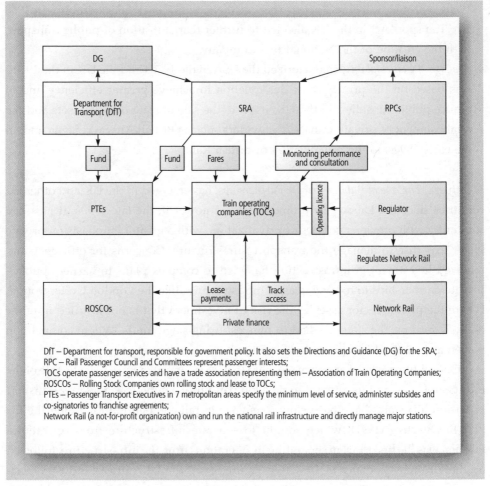

Figure 5.4   The UK rail passenger industry structure (source: Page, 2002; © Mintel)

to success in some new high-speed operations (e.g. Spain's AVE route from Madrid to Seville saw the share of air traffic drop from 40 per cent to 13 per cent, and the Paris–Brussels THALY service led to a 15 per cent drop in car usage), these are the exception rather than the norm.

The discussion of policy issues that, in the wider business environment in which transport companies operate, government policy direction can directly affect the supply of transport services in its use of regulation–deregulation measures. Notable entrepreneurs in the transport sector have responded to the opportunities afforded by transport policy changes (e.g. the deregulation of the bus industry after 1985 and railway system), as the rise of Stagecoach as a global transport operator and of the Souter family in the UK has shown. The rise of Virgin as a transport brand has also followed a similar direction. Policy changes such as deregulation have also altered the shape and nature of transport provision for tourists (see Chapter 6). In some cases it has increased choice, and in other instances consolidation has actually reduced choice. Recognizing the linkages between transport and tourism can also yield invaluable business opportunities (consider, for example, the growth in airport shuttle companies). In some cases airport authorities have taken the lead, as in the British Airport Authority in the UK with the construction of the Heathrow Express, a fast rail link from Paddington in Central London to Heathrow. With these issues in mind, attention now turns to land-based transport.

Land-based transport

Land-based transport is often neglected in discussions of transport and tourism, although it forms the dominant mode of travel for many domestic tourist trips. Air travel normally attracts more attention owing to the scale and pace of development in this market since the early 1970s. However, land-based transport has a long history and covers a number of distinct forms: the car, the bicycle, bus and coach travel, and rail travel.

The car

Since the war, the increase in car ownership has not only made tourist travel more flexible; it has also induced over-use at accessible sites. This ease of access, fuelled by the growth in road building and the upgrading of minor roads in many developed countries, has been a self-reinforcing process, leading to overuse and the greater dominance of passive recreational activities. Car ownership expanded rapidly in most countries in the 1970s and 1980s, adding to pressure on the road network, especially at holiday times. Among the key factors that affect the use of roads by tourists are access, the quality of the infrastructure, grades of roads, and signage to guide tourists to tour areas, which may be off the beaten track. This is evident in New Zealand, where Destination Northland's Twin Coast Highway's initiative to encourage tourists to travel on a circuit has spread the distribution of visitors by encouraging them to explore heritage, wineries and golf on less-used roads. Intermodal connections (i.e. between different modes of transport) between airports, ports and rail termini and tourist areas are also important. There is recognition that tourist areas need to develop new linear land and water corridors that integrate various forms of transport to explore scenic regions.

Regions and countries also need to consider the concept of seamless transport systems for tourists. This means that the individual transport networks that for each mode of tourist transport need to be planned and integrated into a holistic framework. This will ensure that the tourists' experience of transport is a continuous one that is not characterized by major gaps in provision and a lack of integration (e.g. airports need to be linked to tourist districts so that visitors transfer from one mode of transport to another with relative ease).

Probably the most influential study of car usage among recreationalists was Wall's (1971) study of Kingston-upon-Hull in the UK. This highlighted the importance of seasonality and the timing of pleasure trips by car, and the dominance of the car as a mode of transport for urban dwellers. It also considered the role of the journey by car as a form of recreation in itself, as well as the importance of the car as more than just a means of transport. Wall found that the majority of pleasure trips were day trips to areas less than 100 km from Hull, being spatially concentrated in a limited number of resorts along the Yorkshire coast and the southerly part of the region.

More recent research by Eaton and Holding (1996) identified the growing scale of visitors to the countryside travelling by car. In 1991, 103 million visits were made to National Parks in the UK (Countryside Commission, 1992), the most popular being the Lake District and Peak District Parks. It was estimated in 1992 that car traffic would grow by 267 per cent by the year 2025. Rising car usage has coincided with the decline in public transport usage for tourist and recreational trips. However, many National Parks seem unlikely to be able to cope with the levels of usage predicted by the year 2025, given their urban catchments and the relative accessibility by motorway and A roads in the UK. Eaton and Holding (1996) reviewed the absence of effective policies to meet the practical problems of congestion facing many sites in the countryside in Britain. Furthermore, there is a failure to design public transport that will suit the needs and perception of users in order to achieve reductions and solutions to congestion in National Parks. This problem is worse when spatially concentrated at 'honeypots' – locations that attract large numbers in a confined area – in the National Parks.

The UK Tourism Society's response to the Government Task Force on tourism and the environment (English Tourist Board/Employment Department, 1991) highlighted the impact of the car by commenting that:

... no analysis of the relationship between tourism and the environment can ignore transportation. Tourism is inconceivable without it. Throughout Europe some 40 per cent of leisure time away from home is spent travelling, and the vast majority of this is by car ... Approaching 30 per cent of the UK's energy requirements go on transportation ... [and] ... the impact of traffic congestion, noise and air pollution ... [will] ... diminish the quality of the experience for visitors.

Chubb (1989) also highlighted the central role of the car in tourism in his study of the Great Lakes region of North America and cross-border travel between Canada and the USA. This region, which contains the world's largest complex of fresh water, also has a diversity of recreational and tourism resources, including lakes, forests, large park areas, cottages and resort complexes. Recreational cottages line many of the lakes as second-home developments, and other seasonal residences are distributed throughout the region and are used for weekends and vacations from May to September. A range of resort areas also exists, and the region experiences a high usage of recreational vehicles such as caravans and campervans. There are a number of straight-line and circuitous routes that cross the international border between Canada and the USA.

One additional area that is worthy of discussion in terms of road transport is the car hire industry. This is neglected in many studies of tourism and transport, and yet it is a major motivator of this car-based activity. The car hire business can be divided into three distinct segments:

1 Airport rentals, which often command a 15 per cent premium over and above other rentals due to the charges imposed by airport authorities. This is based on the principle that there is a captive market, which is able to pay the price demanded. This may be the case for corporate travel, where such prices have been discounted on the basis of volume or business, but leisure travellers pay premium prices. However, in the UK the budget airline easyJet has established a rental brand that has undercut the main hire car businesses.
2 Downtown rental locations
3 Replacement vehicles for corporate and individuals whose cars are off the road being repaired or serviced.

In Europe and the USA, the car hire business is dominated by the main brands – Avis, Budget, National (formed from Eurodollar and Alamo) and Hertz. The scale of the industry is illustrated by the market leader, Avis, which employs 4600 staff in Europe and has a fleet of 80000 vehicles. The traditional ownership patterns, where car manufacturers were key stakeholders, have changed as the manufacturers have reduced their involvement. Many car hire companies have looked at leasing vehicles rather than purchasing now that second-hand car values have dropped in Europe owing to the oversupply of new vehicles.

The cost of car hire for tourists varies considerably by country, reflecting tax regimes and other local factors. In Europe, Finland has the most expensive rental costs, at 48 per cent more than the cheapest rental costs in Belgium and Luxembourg. In the USA, the Internet booking site Travelocity announced a new scheme in 2002 to develop its 'Total Pricing for Cars' package, where Internet bookers are given the all-in price of a booking as opposed to a basic price without the add-ons that arise when looking at hire car tariffs. This reflects varying pricing strategies, a feature observed by the American Automobile Association (AAA) in 2002 when it noted that hire car rates in the same city could vary between 18 and 190 per cent for the same product. Typically, rates varied around 77 per cent for the same type of vehicle depending upon the hire company, with the greatest variations in key tourist destinations in states such as California and Nevada. Overall the most lucrative markets for car rental are France, Germany, Italy, Spain and the UK, which reflects the domestic and international tourism markets in each country.

The bicycle

From a tourism perspective, bicycles are used either occasionally by tourists visiting a destination, who may hire a cycle for a day, or by more determined tourists who undertake long-distance cycling holidays. Lumsdon (1996: 5) defines cycle tourism as cycling that is 'part of or the primary activity of a holiday trip . . . it falls within a categorization of activity holidays'. The UK Department of Transport statistics suggest that up to 40 per cent of cycle journeys are for leisure purposes. As Lumsdon (1997: 115) shows:

> Leisure cycling has great potential for growth, it can be a stimulus to tourism, it is a high-quality way to enjoy the countryside and a good way to introduce people to cycling for their everyday transport needs. To encourage leisure cycling there need to be small-scale improvements, especially near where people live, followed by better signposting, marketing and information. Flagship leisure routes, using quiet roads or disused railway paths, can increase the profile and boost leisure cycling in town and countryside.

But who are the typical cycle tourists, and what motivates them to use this form of transport? The Scottish Tourist Board's (1991) innovative study on the *Tourism Potential of Cycling and Cycle Routes in Scotland* indicated that cycling had grown in popularity as a recreational activity in the 1970s and 1980s, with the Cyclists' Tourist Club having 40 000 members in the UK – an increase of 10 per cent in the previous decade. The more recent study by the Countryside Commission (1995), *The Market for Recreational Cycling in the Countryside*, identified some of the main motivations for cycling, including:

- Keeping fit
- Having fun
- Fresh air
- Access to the countryside.

In a tourism context, Lumsdon (1996) simplifies the market segments involved in cycle tourism to include:

- *Holiday cyclists*, comprising couples, families or friends who seek a holiday where they can enjoy opportunities to cycle but not necessarily every day. They seek traffic-free routes and are independent travellers not seeking a package holiday. While they are likely to take their own bikes on holiday, a proportion will hire bikes. They are likely to cycle 25–40 km miles each day they travel by bike.
- *Short-break cyclists*, who seek to escape and select packages that will provide local knowledge (with or without cycle hire) and comfortable accommodation. They are likely to travel in groups, and to cycle 25–40 km a day.
- *Day excursionists*, who are casual cyclists who undertake leisurely circular rides of 15–25 km and are not prepared to travel long distances to visit attractions or facilities. They prefer to seek quiet country lanes, which are signposted. They tend to comprise 25–30 per cent of the market for cycling, and are increasingly using their own bikes rather than hiring them.

The Royal Commission on Environmental Pollution (HMSO, 1994) identified the role of cycling as a mode of personal transport as a sustainable form of transport with minimal pollution and effects on others. It recommended that cycle trips should be quadrupled to 10 per cent of all journeys in the UK by 2005, which highlights the need for further infrastructure to achieve such growth targets. One of the important findings of the Royal Commission was that local authorities in the UK should have a controlling role in meeting the 2005 targets and in infrastructure provision. In a planning context, this was to be achieved through the existing planning mechanism – the local authority's annual Transport Policies and Programme Submissions (TPPS). While the purpose was to improve the level of cycle use, it has implications for tourism, which can utilize any infrastructure put in place for residents and leisure users in the local areas. A number of UK local authorities appointed cycling officers who have developed strategy documents for local use, but one of the principal catalysts for facilitating the development of a national cycle network in the UK is SUSTRANS.

SUSTRANS is a national sustainable transport and construction company operating as a charity which designs and builds routes. One of its early aims was to develop a 3200 km (2000 mile) national cycle network to link all the main urban centres in the UK, using a combination of traffic-calmed roads, cycle paths, and disused railway lines and river/canal paths. This aim was realized in 1996 by a grant of £43.5 million from the Millennium Commission (comprising 20 per cent of the total cost) to form a 10 400 km (6500 mile) route on the basis of its original vision to become the UK's National Cycle Network. By 2002 it had achieved this, and it has an ambitious target of 16 000 km (10 000 miles) by 2005. In the year 2000 over 60 million trips were made on the network, and estimates indicate that the network has the potential to generate 100 million trips per annum. SUSTRANS (2002) argues that the network generates £635 million income from cycle tourism:

- £146 per domestic trip (based on expenditure of £30–£35 a night)
- £300 per overseas cycling holiday trip
- £9 per cycling day trip
- £4 per local leisure cycling trip.

The UK Leisure Day Visits Survey in the UK recognized that the average cycle day trip is 62.9 km (39.3 miles) in length, 3.6 hours in duration, and a party size of 4.6.

The market segments for cycle tourism trips identified by SUSTRANS (2002) comprise:

- Infrequent leisure cyclists
- Occasional leisure cyclists
- Frequent leisure cyclists
- Cycling enthusiasts.

Each of these has specific product requirements (see Table 5.1).

Table 5.1 Cycle tourism market segments and product requirements (source: SUSTRANS, 2002: 7, reproduced with permission from SUSTRANS, www.sustrans.org.uk)

Market segment	Types of activity required	Product requirements
Infrequent leisure cyclists	Traffic-free cycling Packaged cycle touring holidays	Traffic-free cycle paths Cycle hire Packaged cycling holidays
Occasional leisure cyclists	Day cycle rides (20–25 miles on quiet country roads and traffic-free paths) Centre-based cycling short breaks Access to countryside from town and home	Circular day cycle routes with maps and information Safe places to leave the car while cycling Ideas for cycling short breaks Cycle parking and storage Cycle repair/rescue
Frequent leisure cyclists	Day cycle rides (30–35 miles on quiet country roads and traffic-free paths) Centre-based cycling short breaks Access to countryside from town and home	Circular day cycle routes with maps Safe places to leave the car while cycling Cycle access by train (for some) Ideas for cycling short breaks and cycle touring holidays Cycle friendly accommodation Cycle parking and storage Cycle repair/rescue
Cycling enthusiasts	Day cycle rides (up to 40–50 miles primarily on quiet country roads) Independent cycle touring holidays and short breaks Access to countryside from town and home	Ideas for day cycle rides – cycling enthusiasts tend to plan their own rides, using cycle route leaflets for ideas and information Cycle access by train (generally more important for cycling enthusiasts than for other market segments) Cycle friendly accommodation Cycle parking and storage Cycle repair

The C2C cycle route is indicative of the generative effect the network may have. The C2C route is a 270 km (170 mile) coast-to-coast route in Northern England, which SUSTRANS (2002) estimates has attracted 10 000 cycle tourists to an economically marginally area (West Cumbria and the North Pennines). This has generated an annual expenditure of £100 per person and £1.1 million for the local tourism economy. There is also a European Cycle Route Network, and some of the principal routes are:

- The 5000 km Atlantis route (Isle of Skye, Scotland to Cadiz in Spain)
- The 470 km Noordzee route (Den Helder in the Netherlands to Boulogne-Sur-Mer in France).

According to Lumsden (1996: 10–12), there are three ways in which the National Cycle Network may contribute to sustainable tourism (i.e. tourism that does not further damage or harm the resource base upon which it depends):

1 By encouraging tourists to switch from cars to cycles at their destination, although it needs a cycle-friendly culture to implement such changes in tourist attitudes. This could reduce recreational car journeys at the destination by 20–30 per cent.
2 By reducing car-based day excursions, particularly at 'honeypot' attractions or sites near to resorts and urban areas. The National Cycle Network may offer 'escape routes' to allow tourists to get off the beaten track.
3 By encouraging growth in cycle-based holidays, in both short-break and longer duration categories, by UK residents and overseas visitors.

Cycle tourism is certainly beginning to assume a much higher profile in the UK, and if leisure use encourages people to become more avid cyclists and reduce car usage, it will certainly make a valid contribution to local authority Agenda 21 objectives to achieve more sustainable development in transport and tourism. Indeed, in October 2002 the Dover-based tour operator Continental Car Tours (CCT) launched a Continental Cycle Drive package, given the excellent provision for cycling in many European countries and networks that are ideal for leisure use (see www.continentalcycledrive.co.uk).

Coach and bus travel

Bus and coach travel assumed a growing significance in the 1930s in most countries (see Chapter 2). There is a tendency to interchange the terms 'bus' and 'coach'. Bus travel usually refers to a specific form of urban and rural passenger transport, which tourists may use in the destination at which they are staying. In the UK a bus trip is defined as a trip of 24 km or less, whereas a coach trip is of greater than 24 km. In other European countries, specific terms (such as the Autocar in France) distinguish coach travel from bus travel. However, such a definition does not distinguish between the market for international and domestic coach services. The European Conference of Ministers of Transport (1987) classified the international coach travel market in terms of three categories of service:

1 Scheduled services (lines). These transport passengers at specified times, often based on a timetable, over specified routes. They involve the picking up and setting down of passengers at established stops. Such services are provided, under a licence, for a prescribed period for which the service is offered. Timetables, tariffs and the vehicles to be used are also specified, and particular conditions are attached to the service provided. These services are sometimes called express coach services, and are operated by consortia of companies or individual operators.
2 Shuttle services. These consist of trips for the transport of groups of tourists or individuals from the same point of departure to the same destination. The traveller is also transported back to the original departure point, and the service usually involves accommodation for the group at the destination. The service must comply with the conditions of an itinerary and length of stay, and no passengers are carried on the last outward or first inward journey. These services are often referred to as holiday shuttles.
3 Occasional services. These include a range of different services, such as:
   ● Closed-door tours (where one vehicle is used throughout the journey for the same group and the tour returns to the original point of departure), often referred to as continental coach holidays or continental coach tours
   ● Services with the return trip unladen
   ● All other services.
     These international services are complemented by domestic tourism and day-trip markets, where a variety of market segments exist for:
   ● Day excursions
   ● Extended tours (coach holidays), such as those run by Shearings (which has a £100 million turnover) and Wallace Arnold (which has a £70 million turnover in the UK)

- Private hire (including the market for group travel, which typically involves travel by coach for social reasons as a group outing and educational trips)
- Airport shuttle services
- Urban excursions, such as Guide Friday in the UK and the all-day ticket tours in London, where tourists purchase a day ticket and can board and get off as many times as they wish to and attend visitor attractions.

The market segments to which coach travel appeals are far from homogenous, ranging from the youth travel market, for express domestic and continental services, to the elderly markets, which dominate coach tours. Coach travel has an image of appealing to low-income groups and being a slow mode of surface transport. In recent years a number of new trends have come to dominate coach travel, including the rise of multi-modal operators such as Stagecoach, which has global coach and bus operations (it acquired the long-distance CoachUSA in 1999) and operates over 28 000 vehicles. The coach and bus sector employs a large workforce, with 196 000 employees in Germany, 155 000 in the UK, 126 000 in France and 32 000 in the Netherlands.

There is a tendency to underplay the role of local bus services and urban services in the tourism industry; tourists may use these when staying in a destination. In the UK, the bus industry is largely controlled (since deregulation in 1985, when the National Bus Company was sold off as 70 units for £1 billion) by five major organizations, with a turnover of £3.3 billion. In 1990 these groups had 5 per cent of the market, and by 2002 this had grown to 66.5 per cent as a process of consolidation occurred. In 2002, the ownership pattern was: First Group (22 per cent), Stagecoach (16 per cent), Arriva (15 per cent), Go-ahead (7.5 per cent), National Express (6 per cent); small operators (26.5 per cent); public sector (7 per cent). The pattern of bus use has declined from 42 per cent of all journeys in 1952 to 6 per cent in 2002, while the use of cars has grown from 27 per cent of all journeys in 1952 to 85 per cent in 2002. Public transport on buses in the UK is supported by an central government bus subsidy, with 29 per cent partial rebate for fuel duty and 45 per cent of the cost of concessionary fares (e.g. the old, young and disabled) and for services that are not commercially viable (18 per cent of journeys in 2002), illustrating the effect of government policy on service provision.

Table 5.2 shows the patterns of bus and coach travel in selected European countries, and the variable demand. These statistics do not illustrate the patterns of travel with express services, which tend to be point-to-point (i.e. city to city) or city-to-city via non-urban areas, using major transport corridors wherever possible to gain

Table 5.2 Usage of bus and coaches in selected European countries in 1998 (modified from Eurostat. ©European Commission)

Country	Passengers (millions)	km/person per year
Austria	12.7	1572
Belgium	12.0	1176
Denmark	11.1	2100
France	58.8	999
Italy	89.2	1548
Ireland	5.7	1166
Germany	69.4	846
Greece	21.2	2015
Netherlands	14.5	923
Portugal	14.0	1404
Sweden	9.5	1073
UK	45	731
EU (including Luxembourg)	417.2	1108

economies in order to be price- and time-competitive with rail travel. In contrast, coach tours (particularly packaged tours) tend to follow what are called 'milk runs', following a set itinerary to showcase the main sights and attractions, following well-worn routes – some of which even replicate the Grand Tour in Europe (see Chapter 2). In the UK, these milk runs with a strong heritage appeal might typically depart from London, visit Oxford, Stratford-upon-Avon, Bath, Chester, the Lake District and Scotland, returning on the east coast via York and Cambridge, depending on the length of the tour.

In 2000, coach tourism generated £153 million for the UK economy (an average of £219 per trip and £57 per night). Of this market £28 million came from overseas coach trips to the UK (an average of £280 per trip and £47 per night), comprising 4 per cent of all overseas expenditure in the UK. The majority of these trips are holidays – tours mainly of four to seven nights, with visitors staying in hotels or guesthouses. In 1998, a study undertaken for the Confederation of Passenger Transport noted that:

● UK tourists undertook 4.2 million coach tours, were away for 15.8 million nights, and spent £643 million

- UK residents undertook 36.2 million day trips on coach tours, and spent £844 million
- The UK coach tour industry generated £1883 million and generated over 79 000 jobs (full and part time), equivalent to 59 000 full-time equivalent jobs.

Regarding Scotland, the 100 000 overseas visitors generated £28 million. The majority of tourists travelled from Germany (40 000 tourists) and were responsible for £12 million in expenditure. Most overseas coach tours (54 per cent) arrived via the northeast coast of the UK (typically Hull or Newcastle, with lesser numbers using the new Rossyth–Zeebrugge service), although 28 per cent arrived via Dover (11 per cent using the Channel Tunnel) and a further 5 per cent from the Irish Republic, using Irish Seas crossings. The geographical distribution of UK and overseas tours in Scotland is shown in Figures 5.5(a–c). This shows that the key markets for coach tourism are the Highlands, and the urban gateways and major destinations of Glasgow and Edinburgh. The main differences between the domestic and overseas patterns of visitation are:

- The domestic visitors tend to focus on a limited range of destinations, particularly the Highlands and Stirling, Edinburgh and, to a lesser degree, Glasgow.
- The overseas visitors tend to follow a more dispersed pattern of visits, reflecting the tendency to tour and also to visit a wider range of destinations; they focus particularly on the Glasgow–Edinburgh gateways, followed by the Highlands as part of a circuit. The circuit has a tendency to include only smaller city destinations on more extended tours.

The structure, organization and management of coach and bus operations in each country is specifically shaped by the history, regulations and policies towards transport, and by a strong tradition of visiting established destinations – except where a major draw such as the Eden Project in Devon or new attractions in cities act as a hub for day excursions or visits. In most countries (excluding the UK) protection of the rail network has meant that bus and coach travel has not competed on an even basis, although there is evidence that this is changing. More recently the liberalization of European coach travel so operators can operate in different countries and the rise of new markets, such as the shuttle and long-distance markets opened up by the Channel Tunnel, have directly impacted on the further growth and expansion of coach travel.

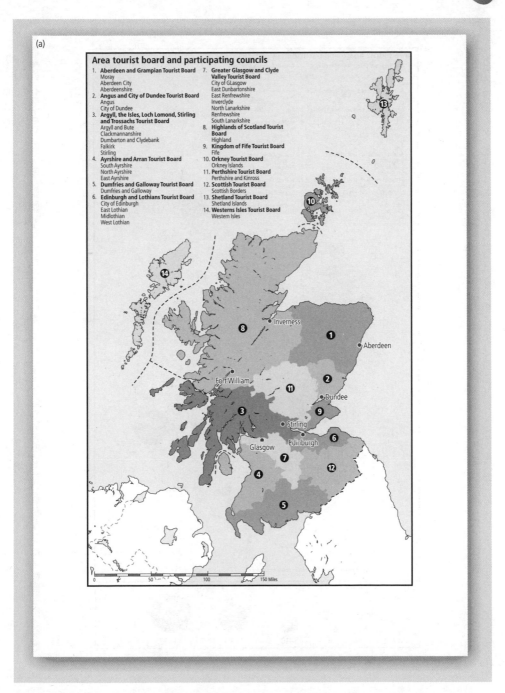

(a)

Area tourist board and participating councils

1. **Aberdeen and Grampian Tourist Board**
   Moray
   Aberdeen City
   Aberdeenshire
2. **Angus and City of Dundee Tourist Board**
   Angus
   City of Dundee
3. **Argyll, the Isles, Loch Lomond, Stirling and Trossachs Tourist Board**
   Argyll and Bute
   Clackmannanshire
   Dumbarton and Clydebank
   Falkirk
   Stirling
4. **Ayrshire and Arran Tourist Board**
   South Ayrshire
   North Ayrshire
   East Ayrshire
5. **Dumfries and Galloway Tourist Board**
   Dumfries and Galloway
6. **Edinburgh and Lothians Tourist Board**
   City of Edinburgh
   East Lothian
   Midlothian
   West Lothian

7. **Greater Glasgow and Clyde Valley Tourist Board**
   City of Glasgow
   East Dunbartonshire
   East Renfrewshire
   Inverclyde
   North Lanarkshire
   Renfrewshire
   South Lanarkshire
8. **Highlands of Scotland Tourist Board**
   Highland
9. **Kingdom of Fife Tourist Board**
   Fife
10. **Orkney Tourist Board**
    Orkney Islands
11. **Perthshire Tourist Board**
    Perthshire and Kinross
12. **Scottish Tourist Board**
    Scottish Borders
13. **Shetland Tourist Board**
    Shetland Islands
14. **Westerns Isles Tourist Board**
    Western Isles

Figure 5.5a   The geographical distribution of overseas and domestic coach tours in Scotland in 2000 by destinations visited – area tourist board regions (source: VisitScotland data)

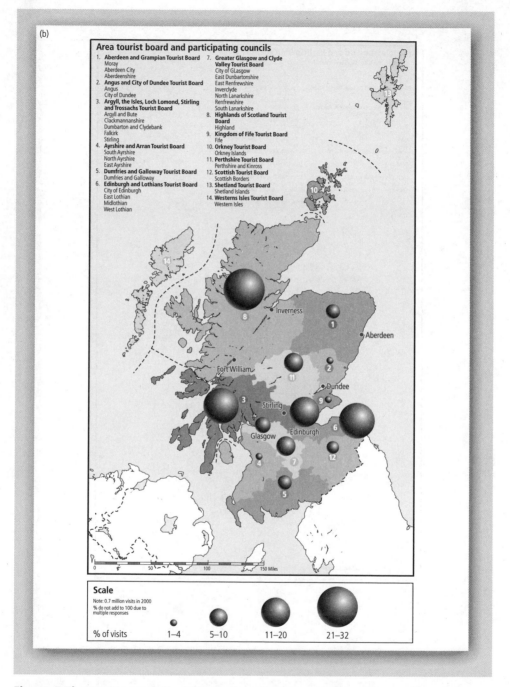

Figure 5.5b   The geographical distribution of overseas and domestic coach tours in Scotland in 2000 by destinations visited – distribution of domestic coach tourism (source: VisitScotland data)

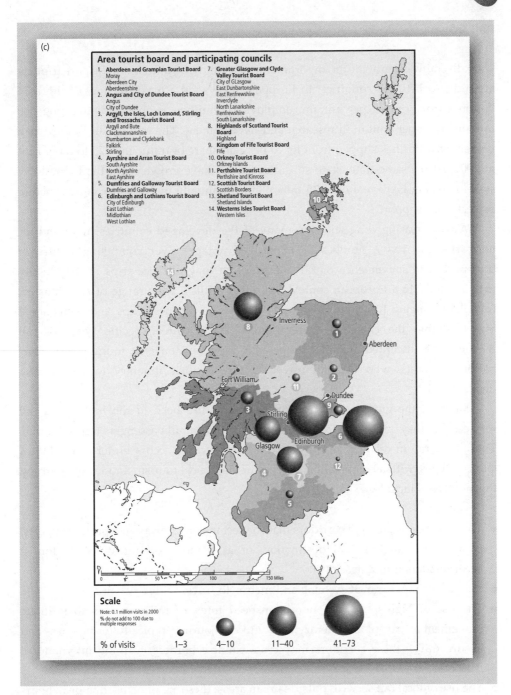

Figure 5.5c   The geographical distribution of overseas and domestic coach tours in Scotland in 2000 by destinations visited – distribution of international coach tourism (source: VisitScotland data)

Rail travel

Globally, railways provide an important means of moving tourists and leisure trippers around and between countries. In Europe railways are a major business, with a 75 billion euro turnover per annum, employing 1 million people and investing 250 million euros per annum in research and development. The role of rail in European passenger traffic has slipped from its 10 per cent share of traffic in 1970 to 6 per cent in 2001. At the same time, state subsidies for rail have grown, with the EU railway system costing taxpayers over 35 billion euros annually in grants for infrastructure projects and support.

With increasing congestion on many of the developed countries' road and air networks, rail has a number of natural advantages over competing modes of transport. The convenience of rail for short- to long-distance trips on city-to-city trips remains. In a European context rail travel fulfils a wide range of functions for travellers, ranging from daily commuting needs to business trips and recreational travel. Within the category of recreational travel, three specific types of rail user can be discerned within Europe; day-trippers, domestic tourist, and international tourists, who use rail travel as part of their itinerary to visit tourist destinations.

Much of the growth in European rail travel has been in the high-speed rail services, but they only carry 13 per cent of all European rail passengers (see Table 5.3). The use of rail in relation to tourism and leisure travel occurs under a number of journey types, with a combination of types in the typical tourism and leisure journey. Journey types include:

- The use of dedicated rail corridors that connect major gateways (airports and ports) of a country to the final destination, or as a mode of transit to the tourist accommodation in a nearby city
- The use of rapid transit systems and metros to travel within urban areas
- The use of high-speed and non-high-speed intercity rail corridors to facilitate movement as part of an itinerary or city-to-city journey, typically for business and leisure travel; these corridors may cross country borders, forming international networks
- The use of local rail services outside urban areas; these are often used in peak hours by commuters travelling to or from mainline or intercity rail terminals en route to other destinations

Table 5.3 Passengers carried by railways in the European Union, 1997–2000 (millions). (Source: modified from UIC)

Country	1997	1998	1999	2000	% change 1999–2000
Germany (DB)	1346.8	1332.0	1671.4	1712.6	2.5
UK (25 TOCs)	845.5	892.0	688.0	730.6	6.1
France (SNCF)	797.4	811.8	807.3	861.2	6.7
Italy (FS)	461.2	440.05	461.8	474.2	2.7
Spain (Renfe)	395.3	409.5	418.9	437.8	4.5
Netherlands (NS)	315.7	318.9	328.3	305.7	−6.9
Portugal (CP)*	178.2	178.0	151.7	148.6	−2.1
Denmark (DSB)	144.4	148.7	149.3	153.2	2.6
Belgium (SNCB)	143.5	145.9	147.3	153.3	4.1
Sweden (SJ)**	106.7	110.9	114.9	49.9	
Finland (VR)	50.0	51.4	53.2	54.8	3.0
Ireland (CIE)	29.5	25.4	15.6	15.7	0.9
Greece (CH)	13.3	13.2	5.5	5.4	−1.5
Total	4827.5	4878.2	5103.3	5102.4	

*Passenger data for 1999 and 2000 are not directly comparable
**Since January 2000, private train operators have taken over some of SJ's passenger traffic.

- The use of rail services to peripheral tourist destinations (e.g. the Caledonian Sleeper, which serves the London to the Highlands of Scotland market); these sometimes have a scenic value as tourist journeys in their own right (e.g. the Central Otago, New Zealand, Taireri Gorge half-day rail tour)
- Purpose-built rail excursions/holidays on historic services such as the Orient Express.

It is clear that rail travel, aside from commuting, provides a wide range of options for tourist and leisure travel. In a European context rail continues to have a slow rate of overall growth, with 4827.5 million passenger journeys in 1997 rising to 5102.4 million in 2000. Thus at a pan-European level, rail travel is constantly outperformed by the increase in air- and car-related travel.

Despite the declining importance of rail (excluding high-speed services), a wide range of issues have been suggested as important in trying to attract more tourists to use rail as a mode of travel. These include improved marketing to raise awareness of new services, better ticketing options such as through tickets, more seamless travel across rail networks, e-commerce, frequent traveller schemes, and greater attention to service quality issues. In addition, a wide range of business issues has been highlighted for railway companies, including widening their distribution channels (e.g. in 2002 the Caledonian Sleeper adopted e-ticketing and paperless check-ins in line with innovations from the airline sector). Attempts to improve customer usability of rail services (e.g. simplification of ticketing systems to remove confusion over tickets and prices, such as the SNCFs Découverte (Discovery) fares, launched in April 1998) have been proven to generate a substantial volume of business in their first year of operation. It is also notable that rail operators are slowly recognizing the link between transport and tourism, with value-for-money fares for leisure travel stimulated in Europe by the onset of the low-cost airlines. Physical improvements to the travel environment have also illustrated the need to invest in a better travelling environment for tourists, with new rolling stock and state-of-the-art travel facilities – highlighted by Virgin Trains' new service enhancements on trunk routes and cross-country services, such as music channels, laptop sockets and the segregation of mobile phone users. Developments in e-commerce such as the Trainline.com (in which Stagecoach has a controlling interest) have been important in making rail a more accessible option for travellers. Partnerships and collaborations have also been developed; for example, the Midland Mainline railway company and the short-break operator Supabreak in the UK have expanded the seamless approach to integrated tourist travel, using e-commerce and packages that are harmonized and more accessible.

Water-based transport

The potential of water or sea-based transport has been greatly overlooked in most analyses of tourism, largely because much attention has been given to the growth in tourism by air post-1945. Yet prior to the development of rail and air travel, water-based travel was of major importance to cross water (e.g. ferries), for pleasure on inland waterways (e.g. canal boats), or as a mode of tourist travel (e.g. cruising).

Many modern-day shipping companies such as P&O developed water-based transport as a means of travelling between continents, linking the UK with its Empire in India and the Far East during the nineteenth century. In 1842, the P&O passenger ship

Hindustan sailed on her inaugural trip, stimulated by the company's contract to carry mail from Southampton to Calcutta. By 1844 the company had also begun deep-sea cruises in the Mediterranean, and in the late 1880s other companies began cruises. In 1886 the North of Scotland and Orkney and Shetland Company began cruises to the Norwegian fjords at a cost of £10, while in 1889 the Orient Line began cruises to Norway and the Mediterranean. By 1890 the P&O line had developed a global network of direct and connecting services for passenger services (see Figure 5.6), which remained largely unaltered (with the exception of the withdrawal of Indian services after the country's independence) up until the 1960s, when air services began to challenge passenger liners. What is apparent from Figure 5.6 is the demand for business travel between the UK and its Imperial territories. P&O became a global brand in the Victorian period, considerably earlier than many of the marketing debates on the internationalization of the tourism industry in the 1960s, although monopoly contracts on mail services did help to support the expansion of the passenger routes. What is evident in this example is that the company reconfigured its business activities after the development of passenger airliners. For example, in the 1970s the company invested in its North American market and the growing demand for cruises as the passenger liner business declined. The company has a history of adapting to new business environments. For example, in 1904 it adapted a ship no longer needed for mail services for the cruise line Vectis – this was the first time it developed a dedicated cruise liner, which carried 160 First Class passengers in absolute luxury. Cruising is therefore not a new concept, although it has certainly seen a revival at a global scale in the 1990s and new millennium, becoming a more popular activity and no longer just the pursuit of elderly customers or the wealthy.

In 2000 the number of berths operated by cruise ship companies globally was 241 000, a 10.8 per cent increase on 1999, and they carried 10 million passengers, comprising a 10 per cent growth. This reflects the trends towards growing consolidation in the cruise market with larger companies and an increasing size of vessels. Despite the impact of the terrorist activities of 11 September 2001 on tourism, between 2000 and 2009 cruise ship capacity is forecast to grow by 66 per cent while passenger volumes may grow by 58 per cent. On a global scale three companies now dominate the cruise market, controlling almost two-thirds of the market:

- Carnival Corporation, with nearly 28 per cent of the market
- Royal Caribbean International, with just over 22 per cent of the market
- P&O Princess, with 12 per cent of the market.

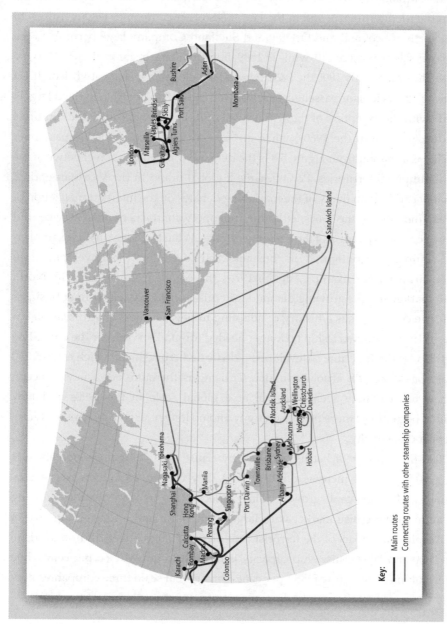

Figure 5.6 Schematic diagram of the steamer routes operated by the Peninsular and Orient (P&O) Steam Navigation Company in 1890 (redrawn and redesigned from Horwath and Horwath, 1986 *The Story of P&O: The Peninsular and Oriental Steam Navigation Company.* London: Weidenfield and Nicolson

Key:
—— Main routes
—— Connecting routes with other steamship companies

However, the impact of 11 September 2001 accelerated problems for some smaller cruise lines competing with the larger companies, whilst the three largest companies are seeking to enter into a mergers/acquisitions with each other and are the subject of monopoly/merger investigations regarding P&O Princess and Royal Caribbean International, and Carnival Corporation's takeover bid for P&O Princess. With many cruise ships now costing in excess of US$300 million – many over US$400 million – and being able to accommodate up to 3000 passengers, capital costs for this area of tourist transport are massive. In 2000 7 million passengers undertook US cruises, of whom 60 per cent joined their cruise by flying to the ship. In fact the worldwide cruise ship business is worth US$14 billion, with the main market being North America. Operating cruises is a vastly expensive business, with Royal Caribbean estimating in 2001 that the cost of cancelling eight cruises was US$12 million. Whilst much of the cruise business is focused on the Caribbean, followed by Europe, the Far East has entered the market with Australasian/Pacific Island cruises challenging traditional patterns of cruising. The cruise line industry is constantly innovating to attract a growing variety of passengers.

Ferries

Ferries are more functional modes of tourist transport used to cross stretches of water. In the lead up to the opening of the Channel Tunnel, many ferry operators attempted to market many of the UK's short-sea ferry crossing as cruises. In reality, ferries offer travellers a different element in their holiday, trip or excursion, and a time for rest, relaxation and a break from their main form of transport. One of the most frequently crossed waterways is the English Channel, which saw the construction of the Channel Tunnel to offer an all-weather crossing. Despite the concerns over the Channel Tunnel's impact on UK ferry services, passenger volumes through the Port of Dover rose from 11 million in 1994 to 16.2 million in 2000. Over the same period the number of tourist vehicles grew from 1.4 million to 2.6 million, while the number of coaches increased from 62 000 to 148 000. One consequence of increased competition from the Channel Tunnel was the merger of the two Dover–France ferry companies, Stena Line and P&O Ferries. The major blow for the ferry companies was the loss of duty-free sales on board ferries in 1999, which had accounted for 65 per cent of profits from short sea-ferry routes. This gave an estimated loss of revenue of £350 million for UK-European services, which, together with rises in fuel costs, led to fare increases of up to 40 per cent and a drop in passenger volumes of between 16 and 20 per cent.

However, ferry companies see this as a temporary problem despite the impact of low-cost airlines on ferry business. For example, it has been estimated that the 92.6 million passengers who went from the UK to France, Holland, Germany and Belgium in 2000 travelled thus:

- 68.6 per cent flew
- 31.4 per cent went above or under the English Channel, of whom the ferries carried 18.2 per cent (24.1 million passengers) and the Channel Tunnel carried 13.3 per cent (18.3 million passengers).

Although ferry traffic continued to increase from the mid-1990s, between 1996 and 2000 air travel increased by 388 per cent, reflecting the new markets that budget airlines have generated. The majority of ferry travellers in 2000 used the short sea routes across the English Channel (66 per cent), the Western Channel in the southern/southwestern Irish Sea (25.8 per cent) and the North Sea (7.6 per cent). In the short-crossing sector, a number of smaller, peripheral ferry services from Sheerness, Folkestone and Ramsgate have been cut as the industry has focused operations on Dover. In addition, the company Hoverspeed withdrew its Hovercraft services in September 2000 after 32 years of operation. Again, a rapidly changing competitive environment in the short sea-ferry routes with the impact of Eurotunnel, the loss of duty free sales and low-cost airlines has meant that tourism managers have had to set out future strategies carefully to ensure the viability of their business, and in some cases operations have been closed, rationalized, merged or sold. In addition, businesses have had to keep sight of their existing and future passengers by more active marketing campaigns to extol the virtues of cross-channel ferry travel now that Eurotunnel and lost-cost airlines are in operation. A rapid period of change in the holiday market and turmoil in the operating environment highlights the importance of being proactive in managing the tourism business. In each case, operators have sought to add value to the services they provide by upgrading on-board facilities, particularly food and beverages, children's lounges and business lounges, and increasing the size of ferries so they can carry over 2000 passengers in some cases.

Inland waterways

Inland waterways are a relatively neglected area of study in tourism research, as a product of a bygone era. They are linked to industrialization in the late eighteenth

Box 5.1   Boating on the Norfolk Broads

The Norfolk Broads ('the Broads') is a wetland region in East Anglia, which was created in the medieval period through a series of flooded peat diggings. The region is focused on a number of rivers (such as the Bure, the Yare and Waveney) and their tributaries in the eastern part of Norfolk and northern part of Suffolk, giving 200 km (125 miles) of lock-free waters to explore by boat. In 1989 the area was accorded virtual National Park status when the Broads Authority was established by the 1988 Norfolk and Suffolk Broads Act, and the area now receives in excess of a million visitors a year. The Act granted the Broads Authority the same autonomy as a National Park in terms of finance, policy and administration, and thus it receives a 75 per cent grant from central government. Boating for pleasure dates back to the 1870s, when the early wherries (local sailing cargo vessels) began to carry passengers. In the 1880s John Loyne pioneered the hire boat industry, and in 1908 the present-day H. Blake and Co. was established to rent purpose-built vessels to visitors who travelled to the area by rail. Thus the use of transport for recreation and holidays led to the development of a form of water-based tourism that is transport-dependent. In 1995 boat companies owned 1481 motor cruisers and launches, which were hired to approximately 200 000 visitors a year. The industry is dominated by the two main holiday companies, Hoseseasons and Blakes Holidays. There are a further 4 independent boatyards, 51 day-hire boatyards, and 6 boatyards operating tours.

Very heavy usage occurs at weekends in the northern parts of the river system (e.g. The Thurne Mouth and the middle reaches of the River Bure at Horning and Wroxham/Hoveton). A Broads Authority boat movement census highlighted that on one peak Sunday in August there were 6296 craft movements recorded at 14 census points. In contrast, the upper reaches of many rivers are protected by their relative inaccessibility and, in a few cases, by low bridges. The hire boat industry is estimated to contribute £25 million to the local economy, with boating employing over 1622 people (884 full time, 148 part time, and 590 people on a seasonal basis). Furthermore, recreational and tourist spending indirectly employs 5000–5500 people in the hospitality sector and local tourist attractions, as well as in the local marine industry. Therefore, the example of the Broads shows that inland waterways offer a major resource for transporting tourists and as an attraction and holiday in their own right.

century, when canals and waterways were developed to transport products from source areas to market in many European countries. Yet many towns and cities with waterway and river networks have seen a renaissance in their regeneration for tourism purposes in the late twentieth century, with Birmingham in the UK being a case in point. Much of this regenerative activity has been a as a result of successful partnerships of waterway agencies such as the British Waterways Board and local authorities, often supported in the UK by grants from Lottery and Millennium funds. This has led to a well-developed riverboat and canal-based holiday market that is exemplified by the Norfolk Broads, where a major holiday and boating industry exists (see Box 5.1).

Summary

This chapter has highlighted the diversity of transport and its wide range of uses in tourism, from linking the home to the nearest departure point to using it as a holiday context (e.g. a cruise). Integrating the transport modes to ensure a seamless travel experience without major service interruptions is a major challenge for the tourism industry, since transport functions are often contracted out to suppliers who may not have a tourism ethos (e.g. coach operators or taxis). In each case transport providers interface with tourists, and thus ensuring that they are good ambassadors for tourism has become a priority for many destination areas. Within the transport sector there is also a management function for operators in ensuring that those people who interface with tourists recognize the service standards that travellers now experience in other areas of the service economy. The transport sector has been very slow to embrace these ideas, since they have been operationally led and have focused on operating vehicles, plant and capital investment rather than on the tourist as a customer. This issue permeates most forms of surface-based transport, as tourism and service provision in air travel has been more innovative.

Much of the planning and integration of surface transport has been achieved in many European capitals by innovative and forward-looking planning in the post-war period, with purpose-built infrastructure. However, in some older European capitals the existing infrastructure still has gaps in the provision of terminals, with visitors often having to travel from central areas to airports on systems that are not integrated and are complicated to use. Transport provision needs champions within each destination area so that the tourist can be easily connected with terminals, attractions, accommodation and gateways, such as ports and airports.

Airports provide the most obvious example of the private sector taking the lead in integrating transport and tourism, as the work of BAA in the UK illustrates, with each airport having a surface transport strategy, working within the UK government's encouragement of public transport for more journeys. In the case of BAA, a third of passengers travel to its three London airports by public transport, and it is seeking to expand that to 50 per cent. Specific initiatives include: the development of the Heathrow Express, the St Pancras Express (to be launched in 2003) and the M4 spur road bus lane; airport staff-discounted London Underground travelcards; public–private sector partnerships to improve railway stations and enhancements to bus services (including a subsidy to the Glasgow Airport link); and environmental levies on car parking to support public transport initiatives. This is considered in more detail in Chapter 6.

References

Button, K. J. and Gillingwater K. (eds) (1983) *Future Transport Policy*. London: Routledge.

Chubb, M. (1989) Tourism patterns and determinants in the Great Lakes region: population, resources and perceptions. *GeoJournal*, **19**(3), 291–96.

Countryside Commission (1992) *Trends in Transport and the Countryside*. Cheltenham: Countryside Commission.

Countryside Commission (1995) *The Market for Recreational Cycling in the Countryside*. Cheltenham: Countryside Commission.

Eaton, B. and Holding, D. (1996) The evaluation of public transport alternatives to the car in British National Parks. *Journal of Transport Geography*, **4**(1), 55–65.

English Tourist Board/Employment Department (1991) *Tourism and the Environment: Maintaining the Balance*. London: English Tourist Board.

HMSO (1994) Royal Commission on Environmental Pollution. Eighteenth Report, Transport and the Environment, Cmmd. 2674. London: HMSO.

Horwath, D. and Horwath, S. (1986) *The Story of P&O: The Peninsular and Oriental Steam Navigation Company*. London: Weidenfield and Nicolson.

Lamb, B. and Davidson, S. (1996) Tourism and transportation in Ontario, Canada. In: L. Harrison and W. Husbands (eds), *Practising Responsible Tourism: International Case Studies in Tourism Planning, Policy and Development*. Chichester: Wiley, pp. 261–76.

Lumsdon, L. (1996) Future for cycle tourism in Britain. *INSIGHTS*, A27–32.

Lumsdon, L. (1997) Recreational cycling: is this the way to stimulate interest in everyday urban cycling? In R. Tolley (ed.) *The Greening of Urban Transport Planning for Walking and Cycling in Western Cities* (2nd edn). Chichester: Wiley, pp. 113–27.

Page, S. J. (2002) European rail travel: special feature. *Travel and Tourism Analyst*, **2**, 1–39.

Scottish Tourist Board (1991) *Tourism Potential of Cycling and Cycle Routes in Scotland*. Edinburgh: Scottish Tourist Board.

SUSTRANS (2002) Cycle Tourism: Information Pack TT21. SUSTRANS online www.sustrans.org.uk, accessed 11 October 2002

Wall, G. (1972) Car owners and holiday activities. In P. Lavery (ed.) *Recreational Geography*. Newton Abbot: David and Charles.

Further reading

Page, S. J. (1999) Transport and Tourism. Harlow: Pearson Education.

Questions

1 How would you develop a model of tourist transport and its relationship to tourist activity?

2 Why is the car so important to tourist activity patterns? What advantages and disadvantages does it have compared with other modes of surface travel?

3 What role does transport play as a focus for tourist activities?

4 How important is the integration of different forms of transport to achieve a seamless tourism experience?

Chapter **6**

Transporting the tourist: II The aviation sector

Learning objectives

This chapter examines the role of the aviation industry in tourism as a global phenomenon that is responsible for enabling people to travel to destinations worldwide. After reading it, you should be able to understand:

- the structure and organization of the aviation sector and the role of airports in the handling of tourists as travellers;
- key trends in the airline sector and the importance of the low cost airlines as a new business sector in Europe;
- the way in which airlines market their businesses to travellers.

Introduction

In Chapter 5, the role of surface transport highlighted the fundamental link between tourism and transport in a number of different contexts. One of the underlying themes was how transport (the industry) is linked to the tourist (the consumer), which in simple terms raises a fundamental question: how are these two elements managed so that consumer needs are met? This returns to many of the issues initially developed in Chapter 1 regarding the role of tourism management, and who should manage such issues. This chapter addresses these issues by focusing on the aviation sector, which has seen the greatest growth in volume of passengers of all forms of transport excluding cars. It focuses on a complex transport system that has a direct impact upon tourist experiences. This is shaped from the point they enter an airport through to the point when they disembark at the destination – a process that is repeated on the return journey. In other words, the management of the tourist by the airline industry reveals an integrated transport system, which can largely be defined as (Page, 2002: 209):

> ... the process whereby individual (and groups of) airlines seek to organize, direct and harness their resources, personnel and their business activities to meet the needs of their organization and customers in an effective and efficient manner.

This also involves the close working relationship of the airlines with airports to ensure the smooth, safe and reliable processing and transfer of tourists through the system with the minimum of disruption and inconvenience. This is crucial, as the airline industry carries a large volume of passengers and the airport system has to be able to process them in an efficient manner so that the system continues to have the capacity to allow the flow of travellers through the system.

This chapter commences with a discussion of the role of the airport as a terminal facility that links the tourist with the supply of air transport. In principle it offers a seamless travel process from departure to arrival, although sometimes service interruptions and unavoidable delays may cause problems in the system. This is followed by a discussion of air travel, emphasizing its growth and significance as a mode of tourist transport, and explaining how it is regulated, the role of airlines operations and the significance of recent developments in the airline market, including the rise of low-cost airlines and future prospects for global air travel.

The role of the airport as a tourist terminal facility

For tourists, airports are one of the most highly developed and complex environments that they will experience. Airports operate as well-developed systems where a wide range of tourist interactions occur. At a simple level the airport is the point of processing for travel to a destination, although it may also be a highly developed shopping and retail environment. Other analogies of airports as post-modern citadels of tourism and consumption have led commentators to examine the architecture, subtle design features and careful management measures devised to encourage consumers to spend their money, with layouts designed to nurture a captive audience. Airports are more than just transport termini, where tourists transfer from a ground-based form of transport to one that is air-based. In larger capital cities airports are major integrated transport hubs, with a wide range of feeder routes by public transport and road from which travellers (including air travellers in transit) are sorted, sifted, channelled and directed towards departing flights as part of their tourism experience. Airports have changed out of all recognition from the early 1930s, when they originated as simple buildings that provided a waiting area for flights. Today they are multi-million pound businesses, with vast capital investment in the transport infrastructure to facilitate the air travel function as well as many other purposes – including retailing, support services, car hire, onward travel by other modes of transport and large car parking facilities, as well as a cargo function.

The scale of these activities in terms of passenger movements through airports is illustrated in Table 6.1, which shows the volume of passengers passing through the busiest twenty airports in the world. It highlights the management challenge for airport operators in ensuring that business activities run smoothly, given the numbers of travellers using these terminal areas. The Airport International Council (AIC, at www.aic.org), which represents 550 airport operators worldwide with 1441 airports in 165 countries, identified the following key issues as challenges for airports in ensuring that a positive visitor experience is maintained:

- The need to cope with larger aircraft size, as 600-seater aircraft are likely to be introduced on long-haul routes.
- The need to embrace technological change such as new navigation systems so that the capacity at individual airports can be increased to cope with demand. This is important given that the Boeing Commercial Airplane Group (2002) *Current Market Outlook 2001* indicated that future demand will lead to a greater

Table 6.1 Top twenty world airports in 2001 (modified from ACI and other industry sources)

Airport	Passenger flow
Atlanta (ATL)	75 849 375
Chicago (ORD)	66 805 339
Los Angeles (LAX)	61 024 541
London Heathrow (LHR)	60 743 154
Tokyo (HND)	58 692 688
Dallas/Fort Worth Airport (DFW)	55 150 689
Frankfurt (FRA)	48 559 980
Paris (CDG)	47 996 223
Amsterdam (AMS)	39 538 483
Denver (DEN)	36 086 751
Phoenix (PHX)	35 481 950
Las Vegas (LAS)	35 195 675
Minneapolis/St Paul (MSP)	35 170 528
Houston (IAH)	34 794 868
San Francisco (SFO)	34 626 668
Madrid (MAD)	33 984 413
Hong Kong (HKG)	32 553 000
Detroit (DTW)	32 294 121
Miami (MIA)	31 668 450
London Gatwick (LGW)	31 182 361

use of medium-haul aircraft (e.g. the Boeing 767), increasing the number and frequency of aircraft wishing to take off and land at airports worldwide.

- The recognition that air travel has now begun to serve a mass market rather than having the elite status it had in the 1950s and early 1960s.
- The need to speed up the passenger flows at airports, including the removal of bottlenecks and delays with baggage handling, by introducing new technology and smart technology to track travellers and their personal belongings.
- Addressing security issues at airports, which are seen as one of the weakest links, as well as enhancing safety matters for travellers.

In each case the AIC recognizes the importance of investing in the airport system and its constituent parts so that the interface with the traveller is enhanced. Perhaps one of the greatest challenges for the airport sector is in recognizing and acknowledging the fact that:

> The airport cavalcade can baffle or startle the inexperienced passenger . . . Laden with suitcases and packages, calm and rational people grow uptight, defensive with aggression, fail to allow themselves time to familiarize themselves with the layout or study the free guides to terminals.
> (Barlay, 1995: 48)

This quotation illustrates the importance of designing passenger-friendly environments that are welcoming, have a relaxed feel (such as London Stansted's terminal building designed by Sir Norman Foster) and provide opportunities for travellers to reduce the stress, anxiety and uncertainty associated with air travel.

For the airport sector various issues affect how the traveller perceives the terminal, including:

- Speed of check-in
- Efficiency of passport control and customs clearance
- Ease of luggage retrieval
- Availability of shops, duty-free and associated services
- The environment in which they wait to board the aircraft.

(Barlay, 1995: 49; cited in Page, 1999)

This identifies the themes that airport managers need to address as they become more customer oriented as investment in new terminals and redevelopments integrate the latest thinking regarding passenger-friendly environments. This is somewhat of a culture change for airports, as traditionally they have been largely operationally focused and only paid lip service to the needs of travellers. The airport manager's focus has changed out of all recognition since the impact of privatization and the need for a greater consumer orientation in order to generate profits for shareholders and other investors.

The greater commercialization in airport operations is coupled with the development of global airport companies (such as BAA plc and Amsterdam Schipol) and the non-airport transport companies that have entered airport management (e.g.

FirstGroup and Stagecoach in the UK). As a result, airports have also become part of the wider globalization of transport and tourism activities. Such companies recognize that managing airports is not just about providing some of the services and facilities that travellers need; it is also about coordination, planning, leading and communication between the airport and a diverse range of ancillary services, including handling agents, concessionaires (i.e. businesses that operate under licence or franchise on airport premises), government bodies (e.g. the Federal Aviation Authority in the USA) and industry bodies (e.g. ACI), as well as the airlines themselves. Airport operations have certainly seen a greater emphasis on business skills and communication than on its traditional operationally led focus since the wave of commercialization has swept through the airport sector. This is also reflected in the evolution of airports as business entities that recognize their different revenue streams.

What is an airport and how is it operated?

In physical terms, Doganis (1992: 7) defines an airport as:

> Essentially one or more runways for aircraft together with associated buildings or terminals where passengers . . . are processed . . . the majority of airport authorities own and operate their runways, terminals and associated facilities, such as taxiways or aprons.

The evolution of airports in many countries has been a complex pattern based on historical, legal and other factors (e.g. changing government policy, and the different roles of public and private sector involvement). Airport development has in many instances been associated with opportunities for the expansion of gateway airport terminals and post-war re-use of former military bases and available sites, as well as new-build projects. Airport development in part mirrors the expansion of tourism in the post-war period, but the lead times for airport development, owing to the capital-intensive nature of their sunk costs, means that development horizons are at least 10 years for new runways and terminals and the associated infrastructure (such as expanding the road infrastructure to cope with demand).

Doganis (1992: 7) distinguishes between the three principal activities of airports:

1 Essential operational services and facilities
2 Traffic-handling services
3 Commercial activities.

Whilst the dominant activity to be considered for the safe and efficient management of the airport as a terminal area is its passenger flow, it is clear that the airport is a complex system in which a wide range of inter-related activities take place. The scope of activities broadly encompass (Page, 1999):

- Ground handling
- Baggage handling
- Passenger terminal operations
- Airport security
- Cargo operations
- Airport technical services
- Air traffic control
- Aircraft scheduling (take off/landing slot allocation)
- Airport and aircraft emergency services
- Airport access.

The way in which airports are managed is also partly determined by their pattern of ownership. New forms of ownership have emerged as the demand for air travel has grown and state involvement in airport provision has been reduced, allowing owners to pursue commercial strategies so they can invest and increase their capacity and ability to respond more quickly to the market. There are four main types of ownership:

1 *State ownership with direct government control*, characterized by a single government department (e.g. a Civil Aviation Department) that operates the country's airports. The alternative to a centralized government pattern of control and management is localized ownership, such as municipal ownership.
2 *Public ownership through an airport authority*, usually as a limited liability or private company.
3 *Mixed public and private ownership*, which is an organizational model adopted at larger Italian airports, where a company with public and private shareholders manages the airport.
4 *Private ownership*, which was a model of limited appeal prior to the wave of privatization in the 1980s, reflected in the UK government's privatization of BAA in 1987.

Privatization is seen as a politically sensitive issue, since it involves the transfer of state assets, accumulated from taxpayers' revenue, that may give the private sector significant commercial opportunities.

However, the fundamental issues that are involved in any airport development are:

- Costs
- The economic features of airports
- Sources of revenue
- Methods of charging and pricing airport aeronautical services
- The type of commercial strategy adopted
- Potential sources of commercial revenue
- The most appropriate management structure for an airport as a commercial/non-commercial organization
- Financial performance indicators.

(Source: based on Doganis, 1992, and Ashford, Stanton and Moore, 1991)

Aside from revenue issues, managers of airport facilities need to understand the costs and economic characteristics of airports so as to recognize both the commercial potential and where fixed costs exist. By far the largest cost, as expected in line with tourism as a people industry, is staffing costs. These are often in excess of 40 per cent of the operational costs, and are followed closely by ongoing capital charges (i.e. interest payments on loans and the cost of depreciation on the capital assets). Other operational costs (e.g. electricity, water and supplies) typically comprise 11 per cent of the total, while maintenance and administrative costs can account for the remaining costs.

In contrast to costs, revenue can be divided into two categories:

1 Operating revenues, which are generated by directly running and operating the airport (e.g. the terminal area, leased areas and grounds)
2 Non-operating revenues, which include income from activities not associated with the airport core business and are divided by airport analysts into aeronautic or traffic revenues, and non-aeronautical or commercial revenues.

For the airport there is a range of possible revenue sources (although not all airports necessarily collect or use the revenue in a set way), including:

- Landing fees (which the AIC have suggested do not exceed 4 per cent of airlines operating costs)
- Airport air traffic control charges
- Aircraft parking
- Passenger charges
- Freight charges
- Aircraft handling services.

In terms of non-aeronautical revenue, Doganis (1992) outlines the following sources:

- Rents or lease income from airport tenants
- Recharges to tenants for utilities and services provided
- Concession income (e.g. from duty-free and tax-free shops)
- Direct sales in shops operated by the airport authority
- Revenue from car parking where it is airport-operated
- Miscellaneous items.
- Non-airport related income (e.g. from land or hotel development).

Within a European context, Doganis noted that aeronautical revenue accounted for 56 per cent and non-aeronautical revenue for 44 per cent of income. In the USA, airports generated more revenue from commercial sources (e.g. concessions, 33 per cent; rents, 23 per cent; car parking, 4 per cent; other non-aeronautical sources, 17 per cent; aeronautical fees, 23 per cent). In terms of non-airport revenue, airports need to understand the scope of airport users, who comprise:

- Passengers (departing, arriving and transferring between flights)
- The airlines, which are major consumers of space for storage, maintenance, staff and catering
- Airport employees
- Airline crews
- Meeters and greeters (i.e. those who are accompanying or meeting friends and relatives departing or arriving by air)
- Visitors to airports, particularly where airports market their shopping facilities and provide opportunities to observe aircraft activity in purpose-built viewing areas
- Local residents
- The local business community.

(Based on Doganis, 1992: 115)

Among some of the more contentious issues that airport management has to deal with are passenger safety and security, and environmental issues.

Safety, security and environmental concerns

Safety and security aspects are firmly lodged in the travelling public's minds following the 11 September 2001 terrorist incidents across the USA. A number of agencies within and outside airports are responsible for passenger safety on the ground and in the air. At the airport, principal concerns are associated with ensuring the integrity of the perimeter fence and that intruders do not penetrate the security cordon. Within the airport, prevention of terrorism has become an issue and security has been enhanced in recent years with the introduction and greater use of closed circuit television cameras (CCTV). New technologies such as biometrics (the use of technology that recognizes passengers' unique features based on physiological characteristics such as the eye, fingerprint or iris pattern) are being trialled, along with passenger profiling by crime detection agencies, enhanced baggage screening (such as Munich's double baggage screen) and greater collaboration between airline agencies to deter would-be terrorists.

Among the major constraints facing airports in the future are community objections to noise and pollution emissions. These are increasingly being documented by airports (see BAA's reports for each airport it operates at www.baa.co.uk, which consider the mitigating measures they are taking to address these concerns). As major land users and consumers of space, and being a focal point of transport activity, it is inevitable that airports will provide a focus of attention for transport-related pollution problems, particularly illustrated in the recent inquiry into the development and expansion of Heathrow's Terminal Five. This debate has been re-examined with the announcement in July 2002 by the UK government's national consultation regarding the future airports policy for the UK (www.dft.gov.uk). This preceded the new Airports Policy White Paper, due in 2003, which is likely to herald the largest airport expansion programme in the UK since the privatization of BAA, with new runways and airports across the UK to accommodate the forecast growth in demand. The environmental effects of such development are summarized as:

● Those effects that impact on people who live close to airports or under flight paths
● Emissions that affect the built and natural environment

- Increased land-take from new development, especially where green belt land or ecologically sensitive areas are affected – for example, one plan is for a new airport in southeast England on a wildlife site in Cliffe, Kent
- The additional congestion that will result from additional passengers travelling to the airports.

Much of the initial discussion has focused on statistics that suggest that up to 50 per cent of the UK population travel by air once a year, whilst the economy has been expanding. Yet interestingly the UK government has made no mention of demand management measures, such as realistic pricing policies to limit the demand from low-cost airlines, who have generated large volumes of price-sensitive business. In addition, the discussion paper does not examine the implications of hidden subsidies such as aviation fuel, which is exempt from tax under international agreements. As a result, the full costs of pollution are not charged to the users and suppliers. It is estimated that subsidies such as this may subsidize the UK aviation industry by £7 billion a year and give it unfair advantages over and above other forms of transport, although research shows that substituting air travel for rail is only successful where journey times are no longer than three hours. Whatever the case, airports have been in a very enviable position in terms of their growth prospects for future air travel, and this seems set to continue. The environmental consequences of such development are likely to be controversial at a time when the demand for air travel continues to outgrow the rate of expansion of national economies.

At a local level, the national consultation highlights the need for a new runway in Scotland and a new integrated transport infrastructure at either Glasgow or Edinburgh airport, as low-cost air travel has led to growth rates of up to 12 per cent per annum in air travel at Edinburgh airport. Therefore airport development is likely to have a national impact, since future development is being directly linked to economic growth in the UK as large lobby groups such as the aviation industry make a case for continuing prosperity based around the air transport sector.

The international airline industry

The airline industry developed as a commercial enterprise during the 1930s as technological advances in aviation enabled companies to develop regular passenger services, cross-subsidized by the provision of freight and air postal services. In the post-war period, modern-day air transport emerged as an

international business, providing services and products for a diverse group of users including scheduled and non-scheduled (charter) transportation for air travellers and cargo transportation for businesses.
(Page, 2002: 209)

The airline industry is truly a global business, and the effects of 11 September 2001 and the ensuing financial problems experienced by many airlines only led to a slight drop in international tourist arrivals to 689 million in 2001, from 697 million in 2000. It is clear is that the pace of change in the aviation sector is rapid, and understanding the nature of underlying and current trends is important from a tourism management perspective so that managers and the industry can understand how to respond to such issues.

Trends in the airline industry in the new millennium

The airline industry in its broadest form, as shown in Figure 6.1, is a complex amalgam of transport-related sectors and interest groups that operate, regulate and interact with the aviation sector. The previous section reviewed one of these sectors – the airport – and in this section the focus is on the trends and patterns of development

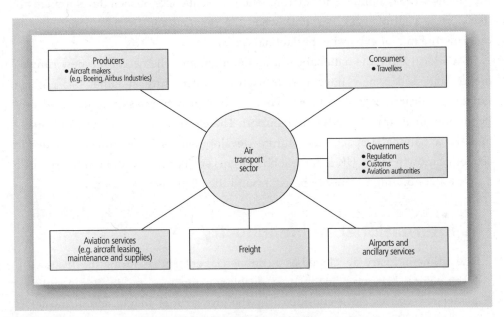

Figure 6.1   The dimensions of the air transport sector

of the airline sector, namely passenger airlines. These can be divided into two distinct groups:

1 Scheduled services, which operate between destinations to a predetermined timetable, with two types of services operated by domestic airlines and inter-national airlines. There are over 650 airlines that provide scheduled services internationally. Quite often a country may run a state-owned airline, and this is known as a flag carrier, which safeguards the tourism market for the destination and air access. Other airlines can be part publicly owned and part privately or wholly privately owned. Where airlines operate on high-volume routes between major destinations, these are termed trunk routes, which are fed by feeder or regional airlines. This is illustrated in Figure 6.2. Yet one recent innovation that the Boeing Commercial Airplane Group (2002) notes is the rise in point-to-point or city pair flights, using medium-sized aircraft that remove the hub and spoke pattern of development observed in Figure 6.3. These point-to-point flights are also illustrated later with reference to the low-cost carriers that have pioneered this concept, often using secondary, lesser known airports at a distance from the major tourist destination, with lower landing costs.

2 Charter airlines, which do not operate to published timetables, being chartered to tour operators (travel intermediaries) who then sell the seats. In recent years charter aircraft have also pioneered the sale of seat-only sales, which account for up to 20 per cent of their sales, particularly on Mediterranean holidays. Charters have therefore been associated with leisure travel (see Chapter 2) and one example of

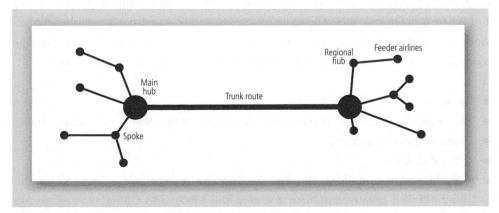

Figure 6.2   Hub and spoke operation (© Boeing, 2001: 41)

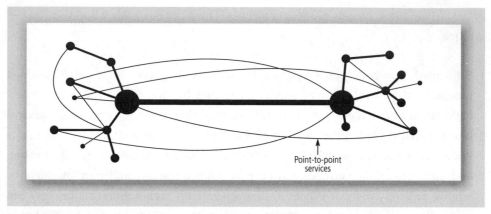

Figure 6.3   Hub and spoke service with point-to-point services (© Boeing, 2001: 41)

their large-scale use is for the Hajj pilgrimage to Mecca, where up to a million visitors travel for a religious event each year. Many scheduled carriers or tour operators also have their own charter airlines as part of an integrated tourism business.

Globally, the airline industry carried 1600 million passengers in 1998 on 18 000 aircraft operating to and from 10 000 airports. In Europe the total demand for air traffic in 1998 was 541 million passengers, and this is expected to rise to 1101 million in 2015. The UK remains the dominant market for traffic in European air travel, with expectations that by 2015 passengers will travel to, within and from the UK. The next largest markets are Germany, Spain, France and Italy; there is thus a clear relationship with the key European tourism markets. The scale of growth in air travel has been phenomenal since the 1960s, and the Air Transport Action Group (ATAG), a lobby group for the aviation sector, has used a list of factors to explain this growth. These include:

● The falling real cost of air travel
● The increased international trade and economic activity, which necessitates travel
● Rising disposable incomes
● Political stability
● A gradual relaxation of travel restrictions in many countries (e.g. South Korea and China allowed greater outbound travel in the 1990s, and China allowed greater inbound travel in the 1990s)

- Greater leisure time and tourism promotion
- Rising air transport liberalization
- New countries with low levels of air transport activity have expanded their traffic volumes (e.g. East Asia-Pacific).

These factors are reflected in a series of trends in air travel since the 1970s, which Doganis (2001) explains in terms of:

- The effects of increasing liberalization (at the same time as airports were being privatized to accommodate changes in demand), which have removed many of the existing controls on air route capacity and frequency of services, where monopoly, duopoly or collusion previously prevented fair and open competition.
- The relatively low price of aviation fuel since the mid-1980s, which typically accounts for 30–33 per cent of airline operating costs.
- Actual declines in the growth rate of air travel – from growth rates of up to 12 per cent per annum in the 1960s and 7.8 per cent per annum prior to 1987, to 4.8 per cent per annum between 1987 and 1997. ATAG predicts growth rates of 4–5 per cent in the 2001–2010 period, which shows a global slowdown, but the rate of growth is still in excess of the growth in many countries' GDP, which is often seen as a driver of air traffic. Even so, some region such as Asia-Pacific will certainly outperform these rates.
- Major restructuring in the nature of the supply and market demand for air travel since the 1970s. Doganis (2001) found that in 1972 the USA and Europe were dominant, with 66 per cent of all international air travel. By the 1990s this had dropped to 50 per cent as Asian airlines with lower cost bases (and hence greater flexibility in staff utilization and lower salary and operating costs) reconfigured the nature of air transport supply as demand from Asia Pacific also expanded.
- The yields (the actual profitability of an airline seat or flight) dropped in the 1990s, reflected in lower revenue per passenger km, due to the increased capacity on many flights/routes and lower prices. Doganis (2001) found that the percentage of passengers travelling on promotional fares (i.e. discounted rates) rose from 51 per cent to 71 per cent in the early to late 1990s. To address the falling yields, airlines have had to reduce the unit costs of operation (i.e. the cost of each individual input that goes into a flight, including in-flight service, staffing and associated costs). Where airlines failed to reduce costs quicker than drops in yields, they have been forced to raises the number of passengers they carry (loadings) or face financial problems.

- Growing globalization and international ownership of airlines as governments sell interests or whole airlines off to reduce their liability and need for investment, in much the same way as the airports have been privatized in the 1980s and 1990s. The most notable privatization in the 1980s was of British Airways. Accompanying these changes are greater involvement in collaboration and partnerships (e.g. airline alliances), greater concentration of airlines in a large number of global carriers, and increased numbers of mergers and agreements for working together.
- A constantly downward decline in fare levels and a response by the airline industry in bypassing travel agents and their commissions, which have been as high as 12 per cent of operating costs. This is known as disintermediation, and involves selling direct to the customer and the use of paperless tickets, which remove the role of a travel agent.
- Infrastructure constraints, induced by liberalization and more airlines seeking take-off and landing slots at congested gateway or hub airports, as well as pressure on airlines to be more environmentally responsible and reduce noise emissions.

ATAG estimates that by 2010 the global airline industry will generate 28 million jobs and account for an economic impact of US$1800 billion, with 2.3 billion passengers travelling.

Managing the airline industry

From the previous discussion, it is evident that the aviation sector has experienced and continues to undergo rapid change. Adapting to such change is a key challenge for management in order to ensure profitability. Many airlines began life as state-owned enterprises, indicating the need for massive investment, as the airline industry is a very capital-intensive activity that requires a steady and predictable long-term stream of revenue to absorb the high capital and operating costs. For example, a Boeing 737 can cost US$30 million to purchase new, and that excludes some of the fit-out costs; hence it is critical that such resources are deployed optimally. The airlines of many smaller countries are still subsidized and maintained for political reasons, especially in Asia-Pacific and South America.

Airline management requires that airlines balance those issues they have to deal with on a day-to-day (operational issues) and a longer-term basis (strategic issues) together with the marketing of airlines. In reality, the management process for airline companies is an ongoing activity that requires a predetermined structure within the organization to ensure that all the business activities are adequately integrated to meet the needs of its internal customers (those within the organization) and external business needs (the customer or purchaser of services and products). This involves overseeing the activities of both airline operations (domestic and international airline business) and the diverse activities that affect the organization's main business (e.g. ground handling, planning, human resource management and reservations). To streamline the parts of an airline and ensure that they work efficiently, many larger companies have been organized into functional business units and in some cases have outsourced, franchised or disposed of elements of the business that are not profitable or central to core activity. This is most noticeable in low-cost airlines, which have stripped out all but the basic elements needed for the business to function.

Yet:

> ... airline managers are not free agents. Their actions are circumscribed by a host of national and international regulations. These are both economic and non-economic in character and may well place severe limitations on airlines' freedom of action.
>
> (Doganis, 1991: 24)

As a result regulation is a major factor affecting the business environment for aviation, and this is a very complex area that involves politics, decision-making, governments, airlines and changing international pressure for greater liberalization.

Regulating international air transport

Many countries' airlines have seen growing pressure over the last twenty years for the state to be less involved in the protection of national flag carriers and to allow other airlines to fly between countries and compete for traffic. Within many sectors of the tourism industry there is a great debate on why certain activities need to be regulated. In the case of air travel, regulation is needed for a number of reasons concerned with passenger safety. Appropriate international regulation and supervision of the industry ensures that airlines do not operate in an unsafe manner. Regulations set minimum standards for operating aircraft, and non-economic regulations are designed to cover the safety and operational guidelines for airline services. There are regulations concerning, for example:

- The airworthiness of aircraft, their maintenance and overhaul and the training of engineers who undertake this work
- The numbers and type of flight crew and cabin staff required on specific types of flight together with their qualifications and training
- The aviation infrastructure, such as airports, meteorological services, en route navigational facilities and safety standards.

Technical and safety standards are developed and policed by civil aviation bodies in each country (for example, the Civil Aviation Authority in the UK). Technical standards and safety procedures are incumbent upon airline managers, and adhering to high standards of technical expertise and safety is now seen as essential to maintaining a competitive advantage. Other forms of regulation include environmental regulations associated with the noise and emissions that airlines create, and the effects in and around airports and their local population. As mentioned above, many airports have begun to develop stringent environmental conditions that airlines must meet if they operate from their airports – otherwise they may be fined or banned.

The economic regulation of airlines can be traced back to the Paris Convention (1919), which established the principle that states have sovereign rights over their territory (i.e. their airspace). This led to the eventual development of bilateral agreements between countries to allow other airlines the right to overfly their airspace and them the right to operate into and out of other countries. In 1944, the Chicago Convention led to multilateral agreement on the:

- Exchange of air traffic rights, or 'freedom of the air' (see Table 6.2)
- Control of fares and freight tariffs
- Control of frequencies and capacity.

As a result the operating environment for air travel was rigidly regulated, although agreement on the first two freedoms was not completed until the International Air Services Transit Agreement (1944). The outcome of the Chicago Convention was the establishment of the International Civil Aviation Authority (ICAO), an inter-governmental agency designed to act as a forum to discuss major aviation issues. In addition, the International Air Transport Association (IATA) was established in 1945 to represent the interests of airline companies, as a rival to ICAO. IATA's primary purpose remains coordination and standardization of airline operations, representing airlines in a diverse range of negotiations with airport authorities, ICAO, govern-

Table 6.2 International cooperation in air travel (based on Mill, 1992: 18). Reproduced with permission of the author

International air travel requires countries to cooperate so that the movement of aircraft and people can occur in a reasonable flexible manner. To provide a degree of regulation and coherence in air travel, two important international agreements underpin present-day air travel: the 1944 Chicago Convention, which established the principle of freedoms of the air and the 1946 Bermuda Agreement, which provided a framework for bilateral agreements to implement freedoms of the air. A bilateral agreement is where two countries agree to provide an air service on a reciprocal basis, and it helps to facilitate and protect the rights of each country's airline irrespective of whether it is a profit-making or non-profit venture. Consequently, the following 'Freedoms of the Air' can be observed:

Freedom 1   The right of an airline to fly over one country to get to another

Freedom 2   The right of an airline to stop in another country for fuel/maintenance but not to pick up or drop off passengers

Freedom 3   The right of an airline to drop off in a foreign country traffic from the country in which it is registered

Freedom 4   The right of an airline to carry back passengers from a foreign country to the country in which it is registered

Freedom 5   The right of an airline to carry back passengers from two foreign countries as long as the flight originates or terminates in the country in which it is registered

Freedom 6   The right of an airline to carry passengers to a gateway in the country in which it is registered and then on to a foreign country, where neither the origin nor the ultimate destination is the country in which it is registered

Freedom 7   The right of an airline to operate entirely outside the country in which it is registered in carrying passengers between two other countries

Freedom 8   The right of an airline, registered in a foreign country, to carry passengers between two points in the same foreign country

According to Mill (1992), freedoms 1 and 2 are accepted internationally, freedoms 3–6 are the subject of bilateral agreements, and freedoms 7 and 8 are rarely accepted.

ments and even hijackers. It also operates the clearing-house for inter-airline debts arising from inter-airline traffic (carriage of airline passengers or freight on a service holding tickets issued by other airlines).

Airlines also use bilateral agreements, based on the principle of reciprocity (a fair and equal exchange of rights) while pooling agreements exist (except in the USA, where US antitrust legislation prohibits such agreements – which are viewed as being anti-competitive). Pooling agreements have been used in duopolistic situations to share the market between two airlines. Where business may not be sufficient to justify a two-airline operation, a revenue cost pool may be used where one airline operates the service on behalf of the pool partners. Airlines may also enter into inter-airline royalty agreements where airlines wish to pick up 'fifth freedom' traffic (see Table 6.2) from areas where they do not have such rights. By making royalty payments to the airline of the country involved, it may gain such rights. Such a range of regulatory measures means that the management of airlines is a complex process when dealing with the international aviation market. A further change to this regulatory environment was the decision of the US government in 1978 to deregulate its domestic airline industry. A more recent development is the evolution of 'open skies' policies since 1992. These have emerged because:

- There has been increasing concentration in the US airline market following deregulation, with former domestic airlines emerging as major international carriers
- International airlines are searching for marketing benefits from mergers in their home country and minority share purchases/strategic alliances to operate in other markets (which are discussed further below)
- There is a growing trend towards privatization of national flag carriers.

Open skies policies involve bilataral air service agreements where market access and price controls are removed. According to the Boeing Commercial Aircraft Company (2002), 50 per cent of the world's airline traffic is now based on open skies agreements, illustrating the scale of change in just over a decade.

Deregulation in the USA aimed to achieve greater competition, and resulted in a 62 per cent increase in domestic passenger traffic between 1978 and 1990 followed by greater integration and concentration within the industry. It led to a new business environment where airline companies reorganized their activities to achieve cost reductions, least-cost solutions and network maximization to achieve cost-effective operations. 'Hub and spoke' operations (see Figure 6.2) allowed airlines to develop a network to serve a large number of people over a wide area, with the hub acting as a switching point for passengers travelling on feeder routes along the spokes, which cannot sustain a trunk route. This has resulted in the geographical concentration of hubs in major US cities and the six largest US airlines developing four major hub cities – Atlanta, Chicago, Dallas and Denver. The more competitive and unregulated the market, the greater the degree of planning and adjustment needed to match supply and demand. This is normally undertaken under the auspices of the marketing process.

Airline marketing: its role and recent innovations

Growing global competition in the air travel market meant that the 1990s were the decade of the air traveller as a consumer seeking enhanced service quality. This has gone a stage further in the new millennium as the price-sensitive customer is a dominant element, especially in domestic air travel, and is concerned with a minimum standard of service. Airlines been forced to reduce operating costs and compete aggressively for business, and also to focus on the needs of their customers. Airline marketing is now more complex as it is vital to the management process of deciding what to produce and how it should be sold. Thus: '. . . the role of airline marketing is to bring together the supply of air services, which each airline can largely control, with the demand, which it can influence but not control, and to do this in a way which is both profitable and meets the airline's corporate objectives' (Doganis, 1991: 202). BA explained its financial turnaround from a loss of £544 million in 1981–1982 to a profit of £272 million in 1983–1984 in terms of a more focused marketing orientation involving recognizing customers' needs and setting about satisfying them. This has now come full circle, with a re-evaluation of the company's core business and marketing focus as its business has been significantly affected by the rise of low-cost carriers on short-haul domestic and European routes. BA has had to align its fare structure to what customers are prepared to pay, and also to rationalize its operations. For example, up to July 2002 BA had reduced fares on 71 routes and removed restrictions on lower priced tickets to stimulate demand. This was a result of the company's poor financial performance for the year ended 30 March 2002, where a £200 million loss before tax compared to a £150 million profit in 2000. In February 2002 the company announced its 'Future Size and Shape' study, which began a process of realigning the company to demand by removing unprofitable sections of its business through capacity and overhead reduction. One notable outcome was the decision to reposition its short-haul routes to compete with the low-cost airlines.

How airlines use marketing functions

Marketing in the management of airline services can be summarized as a four-stage process:

1 Identify the markets and market segments using research methods and existing data sources and traffic forecasts.
2 Use the market analysis to assess which products to offer, known as product planning. At this stage price becomes a critical factor. Therefore product planning is related to:
   - Market needs identified from market research
   - The current and future product features of competing airlines and the cost of different product features
   - Assessing what price the customers can be expected to pay for the product.
3 Develop a marketing plan to plan and organize the selling of the products. Sales and distribution outlets need to be considered, together with a detailed programme of advertising and promotion, such as the impact and effect that advertisements on the side of taxis may have on the travelling public.
4 Monitor and review the airline's ability to meet service standards, assessing this through sales figures, customer surveys, analysis of complaints, and long-term planning to develop new service and product features (Page, 2002).

The role of marketing, particularly advertising, has also assumed an increasingly important role in the evolution of the low-cost carrier market.

The low-cost carriers: aligning service provision with demand

Airlines have traditionally targeted service quality in the business travel and luxury market for first-class travel. This is because it is the most profitable segment of the market for scheduled airlines, with premium pricing and high profit margins per seat, compared to lower yields in economy class, where profitability is attained by achieving high load factors. However, this traditional strategy has been significantly challenged in many markets that have allowed liberalization of services, permitting new entrants to compete for business – notably low-cost carriers, as more travellers now seek budget fares (see Box 6.1).

Box 6.1   The low cost carrier: the SouthWest phenomenon

Low-cost air travel, often termed no-frills or budget airline travel, is a relatively new phenomenon in Europe, despite the ill-fated attempt in the 1970s by Freddie Laker and his Skytrain concept, which sought to compete on the North Atlantic market. Yet low-cost air travel was well established in the USA long before deregulation, with certain airlines specializing in this niche market. Indeed, the growth of SouthWest Airlines in the USA since 1971 epitomizes the traits of the low-cost carrier and established many of the basic business principles of streamlined airline operations (see Table 6.3 for key data on SouthWest, and Plate 6.1).

SouthWest entered new markets at a low price, using lesser-known secondary airports, and demand outstripped supply. Following deregulation in 1978, SouthWest expanded across the USA in a cautious manner as many other carriers went bankrupt or were taken over. It avoided head-on competition with the major carriers, although when it had to face such competition (such as when United launched its shuttle services in California) it initially saw market share drop and then business recovered (as United could

Plate 6.1   A SouthWest Boeing 737 in corporate livery © SouthWest, reproduced with permission

Table 6.3 Key facts on SouthWest Airline operations (based on data provided on www.southwest.com)

- In 2002, the airline served 58 cities in 30 US states, with a fleet of 366 Boeing 737s
- It had a net income of US$5111.1 in 2001
- In 2001 it carried 64.4 million passengers with an average load factor of 68.1 per cent
- In 2002, its average fare was US$82.84 for a one-way trip on an average flight length of 715 miles
- In 2001, SouthWest booked 7.2 million passengers monthly
- It provides 90 per cent of all discount air travel in the USA
- In May 2002, the *Wall Street Journal* ranked the airline first for customer service based on the American Customer Satisfaction Index
- The airline was ranked among the top four US airlines for National Airline Quality Ratings of 11 airlines in April 2002, based on punctuality, baggage handling, overbooking and customer complaints
- SouthWest was the first airline company to establish a home page on the Internet (www.southwest.com)
- The airline's booking costs are $1 for an Internet booking and $6–8 for a travel agent booking
- According to search engines such as Lycos, SouthWest is one of the commonly searched airlines on the web
- It has 2800 departures a day
- The year 2001 marked 29 consecutive years of profit
- The company employs 35 000 staff

not operate services viably) to the point where SouthWest was the dominant intra-state carrier in California. *So how does SouthWest manage to operate a viable business where competitors fail?*

In terms of the economics of airline operation (see Figure 6.4 for an illustration of the main costs in airline operation), it manages to operate at a cost structure well below its revenue. This means it can operate at a cost base, which is often 25–40 per cent below that of its competitors where unrestricted fares are low. Yet for the airline, many

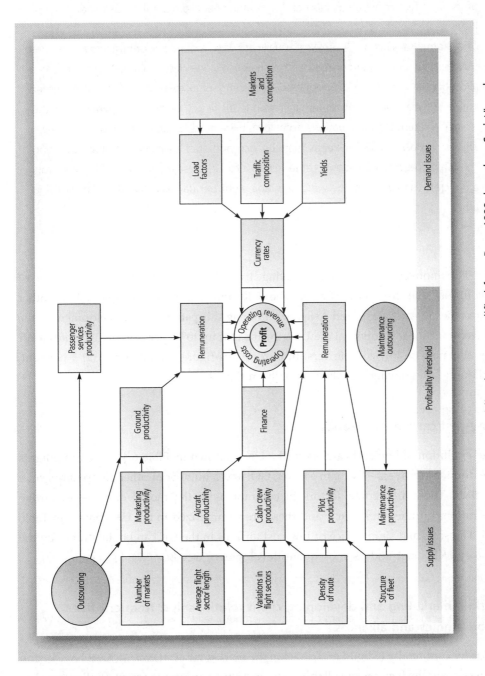

Figure 6.4 The main costs in operating an airline (source: modified from Page 1999, based on Seristö and Vepsäläinen 1997)

of its flight sectors are often short and so revenue per kilometre flown is relatively high. It has a simple fare structure, high levels of punctuality and correspondingly high levels of customer satisfaction. SouthWest usually attracted a good mix of business and leisure travellers, despite being no-frills, with high-density, one-class seating. There is no seat allocation, and only snacks are offered to passengers to keep costs down. Pilots enter into a ten-year agreement on remuneration levels (a key element of operation for the airline) in return for share options, to help stabilize costs. By standardizing its fleet type with only Boeing 737s, it keeps maintenance and staff training costs low. By using 15–20-minute turnaround times at terminals it can increase the number of flight sectors an aircraft can fly in a day – which average eight per day, and twelve hours of flying time.

The innovations in low-cost flying have been translated into the low-cost revolution that has now affected the UK and mainland Europe, whilst other companies in Australasia and Asia are following this pattern. The development of the low-cost airline revolution in the USA means that up to 15 per cent of all domestic air travel is now on low-cost carriers. In Europe this figure is much lower at 3 per cent, although it is growing rapidly, especially in the UK.

Low-cost carriers in Europe

The evolution of low-cost carriers in the UK is shown in Table 6.4, which highlights the dominant players – Ryanair, easyJet, GO, and a number of other competitors such as BMI. There are certain factors in common with the model of low-cost airline operations outlined in Box 6.1, and these are summarized in the UK context in Table 6.5. The scale and significance of low-cost airlines in the UK can be illustrated by the history of Ryanair and its subsequent development (see Box 6.2).

Airline marketing and developing client relationships: frequent flyer programmes and alliances

In order continually to build and develop the market for air travel, airlines have begun to recognize the benefits of collaboration and joint working in terms of alliances. The concept of frequent flyer programmes (FFPs) is one example of building good client

Table 6.4 A brief history of low-cost airline development in the UK

Date	Event
1985	Ryanair established
1991	Ryanair losses £18 million
1992	Ryanair move its UK hub from Luton to London Stansted. It makes a pre-tax profit
1995	easyJet established in October Ryanair begins a new UK domestic service from Prestwick Airport, Ayr, Scotland
1996	Debonair established in June
1997	Virgin Express established Ryanair flotation on stock market Ryanair pre-tax profit of US$53 million for 1997–1998 Ryanair adds four new European routes to its UK–Ireland flights
1998	Ryanair adds seven new European routes British Airways established GO in May
1999	Debonair goes into receivership in September
2000	BUZZ, a subsidiary of KLM, is established GO is sold off by British Airways to venture capitalists 3i for £100 million through a management buy-out after losses of £20 million in each year of operation
2001	British Midland establishes its BMIbaby low-cost carrier, based at East Midlands airport
2002	easyJet purchases GO for £400 million Ryanair places the largest aircraft order ever for a low-cost carrier: 100 new Boeing 737s

relationships to encourage customer loyalty. These programmes were originally developed in the USA in May 1981 by American Airlines (AA), where FFPs were developed to attract business following deregulation. AA used its database of passengers to identify frequent flyers, who were enrolled into a 'Very Important Travellers Club'. The reward for loyalty was free air travel on a route that consistently

Table 6.5 Key characteristics of low-cost carriers that make them more competitive than other carriers

---

- Some carriers have introduced single/one-way fares not requiring stopovers or Saturday night stays to get advanced purchase (APEX) prices
- No complimentary in-flight service (no frills), which often reduces operating costs by 6–7 per cent
- One-class cabins (in most cases)
- No pre-assigned seating (in most cases)
- Ticketless travel
- High-frequency routes to compete with other airlines on popular destinations, and up to three flights a day on low-density routes
- Short turnarounds (often less than half an hour) with higher aircraft rotations (i.e. the level of utilization is higher than other airlines) and less time charged on the airport apron and runway
- The use of secondary airports where feasible (including the provision of public transport where none exists)
- Point-to-point flights
- Lower staffing costs, with fewer cabin crew because there is no complimentary in-flight service, which also reduces turnaround times due to the lack of cleaning caused by food service
- Flexibility in staff rostering, a lack of overnight stays for staff at non-base locations, and streamlined operations (e.g. on some airlines toilets on domestic flights are only emptied on cabin crew requests rather than at each turnaround to reduce costs)
- Many of the aircraft are leased, reducing the level of depreciation and standardizing costs
- Many airline functions are outsourced, such as ground staff and check-in, minimizing overheads and reducing costs by 11–15 per cent
- Standardized aircraft types (e.g. Boeing 737s) to reduce maintenance costs and the range of spare parts that need to be held for repairs
- Limited office space at the airports
- Heavy emphasis on advertising, especially billboards, to offset the declining use of travel agents as the main source of bookings
- Heavy dependence upon the Internet and telephone for bookings
- Small administrative staff, with many sales-related staff on commission to improve performance (as well as pilots in some cases)

Box 6.2   The history and development of Ryanair

Ryanair is the airline founded in Ireland in 1985 by the Guinness Peat Aviation aircraft leasing company. The airline's traffic grew from 80 000 passengers in 1986 to 600 000 in 1989, when it introduced aged jets – BAC-111s – to expand capacity. In the first four years of operation, up to 1989, Ryanair lost £20 million. By 1994 it was transporting 1.5 million passengers a year after reconfiguring its operations, replicating the success of SouthWest by standardizing its fleet, and purchasing used Boeing 737s from Britannia and Lufthansa. By 2000 it had managed to achieve the same rate of growth per annum as SouthWest – 25 per cent per annum – reaching seven million passengers in 2002. As a result, it has set a growth rate that other low-cost carriers have sought to emulate – particularly easyJet, which had a turnover of £357 million in 2002 and carried 7.1 million passengers. The majority of its flights are booked on the Internet, and the scale of growth in low-cost carriers in the UK has led to the development of new markets, often with loss-leading fares initially to develop a market presence. Its methods have been termed 'ambush marketing' – i.e. taking the market from the larger established carriers with larger overheads and less flexibility (consider British Airways' declining profitability in the new millennium). This illustrates how volatile and changeable the airline market is, particularly regarding the scale and pace of change, where dominant market players can be severely affected by new trends such as the low-cost airline phenomenon.

had a high ratio of unsold seats – Hawaii. AA's Advantage FFP aimed to maximize revenue yield and its load factor; it helped to develop Dallas as a logical hub; and it also succeeded in capturing business from their competitors' airlines. AA's Advantage scheme was closely followed schemes launched by other companies (United, TWA and Delta), though BA was added to the AA FFP to give it an international dimension, with Qantas joining to form the One World Global Alliance.

To broaden the marketing appeal of FFPs, non-airline travel services (e.g. car rental companies, tour operators and hotel chains), airline-affiliated credit card purchases (mileage credits added according to the volume of spending) and other services now attract FFP points. It is a basic element of airline marketing strategy in the USA, and European and other global carriers have also introduced it. In the

Asia-Pacific region there is a major airline alliance to challenge the One World Global Alliance discussed above; this is the Star Alliance, which is a combination of Air New Zealand, United, Lufthansa, Thai Airways International, SAS, Varig and Air Canada, offering services to over 700 destinations in 111 countries. In 2001, 51 per cent of the world airline capacity was linked to airline marketing alliances, and this reflects a growing consolidation in the market. The Star Alliance now dominates the alliance networks, with 20 per cent of capacity; One World has 15 per cent; SkyTeam has 10 per cent; and KLM/NorthWest has 6 per cent. The remaining 46 per cent are in non-aligned groupings. This allows partner airlines to grow their network, achieve economies of scale in ticketing, maintenance and purchasing, and provide the consumer with seamless travel.

Doganis (2001) has identified two types of airline alliance in existence:

1 Commercial alliances, which are operationally driven and focus on the early stages of alliance development
2 Strategic alliances, leading towards a full merger of airlines.

This is reflected in the three stages to alliance development. The first phase is revenue generation, where partners can enter and exit easily, and involves a series of code shares, joint FFPs, network coordination, joint sales, shared business lounges and an alliance logo. In the second phase the alliance is cemented together, seeking to make cost savings for its members from common ground handling, joint maintenance, sales and call centres, purchasing and fleet harmonization. Exit is difficult at this stage. In the last phase, a joint venture situation, and exit is almost impossible as it involves franchising, joint product development, sharing of aircraft and crews and a single alliance brand. The emergence of alliances reflects a more sophisticated business approach to airline development, although some airlines still seek to differentiate themselves on the basis of unique selling features or propositions – especially in the luxury market, through in-flight food provision.

In-flight catering: a marketing opportunity?

It is estimated that food provision accounts for 5–10 per cent of the total cost of the fare, and some airlines recognize that it is an important element of the in-flight experience – particularly in business and first-class, where customer expectations are high as a result of advertising campaigns. In contrast, economy travellers often view in-flight food as a sign of value for money, although critics have questioned the need for food as a sign of service quality. However, airline managers have universally endorsed the role of food as a vital element in airline marketing as recent advertising campaigns have attempted to differentiate airline services. For example, Emirates has advertised that 'whatever class you fly, you'll enjoy award-winning food and the finest selection of wines', while other airlines advertise their business class service in top cuisine magazines.

Some airlines perceive food provision as more than a simple element of their product or service, and this may explain why customers focus on it as a source of dissatisfaction when their expectations are not met. Yet catering at 30 000 feet is not easy because passengers' taste buds respond differently owing to pressurization, their digestive systems become sluggish due to humidity levels and dehydration, and reheating airline meals successfully can be a challenge. Whilst many short-haul budget airlines do not offer in-flight meals due to the cost savings of £5–6 per passenger (passengers can purchase snacks and sandwiches), food provision on long-haul flights is seen as a way of occupying travellers' time to create the illusion that the flight is shorter than it actually is. The growth in contract catering (for example, Lufthansa's LSG Sky Chefs in Europe) has removed the problem of food provision from the immediate remit of airline managers, and has created a new business activity for large companies able to meet the exacting requirements of airlines (for example, a Boeing 747 requires 50 000 catering items per flight). Despite the logistical and technical problems of providing quality food on board aircraft, it remains essential in the expectations of consumers on flights other than with low-cost carriers, and continues to assist airline managers in the perceived differentiation of their products and services.

Future trends

Airlines are a complex industry, especially as they are working in a constant state of flux and change. As Page (1999) indicated, the main challenges for airline managers in the new millennium are:

- Technical change (i.e. the greater use of technology such as Computer Reservation Systems (CRS) and global distribution systems, which are more complex and all-embracing than the former CRS)
- Regional change, where new trading blocs (for example, ASEAN) are posing new challenges for patterns of trade and business travel.

For the traveller, there are ongoing risks with air travel from a health perspective. This has been highlighted by recent concerns regarding deep vein thrombosis on long-haul flights, and cramped conditions and a lack of movement by passengers during the flight. In addition, there has been a worrying growth in disruptive behaviour, commonly known as air rage, on board flights. The Civil Aviation Authority in the UK indicates that whilst this is not a widespread problem, with a total of 1055 reported incidents in the year ended 31 March 2002, violence occurred in 10 per cent of cases and alcohol was involved in a further 45 per cent of cases, with smoking (which is banned on most European flights) in the toilets also creating problems. Although air rage is downplayed by airlines and the CAA it can nonetheless be a very disruptive and potentially dangerous situation, which is exacerbated when drunk passengers are carried by airlines despite guidelines that are supposed to prevent them from boarding. The majority of such offences were committed by males (77 per cent of cases), largely 20–40 years of age, and only 5 per cent of cases occurred in first or business class. Typical problems included disruptive passengers who were verbally abusive and offended by airline regulations. Only a small number of incidents led to physical restraints being used or requiring an aircraft to divert. The likelihood of an offence occurring in UK airspace or on an UK outbound/inbound flight was 1 : 22 000 for a serious incident. Greater health risks were encountered in the quality of recirculated cabin air provided to passengers in flight, and the ongoing debates over the problems of dehydration owing to dry air as well as the potential for the spread of communicable diseases.

Summary

The future global aviation industry is likely to contain a limited number of global mega-carriers, with smaller airlines integrated into their operations by strategic alliances and other devices (for example, part ownership by the larger carriers). The major constraint on this rapidly evolving business activity for airline managers will be the availability of uncongested airspace and airports with sufficient capacity – a feature that the low-cost carriers have addressed through the use of secondary airports. This is already affecting air travel in Europe and the USA, while the environmental lobby regularly opposes airport expansion near to major urban centres. These managerial issues have to be addressed and accommodated within the day-to-day operation and longer-term planning by airline managers, so that passengers are not adversely affected by delays, congestion and inadequate planning.

References

Ashford, H. Stanton, H. and Moore, C. (1991) *Airport Operations*. London: Pitman.

Barlay, S. (1995) *Cleared for Take-off: Behind the Scenes of Air Travel*. London: Kyle Cathie Limited.

Boeing Commercial Airplane Group (2002) *2002 Current Market Outlook*. Seattle: Boeing Commercial Airplane Group.

Doganis, R. (1991) *Flying Off Course: The Economics of International Airlines*. London: Routledge.

Doganis, R.(1992) *The Airport Business*. London: Routledge.

Doganis, R. (2001) *The Airline Business in the 21st Century*. London: Routledge.

Mill, R. C. (1992) *Tourism: The International Business*, New Jersey: Prentice Hall.

Page, S. J. (1999) *Transport and Tourism*. Harlow: Addison Wesley Longman.

Page, S. J. (2002) Airline management. In: M. Warner (ed), *Encyclopaedia of Business and Management*, Vol. 1, 2nd edn. London: Thomson Learning, pp. 209–18.

Seristö, H. and Vepsäläinen, A. (1997) Airline cost drivers: cost implications of fleets, routes and personnel. *Journal of Air Transport Management*, **3**(1): 11–12.

Further reading

Doganis, R. (2001) *The Airline Business in the 21st Century*. London: Routledge.

Hanlon, P. (1996) *Global Airlines: Competition in a Transnational Industry*. Oxford: Butterworth-Heinemann.

Questions

1 Why are airports so important as staging points for international travel?

2 What range of issues would you have to deal with as an airport manager?

3 Why is the US airline industry facing a crisis?

4 How have the low-cost carriers affected the business of leisure travel?

Chapter **7**

Accommodation

Learning objectives

This chapter examines the significance of the tourist accommodation product consumed by tourists, and outlines the diversity of accommodation types and a number of current trends in the accommodation sector. After reading it, you should be able to understand:

- the scope and nature of tourist accommodation;
- the range of operational issues affecting the accommodation sector;
- the differences between serviced and non-serviced accommodation;
- the importance of environmental issues in the management of hotels.

Introduction

Accommodation provides the base from which tourists can engage in the process of staying at a destination. Accommodation is the focal point for the hosting of guests and visitors, where a guest may pay a fee in return for a specified service, grade of accommodation, and associated services such as food and beverages. The accommodation establishment as a commercial venture, especially the evolution of the commercial hotel in the Victorian period, has dominated the literature on the subject as entrepreneurs responded to the demand for serviced accommodation of a high standard. The development of accommodation has normally accompanied the growth of resorts and areas of tourism activity, and in the demand for visiting specific areas. Like the tourist, accommodation assumes many forms and not all of them fit the conventional image of the hotel. Indeed recent trends in accommodation have seen great changes in the form and nature of accommodation provision.

This chapter examines the scope and nature of accommodation, the impact of globalization, and the operational issues that affect the accommodation sector. The characteristics of the accommodation sector are examined in a case study of German hotels. The discussion then turns to the growing differentiation of accommodation in the serviced and non-serviced sectors. The accommodation sector is part of the capital-intensive infrastructure that tourists utilize, and is very labour-intensive in servicing visitors' needs. However, it has an advantage in that by hosting guests it also has the potential to generate additional revenue from food and beverage services.

Globalization and operational issues

Chapter 1 briefly introduced the growing globalization of the tourism sector, where global companies are responding to consumer trends. Globalization has resulted in various forms of companies that operate in a globalized or transnational manner. These comprise:

- Global corporations that operate throughout the world, such as the Holiday Inn
- Multinational corporations with operations in countries outside that of the main base or headquarters
- Smaller multinationals that operate in a limited number of countries.

An organization can adopt transnational strategies by:

- Franchising its operation to other businesses in different countries
- Licensing other companies to operate using its brand, logo or trademark
- Non-investment management agreements
- Acquisitions of overseas properties and interests
- Mergers to integrate business interests horizontally to operate in a number of countries.

These changes have led to nearly 30 per cent of all of the world's accommodation stock being chain-controlled (i.e. international businesses operating globally). In many cases chain hotels expatriate profits back to the country in which the hotel chain is based. Many of the chains have highly developed distribution channels, being affiliated to major Global Distribution Systems that distribute the product electronically to travel agents. The Horwath and Horwath Worldwide Hotel Industry report has predicted that by 2050 up to 60 per cent of hotels will be affiliated to global chains, continuing the consolidation trend discussed in Chapter 4.

The Horwath and Horwath study indicated that in the late 1990s average daily room rates were US$90.89, yielding revenue of US$62.96. The chain hotels consistently recorded higher revenue than independent hotels, with occupancy rates of 69.8 per cent for luxury hotels. In economy hotels, occupancy rates were 63 per cent and the revenue yielded was less than half that of luxury hotels. Some of the highest occupancy rates occurred at airport hotels, with rates of 74 per cent. The survey also confirmed that hotels derive a significant proportion of their trade from business travellers at the luxury end of the market, while leisure travellers traditionally dominate the economy segment. However, Horwath and Horwath also highlighted a number of other markets for hotel accommodation, including:

- Airline crews on layovers in between flight schedules, resting before continuing their duties
- Conference delegates
- Tour groups
- Government officials
- Other categories of travellers..

Business travellers are the premium market for hotels, since they stay for shorter periods than leisure travellers but spend higher sums per visit. The Horwath and

Horwath study also found that the balance of domestic to international visitors in chain hotels was 48:52 compared to 51:49 in independent hotels. In this respect, the Horwath and Horwath study highlights the diversity of the markets that hotels serve, although some accommodation (e.g. boutique hotels) may specialize in certain sectors. In a European context, private accommodation still remains the most important for certain nationalities such as Greeks, Spanish, Italians, Portuguese, Finns, Swedes and British. In contrast, Danes, Germans, Irish, Austrians and visitors from Luxembourg have a propensity to use hotels for both domestic and international travel. This highlights the divergence among different countries, which illustrates the appeal of different elements in the accommodation industry.

The characteristics of the accommodation industry

Accommodation has been conceptualized by some researchers as a product. This is illustrated in Figure 7.1, which depicts the principal factors that can impact upon the way in which the product is constructed, portrayed and sold to customers. For example, large luxury hotels will emphasize facilities, service and image to certain market segments, such as business travellers, to secure business. In contrast, economy hotels will ultimately emphasize price as the key determinant of the product

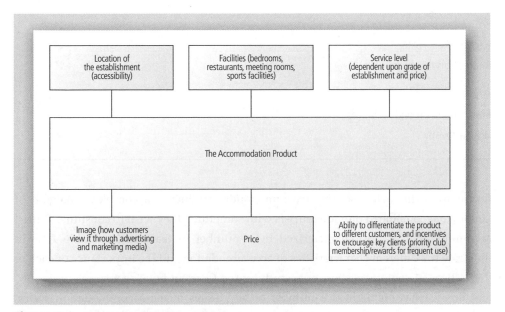

Figure 7.1   Accommodation as a product

Table 7.1 Forms of tourist accommodation (developed from various sources)

	Business usage	Leisure usage
Serviced accommodation		
Hotels	✓	✓
Resort hotels		✓
Educational establishments	✓	✓
Airport hotels	✓	✓
Motels	✓	✓
Inns	✓	✓
State-run hotels	✓	✓
Bed and breakfast		✓
Apartment hotels	✓	✓
Non-serviced accommodation		
Holiday villages/centres/camps		✓
Caravans		✓
Campsites		✓
Gîtes		✓
Holiday cottages		✓
Villas		✓
Youth hostels		✓
Backpacker hostels		✓
Recreational vehicles		✓
Other		
Staying with friends/relatives	✓	✓
House swaps		✓

formulation. In each case, the accommodation product is a complex amalgam of factors that combine to provide tourists with something they wish to consume. Tourist accommodation is also characterized by a number of features (see Table 7.1). To illustrate the different characteristics of accommodation and the importance of each of these, Box 7.1 contains a short case study of the German hotel sector.

Box 7.1 has highlighted a number of key issues in the accommodation sector, including occupancy levels and the importance of location. It has also shown that

Box 7.1 Case study: the German hotel industry

The German hotel sector is an interesting example to use to illustrate the operation and nature of tourist accommodation because it has a very decentralized distribution of properties, since it is not dominated by a single city – as is the case in many other European countries. Berlin, Hamburg, Munich, Cologne and Frankfurt am Main are the principal cities that dominate patterns of hotel supply. Although Germany had a problem of oversupply, tourism demand is expanding to fill surplus capacity following reunification. Much of the market for German hotels consists of domestic visitors, but it is also the largest country in the world for trade fairs, festivals and special events such as the Munich Oktoberfest (a beer festival), which attracts 6 million visitors annually.

Hotel arrivals grew by 13.1 per cent between 1998 and 2000, while overnight stays expanded by 13.6 per cent in the same period. In 2000, 47 million Germans stayed in hotel accommodation compared to 12 million overseas visitors (an 80:20 split), with nearly 60 per cent of overnight stays generated by business travellers. Significant market differences exist in German cities between the international hotel guest market and the domestic market. Frankfurt, which has the second largest European airport and is a key business centre, concentrates on the business sector; in contrast, Hamburg is predominantly a domestic market. Berlin is somewhere between the two extremes, as it re-establishes itself as an international location for visitors.

In 2000, a City Survey by the consulting firm Parnell Kerr Foster (PKF) provided a breakdown of the business mix in upscale city hotels in Europe and Germany. In Europe, it identified the following segments (based on 1999 survey data):

- Full rate (11.1 per cent)
- Corporate discount rate (34.5 per cent)
- Tour operator/group rate (15 per cent)
- Leisure break (13.3 per cent)
- Conference/incentive travel (13.5 per cent)
- Airline crew (8.2 per cent)
- Other (4.4 per cent).

In the case of Frankfurt, among the nineteen hotels surveyed, PKF found:

- 16.6 per cent paying the full rate
- 19.9 per cent were aircrew

- 13.6 per cent were conference/incentive business
- 31.8 per cent enjoyed a corporate discount rate
- 8.1 per cent were on a tour operator or group discounted rate
- 8.5 per cent were taking a leisure break
- 1.5 per cent others.

Table 7.2 shows some of the principal operational data based on occupancy rates and the average annual room rate (in Deutschmarks) among Germany's main city hotels. The latter can be compared to the revenue per average room rate (the yield, or income per room). What these rates show is that different client mixes generate different yields per room, and average rates do not easily reflect the different rates charged to specific markets. The major German cities outperformed the German average, led by the airport hotel sector. However, in terms of profitability, a survey of worldwide hotels by the consulting firm Arthur Andersen found that the average German hotel profit margin (income before fixed charges are deducted) was only 31 per cent compared to 43 per cent in the UK and 38 per cent in Amsterdam. Even this average profitability measure varies between cities, with Frankfurt (36 per cent) and Munich (37 per cent) experiencing higher yields than Hamburg (28 per cent). A higher proportion of revenue in part explains the higher profitability in Frankfurt and Munich, from rooms as opposed to non-room revenue (i.e. food and beverages). These revenues have to be set against the costs of producing rooms/food and beverages, together with the operating expenses of

Table 7.2 Operational data for principal hotels in Germany in 2000 (modified from Hotelverband Deutschland (IHA) and Marvel, 2001)

	% Occupancy rate	Average annual room rate (DM)	Revenue per average room (DM)
Berlin	69	201	139
Cologne	71	207	147
Frankfurt	72	193	139
Hamburg	73	184	134
Munich	77	197	152
Average	65	167	109

running the hotel, which include administration, marketing, maintenance and energy costs. Arthur Anderson found that average operating costs for German hotels were as follows in 2000:

- Administration/general costs (9 per cent)
- Marketing (4 per cent)
- Maintenance (4 per cent)
- Energy (4 per cent).

The German hotel market has also experienced gradual consolidation, and the number of hotel groups increased from 41 in 1985 to 130 in 2001. The number of hotels affiliated to specific chains/groups has risen from 1068 to 3166 in the same period. The significance of these statistics is that whilst affiliated hotels only represent 7 per cent of German accommodation establishments, they account for 27 per cent of turnover (comprising DM32.6 billion). Hotel chains continue to expand through joint ventures with other companies as increasing yield from the hotel sector is reflected in rising room prices. However, the future prospects for the German hotel sector, which has a strong domestic market, is uncertain owing to an economic slowdown, and a weak currency (the euro) in relation to sterling and the US dollar.

hotels are complex business ventures, and has demonstrated the importance of certain costs as well as the benefit of operating in a buoyant economy that has accepted rising room rates, helping to improve profitability in the major cities. Attention now turns to the diversity of accommodation types.

Types of tourist accommodation

The accommodation sector has undergone profound changes since 1945, having been characterized by constant innovation, evolution and diversification of the product range. The pre-1945 pattern of tourist accommodation was dominated by serviced accommodation, while post-1945 there was a rapid growth in non-serviced types of accommodation. Yet even the distinction between serviced and non-serviced accommodation is blurring with the growth of apartment hotels that permit self-catering, but also have arrangements with local restaurants so that clients can enjoy food and beverage services and have them charged back to their hotel account. However, the two sectors will be considered separately here.

Serviced accommodation

Throughout this chapter much of the discussion has focused on the most recognizable element of the serviced accommodation sector – the hotel. Although the greatest changes have occurred in the non-serviced sector, hotels have not been immune. A hotel does not simply consist of premises with rooms, food and beverage services, but is also a business oriented towards a constantly changing clientele. In some countries (e.g. Iceland and Estonia) there has been a rapid expansion of hotels into the fast-growing health resort market. In other cases, the business of hotels has become highly competitive and independent. Small hotels of less than 50 rooms and of one- to three-star status have become much more prone to insolvency, typically due to cash-flow problems where inadequate revenue cannot cover fixed costs. Owners need to plan for regular refurbishment and investment to remain competitive, but such costs are often deferred due to poor financial performance. Some luxury hotels will refurbish their properties every five to ten years.

Hotel managers need to understand how the operation of their establishment(s) generates revenue, and the scale of costs. Some of these costs were outlined in Box 7.1, but it is important to understand the causes of low profitability – employee costs, the cost of staff per room, restaurant costs, supply costs and debt costs that have to be serviced. How the hotels generate their business is also significant for the hotel manager, particularly when underlying issues of seasonality are considered. Hotels located in city areas suffer less seasonality in occupancy levels than those located in mountain areas, where unreliable weather may impact upon the levels of business that can be generated.

Important considerations for hotel managers are the global demand and the resources and marketing efforts needed to generate business. Location of the hotel and its size are important determinants of profitability, and affiliation to distribution channels can offer global booking systems (e.g. Global Distribution Systems). These affiliations help to generate business that is supported by promotions, loyalty programmes, and links to other tourism businesses and services as part of the distribution system. There are two basic types of affiliations for hotels:

1 *Voluntary chain associations*, which have limited marketing activities for members, low fees and shorter member contracts, and are aimed at smaller independent hotels

2 *Franchised products*, run by the larger integrated hotel chains, which have complex purchasing facilities and higher fees for members. The participating companies often have ten- to fifteen-year contracts.

Of the voluntary chain associations the most well known is Best Western, which has a non-profit approach, being American-based but organized on a country-by-country basis. It has global brand recognition and charges an initial entrance fee to members. It then charges a yearly flat fee, plus a fee per room booked. Up to 10 per cent of its business is generated by company reservation systems, and Best Western charges a reservation fee for call-centre bookings. Other voluntary associations tend to operate on a country basis or across a number of countries, such as Alpine Classic, which operates in Austria, France, Germany, Switzerland and Italy. In contrast, franchise chains are more global. Notable examples include Holiday Inn, owned by Six Continents, which is the largest global hotel brand (based on room capacity). The second largest is the Comfort Inn chain, owned by Choice in the USA. The Holiday Inn chain charges an initial fee based on the number of rooms in an establishment, plus a number of other charges including:

• A 5 per cent royalty based on an establishment's gross room revenue
• A 2.5 per cent royalty based on gross room revenue to cover marketing costs
• A reservation charge per room per month.

Joining a chain not only generates business from reservation systems; the image of the chain is also important, as well as client relationships, because Holiday Inn has global agreements with 55 multinational companies and four operators. As a recognizable brand it also receives a large proportion of bookings made by telephone and email as well as in person (known as 'walk-ins'). The Internet is estimated to generate around 5 per cent of hotel bookings, although this is expected to grow rapidly in future years.

To develop profitability, larger hotels have also adopted the revenue or yield management strategies that were pioneered in the airline industry. By identifying peaks and troughs in hotel bookings from previous years, hotels can then provide for a predicted pattern of demand based on experience. Using such models, hotels can then charge prices based on likely demand for future room capacity and seek to balance supply with demand to maximize occupancy. The hotel monitors the booking rate and can adjust prices according to future demand, thus flexibly responding to market conditions. This takes into account the expected business mix, as outlined in the German hotel case study, and the profitability of each segment, since filling a hotel with low-yielding sectors such as air crews is unviable and these need to be mixed with full-price and discounted business. For smaller hotels investment in yield management computer systems (as well as the training and know-how) may previously not have been attractive, but these systems can now be accessed by non-chain hotels via the Internet for a monthly fee. Yield management has been largely used in the larger urban-based and resort hotels.

Trends in hotel development indicate that mega-hotels (those with over 5000 rooms) have also been constructed, such as the MGM Grand Hotel and Casino in Las Vegas. Yet estimates by tourism authorities in Las Vegas indicate that if 1000 new rooms are opened, an additional 275 000 tourists are needed each year to fill them. This in turn needs significant investment in transportation to allow visitors to access Las Vegas, and increased marketing efforts to attract visitors. The hotel manager, hotel chain and developer therefore need to be aware of existing levels of supply so that markets do not become saturated and occupancy rates drop, impacting upon profitability. In some New Zealand resorts, such as Queenstown, a distinct cycle of development in hotel and motel development from the 1970s can be discerned: demand led to a growth in supply to fill shortages; this was followed by oversupply, given the lead-time in approval and construction of hotels. Supply was then filled by demand, and the cycle began again. Such patterns can be discerned in other destinations, as the tourism market does not operate in an ideal competitive environment owing to the development process, which can lead to shortages and then oversupply in capacity.

Much of the discussion of hotels and trends has indicated that larger chain properties provide the future direction for profitability, given the process of consolidation. However, there are other successful sectors, such as:

- Boutique hotels.
- Budget accommodation and hotels.
- Small, family-run properties with less than twelve rooms, which dominate the bed and breakfast/small hotel sectors. This form of serviced accommodation has also been developed into the 'homestay' concept in countries such as New Zealand, where the farm-stay idea has been devised for rural farms to supplement their income.
- Resort hotel complexes, popularized by Club Med, where all tourist services are included and prepaid at the time of purchasing the holiday.

Boutique hotels

An interesting new trend is the growth of boutique hotels. These have been described as townhouses or small style-led properties that are fashion-conscious and are modelled on the concept of a 1960s clothing boutique, based on unique products and goods. Such properties defy conventional star ratings, with their attraction to the consumer seeking a unique experience that is different from the chain hotel. In this respect it is a lifestyle product, with unique architectural or style features in the property. In the USA, the operators in this market are Ian Schrager, Kimpton, Joie de Vivre, Starwood and the South Beach Group. Such operators have styled their properties as fashionable properties to stay in, being associated with consumers who are trendsetters in the music, media and film industries. In some boutique hotels, such as the Malmaison chain in the UK (which has five properties), there is no room service and there are less 'frills' in the eating establishments. Some owners have even reduced the fitting-out costs of hotels by adopting a minimalist strategy. In the USA, occupancy levels in boutique properties grew steadily from 69 per cent in 1995 to 71 per cent in 2000, which represents a good performance. In some instances boutique hotels have reduced costs by reducing service levels, compensating for this by marketing the style features and the limited services as positive elements. For example, the recently opened property in Knightsbridge, London, owned by Firmdale, has marketed itself as an exclusive bed and breakfast, with no restaurant. Many boutique operators are also responding to the market more flexibly than are larger chain hotels, by a process of continuous improvement. A number of factors are promoting a continued growth in boutique hotels, and these include:

- The Internet, which makes it simpler for customers to access this new form of hotel
- The entry of a number of larger hotel chains into this market, such as the Hilton Group and Marriot International.

The entry of chains to the boutique market may be a contradiction in that the individuality of each hotel might be compromised by the homogeneity of chain principles (i.e. that the experience should be uniform in each property regardless of location). However, the principles of boutique hotels are being embodied to emphasize the individuality of the property. In Europe, a 2002 report by Price-waterhouseCoopers consultants forecast that this sector would grow by 85 per cent over the period to 2007. The study identified operators who stated they were planning to build up to 6800 new bedrooms by 2007 in addition to the 8000 already in existence. The number of boutique properties had grown to 92 properties in the previous five years, raising the key question: how can these unique properties continue to expand without becoming ubiquitous, like the chain-owned hotels?

Budget accommodation and hotels

The hotel sector has been overshadowed by one further trend – the rise of the budget accommodation market. The North American market, with its large car-based domestic tourism traffic saw the motel evolve as a cheaper and more flexible form of accommodation. Normally located on principal routeways and roads, the motel evolved as a cost-effective way to accommodate a range of budget-conscious travellers who did not want to pay hotel prices. Motels have developed outside of North America, particularly in Australia and New Zealand, and have become a ubiquitous feature of the accommodation sector in these countries, filling a niche for budget serviced accommodation. Motels often provide catering facilities for travellers, but are typically smaller than the average 50-room hotel. Most are run or managed as stand-alone or family businesses, although some may be affiliated to chains such as Best Western.

In Europe there are other forms of budget accommodation, such as youth hostels. Youth hostels opened in the UK in 1931 and now operate at 230 locations in England and Wales; there are 4500 globally. However, this traditional market for budget accommodation has been challenged in recent years by the rise of the budget hotel. The budget hotel market is most highly developed in France, where two companies – Accor and Group Envergure – run two-thirds of Europe's branded budget hotel rooms. Accor own the largest European brand, Ibis, with 45 per cent of its rooms located in seventeen countries aside from France. In contrast, Group Envergure's eight budget brands are almost entirely based in France. The UK is emerging as the second largest budget hotel market in Europe. In 2000 there were over 47 000 beds in budget hotels in the UK, and this is forecast to expand to 103 000 by 2005. Hotel chains have entered this market in Europe, with major brands such as Travelodge and Express by Holiday Inn now comprising 6 per cent of the UK accommodation market. The budget operators are leisure- and hospitality-integrated companies, with Whitbread owning the Travel Inn chain and Compass (a leading contract catering business) operating the Travelodge brand (which controls 53 per cent of the budget market in the UK). The third largest budget hotel market in Europe is in Germany, and is dominated by Accor's brands (Ibis and Etap).

On a pan-European scale, the top budget hotel management companies are:

1 *Accor*, based in France, with 1082 hotels and 91758 rooms (three leading brands – Ibis, Etap and Formule 1)
2 *Group Envergure*, based in France, with 870 hotels and 52294 rooms (three leading brands – Campanile, Premiere Classe and Kyriad)
3 *Choice*, based in the USA, with 239 hotels and 14643 rooms (Comfort Inns)
4 *Whitbread*, based in the UK, with 266 hotels and 14000 rooms (Travel Inn)
5 *Compass*, based in the UK, with 208 hotels and 10825 rooms (Travelodge).

The hotel chain domination of the European budget sector reflects its profitability; this sector has low staffing requirements (a full-time staff of 20 can operate a 100-room hotel) and the costs of construction are modest. For example, modular construction techniques, which allow prefabricated rooms to be built and fitted out relatively cheaply, have seen UK costs per room of £40000 for new-build properties. This is a fraction of the cost of building an in-town luxury hotel, since many new-build budget hotels have located at out-of-town sites or adjacent to motorway junctions to meet the needs of car-borne traffic. Major city budget hotels have often converted older properties, with low fit-out costs per room (typically £5000 in the UK), given the basic standard of accommodation offered. This expanding segment is taking business away from existing budget providers, such as the youth hostel market, and from the mid-range hotels (three-star hotels) because prices are set competitively per room (e.g. £39–45), mirroring the North American and Australasian motel sector. The success in Europe of the budget hotel market can be related to the guarantee of quality and minimum standards through the involvement of credible consumer brands, the convenience of car parking and location (adjacent to intersections or out-of-town sites) and value for money. Whilst the budget market has experienced considerable growth in recent years, the non-serviced sector has also seen major changes.

The non-serviced sector

In the Victorian and Edwardian eras, the growth of coastal seaside resorts saw the rise of commercial accommodation such as hotels, guesthouses and boarding houses. The seaside landlady, with her rules and conventions for guests (e.g. set mealtimes and the need to vacate the room each day) heralded an age when regimentation and rigid social rules dominated. In the inter-war period, holiday homes also known as 'second homes' developed in many countries throughout the world as the new middle classes developed leisure habits.

However, in the post-war period these forms of accommodation began to be replaced by innovations in the non-serviced sector. A new genre of non-serviced accommodation developed, ranging from the caravan park to the self-catering village and, more recently, holiday parks (such as Center Parcs and Oasis in the UK). Since the 1970s Mediterranean apartments in Spain and other destinations have been developed for self-catering holidays, along with timeshare developments as a new form of limited ownership 'second home'. In France, gîte holidays have been a time-honoured tradition for urbanite French workers in Southern France, and novels such as Peter Mayle's *A Year in Provence* have portrayed the virtues of such holidays.

Specialist operators have nurtured each niche in the category of non-serviced accommodation (take, for example, Eurocamp's sited tents and caravans, Hoseasons' boating holidays on canals and waterways). It is notable that major capital investment and large corporations have also entered this market, with Center Parcs owned by Scottish and Newcastle Breweries and Oasis by the Rank Group. Each leisure company has other tourism interests; the Rank Group also operates holiday camps/villages using the original brand names (Butlins, Haven and Warner) in the UK. A further development in the non-serviced sector is the rise in the use of university campuses for holiday letting, aside from a well-developed conference business. For example, the University of Stirling in Scotland has over 3000 bedspaces that it lets to holidaymakers as well as to other educational providers such as the Open University, and its wider economic impact on the Stirling region is estimated at £12 million.

One sector that has seen substantial growth in recent years is caravans. In the UK, the Caravan Club boosted its membership in 2002 by 50 000 to a total of over 800 000, and these people use the 7000 or more campsites in the UK. An increasing number are using caravans that cost around £8000–£30 000 to purchase new. The image of caravanning as being a low status and low quality holiday market business has been adjusted by the higher standards of comfort now enjoyed in fixed and touring caravans. They are very popular among young families and the retired. Since the first caravan – the Wanderer – was built in Bristol in 1885, the image and use of caravans has developed into a substantial element of the European holiday industry. In the UK this generates around £2.5 billion as an industry through retail sales, products and holidays employing 90 000 people (many on a seasonal basis). The expansion of sites since the 1930s mainly predated planning restrictions, and the sites tend to be located near to or in coastal areas, as well in forest and valley areas. Fixed caravans (known as holiday homes) are located in the UK's 2200 holiday parks.

Registrations of motorhomes, which are favoured in the USA and Australia, have increased from 3539 in 1988 to 4798 in 2000 in the UK. This is part of the wider growth in caravans, motorhomes and holiday homes in the UK; the total stock of 710 000 in 1975 has grown to 1 054 000 units in 2000. As a result, some 63.5 million nights were spent in such accommodation in the UK in 2000, making it the most popular paid form of accommodation after VFR. Accommodation accounts for 17 per cent of holiday spend in the UK (around £1.6 billion). The majority of the nights are spent in England (45.7 million), Wales (12 million), Scotland (3.9 million) and Northern Ireland (2 million). In Europe there are approximately 4 275 000 tourism caravans in use and 920 000 motorhomes, being most popular in Germany, the Netherlands, France, Italy and Finland. Many analysts tend to overlook this sector even though it has seen a massive re-imaging and development since the 1970s, with flexibility and less need for planning cited as key reasons for using such accommodation.

Other issues for the accommodation sector

Whilst accommodation establishments provide the focus for hosting and hospitality for guests, not all accommodation premises/sites have hospitality services. These are often provided by restaurants, fast-food establishments, cafés, bars, clubs and canteens. As with consolidation in the hotel sector, similar trends can be observed in the hospitality sector with the rise of contract caterers (such as Compass Catering in the UK) and franchisees in the fast-food market (McDonald's, KFC, Burger King, Wendy's and Pizza Hut). These outlets have posed a threat to conventional food retailing. Restaurants and cafés have had to respond with innovative marketing and formula-style café's – such as Starbuck's and Costa, which emphasize quality coffee consumption and relaxation in contrast to the fast-food experience. In more innovative forms of marketing of cities, regions and districts, food consumption has been heralded as a main attraction or theme for the tourism sector. For example, regional food and wine festivals have been used to pump-prime the tourism sector, yielding business for the accommodation sector, with local products showcased and promoted. In Perth (Scotland), an annual food festival is used to promote the district's tourism industry and is supported by the regional tourism organization and by public sector funds as a means of encouraging visitor activity and to promote local products. In this way, hospitality services can be developed as the prime attraction for a region.

Table 7.3 Characteristics of tourist accommodation

- Seasonality, where periods of demand are typically buoyant in the peak season with a drop in the low season, is significant.
- Occupancy levels should be high. Demand for rooms is spread across seasons, but is more precisely accorded to weeks and days. Accommodation seeks to sell its rooms, as they are a perishable product that cannot be stored or sold at a later stage.
- Location often determines the appeal and accessibility of properties. Typically, a distance-decay principle exists in accommodation locations, with the luxury properties being located in the prime in-town sites with greatest access to attractions and facilities. Similar micro-locational factors also operate at airports, with the most accessible and prestigious properties within easy reach of the airport.
- Different grading systems exist, which may be statutory or voluntary, to denote the quality of the establishment.
- Properties can range from complex business ventures at the luxury end of the market through to basic hostel accommodation. Accommodation has a high capital asset value relative to the prices charged to customers, with yield per client relatively modest in relation to cost structures.
- Accommodation has high fixed costs to service, and owners/managers seek to optimize occupancy levels to cover costs.
- Accommodation provision is subject to numerous regulatory codes and laws in terms of the fixed plant (e.g. health and safety legislation), as well as specialist laws governing food safety where food is served. Larger premises require a wide range of skilled staff to operate key departments, such as front office, food and beverage services, housekeeping services, and concierge and portering staff. In some cases unskilled staff are employed in menial roles, but skilled staff are needed to operate and manage each department.

Environmental issues

Many accommodation providers have also had to respond to global concerns associated with environmental issues. Some hotels have embraced the principles of sustainable development, to mirror customers' concerns regarding the energy consumption of their stay. For example, recycling and reusable linen and towels are minor measures that hotels have introduced. Much bigger measures include undertaking environmental audits to assess the environmental costs of hotel activities in relation to:

- Energy consumption
- Transport
- Waste
- Purchasing
- Health
- The local environment.

For example, in 1991 the Inter-Continental Hotels Group developed an *Environmental Reference Manual* to provide staff with guidance on environmental management measures. In 1992, the International Hotels Environment Initiative developed *Environmental Management for Hotels: The Industry Guide to Best Practice*. In Scotland, the Green Tourism Business Scheme operated on behalf of VisitScotland has embraced the hotel sector and other accommodation providers, as part of VisitScotland's Quality Assurance Scheme. To join the scheme an accommodation provider must be a member of an Area Tourist Board, and it is a voluntary accreditation scheme based on an assessment by an independent environmental assessor. The scheme is based upon the implementation measures a business applies in its business. It can help raise market appeal for the business' products, and some examples cited by the scheme include making savings of up to £3000 a year in large hotels through using a compactor for waste disposal, and of £300 a year in family-run hotels by installing low energy candle bulbs in chandeliers. It is estimated that businesses can save between 10 and 20 per cent of their operating costs by using such measures (see www.greenbusiness.org.uk).

Human resource issues have also assumed a growing significance for the hotel and hospitality sector, owing to its poor image as an employer. This is partly linked to pay and rewards, but also highlights cultural issues – where images of servility are conveyed by perceptions of what hotel work involves. Problems of training, shortages of skilled senior and technical staff, and managerial concerns over service and product quality dominate the ongoing debates regarding the continued problems faced by this sector. Recruiting and retaining good staff remains a perennial problem for the global accommodation sector, in a business where high levels of staff–guest interaction not only determine the levels of satisfaction with the accommodation product, but can also impact upon images and on levels of repeat visitation.

Summary

The accommodation sector is a central element of the tourist experience of a place. It is often pre-purchased in a package holiday, and it is one of the most frequent areas of disquiet when consumer complaints are made. Yet the international growth of chain activity in the accommodation sector highlights the potential profitability in this market when the product mix, visitor mix and supply–demand interactions are well managed. Accommodation provides a containing context for the visitor, and one where tourism managerial skills need to be harnessed at two levels:

1 Within the organization, so that operational issues are addressed to maintain profitability. The accommodation manager needs a good understanding of business issues (e.g. hotel operations, finance, accounting, food and beverage issues and marketing).
2 In a customer-focused role, so that guests are satisfied with their visit and can be good ambassadors for the hotel product.

Increasingly, accommodation managers need to be aware of competitive pressures in a rapidly evolving marketplace, as reflected in the case of budget and boutique hotels. Customer attitudes and needs are also important, as in the growth of environmental awareness among hotel chains – some of which have recognized the cost savings that greater environmental responsibility can confer. One thing is certain in the accommodation sector – the consumer's tastes and needs are constantly evolving, and this is reflected in recent trends and developments. Managers and property owners unable to respond to change will find that they will be passed by as innovations, market changes and price competition redefine the business environment for accommodation providers.

Reference

Marvel, M. (2001) The German hotel sector. *Travel & Tourism Analyst*, **4**, 19–38.

Further reading

Verginis, C. and Wood, R. (eds) (1999) *Accommodation Management: Perspectives for the International Hotel Industry*. London: Thomson Learning.
Yu, L. (1999) *The International Hospitality Business: Management and Operations*. New York: Haworth Press.

Questions

1 Why does hotel accommodation play such an important role in the business travel market?

2 What are the wide range of uses for serviced accommodation?

3 How has the non-serviced accommodation sector developed since 1945? What are the main explanations for growth in certain sections of this market?

4 What is the future for boutique hotels?

8

Tour operating and travel retailing

Learning objectives

This chapter examines the way in which tourism products and services are sold to the consumer, and evaluates the role of the tour operator and the travel agent in terms of their respective roles in the supply chain. After reading it, you should be able to understand:

- how the distribution chain operates in tourism;
- how tour operators package holidays;
- the role of travel agents in retail operations;
- the use of Information Communication Technology (ICT) in travel retailing;
- the managerial skills needed to manage a travel agency and to present holiday products to consumers.

Introduction

Operating tours and retailing tourism products to consumers are key elements in the production, selling and distribution of tourism services. Organizations that do this link the supply to the source of demand. However, tourism is not like many other products or services. It is intangible, and is often an experience or product that cannot be stored, tried or tested before purchase, and so the consumer often buys as an act of faith in the hope that what the tourism industry supplies is in line with their expectations and needs. This is epitomized in the following quotation:

> The travel industry, according to everybody outside it, is run by cowboys. Despite the abundance of professionally run companies, both big and small, the perception is still that holiday firms rip off unsuspecting customers ... ABTA fights gamely to defend the industry, but it's like pushing water uphill. Even though a lot of criticism is unfair, you can't help thinking that the industry has brought a lot on itself ... But the biggest problem is that operators are often selling a product where the gap between perception and reality is huge. Mass-market holidays are often sold as a dream vacation when they are often anything but.
> (Source: www.travelmole.com, Issue 226, 17/9/2002: Comment)

One of the main ways in which the tourism industry communicates, trades and interacts with the tourist is through the distribution chain (i.e. how it is sold to the consumer) using intermediaries – agents that sell products for the industry. Historically tourism products have been retailed through travel agents, who offer products from tour operators, known as principals. In a European context, the official EU statistical agency Eurostat estimated the scale of the tour operator and travel agency sector as consisting of 36 353 businesses involved in these activities within the fifteen countries of the EU. The largest concentration of activity exists in the four main countries of Germany (9033 businesses with a €5925 million turnover per annum), Italy (6350 businesses and €6481 million turnover), France (2279 businesses and €6866 million turnover) and the UK (6050 businesses and a €14 710 million) turnover. The use of different means of acquiring travel products varies across the EU, with Belgian, Danish, German, Greek and Austrian tourists preferring to book direct with operators whereas in other countries travel agents are a preferred form of booking – usually for package holidays. The exception is Spain,

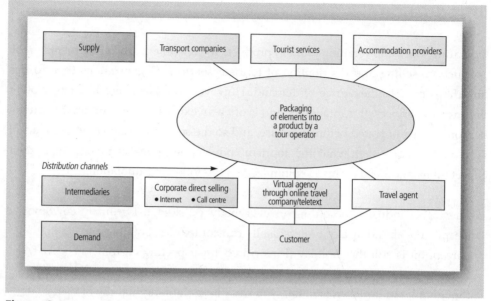

Figure 8.1 How tour operators link the elements of a holiday together to produce, assemble and distribute the package to the consumer

where travel agents are also used to book domestic travel, especially for late booking in Spain and Italy.

More recent trends, such as direct selling by companies such as Portland Holidays, began to change the relationship between the tourism sector and the public, cutting out the travel agent. In recent years this relationship has changed again with the impact of information communication technologies (ICT), such as the World Wide Web and email, creating a new a new form of distribution – a virtual distribution channel.

The basic principles of distribution are illustrated in Figure 8.1, which indicates the role of two critical bodies, the tour operator and the travel agent, which are the focus of this chapter.

The tour operator

Defining the tour operator is a far from easy process, because the role, activities and form have changed dramatically from the early days when Thomas Cook first organized a package trip by rail in the 1840s. One useful approach is to identify what tour operators do as means of establishing their characteristics and form. In simple

Table 8.1 Elements of an inclusive tour (a package)

Basic elements:
- Aircraft seat
- Accommodation at destination
- Return transfer from airport to accommodation
- Services of a tour operator representative
- Insurance

Optional add-ins:
- Car hire
- Excursions

Alternative forms:
- Multi-destination packages that visit more than one destination/country
- Optional extensions to the package to expand the itinerary
- Linear tours by coach operators

terms, tour operators will organize, package (i.e. assemble) different elements of the tourism experience (see Figure 8.1) and offer them for sale to the public, through the medium of a brochure, leaflet, advertisement or the use of ICT. A package, also known as an inclusive tour, will normally have at least two elements that are offered for sale at an inclusive sale price, and will involve a stay of more than 24 hours in overnight accommodation. These elements generally include transport, accommodation and other tourist services (see Table 8.1).

Holiday packages that include flights may be divided into two types: those that use traditional charter flights and those that use scheduled flights, where it is uneconomic for the tour operator to purchase charter flights.

The type of packages are often segmented according to:

- Mode of travel, such as a ferry or coach holiday (typified in the UK by Shearings and Wallace Arnold). It may also be based on twin-transport packages, such as fly-drive, which are very popular with inbound tourists to the USA.
- Mode of accommodation, where hotel chains become tour operators by packaging their surplus capacity to offer weekend or short breaks in business-oriented hotels, and sell rail or air transport and visits to attractions as an all-inclusive package.

- Whether they are international or domestic packages.
- Length of holiday (whether a short break, i.e. less than four nights away, or a long holiday, of more than four nights is offered).
- Distance, where the market is divided into short haul and long haul; over 90 per cent of UK outbound packages are short-haul.
- Destination type (e.g. city breaks, beach holidays, adventure holidays).

The tours may be organized by small, independent tour operators, who specialize in certain segments (e.g. youth operators such as PGL in the UK), or by larger operators (such as MyTravel Group) who have trans-European or global operations. In addition, there are over 300 tour operators who organize the itineraries, activities and logistics of inbound visitors to countries such as the UK, and who are represented by their own trade organization – the British Incoming Tour Operators Association (BITOA).

Why do tour operators exist, and why do people use them? The answer to this is seen in the way in which they operate, and the economic benefits that they provide to the customer.

Economics of tour operation: managing for profit

Tour operators have the ability to purchase services and elements of the tourism experience from other principals or suppliers at significant discounts by buying in bulk. They fulfil a major role in the tourism sector, as they allow the different tourism groups in Figure 8.1 to sell their capacity in advance – often a long time in advance, as contracts are drawn up a year prior to tourists using accommodation or services. This obviates the need for smaller, specialized businesses to market and distribute their product to a wide range of potential retailers, hoping that customers will choose their product or service over and above others. The bulk purchase agreements in large resort areas mean that in the summer season the complete capacity of hotels, self-catering and other forms of accommodation may be block booked, leaving organizations free to develop their own expertise in running or managing their businesses. Similarly, the tour operator connects with all the ancillary services to negotiate contracts and deals that will allow a holiday to be sold and be delivered on the ground.

In terms of transport, the tour operator will bulk purchase airline seats, airport transfer services from coach operators, and taxis in the destination area, as well as a whole host of local entertainment and visitor attraction opportunities to be pre-sold to clients at the booking stage or in the destination. The result is that tour operators traditionally provided a guaranteed level of sales that allows principals to fix their costs in advance and operators to achieve economies of scale by heavily discounted rates on their purchase. The outcome is a business opportunity for the tour operator, which creates a package, product or experience through assembling the elements together, advertising and selling them, and using third-party agents to deliver each element on the ground. It is obvious to see why tourist levels of dissatisfaction can occur – if there are service interruptions or breakdowns in the delivery, the seamless experience does not occur. Therefore, managing the tourist experience to ensure that the holiday experience is an enjoyable and rewarding one is a key element of customer care for tour operators.

Having calculated all the input costs and overheads, tour operators will add a profit margin and then produce a price.

The process of establishing a tour through from the initial idea to its sale and delivery to the client is shown in Figure 8.2, which uses a timeline to highlight the long timeframe involved in researching, planning, developing, administering and implementing a tour programme. Figure 8.2 also illustrates the vast range of risks that the tour operator takes in planning a holiday, including:

- Estimating the likely market
- Competing with long-established tour operators, with a recognizable brand, in a destination
- Major investment in human resources and infrastructure to set up a destination.

Given these risks, it is important for tour operators to recognize how important it is to set up and operate their business in a competitive and sustainable manner so that the investment pays a dividend over and above the costs of operation.

Tour operating business performance

Tour operating business performance is determined by the skill of the company in buying its product components (e.g. aircraft seats, accommodation and transfers) at a competitive cost, and reselling at a price that is lower than that for which a consumer could assemble the same product. One consequence is that tour operators standardize packages (which differ little between destinations) to keep prices low.

	January	April	June	September	December
Year 1			Research ▩▩▩	Research ▩▩▩▩▩	
Research and planning			• Package holiday prospects • Destination selection	• Analysis of competing choice of destination	
Year 2	Select destination ▩▩	Brochure production ▩▩ (design, development, printing contracts agreed)	Printing of brochure proofs		
Negotiation	• Hotel capacity determined • Departure dates identified • Brochure production decisions	• Negotiate with airlines for charter seats, transfers and hotel rooms	• Contracts concluded		
Administration			• Determine exchange rates • Estimate selling prices • Proofs of brochures from printers • Recruit booking staff	• Final tour prices added to brochure • Printing of brochure	
Marketing				• Brochure distributed to agents and launched • Publicize to press and media	
Year 3	January	April	May	September	December
	Peak advertising ▩▩▩▩ Recruitment and training ▩▩▩▩ of holiday reps		First tour departs ▩▩▩▩		

Figure 8.2 Planning horizon for a tour operator's summer programme (modified from Holloway, 2001)

Tour operators may keep their prices low by:

- Negotiating low prices from supplier
- Reducing profit margins
- Cutting their cost structures.

Where tour operators have become integrated tourism companies and operate aircraft, prices for air travel can be reduced by heavy usage of the transport (i.e. the number of flights it can achieve each day). This typically involves an aircraft flying from a base in the UK to another destination, bringing a planeload of passengers back

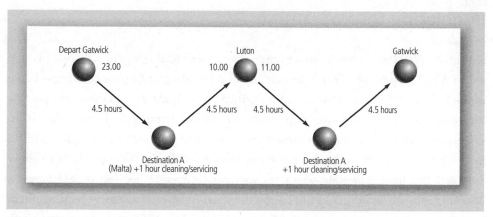

Depart Gatwick   Luton   Gatwick

23.00   10.00   11.00

4.5 hours   4.5 hours   4.5 hours   4.5 hours

Destination A   Destination A
(Malta) +1 hour cleaning/servicing   +1 hour cleaning/servicing

Figure 8.3   A hypothetical W flight pattern for a charter aircraft

to a return destination in the UK, and then flying to the same destination again and back to the original base – known as a W flight pattern (see Figure 8.3). This flight scheduling is very efficient until flight delays (e.g. by air traffic control) occur, which throw the entire schedule back and cause knock-on effects for passengers on other flights.

To achieve cost reductions, charter flights need to have high load factors in order to break even – typically 80–90 per cent, compared to 50–70 per cent for scheduled flights (depending on the cost base of the carrier). This means that any unsold seats may be unloaded on to the market at cost or less to fill the aircraft, either as seat-only sales/cheap holidays or for purchase through consolidators (airbrokers). Consolidators purchase surplus capacity and have the responsibility for marketing and selling such seats. For the airline/tour operator, additional passengers may yield extra revenue from on-board duty-free sales or by purchasing the company's holiday package, even if a loss is made on the flight itself.

For charter operators, costing their price is a complex process because 'dead legs' at the beginning and end of a season have to be incorporated. At the beginning of a season an aircraft on a 'W' pattern will fly out with tourists but return empty, and the reverse applies at the end of the season. To extend the season, operators may provide inducements such as low-cost accommodation to attract business to fill capacity. One such example is the winter flow of elderly people from Northern Europe to winter in the Mediterranean at the beginning of the season. Hotels discount their rates, hoping that guests will spend money in their premises to compensate for the discounts given.

Regulating tour operating

Since the 1960s the UK has seen a number of massive tour operator collapses, which led to ABTA (the Association of British Travel Agents) setting up its bonding scheme in the 1970s. In 1975 the government introduced a compulsory 2 per cent of operator turnover contribution by tour operators to ABTAs bonding scheme. This is to safeguard tourists from company insolvencies and being stranded overseas – as it did in the 1990s with the collapse of the International Leisure Group, which severely depleted the fund. For tour operators wishing to operate specific programmes, a licensing scheme (operated in the UK by the Civil Aviation Authority) requires them to obtain an Air Travel Organizer's Licence (ATOL). The ATOL data are very useful, as they identify some of the dimensions of this market.

The European holiday market

The European market is one of the most highly developed and complex areas of activity in the development of tour operators. It has seen a great deal of action, particularly in investment, acquisitions and mergers. This is reflected in the scale of tourism activity. In 1999, the European Travel Monitor estimated that 326 million outbound trips were taken, involving 2947 million nights away. This generated 276 billion euros. The European leisure travel market found that 53 per cent of Europeans had been away on a holiday, with a greater likelihood among the more affluent Western European regions than the Southern regions (such as the Mediterranean). Outbound travel was growing at around 5–6 per cent per annum in the late 1990s, with most European holidaymakers spending a week or more on overseas holidays. For example, of the 326 million outbound trips the main components were:

- 209 million which were for holidays, of which 173 million were long holidays and 36 million were short breaks
- 12 million which were business trips
- 55 million which were VFR/other trips.

The scale of the demand and the destinations chosen by outbound travellers are shown in Table 8.2. Germany, the UK and Scandinavia dominate outbound travel. A significant proportion of the holiday traffic travels on inclusive tours to the main destinations of: Spain, France and Germany, with Asia-Pacific the fastest growing area

Table 8.2 Top ten origin markets and outbound destinations for Europeans (source: European Travel Monitor, ©European Commission)

Origin market	Number of outbound travellers (millions)	Percentage	Outbound destination	Number of outbound travellers (millions)	Percentage
Germany	91.3	28	Spain	39.1	12
UK	45.6	14	France	35.9	11
Scandinavia	32.6	10	Germany	26.1	8
France	22.8	7	Italy	26.1	8
Italy	19.6	6	Austria	19.6	6
Netherlands	19.6	6	Asia-Pacific	16.3	5
Belgium	13.0	4	UK	16.3	5
Sweden	13.0	4	Greece	13.0	4
Switzerland	13.0	4	North America	13.0	4
Spain	9.8	3	Poland	13.0	4

of activity. These trends and travel patterns can be explored further in the case of the UK using the ATOL data.

According to Table 8.3, the total outbound market has expanded since 1999, with summer traffic growing at 5 per cent per annum with a rise to 7.6 per cent in 2000. But the winter market has stabilized or declined, which has dampened growth overall. Yet the revenue earned from ATOL-related traffic has continued to increase, although much of the expansion in low-cost carriers is not covered by ATOL. What is interesting is the steady increase in the average price of holidays from £426 in 1999 to £451 in 2002 at a time of low inflation.

Table 8.4 shows the 2001 and 2002 ATOL license figures for the top 30 operators, and illustrates the dominance of the integrated companies (i.e. TUI, MyTravel Group plc, Thomas Cook and First Choice). This reflects the high level of mergers and takeovers, and the purchase of North American operators to offer a better spread and usage of aircraft. This is not surprising, given the Monopolies and Merger Commission approval in the UK in 1997 for further mergers. This most telling impact

Table 8.3 Passengers carried and revenue earned on ATOL licences in the UK, 1999–2001 (modified from CAA, 2002, *ATOL Business*, **20**; ©CAA)

	Number of passengers	Revenue (£ billions)	Percentage change	Average price of holiday (£)
Summer season (April–September):				
1999	16.7	6.9	7.4	416
2000	17.9	7.8	13.1	437
2001	18.8	8.3	6.0	441
Winter season (October–March):				
1999/00	9.6	4.2	3.0	443
2000/01	10.4	4.7	12.2	456
2001/02	10.2	4.8	0	470
Year to March:				
2000	26.2	11.2	5.7	426
2001	28.3	12.6	12.8	444
2002	29.0	13.1	4.1	451

came in 2000, when the Department of Trade and Industry Foreign Package Holiday Order stated that travel agents owned by a tour operator controlling more than 5 per cent of the package market should identify their links with suppliers in brochures and shop interiors. These trends in integration are illustrated more clearly in Table 8.5, where the corporate groups and their companies are listed. A more detailed illustration, in the case of MyTravel Group plc is shown in Table 8.6.

A quick comparison with Figure 8.1 at the outset of the chapter shows that MyTravel Group plc controls most aspects of the model, providing a highly integrated company that rivals the TUI group in the UK as market leader. Within Germany Pressaug (which owns TUI) is the dominant player, having sold over 13 million packages in the late 1990s, and controlling 60 aircraft and four cruiseships and 3500 travel agencies. German operators also play a dominant role in Belgium, the Netherlands and Luxembourg, while mergers have provided transnational operators.

Table 8.4 Passengers carried under top 30 largest Air Travel Organizers' Licences (modified from CAA, 2002, *ATOL Business*, **20**; ©CAA)

Twelve months to March	2001	2002	Percentage change
1 TUI UK Ltd[1]	3 985 480	3 925 198	−2
2 MyTravel Group plc[2]	3 632 031	3 784 811	4
3 Thomas Cook Tour Operations Ltd[3]	2 838 715	2 834 895	0
4 First Choice Holidays & Flights Ltd	1 909 134	1 918 424	0
5 Unijet Travel Ltd	981 710	996 107	1
6 Avro plc	640 405	689 534	8
7 Direct Holidays plc	440 915	650 259	47
8 Trailfinders Ltd	629 203	606 786	−4
9 Gold Medal Travel Group plc	446 340	481 430	8
10 Cosmosair plc	452 024	457 094	1
11 Virgin Holidays Ltd	518 985	449 065	−13
12 Panorama Holiday Group Ltd[4]	354 439	425 972	20
13 Thomas Cook Retail Ltd	509 019	410 285	−19
14 Libra Holidays Ltd	276 220	336 535	22
15 Lotus International Ltd	282 046	310 595	10
16 Specialist Holidays Ltd	301 147	309 227	3
17 Accoladia Ltd[5]	394 521	308 622	−22
18 Kuoni Travel Ltd[6]	348 206	290 181	−17
19 Kosmar Villa Holidays Ltd	205 741	250 851	22
20 Travelworld Vacations Ltd	162 920	235 651	45
21 HCCT (Holidays) Ltd	170 764	219 025	28
22 Travel 2 Ltd	199 470	210 654	6
23 Golden Sun Holidays Ltd	158 024	205 462	30
24 Lunn Poly Ltd	171 499	183 324	7
25 The Really Great Holiday Company plc	151 649	179 187	18
26 Travelbag plc	168 594	169 109	0
27 Cresta Holidays Ltd	156 497	168 952	8
28 Hotelplan Ltd	146 406	168 313	15
29 Air Miles Travel Promotions Ltd	186 946	167 134	−11
30 Saga Holidays Ltd	151 413	159 447	5

[1]Since last edition, Thomson Holidays Ltd has changed its name to TUI UK Ltd
[2]Since last edition Airtours plc has changed its name to MyTravel Group plc. The 2001 figure includes passengers carried by Jetset Europe plc
[3]Since last edition JMC Holidays Ltd has changed its name to Thomas Cook Tour Operations Ltd
[4]The 2001 figure for Panorama Holiday Group Limited includes passengers carried by Mano UK Ltd
[5]Accoladia Ltd is the merged business of British Airways Holidays Ltd and Thomas Cook Holidays Ltd
[6]The 2001 figure for Kuoni Travel Ltd includes passengers carried by Travel Promotions Ltd.

Table 8.5 Passengers licensed to top ten groups and companies for the twelve months to September 2002 (Source: CAA, 2002, *ATOL Business*, **20**; ©CAA)

Group and licence holders	Passengers licensed at June 2002 for 12 months to September 2002	Percentage of total	Passengers licensed at June 2001 for 12 months to September 2001	Percentage of total	Change (%)
1 MyTravel Group Total (MyTravel Group plc; Going Places Leisure Travel Ltd; Cresta Holidays Ltd, Bridge Travel Services Ltd; Panorama Holiday Group Ltd; Direct Holidays plc; Leger Air Holidays Ltd)	5 472 740	17	5 319 273	17	3
2 TUI Group Total (TUI UK Ltd; Lunn Poly Ltd; Something Special Holidays Ltd; Port Philip Group Ltd; Specialist Holidays Ltd; Callers-Pegasus Travel Service Ltd; The Magic Travel Group (Holidays) Ltd; Simply Travel Ltd; Bass Travel Ltd; Manchester Flights Ltd; The Original Travel House Ltd)	4 889 588	15	4 725 732	15	3
3 First Choice Holidays Group Total (First Choice Holidays & Flights Ltd; SkiBound Ltd; Schools Abroad Ltd; Globesavers Ltd; Unijet Travel Ltd; Hayes and Jarvis (Travel) Ltd; Bakers World Travel Ltd; Bakers Dolphin Group Tours Ltd; FlexiGroup Travel Ltd; Sunsail Ltd; Meon Travel Ltd; Sunquest Holidays (UK) Ltd; Crown Travel Ltd; Exodus Travels Ltd*; Citalia Holidays Ltd)	3 566 990	11	3 270 324	10	9
4 Thomas Cook Group Total (Thomas Cook Retail Ltd; Thomas Cook Tour Operations Ltd; Style Holidays Ltd)	3 289 093	10	3 504 043	11	(6)
5 Cosmos Group Total (Cosmosair plc; Cosmos Coach Tours Ltd; Avro plc; Archers Tours Ltd; The Charter Warehouse Ltd; Monarch Air Travel Ltd; Pullman Holidays (UK) Ltd; Urbanweb Ltd)	1 273 082	4	1 298 072	4	(2)
6 Trailfinders Limited	655 678	2	691 591	2	(5)

Table 8.5 (Continued)

Group and licence holders	Passengers licensed at June 2002 for 12 months to September 2002	Percentage of total	Passengers licensed at June 2001 for 12 months to September 2001	Percentage of total	Change (%)
7 Gold Medal Travel Group plc	620 000	2	560 000	2	11
8 Libra Holidays Group Total (Libra Holidays Ltd, Sky Holidays Ltd)	457 450	1	455 116	1	1
9 Accoladia Group Total (Thomas Cook Holidays Ltd; Time Off Ltd; A.A.H. (1997) Ltd; Accoladia Ltd)	421 895	1	443 254	1	(5)
10 Virgin Travel Group Total (Virgin Holidays Ltd; Virgin Atlantic Consol Ltd; Worldwide Travel of East Anglia Ltd)	367 137	1	599 050	2	(39)
Total passengers licensed to the top ten groups and companies	21 013 653	64	20 867 055	65	1
Total passengers licensed to the top four groups	17 218 411	53	16 819 372	53	2
Passengers licensed to all ATOL holders	32 208 246	100	31 619 165	100	2

*New ATOLs in the group since last edition, not included in the 2001 figures for the group.

How do these companies compete for business?

In June 2002, MyTravel initiated a price war over its 2003 summer holiday brochure by claiming that prices in its first edition brochure (i.e. 306 of them) were lower than those of its rivals (Thomson and First Choice). This is a very characteristic response from the tour operator sector, especially the larger companies, as they:

● Seek to expand market share, market dominance and market position in consumers' minds
● Seek to convert domestic holiday taking to outbound travel by conveying images of low-cost overseas holidays
● Drive down the cost from suppliers, and re-package the product so that no-frills options (i.e. no airport transfers, no holiday representative or in-flight meals) are provided in the market, appealing to the lower end of the consumer spectrum.

Table 8.6 The MyTravel Group Plc tourism companies (source: based on and modified from MyTravel Group plc Annual Report 2002)

Region	Distribution	Tour operating	Airlines	Other services
UK/Ireland	Going Places, Late Escapes, Travelworld, Holidayline, Go Direct, MyTravel	Airtours Holidays, Aspro, Direct Holidays, Panorama, Jetset, Manos, Bridge, Cresta, Tradewinds, Eurosites, Leger	Mr Travel, Airways UK	Globales, Hotetur*, Aquasol*, Sun Cruises, My Travel Money, Tenerife Sol*
Northern Europe	Ving, Spies, Tjaereborg, MyTravel Reiswinkels, MyTravel, Gullivers, Saga, Skibby	Ving, Always, Spies, Saga, Tjaereborg, Sunair, Trivsel, Globetrotter, Marysol, Travel Trend, Gate Eleven, Bridge, Skibby	MyTravel Airways, Northern Europe	Sunwing, Sun Cruises, Aquasol*
Germany, Austria, Switzerland	Allkauf, 5 vor Flug, Flugboerse, Club Valtur, LAL Sprachreisen, Fti Touristik, Megatours	Fti Touristik, Air Maritime, Seereisen, Club Valtur, LAL Sprachreisen		LAL Sprachreisen, Hotetur*
North America	Travel 800, Auto Europe, Diplomat Tours, FlyCheap, Lexington Services, Cruises Inc., WorldChoice Travel, Cruises Only, CruiseOne, Lifestyle Vacation, Incentives, MyTravel, DFW Tours, Landry and Kling, ABC Corporate Services, Cruise Masters, Resort Escapes, Kemwel, Fly Cheap Vacations, Drive Away Holidays†, Canadian Retail Division	Sunquest, AHI, Suntrips, Alba Tours, Vacation Express, The Holiday Network, Ship 'N' Shore, Alumni Holidays	Sun Trips USA‡, Skyservice‡	Blue Bay *, Sun Cruises

*Joint ventures and part owned; †based in Australia; ‡strategic alliance.

- Attempt to drive out the smaller operators in the long term, to consolidate market dominance further.

In the latter case, such predatory behaviour has not affected dramatic change. For example, following the collapse of the ILG group other companies were formed to fill market niches as business opportunities emerged. In addition, more complex economic forces such as currency fluctuations and changing consumer behaviour have led to companies re-thinking how they operate and compete. For example, most tour operators issue holiday brochures in multiple editions. In the 1970s and 1980s consumers were encouraged to book early for discounts and price guarantees. In the late 1980s the traditional booking period was in late December (after Xmas), when much of the tour operators advertising on television and in the press was mobilized to stimulate consumer activity. This provided operators with client funds from early in the year until bills were due from suppliers, often as late as September, providing up to nine months' interest. With increased availability of ICT, in the 1990s clients recognized the value of late bookings, as supply normally exceeded demand for outbound inclusive tours from the UK and many European countries.

Tour operators of course suffered reduced income, losing the interest previously gained by investing clients' income. This led Thomson to introduce fluid pricing in 1996 – larger discounts were offered for early booking, and there were price increases in later brochure re-issues. This cost MyTravel an estimated £5 million in 2002, for a second edition re-launch for its summer 2003 programme. Other strategies have been to develop new markets, such as long-haul holidays (which now exceed 20 per cent of outbound UK business). Seat-only sales on charter flights have also seen some operators expand their business. More common strategies are to seek new, cheaper destinations, as the European industry did in the 1980s with Greece and then Turkey, as sun, sea and sand packages remain popular. With over 50 per cent of UK holidaymakers choosing packages when travelling overseas abroad at some time, it is evident that operators have had to switch attention from the first-time, novice travellers of the 1950s and 1960s to repeat travellers. The result has been product diversification, increasing the range of possible holiday options to include:

- City breaks and additional short breaks, as secondary airports open up new potential destinations (e.g. Iceland Air's service to Reykjavik)
- Long-haul and adventure travel, such as ecotourism and nature holidays
- Greater flexibility and tailoring of the packages to the client's needs.

Increased competition is likely to lead to further consolidation in the marketplace among tour operators, especially as virtual tour operators sell more capacity on the World Wide Web as part of a growing e-business strategy. However, the tour-operating sector is not simply characterized by constant growth and profitability among the businesses working within it. For example, 23 ATOL licensed companies went bankrupt in 2001 and £3 million in compensation was awarded to travellers. In the period 1985–2001, £159 million was paid to 190 000 people following the failure of 300 ATOL operators, and this was paid from the ATOL bond retained from tour operators. The CAA pays the shortfalls in compensation from the bond from its Air Travel Trust Fund, which in 2002 was reportedly, £8 million in debt – highlighting the need for a re-evaluation of the role of bonds and the tour operators' solvency.

Much of the activity in further tour operator integration and consolidation is likely to focus upon:

- Expansion via acquisitions
- Integration of air and hotel businesses
- Further widening of distribution channels
- Widening of geographical coverage of markets and tour operators merging/ entering into strategic alliances
- The impact of the euro, which may allow operators to buy capacity cheaper from weaker currencies and thus provide lower-priced holidays
- A gradual levelling of package holiday prices across the EU
- Greater cost controls
- New business strategies towards products (e.g. a focus on core business versus diversification)
- A greater alignment of business towards changing consumer behaviour.

Consumer trends affecting the future of tour operating

For the travel retailer, one of the principal changes observed over the last decade is the diversification away from the preoccupation with mass tourism as the market (i.e. the demand) for tourism products has changed. Industry commentators such as Auliana Poon have described this as a transition within tourism retailing from 'old' to 'new' forms of tourism.

'Old' tourism was best described as driven by consumers who were inexperienced travellers and were satisfied with homogenous tourism products (i.e. similar mass-produced packages) that were predictable, based on sun-based destinations (such as the Mediterranean resorts), and provided escape from the routine of everyday life – especially work. In contrast, 'new' tourism is characterized by more experienced travellers who have a growing environmental concern about the impact of their holidays on the places they visit. 'New' tourists also seek more individualized products that are less predictable, are full of surprise and discovery, and provide a memorable experience rather than simply a repetition of last year's beach holiday. 'New' tourists are looking for something different – a holiday that is an extension of their life rather than a simple escape. In contrast to 'old' tourism, which was very much supply driven (as is shown by the history of mass package holidays), 'new' tourists are seeking to define what they want. Whilst 'old' and 'new' tourism coexist, 'new' tourism offers the industry many growth opportunities, given that tourism businesses can react to the demand for increased flexibility through greater use of ICT.

Demographic factors

One very visible factor that is present in most western countries is the ageing population, with a corresponding increase in the number of people aged 50 to 70 years. Many of these people now enjoy a higher standard of health care, are less sedentary, and have experience of travel. This has led to the rise of the senior (or 'grey') market. It is notable that this section of the travelling population tends to spend up to 30 per cent more on travel than other age groups, given their greater disposable income. Many people in this age group are described by marketers as 'empty nesters' – i.e. their children have grown up and left home – who are taking early retirement, are mortgage-free, and have more free time – which means they have a greater propensity to travel. A new term now being used is 'Third Age Travellers'. Senior travellers comprise approximately 30 per cent of the population in France, 28 per cent in Canada, 27 per cent in Japan, 27 per cent in the USA and 20 per cent in Germany. In many countries, tour operators, visitor attractions and accommodation providers have experienced continued increases in the mature market. Indeed, some direct-selling tour operators specialize in this market – e.g. Saga in the UK and Elderhost in the USA. In the USA alone, forecasts suggest that the mature market (those aged 55–74 years) will increase from around 40 million in 2001 to 74 million in 2031. The implications for tourism managers are that not only will the mature market continue to grow, but also they will potentially be tourists for much longer owing to greater longevity. As this age group is generally less technologically able, such travellers are more prepared to rely on travel agents as holiday organizers.

Consumer issues in tour operating

With the growing expansion of the holiday market, reduced costs and the continued growth in the package market (of the 11 million UK trips to Spain in 2001, 4.5 million were package holidays), a number of trends have become evident. The growing variety of destinations has meant that competition between countries has intensified cost pressures. For example, in 2002 Spain experienced a 20 per cent drop in visitor arrivals up to July – the first decline since growth began in the 1960s – which was attributed to cost and to wider issues such as image, and cheaper alternatives such as Morocco, Bulgaria, Croatia, Turkey and Tunisia. At the same time, the reduction in prices and the increase in numbers of travellers taking budget holidays have been accompanied by growing numbers of complaints. According to ABTA, in 2000 almost 5 per cent of the UK's 20 million package tourists were fairly or very dissatisfied with their holidays. This reflects an increasing dissatisfaction with the quality of accommodation, concern over the perceived safety standards of overseas chartered aircraft, the addition of surcharges, and failure to provide what was advertised. Yet the number of actual official complaints made to ABTA is relatively low, at around 19 000 in 1999, although legal recourse and litigation is growing in popularity as a small minority seek legal redress.

In the EU, the 1993 EC Directive on Package Travel has brought a greater degree of precision into the roles and responsibilities of the tour operator. The DTI's response to the Directive led to the following measures were implemented:

- All tours must be licensed
- There must be a greater degree of honesty in holiday brochure description
- Travel agents have a responsibility for the information contained in brochures they stock and for ensuring adequate advice to clients on health, passport and visa requirements, and insurance needs.

In addition, the tour operator is liable for losses resulting from misleading information or where suppliers do not provide the services paid for and contracted. For example, in 2002, 600 holidaymakers in the UK were joining a class action against major tour operators after falling sick with salmonella during their holiday in Torremelinos, with a further 700 considering joining in the action. This is the largest class action to date against the UK tourism industry, and demonstrates the increasing litigation by holidaymakers, as the EC Directive encourages a greater duty of care for visitors. In fact, some law firms now specialize in travel litigation. This also highlights the greater onus on the tour operator in terms of the provision of support staff in the destination, namely holiday representatives (reps).

Holiday representatives

These are useful trouble-shooters who can often remedy problems or complaints *in situ*, although it is a very demanding job being a public relations agent for the company, often on call 24 hours a day, 7 days a week in the peak season. They typically have a number of roles, including:

- Meeting and greeting incoming and departing passengers at the airport to ensure that airport transfers drop the right passengers at the correct accommodation
- Handling a wide range of destination-specific inquiries and requests, and providing social events
- Publicizing company-endorsed tours and services, for which a commission is received by the company
- Dealing with special requests (e.g. arrangements for disabled guests) and acting as go-betweens for the tourist and hotel, local police, medical services and other agencies when required.

Typical assistance includes locating lost-baggage, calling doctors when clients get ill (or, rarely, die) and, in extreme cases, liaising with police and authorities as well as re-booking flights when emergencies arise. At airports, when flight delays occur holiday reps may have to deal with disgruntled passengers and offer company refreshment vouchers. They also address complaints about the accommodation. A recognizable human face in a strange environment, with the ability to offer tourists local advice regarding health and safety issues, and of paramount importance in ensuring the well-being of tourists. Whilst the role, character and ability of the holiday rep are critical in undertaking this key client liaison role, training and excellent interpersonal skills (i.e. an empathy with people and their problems) is essential as the tourist experience and client satisfaction are critical in gaining repeat business. In the UK Thomson Holidays has an enviable reputation for generating repeat business, as is shown by its in-flight customer satisfaction scores.

Marketing and planning the holiday: the holiday brochure

For the tour operator the holiday brochure is its most powerful marketing tool, since the intangible nature of tourism makes it imperative that potential customers can read about what they may want to purchase. It is not uncommon for up to 50 per cent of tour operators' marketing budgets to be spent on brochure production. This has to be viewed in the wider context of planning, organizing and implementing tour programme. In the hypothetical example shown in Figure 8.2, the tour operator has to undertake a series of stages of work including:

● Research and planning
● Negotiation with suppliers
● Administration
● Marketing.

With the exception of the initial research stage, the holiday brochure is an integral part of the planning and marketing process. Figure 8.2 highlights the timeframe involved in brochure production and distribution, and many holiday brochures cost as much as £1 a copy with print runs of millions for large operators such as MyTravel. Yet brochures have high wastage rates, Green Flag International indicated that of 120 million printed in the UK in the late 1990s, nearly 48 million were never used (Holloway, 2001). It is estimated that this adds up to £20 to the average cost of a package holiday.

The form of holiday brochure currently in vogue among tour operators has evolved from its recent predecessor, introduced in 1953 by Thomas Cook. This adopted a similar format to that of women's magazines, reflecting the important role of women as holiday decision-makers. The 1960s saw holiday brochures become glossier and packed with information, and its role has gradually changed to its present one of a holiday catalogue.

Holiday brochures distributed through travel agents seek to achieve a number of objectives:

1 To obtain sales

2 To provide information to assist in decision-making by purchasers in relation to the destination, product offerings, holiday timing (summer/winter), price, ancillary services

3 To afford cost-effective distribution for the tour operator, by having an attractive cover and being prominently racked in travel agents

4 To provide an effective tool to allow agents to sell holidays with detailed products/ booking codes

5 To allow a contract to be agreed between the tour operator and customer, providing information on procedures for changing the booking, complaints, refunds, the details of the product purchased, the client details, and the insurance premium paid.

In the case of direct mail, the brochure seeks to fill some of the objectives above but places more emphasis on the customer deciding on the product offering. It also seeks to appeal to the market segment at which it is targeted, and needs to be easy to use.

A brochure will typically comprise the elements embodied in Figure 8.4, and involves a complex process of design including:

- Identifying the market audience and product
- Utilizing an appropriate company brand
- Designing a mock-up, using a computer, with illustrations and professional photographs of the hotels, destinations, product offerings and services
- Using a desk-top publishing system to help with brochure layout and design
- Producing a proof, which is checked in order to identify and rectify inaccuracies prior to printing.

With increasing consumer regulation in most countries, holiday brochures need to get potential tourists to book a holiday, advertising dreams or images of their ideal holiday, but must also be honest and accurate. Above all they must not make false statements, as this can lead to prosecution under Trade Descriptions legislation in many countries. This is now a more stringent requirement since the EU Directive on Package Travel has made it easier for tourists to litigate against tour operators, who are responsible for the supplier abroad. The need for honesty is endorsed by ABTA in its Code of Conduct for Tour Operators, making the brochure a legal document to which complainants may refer in future claims for compensation.

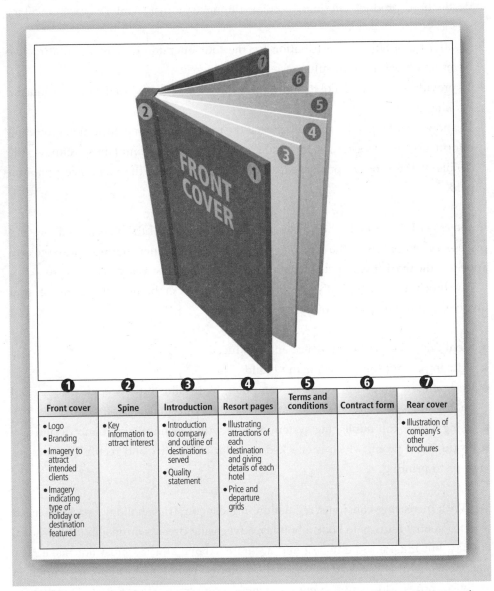

①	②	③	④	⑤	⑥	⑦
Front cover	**Spine**	**Introduction**	**Resort pages**	**Terms and conditions**	**Contract form**	**Rear cover**
• Logo • Branding • Imagery to attract intended clients • Imagery indicating type of holiday or destination featured	• Key information to attract interest	• Introduction to company and outline of destinations served • Quality statement	• Illustrating attractions of each destination and giving details of each hotel • Price and departure grids			• Illustration of company's other brochures

Figure 8.4   Structure of inclusive holiday brochures (© Eric Laws, 1997; redrawn and reproduced with the author's permission)

To meet the obligations of a tour operator's licence, Holloway (2001: 253–54) identifies the following information as being required in a holiday brochure:

- The name of the firm responsible for the inclusive tour (IT)
- The means of transport used, including, in the case of air transport, the name of the carrier(s), the type and class of aircraft used, and whether scheduled or charter aircraft are operated
- Full details of destinations, itinerary and times of travel
- The duration of each tour (number of days/nights)
- A full description of the location and type of accommodation provided, including any meals
- Whether services or a representative are available abroad
- A clear indication of the price for each tour, including any taxes
- Exact details of special arrangements (e.g. if there is a games room in the hotel, whether this is available at all times and whether any charges are made for the use of this equipment)
- Full conditions of booking, including details of cancellation conditions
- Details of any insurance coverage (clients should have the right to choose their own insurance, providing this offers equivalent coverage)
- Details of documentation required for travel to the destinations featured, and any health hazards or inoculations recommended.

Brochures are normally distributed to travel agents, and operators need to build in wastage costs – operators typically have to distribute twenty brochures to gain one booking, although this may be for a group of two to three people. Many agents operate different policies on distribution, including:

- Having brochures available on display with open access
- Displaying one copy only, with consumers needing to ask for a copy.

Even these policies are not a guarantee of success, and operators can classify agents in terms of performance, with high-performing agents selling 100-plus holidays a year while low performers sell less than 5 a year. This appears to hold true for mass package holidays, although the significance of the number of sales obviously depends upon the value of each holiday.

Once the client has decided to make a booking, the tour operator will retail the product through a Computer Reservation System (CRS) or direct to the public (although Internet bookings are on the increase for packages). Over 80 per cent of package bookings are still made via travel agents, who use call centres for manual bookings, or the company CRS system, where a tour operator link is made direct to the travel agent.

As consolidation continues to affect the European holiday market, it is no surprise to find that 80 per cent of inclusive tours are sold through 20 per cent of agents, with commissions paid to agents, plus an override (1–5 per cent), in addition to the basic 10 per cent for high performance. However, in 1998 Thomson cut commissions to a three-tier system, ranging from 7–12 per cent. The evolution of the World Wide Web is likely to put additional pressure on selling through conventional means.

Travel agents

Distributing tourism products seeks to entice customers into purchasing an offering, linking the supply with demand. In technical terms, the distribution is a system that links the various tourism organizations (e.g. operators and agents) together with the objective of describing, explaining and confirming the travel arrangements to the consumer. Explaining the tourism offering to the consumer requires retailers (and operators through their brochures) to recognize, identify and incorporate the following elements of tourism:

● Tourism is intangible, meaning that it is a speculative investment and an expensive purchase where the product is generally conveyed to the customer via a brochure.
● Tourism is perishable, and so can only be sold for the period it is available (it cannot be stored); this highlights the importance of last minute bookings to sell surplus capacity.
● Tourism is dynamic, meaning that it is forever in a state of flux, especially as a product where prices can rise and fall.
● Tourism is heterogeneous, meaning that it is not a standardized product that is produced and delivered in a homogenous manner. It varies, and interactions can enhance or adversely affect it, since it is dependent upon people and many other unknown factors.
● Tourism is inseparable, meaning that in the consumers' mind it is purchased and consumed as an overall experience; hence communicating what is being offered, its

value and scope is important. Since the consumer is transported to the product, it is an unusual form of distribution, where there is a need for timely information on all of the elements as outlined in the brochure.

The traditional package holiday has normally been retailed through agents who have recognized and sold holidays with the above factors in mind. Travel agents remain a key intermediary in the distribution chain, and are characterized by many features.

The evolution of travel agents

When Thomas Cook organized the first tour package by rail from Leicester to Loughborough, the age of travel retailing emerged. Travel agents were mainly independent agents, with the exception of the growing Thomas Cook outlets. Their primary role was in acting as agents selling travel tickets for rail, sea and land-based services, as well as accommodation. Even in the inter-war years travel agents retained this brokerage role, receiving a commission on each sale. The 1940s saw the emergence of air-based travel, but agents had not yet reached a mass market and their travel products were still oriented towards a small section of the international travelling public. The 1960s heralded the greatest changes in travel agencies, with commissions, licensing and greater airline–agency relations, particularly in the sale of group travel. By developing increased levels of information, service and specialized products, agents began to become more involved in the tour operation side of travel by organizing tours and selling cruises from block allocations. During the 1970s these changes saw many travel agents expand with the growth of package travel, basing their business on volume sales. In the 1980s and 1990s many agencies entered into tour operating, with growing numbers of mergers, acquisitions and consolidation. Grouping into formal alliances or consortiums enabled agencies to seek greater commissions, using increased levels of technology to assist in distribution, while the high street saw large chains emerge. Many of these changes are documented in Table 8.7, which highlights the relationship between the trading environment in the post-war period and the style of travel retailing that evolved to characterize each era.

Characteristics of travel agents

In the UK, there are around 7000 travel agency branches and 1890 travel agents. These are affiliated to their industry body ABTA, the Association of British Travel Agents.

Table 8.7 Changes in travel retailing (©Eric Laws, 1997: 122; reproduced with the author's permission)

Period	Trading environment	Type of travel retailing
1950s	Limited demand for holidays or other travel Reconstruction of war damaged city centres	Full-service travel specialists located in major urban and business centres Limited competition
1960s	Gradual increase in city centre travel retailers with the development of demand for leisure travel	Coach and other domestic holidays sold by small coach companies and through newsagents
1970s	Rapid expansion in demand for holidays	Successful retailers expand the number of outlets – proliferation of high street retailers
1980s	Development of out-of-town shopping malls and large-scale town centres Many high streets suffer from shop closures and temporary tenants	First computerized reservations system for inclusive holidays Larger travel agency chains grow by acquiring smaller 'miniples', consolidating ownership and putting pressure on independents Development of specialized holiday shops, and decline of full-service travel agencies
1990s	Increasing financial pressure on travel retailers, increasing rate of acquisition and mergers	Increasingly selective racking policies Technological developments enable customers to create their own holiday packages by booking direct from home

The structure of travel agents has changed over the last twenty years as consolidation has led to greater pressure on independent agents and less choice for the consumer as multiples dominate the retailing of products. Travel agents as businesses carry no stock, act on behalf of the tour operators, and so have little financial risk and do not purchase products themselves. They receive a commission for each sale and, as agents, do not become part of the contract of sale, which is between the tour operator and the customer.

Their role is based upon the products they sell, and they can be either generalist agencies selling a wide variety of products or specialist agencies selling a certain type of product. Some agencies, by virtue of their geographical location or appeal, can be low-cost, low-revenue businesses (i.e. selling low-cost packages), whilst others located in more prosperous areas can be high volume, selling high-value cruises and similar products. Other specialist agents, like Austravel, only sell long-haul travel and so are niche agents.

High-street agents do not specialize in business and corporate travel, although the market for specialist agents is worth over £10.5 billion a year in the UK. One very controversial area of debate in travel agents is the process of racking, where they emphasize/display certain products (perhaps their own company's in the case of integrated businesses) to favour them because of the promise of higher commissions. This perceived favouritism, often described as directional selling, has led the independent travel agents in the UK to launch a Campaign for Real Travel Agents to counter this by claiming that their 300 members will offer impartial, objective advice, and promote smaller, independent operator's products.

Ultimately, the travel agency is a physical location that seeks to offer a convenient place to purchase travel products. It provides a source of information as well as a point of sale, via booking agents. The perceived expert product knowledge (often gained from training and educational trips to the destinations on sale) is seen as offering a competitive advantage, although this is becoming more problematic given the low salaries, young age profile of travel agents, and growing product range now available to consumers.

It is evident that travel agents cannot offer a limitless product range, since research indicates that beyond a certain point, trying to offer too many products erodes agency profitability. As a result, specializing in a limited range of tour operators allows agents to develop product knowledge, tailor the products to the markets they serve, and recognize their own limitations. With the endless possibilities and knowledge available on the World Wide Web, it is apparent that agents are having to compete by developing specialist knowledge and advice to maintain their competitive edge.

The organization of travel agents

Whilst the businesses in this sector can be broadly split into the independent travel agencies and multiples that are owned and operated by tour operators and other tourism concerns, two basic principles characterize success in each: high quality customer service and management.

In terms of management, cost control, the employment of highly motivated staff and building upon a customer base through word of mouth are critical. The independent agencies, which are manager-owned and typically employ less than five staff, contrast with the larger chain agencies, which are located in prominent high street or shopping mall locations and have high passer-by traffic.

Travel agents typically deal with a diverse range of tasks, including:

- Making reservations
- Planning itineraries (including complex round-the-world travel)
- Calculating fares and charges
- Producing tickets
- Advising clients on destinations, resorts, airline companies and a wide range of travel products
- Communicating with clients verbally and in writing
- Maintaining accurate records on reservations
- Ensuring racks are well stocked, or supplies are kept in-house
- Acting as intermediaries when customer complaints occur.

Not only do travel agency staff need technical skills in reading timetables, calculating fares and an ability to write tickets, they also need good interpersonal skills for closing a sale and the ability to use technology (e.g. CRS). With the growing complexity of airfares and the conditions attached to them, staff must also be able to explain these technicalities in simple, plain English. An agency manager will have to be able to manage a group of staff and will also be engaged in the financial management of accounts and cash flow, the invoicing of clients, and in controlling expenditure in running the business.

Above all, it is critical to ensure that all staff provide a high level of customer service so as to make sales and build the client base. To do this:

- Customers must be greeted warmly, typically with a smile
- Staff must have high standards of dress, appearance and personal grooming, as customers are influenced by first impressions; their personal posture, manner and body language are also important, as being alert, attentive and willing to empathize and match client needs with available products is key

- Staff must be polite and able to express themselves clearly, while always maintaining eye contact
- Telephones must be answered promptly and courteously.

Selling a product

In selling a product, a set sequence is usually adhered to as in Figure 8.5. This illustrates the consumer psychology of a holiday purchase, where an agent needs gradually to understand what the consumer wants, how to fulfil that demand and the type of interaction sought. In particular, a process of search, evaluation and re-evaluation goes on in the agency or on a return visit after the client has taken away brochures to assess the product offerings.

It is clear that the agent has a critical role to play, not necessarily in providing definitive answers, but in guiding the consumer and presenting options (and

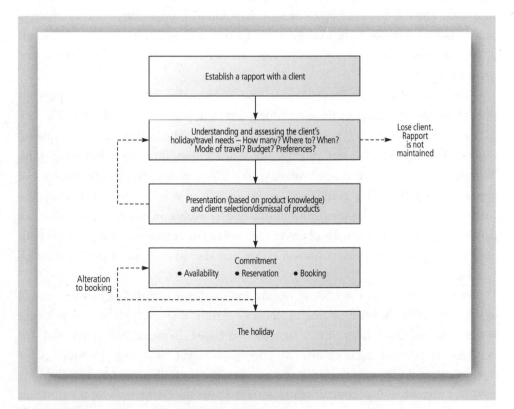

Figure 8.5 The travel agent–client purchase process

managing their dismissal) until a suitable product is located. This is evidently a time-intensive undertaking, and thus it is apparent why many consumers will go through this process using technology such as the World Wide Web as well as in using a travel agency.

Business travel

The process is somewhat different in the case of business travel, where agencies offer this service. Here the client will be looking for time savings, be less price-sensitive and be very demanding of time and service. Bookings are often made at short notice, sometimes outside of office hours, and special help with visas and other documents may be sought. Those agents who offer a business travel service have found this to be a highly competitive market, where tied arrangements with companies exist. In return for agreements on a certain volume of business, travel agencies may provide a set rate of discount or charge a set management fee for all the business it handles for a company. The latter is proving to be very popular with large companies in order to reduce business travel costs. Contracts can be constructed in a number of ways, but above all seem to provide companies with greater cost controls on corporate travel and reduce costs.

The Guild of Business Travel Agents, with 40 members, represents 75–80 per cent of all business air travel in the UK, which is dominated by the multiples. The key players are American Express, Carlson Wagonlit and The Travel Company, among others. These multiples can provide substantial discounts by purchasing bulk volumes of air travel. Where companies employ travel managers instead of agents, the agency is excluded. This is reflected in the growth of a UK professional body, the Institute of Travel Management, and illustrates the evolution of a new trend that has further impacts on the business of travel agents. For larger businesses direct links with airlines in global alliances are possible, so that discounted travel occurs through volume rebates.

A recent study in the USA by Topaz International found that business travel agents provided the best source of cheaper airline fares – typically 19 per cent lower than Internet fares. Even so, Internet-based Expedia has purchased US business travel management firm Metropolitan Travel as a new IT solution for business travel. However, many of the surveys that identify trends in online retailing are somewhat contradictory, as certain travel companies report different fortunes in the online booking market. For example, in September 2002 GetThere, which provides online travel reservation systems, reported that US travel sites in the year ending July 2002 saw US$701 million of sales, with a significant growth in corporate travel.

Travel agents and information communication technology (ICT)

In terms of information technology, there are a number of key elements that impact upon travel agents. Such technology is designed to allow agents to access the principal's supply of products and services, process bookings, and manage corporate performance, but a number of issues are evident:

- CRS' are expensive to maintain for small and medium agencies, so Internet booking may be more cost effective
- CRS' do not necessarily provide agents with improved business levels unless used to their full
- There is inherent bias in CRS', with airlines having to pay fees to have a presence
- New forms of technology are overtaking CRS' in some market segments, such as the development of electronic agencies (e-travel agencies), the World Wide Web, direct selling operators (known as business-to-consumer), and a number of operators selling discounted travel (e.g. Expedia, e-bookers and the low cost airlines online).

E-ticketing has emerged as a new force in global travel markets, and this has the potential to bypass the travel agent and the airlines GDS'. In Europe Lufthansa led the way by introducing this mode of ticketless travel with ETIX, a concept now adopted by many airlines worldwide. It enables passengers with hand luggage only to bypass long check-in counters at airports, and allows consumers to buy tickets over the Internet without paper coupons. Many of the budget airlines, such as GO in the UK, have also adopted paperless e-tickets to reduce administrative costs. Sabre, the GDS company, estimated that almost 70 per cent of its North-American tickets are now issued this way, while in the UK Galileo, the European GDS, reported that in 2001 e-ticketing represented 10 per cent of its business. Yet Galileo also estimate that 70 per cent of UK e-tickets are still issued through travel agents. One response from travel agents, according to Sabre, is a desire for tools that will allow them to access the growing demand for online travel.

A number of travel agencies have been acquiring online booking engines, as forecasts by Internet analysts Jupiter indicate that the value of European online travel for 2006 will be 20 billion euros. In 2001–2002 the use of online travel sites grew by 75 per cent in some European countries, with the UK having the largest market – over 6 million people used such sites in January 2002 alone, followed by 5.1 million in Germany and 2.6 million in France.

In more general terms, e-commerce, promoted by the use of the Internet to establish web sites and direct contact with consumers, has generated online sales for many travel firms that have bypassed the travel agency sector. In Europe, Forrester Research estimated in 2002 that Internet penetration was 46 per cent – only 4 per cent higher than in 2001 – indicating that the increasing number of Internet users is slowing down as a major trend. At the same time the use of the Internet for online shopping is increasing, representing 17 per cent of all European use of the Internet. Although many of the online travel companies have reported slow progress towards the stage of reaching a break-even point in their business, in 2002 the Internet-based company ebookers reported a loss of £7 million compared to a loss of £12 million in 2001 and was expecting to go into profit in 2003. To cut costs it is relocating some of its activities to Dublin, and it has a back office centre in Delhi. This model has also led Delta, the US airline, to relocate call-centre work to India and the Philippines. In October 2002 Delta indicated that using the overseas call centres to handle US domestic travel inquiries would reduce costs by US$15 million. Clearly this may be the beginning of a process whereby ICT allows closer management of overheads by the use of the cheapest location for routine administrative functions. This is a very good illustration of the impact of globalization on the tourism industry and the way in which supply issues are handled. Given these trends, what is the future for retail travel agents?

The future of travel retailing

Chapter 4 examined the theme of disintermediation, which is the ability of tourism suppliers to use ICT to communicate direct with consumers in their home. Travel agents did have a virtual monopoly on the distribution of travel services, especially inclusive tours, but their future is unclear. To eliminate the travel agent completely would require new ICT that could provide all the social, economic and psychological benefits that agencies provide for the travelling public. They will still remain the

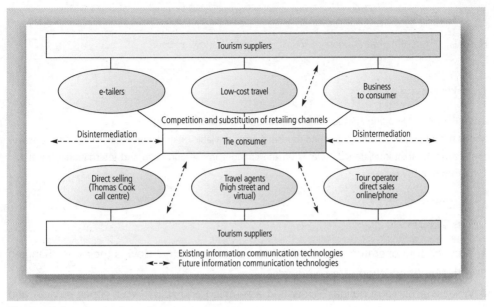

Figure 8.6   The future of travel retailing

public face of the tourism industry in a retail setting as the range of ICT makes travel a more complex process since more options and products are available. Far from disintermediation leading to the demise of travel agencies (see Figure 8.6), it may in fact lead to a resurgence in the holiday market as technology proves to offer too much choice, is time consuming for travellers, and does not provide the psychological benefit of a brochure as a purchase.

Figure 8.6 shows the existing and future forms of travel retailing, spurred on by the evolution of ICT in the re-selling of travel products. Travel agents will constantly have to evaluate how to protect commission levels and how to reach a highly fragmented travel market as ICT establishes more niches. The pressure on independent travel agents in a highly competitive environment is set to continue, but new promotional tools and modes of distribution will see agents use marketing and advertising to maintain a presence. For example, re-branding holidays under agency names such as Thomas Cook's initiative, offering no deposit bookings and home-based sales visits, and using technology to retain face-to-face contact whilst improving ease of sales will certainly be trends for the future.

Reference

Holloway, J. C. (2001) *The Business of Tourism*, 6th edn. Harlow: Pearson.

Further reading

Laws, E. (1997) *Managing Package Holidays*. London: Thomson Learning.

Mintel has a number of useful travel and tourism reports available on its website (www.mintel.com) as well as regular market intelligence updates on the changes in the European and international travel and tourism industry business.

Questions

1 Why are tour operators important in the tourism industry? How is their role changing with the introduction of e-commerce?

2 What is a package holiday? How is it assembled and sold? What other services and support do tour operators offer their clients?

3 How do travel agents operate? What are their main roles and responsibilities? What types of services and products do they sell?

4 What is the future of the travel agent as a retailer? Will their traditional high-street location be maintained?

Chapter **9**

Visitor attractions

Jo Connell and Stephen J. Page

Learning objectives

This chapter examines visitor attractions both as a key element of the tourist's activities and as a business activity that has specific management requirements. After reading it you should be able to understand:

- how to define and classify visitor attractions;
- the marketing and management issues associated with visitor attraction development;
- the importance of managing the visitor experience at attractions, and future issues for tourism managers.

Introduction

Along with transport and accommodation, attractions form one of the central components of tourism, providing a vital element in the visitors' enjoyment and experience. They are important both at destinations and *en route* to a destination. One of the major problems in identifying attractions is that whilst they are patronized by tourists, more importantly, the scale and volume of visits are dominated by leisure and day trippers as well as local residents. In this respect the market for attractions is large, and it forms a vital part of the infrastructure of the destination area. Attractions provide a nucleus for visitor spending in destinations when they are linked to regeneration strategies. Thus a successful attraction industry is vital for a healthy tourism sector so that visitors have sufficient scope to undertake visits and spending during their stay. Attractions are also a major draw for many visits, especially in areas where the regeneration strategies by public and private sector agencies have underpinned future tourism development around such a hub of activity, as shown in the case study in Box 9.1.

Box 9.1   Case study: visitor attractions and tourism development – using heritage to regenerate an area

In the UK there has been a massive investment in visitor attractions using funding available through the Millennium Commission and lottery funds. In many urban and rural locations bids for these funds have been made to justify the use of tourism as a means to achieve urban regeneration objectives – a process that seeks to reverse economic and social decline after local employment has collapsed. This is shown in Figure 9.1, and highlights how many local authorities and public–private partnerships have sought to develop tourism as a means of harnessing new economic life in an area. Since the 1980s there have been both success stories and abject failures, where local authorities have invested upwards of £10 million in one attraction as the pivotal hub for tourism development in an area to stimulate economic development through tourism. However, in the new millennium there has been an over-investment in many areas, saturating the tourism market; this was shown in the case of the Millennium Dome, which cost £850 million and down-scaled visitor numbers from 12 million to 7 million for its year of operation. This mirrors the experience of many other attractions, which undergo a short-term interest-led boom after opening followed

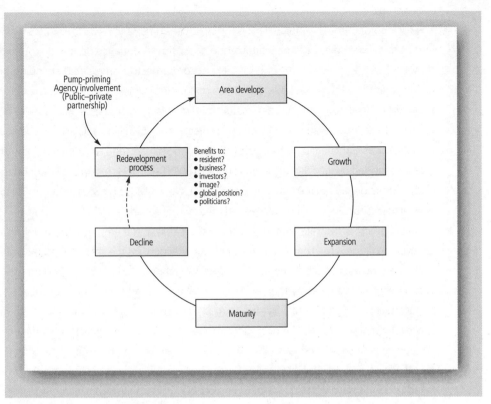

Figure 9.1 Tourism and regeneration

by a decline by the second or third year after opening. In some cases bankruptcy and closure has resulted, and increased competition has meant that many attractions now have to invest in new exhibits and elements in the attraction to reinvent themselves (i.e. invest in innovation) in order both to compete and to remain attractive to the visiting public.

In Scotland, two new projects with substantial public–private sector funding are:

1 The £87 million Millennium Link project in Falkirk (funded by Scottish Enterprise, British Waterways, the European Regional Development Fund (ERDF) and other agencies), which opened in May 2002, and a 68-mile restoration of the Forth & Clyde and Forth Canals, which has re-linked Glasgow and Edinburgh by canal.
2 The Lomond Shores development at Balloch, which is discussed below.

The focal point of the Millennium Link is the large canal lift, which is 35 m long, 35 m wide and 35 m deep, and has a large visitor centre and visitor experience designed around the new engineering project. This project seeks to promote tourism-related spending and development in a town that has experienced major employment loss, and is now seeking to reposition itself using tourism as a means towards reaching that goal. In October 2002, to extend the regenerative effect of the project, a £1.5 million television advertising campaign was launched to promote the attraction to Scotland and Northern England. This was part-funded by the ERDF Structural Fund (£700 000) to seek to expand visitor interest in the attraction (some 300 000 visited the site between May and September 2002) and encourage visitors to visit other places and the town of Falkirk.

The other large-scale that has acted as a catalyst for employment growth and economic change is the Lomond Shores project in Balloch, on the shores of Loch Lomond in the newly created Loch Lomond and Trossachs National Park. This £60 million project was developed as a gateway to the new National Park on a former gravel extraction site and derelict and polluted factory site, with 90 000 square feet of retail and restaurant space. The main feature is the new Kincairn Tower, with viewing galleries, eating areas, an audiovisual show and a tourist information centre nearby (see Plate 9.1). The development has learnt many of the lessons of similar projects in the 1990s (which failed), and has developed leisure shopping on the site to pull visitors in and retain them at the site while encouraging them to spend time and money on a wide range of goods. The gateway visitor centre, operated by the Argyll, Islands, Loch Lomond, Stirling and Trossachs Area Tourist Board, was also opened at a cost of over £2 million to develop a greater understanding of the National Park and visitor potential of the area. A linking sightseeing bus tour also extends the potential experience from Balloch to Luss, a small historic village that has been restored and is a television filming location on Loch Lomond.

The Lomond Shores development illustrates the regeneration process at work in Figure 9.1, since the first well-known visitor to Loch Lomond was the diarist Samuel Johnson in 1773. This began the interest and development cycle for tourism in the area. The Loch's literary associations with the poetry of Walter Scott and the novel *Rob Roy* promoted the area to a larger international audience. This was followed by further development of the Romantic Movement in the nineteenth century with visits from other literary figures such as Wordsworth, Keats, Dickens and Eliot, further extending its growth potential and appeal. These initial interests were followed by substantial

Plate 9.1   Lomond shores development: visitor centre and retail outlets

development and increased access to the area after 1850. In that year, Thomas Cook organized the first group tour to the area, and the increase in Glasgow steamship visits began (see Chapter 2). These developments created both a day trip and a staying market, stimulating a local tourism industry. In the post-war period, this market gradually withered as car and coach tours bypassed Balloch and visitors passed through, although a substantial recreational boating base developed in the town as many vessels were moored on the shores of the Loch. Therefore, the creation of Lomond Shores is an attempt to recreate a destination for visitors on Loch Lomond, to encourage visitors to journey there as a destination in its own right or to stop *en route* at other areas in the National Park. The visitor attraction therefore combines the historical associations of the area and a modern-day visitor experience, building on the heritage and global interest in Loch Lomond and romantic images. The tourism development process has been stimulated, with assistance from public sector agencies, to capitalize on the strengths and appeal of the area, publicized by the creation of the new National Park, using Loch Lomond as the gateway to the area.

The case study in Box 9.1 indicates the significance of visitor attractions to the tourism sector, but also highlights one of the main problems: defining what comprises an attraction. In the Lomond Shores example, both the literary associations with the area and the Loch (i.e. the landscape and environment) have been defined as attractions in their own right due to their popularization by the Romantic movement, while at the same time, facilities physically constructed to attract and service visitor needs are also an attraction. This raises issues of defining and classifying attractions.

Defining visitor attractions

The lack of conceptualization of visitor attractions means that there has been much debate regarding their definition. The debate leads to the identification of three main categories of attractions:

1 *Natural or man-made attractions*, e.g. a National Park (natural) or the Tower of London (man-made). Natural attractions may be further divided into those that are managed and those that are left in a natural state.

2 Attractions that can be *nodal or linear in character* (Holloway, 2001). A nodal attraction may be a capital city, such as London, Rome or Paris, and a focus of the visit and an attraction in its own right – a feature that many tourism organizations utilize in place-marketing strategies, where icons that reflect the place's image are employed (e.g. the Eiffel Tower as representing Paris). The linear resource most used by visitors is the coastal resort. Linear resorts act as attractions in their own right, as is illustrated by the example of Blackpool's Illuminations. The Illuminations attract visitors to the town in the shoulder season, with £2 million spent on promoting this attraction, which can be dated back to its first use in 1912. A number of other UK seaside resorts (such as Southend) also used similar schemes very successfully in the 1950s and 1960s.

3 *Sites as locations, permanent attractions* and *special events*, which are temporary, short term, and may be either constructed or natural (see www.festivals.com for a global listing of festivals and events by category, and a listing of the most unusual sporting events). The America's Cup, held in New Zealand in 1999/2000 and 2002/2003, is an example of an event that rotates to the country of the winning yacht and has a major impact on the local and national economy of the host destination.

Table 9.1 The visitor attraction sector in the UK (source: modified from English Tourism Council, Northern Ireland Tourist Board, VisitScotland and Wales Tourist Board, 2001)

Category of attraction	Percentage of attractions*	Visits to attractions (%)*
Cathedrals and churches	4	5
Country parks	5	16
Farms	3	2
Gardens	6	4
Historic houses and castles	21	11
Other historic properties	6	2
Leisure and theme parks	2	11
Museums and galleries	29	23
Steam railways	2	1
Visitor centres	7	5
Wildlife attractions and zoos	5	6
Workplaces	5	2
Other	6	11
Total	100	100

*These do not sum to 100 on the original

Many classifications and categorizations of attractions exist. One of the most interesting and commonly used classifications is that developed by the English Tourism Council. This is outlined in Table 9.1, and identifies the following attraction types:

- Cathedrals and churches
- Country parks
- Farms
- Gardens
- Historic houses and castles
- Other historic properties
- Leisure and theme parks
- Museums and galleries
- Steam railways
- Visitor centres
- Wildlife attractions and zoos.

Table 9.2 Street markets as visitor attractions: London (developed from Transport for London and London Underground, 2002, *Real London Markets*. London: Transport for London)

Name of market	Speciality
Central London	
Covent Garden	Converted market with antiques and crafts, and a piazza with performers and buskers
The Courtyard, St Martin in the Fields	Ceramics and arts
Gray's Antique Market	Antiques
Berwick Street, Soho	Food
Charing Cross Collectors' Fair	Flea market
London Silver Vaults	Silverware
North London	
Camden Market, Camden Lock	Clothing and all types of items
Camden Passage	Antiques
Chapel Market, Islington	Various items
Nags Head, Seven Sisters	Various
Wembley	Clothing and various
Hampstead Community Market	Various
East London	
Petticoat Lane, Aldgate	Clothing
Spitalfields	Books, fabrics, clothing and food
Billingsgate Fish Market, Isle of Dogs	Fish
Columbia Road Flower Market	Flowers
Brick Lane (The Lane)	Various
Leadenhall Market	Food
Smithfield Market	Wholesale meat
Ridley Road Market (Dalston Market)	Various
Leather Lane	Various
Roman Road Market	Various
Whitechapel Market	Various
Hackney Stadium	Second-hand goods
Walthamstow Market	Various
Kingsland Waste (The Waste)	Second-hand goods

Table 9.2 (*Continued*)

Name of market	Speciality
South London	
Borough Market	Food
Bermondsey Market	Antiques
East Street Market	Caribbean foods
Brixton Market	Handicrafts
Greenwich Market	Clothing and jewellery
Gabriel's Wharf	Clothing
New Covent Garden Flower Market	Flowers
Merton Abbey Mills Market	Weekend market
Riverside Market	Second-hand books
West London	
Bayswater Road Market	Art laid out on pavement
Chelsea Antiques Market	Antiques
Portobello Market	Antiques, clothing and jewellery
Shepherd's Bush Market	Local ethnic market (Afro-Caribbean dimension)
London Farmers' Markets, Notting Hill Gate	Fresh food from farms within 100 miles of London
North End Road, Fulham	Food
Church Street and Bell Street	Various

Various – a variety of food, clothing and mixed retailing.

Note: There are other famous London markets, some smaller and not easily accessible by London Underground, and some that are a major draw for leisure shopping, such as Romford market in Essex. The above table is illustrative rather than all-inclusive.

Yet even this diversity of attraction types, which comprises a simple classification, is not without its problems owing to the diverse range of sites and sights that exist. For example, in London there are 42 markets (see Table 9.2) that act as a distinct element of the local environment for residents and visitors, and are promoted by Transport for London and London Underground as a *Real London Markets* brand in their marketing. This is reflected in their promotion due to the atmosphere, images and character they add to the locality, which visitors wish to experience:

... there are so many reasons to visit, whether it's to savour the sights and smells of the Caribbean, the lure of finding that bargain antique or second-hand book or hearing the wit of a Cockney trader. When you've worked up a hunger from browsing and haggling, stop for a while to eat at an authentic pie and mash shop or snack on a falafel or crepe, before continuing your journey from stall to stall.
(Transport for London and London Underground, 2002: 2)

Furthermore, Pearce (1991: 46) presented an operational definition of a tourist attraction that encompasses a broad spectrum of locations:

A tourist attraction is a named site with a specific human or natural feature which is the focus of visitor and management attention.

Pearce's more conceptual definition is preferable to the specific but widely cited definition offered by the English Tourism Council *et al.* (2001), which states that a tourist attraction is:

A permanently established excursion destination, a primary purpose of which is to allow public access for entertainment, interest or education; rather than being principally a retail outlet or venue for sporting, theatrical or film performances. It must be open to the public, without prior booking, for published periods each year, and should be capable of attracting tourists or day visitors as well as local residents. In addition, the attraction must be a single business, under a single management ... and must be receiving revenue directly from visitors.

This is very complex and specific in terms of operational guidelines. Walsh-Heron and Stevens (1990: 2) confirm and expand the function of a visitor attraction, defined as a place, venue or focus of activity, stating that elements of a visitor attraction are that it:

● Sets out to attract visitors (day visitors from resident and tourist population) and is managed accordingly
● Provides a pleasurable experience and an enjoyable way for customers to spend their leisure time
● Is developed to achieve this goal

- Is managed as an attraction, providing satisfaction to customers
- Provides an appropriate level of facilities and services to meet and cater to the demands, needs and interests of its visitors
- May or may not charge an admission fee.

A point of particular interest from Walsh-Heron and Stevens's (1990) list is that an attraction has a psychological element, as it provides a pleasurable experience and satisfaction to visitors, as well as an appropriate level of services. Walsh-Heron and Stevens (1990: 3) define further criteria relating to management that assist in defining whether an enterprise is an attraction. The criteria are that:

> ... management must: perceive and recognize itself to be a tourist attraction; promote and market the attraction publicly; provide on-site management and staffing; and be recognized as a 'tourist attraction' by the visitor.

Visitor attractions in the UK: recent trends

Within the UK (which is not representative of all countries), there has been noticeable decline in visitor numbers to attractions during the period 1999–2000. In 2001, the visitor numbers fell a further 2 per cent as a direct result of the terrorist activities of 11 September 2001 and the effects of Foot and Mouth on the UK tourism industry. Nevertheless, the scale and volume of visits to UK attractions can be illustrated by reference to Tables 9.3 and 9.4. In the case of visits to paid admission attractions (Table 9.3), the top ten attractions all exceeded a million visits a year; in the case of visits to free-admission attractions (Table 9.4), the number of visits rose from 1 million to 6.5 million at the leading attraction. Some of the decline in the visitor market can be attributed to what analysts describe as a 'softening' of the market, as new developments come on stream to compete with the existing attractions for visitors. This has been accentuated by oversupply in the UK, particularly with the investment of government revenue in attraction-related projects. For example, in the five-year period from 1997 to 2002, over £700 million millennium funding alone was directed towards visitor attractions in the UK. This crowding in the market has led to traditional attractions having to compete with other sectors of the leisure industry – notable retail and entertainment. Much of the competition comes from out-of-town retail developments with entertainment complexes, which vie for leisure spending.

Table 9.3 Top paid-admission attractions in the UK, 2001 (modified and developed from English Tourism Council, 2002)

Attraction	Visitor numbers
London Eye	3 850 000
Tower of London	2 019 210
Eden Project	1 700 000
Natural History Museum, London	1,696,176
Legoland	1 632 000
Victoria and Albert Museum	1 446 344
Science Museum, London	1 352 649
Flamingo Land Theme Park and Zoo	1 322 000
Windermere Lake Cruises	1 241 918
Canterbury Cathedral	1 151 099

Table 9.4 Top free-admission attractions in the UK, 2001 (modified and developed from English Tourism Council (2002)

Attraction	Visitor numbers
Blackpool Pleasure Beach	6 500 000
National Gallery	4 918 985
British Museum	4 800 000
Tate Modern	3 551 885
Pleasureland Theme Park	2 100 000
Clacton Pier	1 750 000
York Minster	1 600 000
Pleasure Beach, Great Yarmouth	1 500 000
National Portrait Gallery	1 269 819
Poole Pottery	1 063 499

In the USA, a different situation exists in the case of its high-profile theme park industry. For example, the decline in theme park attendance in 2002 has had a significant impact on the attraction sector, since theme parks such as Walt Disney and Universal Studio have a heavy dependence upon long-distance travellers staying in their accommodation at the Florida and California sites. In the late 1990s, Disney invested in its theme park and resort division, but external factors such as security concerns and the lack of consumer confidence in leisure spending has dampened the market prospects. Attendance figures in late 2002 dropped by between 6 and 10 per cent, reflecting structural downturns in the US economy. The theme park sector has seen widespread price-cutting measures to attempt to fill surplus capacity with additional day visitors, since operating income has dropped. In addition, there has been a drop in international bookings, and data from the Los Angeles Economic Development Corporation show a drop from 72 per cent to 64 per cent in Disneyland hotel occupancy rates. One immediate response by Disney was 800 cost-containment measures (such as reduced opening hours) at Disney to reduce expenditure, although competition with other theme parks (there are fourteen other theme parks within easy reach of Disneyland) has posed major threats. This is against an investment of US$1.4 billion in the California adventure in 2001. In contrast, attendance figures at Tokyo Disneyland remained buoyant, with 17.7 million visits in 2001.

It is notable that there is a lack of data regarding the visitor attraction sector internationally upon which to gauge comparisons of each sector and the performance in each country. This is complicated by the different ways in which countries classify attractions, although Table 9.5 does provide a number of European comparisons that highlight the diversity of the attraction classifications by country and the problems of drawing parallels in each country. It also highlights the broad product basis of many European visitor attractions.

Visitor attractions: product considerations

Visitor attractions offer both products and experiences. One of the main management issues for operators of visitor attractions is matching the product to the benefits sought by the consumer. Kotler's (1994) view is that products consist of three levels (Figure 9.2), and Swarbrooke (2002) argued that this may be adapted to a visitor attraction setting. The core product is the central component, and comprises the main benefits that will be identified by the visitor as a motivation for visiting. The second dimension of a product is the tangible aspect, which visitors can purchase, and the

Table 9.5 Profile of visitor attractions in selected European countries

Ireland

- There are 397 visitor attractions. Of the fee-paying attractions, 70 per cent have been developed since 1984 with 40 per cent (104) developed since 1989 illustrating the recent investment in this sector.
- Much of the stimulus for development has been linked to government planning and EU structural funding from the Operational Programme for Tourism. This was designed to increase the competitive position of the tourism sector, and many of the projects have a strong cultural and historical linkage. Estimated IR£450 million of investment in tourist facilities, training and marketing in Ireland during 1989–1993.
- Attractions are dominated by historic houses and castles, which account for 35 per cent of visits, with 80 per cent of attractions providing craft and bookshop facilities. A further 60 per cent have food and beverage facilities. Up to 65 per cent of visitors to Ireland felt an attraction was a major reason for visiting the country.
- The volume of visitor demand was 8.6 million visits in 1995, with 37 per cent of visitors from Europe, 14 per cent from North America and 12 per cent UK. In terms of visitor numbers, 5 per cent of attractions had 150 000 visitors or more, 4 per cent had 100 000–150 000, 10 per cent had 50 000–100 000, 31 per cent had 10 000–50 000, and 50 per cent had up to 10 000.

Denmark

- There are 100 attractions with over 50 000 visitors a year, and approximately 200 attractions with over 20 000 visitors a year. Those with less than 20 000 visitors are not recorded, but the Danish Tourist Board estimates that there are about 500 such attractions. In total, the visitor attraction sector receives 30 million visits a year.
- The visitor attractions comprise 75 art museums, 181 museums of cultural history, 58 zoos and wildlife parks, 41 amusement parks, 8 aqua domes, 118 golf courses, and 81 castles and country houses. A further 1800 sq km of conservation areas exist, and there are 3 000 km of cycle routes.
- The majority of attractions are funded by the public sector (80 per cent of the top 100 attractions are funded in this way). Entrance charges apply to the majority of museums, but these are low.
- The government-funded Labour Market Holiday Foundation has funded 30 new attractions, based on a 12.5 per cent tax on employee wages. It has equated to £44 million investment.

Table 9.5 (*Continued*)

Denmark (*Continued*)
- In the last five years a 10–12 per cent growth in attraction visitor numbers has occurred at the 50 largest attractions. The majority of visitation is from the domestic market, which accounts for 85–90 per cent of visitors.

The Netherlands
- There are around 1150 attractions listed in the national museums guide along with other visitor attractions. It has the world's greatest concentration of museums per square metre (Amsterdam alone has 62).
- Museums are operated by the public sector and not-for-profit bodies, with 400 museums being part of the Nederlandse Museumvereniging (museums association).
- Many attractions are highly specialized, and most open all year round. All attractions charge for admission.
- The top seven attractions have over a million visitors a year. A 140 per cent increase in visitation occurred 1985–1995, according to the Dutch NTO, driven by new attractions, events and some growth at existing sites. Much of this is urban-based, especially in the Randstadt (the ringed city urban agglomeration that includes Amsterdam, Rotterdam and the Hague).

France
- There are 40 000 monuments, 4000 prestigious sites and 4000 museums in France.
- As the world's leading international tourism destination the diversity of attractions is not surprising, with a strong linkage to national and regional tourism development plans. The operation of public–private sector partnerships underpins development, together with state funding for high-risk innovative projects. The majority of successful projects (there are few exceptions) are state-funded, given the linkage to economic regeneration.
- French visitor attractions are classified in the state tourism agency guide as caves and caverns, villages of character, gardens, zoos and botanical gardens, rural museums, river tourism and railway tourism. This is certainly different to the many other classifications.
- The market for visitor attractions is largely domestic, since 80 per cent of French people take their holidays within France.

Source: Compiled from Scottish Enterprise and Highlands and Islands Enterprise (2001) *New Horizons: International Benchmarking and Best Practice for Visitor Attractions*. Glasgow: Scottish Enterprise. www.scotexchange.com (Know Your Market section).

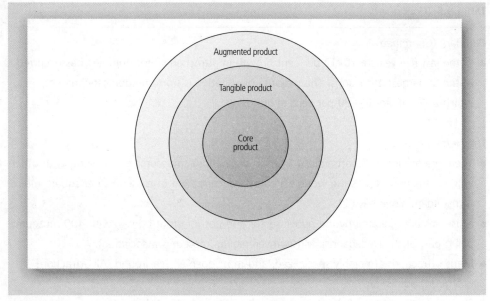

Figure 9.2 The three levels of a product (modified from Kotler, 1994)

third is the augmented aspect, which includes the additional services a visitor receives.

Gunn (1988) also conceptualized a tourist attraction by considering the product basis. He identified three zones in relation to the spatial layout of an attraction: the nucleus contains the core attraction; the zone of closure contains the ancillary services associated with the attraction, such as shops, car-park and tea-room; and the inviolate belt is an area that protects the core product from the commercialized areas of the zone of closure (Figure 9.3).

A more detailed model of attractions as products can be applied, as Figure 9.4 shows in the case of a historic garden such as Kew Gardens in London, with three levels of a garden visitor attraction product.

Attractions as a leisure product

Jansen-Verbeke (1986) developed a framework with which to analyse tourism visits to places, and this can be applied to attractions as places. Still focusing on the idea of a garden as a visitor attraction, the application of the leisure product idea is useful in helping to understand how the structure and presentation of visitor attractions can be

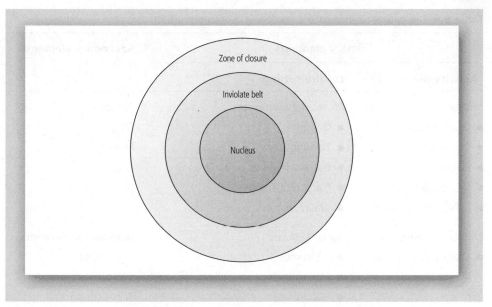

Figure 9.3   Gunn's model of a tourist attraction (based on Gunn, 1972). © 1972, *Tourism Planning*, C. Gunn. Reproduced by permission of Taylor & Francis, Inc., http://www.routledge-ny.com

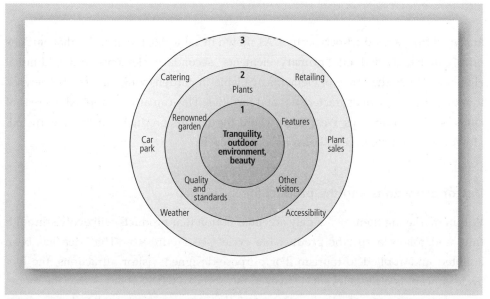

Figure 9.4   A garden as a visitor attraction product. © Jo Connell, reproduced with permission from the author

Table 9.6 The categorization of the garden as a leisure product

Primary elements		Secondary elements
Activity place	**Leisure setting**	
Leisure interest facilities:	*Physical characteristics:*	Tea room
● Guided walks	● Design	Shop
● Exhibitions	● Planting	Nursery
● Routes	● Garden features	Seats
● Self-guided trails	● Garden buildings	
● Events and festivals	● Water features	
Physical features:	*Social features:*	**Additional elements:**
● Children's play area	● Welcome	Accessibility
	● Friendliness	Car parking
	● Helpfulness	Sign-posting
	● Ability to answer questions	Foreign language leaflets
	● Ambience	Information
	● Health and safety considerations	Plant labels

© Jo Connell, reproduced with permission from the author

analysed from a product perspective. As shown in Table 9.6, the facilities that gardens offer can be divided into primary elements, secondary elements and additional elements. While the range of elements available in gardens will vary, the framework identifies the scope of characteristics and facilities. This can also be applied to areas of cities, such as London's West End, where the leisure product can be constructed. However, such products will also have a life cycle.

Visitor attractions and the product life cycle

Within marketing there is a widely accepted notion that products will evolve through time and follow a specific product life cycle (see Figure 9.5). This idea has been adapted and applied to tourism. For purpose-designed visitor attractions, the life-cycle concept is quite relevant. However, Swarbrooke (2002) believes that the model is of less relevance for those attractions that were not originally designed for visitation, because it is difficult to identify the start of the introduction phase.

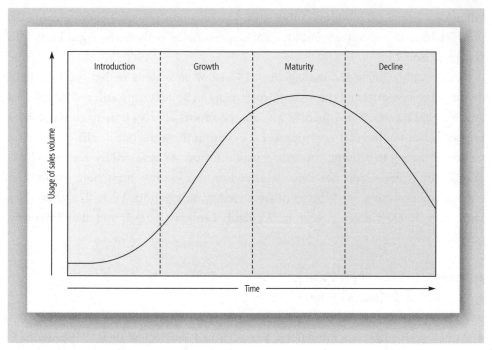

Figure 9.5   The product life cycle (source: Swarbrooke, 2002: 51). Reproduced from Swarbrooke, J., *The Development and Management of Visitor Attractions*. Reprinted by permission of Elsevier

Motivations for opening may be based on the need to derive extra revenue for maintenance or conservation work, and the attraction market is not viewed as the core business. For example, the 'core business' of the National Trust in England and Wales is conservation and education – not running visitor attractions – but it needs visitors to fund its work. However, it is still pertinent for operators of such attractions to be aware of market changes as it becomes more difficult to attract visitors in a market characterized by oversupply.

In a Scottish context, research by Lennon (2001) noted that those attractions that had invested and diversified their product base through retail areas (e.g. merchandizing) were receiving additional benefits in relation to visitor spending at attractions. In Scotland, the average dwell time at an attraction was 2 hours and 42 minutes; this comprised 80 minutes at the attraction, 20 minutes retailing, 28 minutes at a catering outlet, and 34 minutes at other elements of the operation. Therefore, by developing a broader product base attractions were seeking to expand the dwell time at their site.

The significance of attractions is illustrated by the fact that almost 6000 full-time staff were employed in Scottish visitor attractions, with almost 3000 unpaid volunteers helping at trusts and other sites. The economic potential of broadening the product base in expanding employment opportunities is therefore significant – as shown in Box 9.1.

A crucial factor in the management of visitor attractions is that the long-term quality of the product and the visitor experience can be adversely affected by external and internal threats. Consequently, a strategy to focus efforts on managing potential impacts from the internal environment (i.e. within the attraction itself) can assist a visitor attraction in striving towards a viable future. As research by Lennon (2001) found, the competition for leisure spending across the attraction, retail and entertainment sectors has led to a distinct visitor attraction life cycle. For attractions with over 10 000 visitors a year in Scotland, Lennon (2001) found that following opening:

- In years 1–2, growth is apparent
- In year 3, a decline in visitation occurs
- At paid attractions, there is a greater stability in visitor numbers up to year 4
- At non-paid admission attractions, years 3 and 4 see decline then stabilization.

A range of attraction operators and their operational activities and business strategies explain this pattern. For example, there were those who saw an attraction-decline cycle, where a decline set in after two years of growth following initial opening. The decline was a reflection of the failure to innovate and expand their visitor offering, and was typical of many public sector operations in Scotland. In contrast, a series of Year 4 revivalists also existed, where a major refurbishment or reinvestment occurred to nurture the visitor interest again. A further attraction type was also discerned in terms of the constant innovators, where attractions constantly re-invested, seeking to diversify their product offering, upgrade their facilities and pump-prime the attraction lifecycle model by intervening through ongoing reinvestment.

Stevens (1991: 110) notes that attractions provide 'a consumer product which is based upon the unique experience and immediate point of sale consumption' – the implication of which is the need to emphasize visitor care. A clear understanding of the nature of the visitor experience and how it can be enhanced to achieve high levels of visitor satisfaction, according to the type of attraction and types of visitor, are variables over which owners/managers can have a greater degree of control in relation to the management of the attraction.

Visitor attractions: the visitor experience

Swarbrooke (2002) comments that the visitor attraction product is now usually viewed as an experience. The visitor experience is a somewhat nebulous concept, because the tourist experience is a complex amalgam of factors that shape the tourist's feelings and attitude towards his or her visit. The visitor experience is likely to be different for each individual visitor, as it is formed through a series of value judgements based on emotional and physical responses to a site that result in satisfaction/dissatisfaction with one or more components of the site.

Key influences on the visitor experience

Yale (1997) states that the success of a tourist attraction lies in four critical areas: accessibility; opening hours; on-site amenities (such as parking, visitor centre, signs and labels, shops, guides, refreshments, toilets, litter bins, seating and disabled provision); and off-site amenities (such as signposting, local accommodation and local services). Swarbrooke (2002) identified four key factors that influence the success of attractions: the organization and its resources; the product; the market; and the management of the attraction (see Table 9.7), while an intangible quality or 'magic' is necessary as well as highly professional management and innovative concepts.

Swarbrooke (2002) asserts that a range of elements affect the visitor experience on site beyond the core focus of the attraction. These elements include: the tangible elements of the product, such as retail outlets, cafés, toilet facilities and site cleanliness; the service delivery elements, including the appearance, attitudes, behaviour and competence of staff; the expectation, behaviour and attitude of the visitor; and a number of factors that are largely outside the control of either the attraction or visitor, such as climatic conditions and the mix of people using the attraction at one time. The visitor experience is the product of the combination and interrelationship of these factors, and will be different for each individual visitor.

Design issues, such as sign-posting and seating provision, present an image of the attraction to the visitor, and this may or may not be favourable. The contemporary management of an attraction can influence the visitor experience through design and resource issues. Coupled with the physical management of the site is the importance of customer care – acknowledging the crucial relationship between the staff, the service and the needs of the visitor. Each element is important, and a lack of care – whether it is in the signage, car parking, quality of catering or cleanliness of the toilets – can destroy the overall visitor experience.

Table 9.7 Factors influencing the success of tourist attractions (after Swarbrooke, 2002)

The organisation and its resources	Experience of developing and managing attractions	Financial resources	Marketing – see the management of the attraction				
The product	Novel approach or new idea	Location	On-site attraction	High quality environment	Good customer service	Visitor facilities	Value for money
The market	Growth markets – targeting markets that are likely to expand						
The management of the attraction	Experienced professional managers	Adequate attention to market research	Realizing that marketing is not just about brochures and adverts	Long-term strategic view	Accepting importance of word-of-mouth	Planned marketing strategy with proper financing	Staff training

Visitor responses to perceived levels of crowding and impacts on the resource base materialize in terms of dissatisfaction with the site – or, indeed, displacement of the visitor. In reality, the tourist experience at an attraction is likely to be affected by a wide range of factors, some of which are inevitably not linked with the destination *per se* but hinge on the mood and personal circumstances of the visitor. The experience is also likely to be affected by visitors' expectations and preconceived ideas prior to a visit, as well as their cultural origin and prior socialization. The recognition of these individual factors reflects previous consumer product experience or expectations, which influence the satisfaction/dissatisfaction process. It is impossible to control all the factors relating to the visit experience, and it should be recognized that while a visitor may be completely satisfied with the core product and the tangible service elements, an external factor (such as the weather or transport infrastructure) might spoil the experience. In addition, it is worth noting that success in attraction development, particularly within a defined tourism region, can be dependent upon how the various sites are linked together through marketing and information to visitors. Providing brochures and advertising that create an awareness of visitation opportunities can help to spread visitors across a region, especially when there is major investment at an attraction to stimulate tourism development, such as with the Falkirk Wheel.

Creating clusters of attractions can be successful, as with the regeneration of Stirling's Old Town through the public and private sector Stirling Initiative over the last twenty years. This used the drawcard of Stirling Castle, and a number of other attractions were created to fit a heritage theme (e.g. the Old Town Jail, Argyll's Lodgings, and the newly opened Tolbooth Art Centre). Other large-scale projects, such as the Falkirk Wheel, certainly assist in spreading the visitor impact away from the 80 per cent currently focused on the Stirling region as well creating a new destination.

Managing the visitor experience: potential and prospects

Two main factors underpin the need to ensure that customers are satisfied with their visit experience. First, visitor satisfaction can encourage regular and repeat visitation, which is more cost-effective than seeking new visitors. Secondly, positive word-of-mouth recommendations work in the favour of attraction operators since minimal marketing input is required to attract new visitors. Word-of-mouth can of course work negatively too, and the communication of bad experiences to friends and family is also likely to influence visit decision-making. Managing the visitor experience is a vital and complex requirement in the operation of a visitor attraction, and it is essential for attraction owners/managers to recognize the significance of the visit/visitor experience in sustaining visitor satisfaction and, inevitably, visitor numbers. Understanding the visitor experience is a key factor in determining the success of a visitor attraction, and has wider implications for the public perception of specific attraction sectors as day-trip destinations.

A number of models have been developed to evaluate quality and customer satisfaction in business operations, the most notable of which is SERVQUAL (Parasuraman *et al.*, 1985). Considered to be a seminal study in consumer behaviour, the basis of this evaluative framework is the difference between consumer expectations and perceptions of service, based on five generic service quality dimensions necessary for customer satisfaction (see Table 9.8). Parasuraman *et al.*

Table 9.8 Dimensions of service quality based on the SERVQUAL principle

Reliability	Ability to perform services dependably
Responsiveness	Willingness to assist customers and provide prompt service
Assurance	Courtesy, trustworthiness and knowledge of staff
Empathy	Display caring attitude to customers
Tangibles	Presentation of physical facilities

(1985) identified five gaps between service providers and consumers, but later work suggested that another gap existed – that between the customer's and the provider's perception of the experience. These issues form the basis for managing the visitor at attractions and have to be viewed alongside future trends and issues affecting visitor attractions.

The future for visitor attraction management

It is widely recognized that a range of factors impact upon the success or failure of visitor attractions as tourism enterprises. This has to be viewed against growing visitor expectations during their visit and the need for attractions to improve standards in many countries worldwide. It also involves the need to refresh their products in order to retain their market share. Even though some operate as trusts and are based in the not-for-profit sector, their future survival depends upon managing their assets and enterprise in an efficient and robust manner so that they attract visitors and remain viable in an increasingly competitive environment globally. Some of the key factors that will shape visitor attractions in the future have been identified by Swarbrooke (2001) as:

- Coping with the scale and diversity of competition, especially in the leisure market
- Recruiting, rewarding and retaining staff
- Staying ahead of developments in marketing
- Recognizing the role of marketing consortia in achieving economies of cost in advertising
- Satisfying consumers
- Meeting the needs of special groups of visitors such as the disabled
- Offering unique selling propositions and the 'wow factor' at attractions to appeal to visitors.

Many of these factors can be grouped into a number of categories of challenges for the future:

1 Product development and innovation
2 Marketing and promotion
3 Revenue generation and funding
4 Education and training
5 Community and public sector intervention.

Product development and innovation

This is vital to remain ahead of the competition and to take account of trends in the global and national marketplace. Although Chapter 10 examines innovation in more detail, it is notable that most successful attractions seek to identify new concepts, business processes or techniques (such as interpretation or technology) to appeal to a sophisticated visitor audience. One of the greatest developments for many attractions is in the use of film in interpretation and interactive technology to appeal to children, such as in the Newseum in Washington DC – a free admission museum of news and journalism, which cost $50 million to develop. In its first nine months of operation, it attracted 325 000 visitors – which is very interactive and mediaworthy! In a similar vein, the Futurescope in Potiers, France, which opened in 1987, incorporates film as the basis of the theme park's operation, with IMAX, OMNIMAX, and roof projection and seat oscillation. It acts as a public-sector led regeneration project, in much the same way as Lomond Shores, and has generated 1200 direct and 15 000 indirect jobs and received 2.8 million visitors in 1997 – most of whom were largely domestic visitors. In the technology field, virtual reality attractions such as the New York Skyride and the Madame Tussaud Scenerama in Amsterdam offer simulated trips that also orientate the visitor to the destination.

Marketing and promotion

Whilst innovation is a key to success, it is essential that this is communicated to the potential customer through marketing and promotion. Most attractions use limited budgets for public relations (PR) rather than media advertising, with many profile attractions having media kits, websites and virtual reality tours, as well as targeting groups through promotional campaigns that are price-driven. These seek to make the public aware of the role of attractions in leisure spending and as a venue for fun and enjoyment, as well as being safe and interesting. In the USA, the Smithsonian Museum in Washington DC and the Museum of Modern Art in New York both have very sophisticated websites, and these have provided a conduit for electronic trading such as retailing, ticket purchases and corporate hospitality bookings. In some cases, attractions have entered into strategic alliances and partnerships to develop synergies across the attraction and tourism sector to develop their business interests. For example, the Singapore Tourist Board screens all copy produced by attractions and places it in guidebooks and at strategic points of interest for visitors, ensuring the style and image of the tourist board is consistent. In New York, the Convention and Visitor Bureau link attractions and other tourist services with discount schemes and include all attractions on an activities map. Other examples of partnership innovation include museums in Boston cooperating to undertake joint marketing initiatives and ultimately to raise public awareness, or museums sharing best practice. Some attractions have introduced initiatives to extend their life cycle, such as adding new visitor features or in-built regeneration strategies. One of the most interesting examples is Singapore Zoo's development of a nocturnal tour, and others have sought to extend the season through packaging the attraction with other products or services to create all-year-round opening opportunities as well as differential pricing mechanisms. Santa Claus Land in Finland has developed products to appeal to overseas markets at different times of the year, and has created eight peak seasons.

Revenue generation and funding

By presenting attractions as a series of products, managers can expand the scope for increasing the total spend per person while also appealing to the buoyant demand for retailing that has produced opportunities for themed development and linkage to the products and experiences offered by the attraction. Most successful attractions are heavily involved in hospitality, with a prestigious café or restaurant that creates a nice ambience as well as good spending opportunities. In fact, the Singapore Tourist Board has identified and themed food and hospitality into its events strategy for Tourism 21. It uses the Singapore Food Festival as a means to promote the ethnic diversity and 'Asia-ness' of the destination. Other attractions also have well-developed corporate hospitality functions, offering various places to host events, meetings and product launches. Many of the London Museums have embraced this important source of funding, as well as corporate membership. One of the principal tasks of revenue generation from existing visitors is to find ways to extend the dwell time on site. Greater division of attractions into sections/segments and experiences encourages increased on-site time as well as enlarging the range of retailing opportunities.

Education and training

There has been a growth of awareness that many attractions now operate in what is called the 'cultural industries' sector, and of the growing need for education, training and management development activities to recognize the changing nature of attractions as businesses. It is evident that a series of cultural industries exist within a tourism context, and Myerscough (1988) identified the cultural events, artefacts and resources that are of vital significance to the tourism industry. Attractions provide the key element of this system. In an urban context, the cultural industries comprise a diverse group of attractions, including nightclubs, libraries, museums and art galleries. In the UK, these activities employed over 68 500 people in the 1990s, which is reflected in the fact that many countries (such as Scotland), towns and cities now have cultural industries strategies to promote these activities. This is shown in the bids each year for cities to become the European City of Culture, with the perceived focus on attractions as a key element of tourism development and the associated controversy regarding how this will assist the attraction sector in developing its education and training needs to improve service delivery. The use of volunteers provides many useful lessons for employed staff, and some countries (such as France) are exemplars of training in the visitor attraction sector since this is seen as gaining a competitive advantage. As Chapter 10 will show, certain tourism operators in the attraction sector (such as Disney) also lead the world in staff training and motivation to enhance guest care, the visitor experience and product development.

Community and public sector intervention

Visitor attractions are a vital element of any community and its tourism infrastructure, and so local funding support for the low season is often seen as an essential element for success in cultural industry strategies. Off-season visits by local residents, who are also ambassadors for the local area, are important to the market for attractions. There are many good examples of country-level support for attractions in France, and indirectly in the UK through Millennium funds. In contrast, the USA does not directly fund attractions through public funds, since donations, bequests or community efforts are more notable than public sector subsidies. Where the public sector directly intervenes, employment protection or development is usually justified (see Box 9.1). In some cases, states may seek to promote investment in events to help develop an attraction in a destination, and so funding for events and festivals can feature as a major element of public sector intervention in the attraction sector.

Summary

The post-modern age has witnessed a large increase in the range of visitor attractions in Britain and globally, and the visiting public has to make certain decisions about visiting particular venues based on a complexity of factors including location, appeal, cost and perceived benefit, or a combination of these. It is evident that professional approaches to researching visitor satisfaction are necessary as visitors' expectations increase and there is a greater urgency to ensure competitive advantage in the visitor attraction market. One of the major challenges for visitor attractions lies in harnessing new technology, whilst market research agencies such as Mintel argue that visitors are seeking good quality facilities at competitive prices in the leisure sector, with which attractions now compete. Visitors are seeking greater interaction at attractions, which involves the integration of technology and 'high-touch' exhibits to develop a greater degree of social interaction, whilst fulfilling a range of motivations for visiting.

References

English Tourism Council et al. (1999)

English Tourism Council (2002) Tourist Attractions. http://www.staruk.org.uk (accessed 8 June 2002).

English Tourism Council, Northern Ireland Tourist Board, VisitScotland and Wales Tourist Board (2001) *Sightseeing in the UK 2000*. London: English Tourism Council.

Gunn, C. A. (1972) *Vacationscape: Designing Tourist Regions*. Austin, Texas: University of Texas Press.

Gunn, C. A. (1988) *Tourism Planning*, 2nd ed. New York: Taylor and Francis.

Holloway, J. C. (2001) *Business of Tourism*, 6th edn. Harlow: Pearson.

Jansen-Verbeke, M. (1986) Inner-city tourism: resources, tourists and promoters. *Annals of Tourism Research*, **13**(1), 79–100.

Kotler, P. (1994) *Marketing Management: Analysis, Planning, Implementation and Control*, 8th ed. Prentice Hall.

Lennon, J. (ed.) (2001) *Tourism Statistics: International Perspectives and Current Issues*. London: Continuum.

Myerscough, J. (1988) *The Economic Importance of the Arts in Britain*. London: Policy Studies Institute.

Parasuraman, A., Zeithaml, V. and Berry, L. (1985). A conceptual model of service quality and its implications for future research. *Journal of Marketing*, **49**(4), 41–50.

Pearce, P. (1991) Analysing tourist attractions. *Journal of Tourism Studies*, **2**(1), 46–55.

Scottish Enterprise/Highlands and Islands Enterprise (2001) *New Horizons: International Benchmarking and Best Practice for Visitor Attractions*. Glasgow: Scottish Enterprise/Highlands and Islands Enterprise.

Stevens, T. (1991) Visitor attractions. *In*: C. P. Cooper (ed.), *Progress in Tourism, Recreation and Hospitality Management*, Vol. 3. London: Belhaven Press, 106–13.

Swarbrooke, J. (2001) Visitor attraction management in a competitive market. *INSIGHTS*, A41–52, London: English Tourism Council.

Swarbrooke, J. (2002) *The Development and Management of Visitor Attractions*, 2nd edn. Oxford: Butterworth-Heinemann.

Transport for London and London Underground (2002) *Real London Markets*. London: Transport for London.

Walsh-Heron, J. and Stevens, T. (1990) *The Management of Visitor Attractions and Events*, London: Prentice Hall.

Yale, P. (1997) *From Tourist Attractions to Heritage Tourism*. Huntingdon: ELM Publications.

Further reading

Leiper, N. (1990) Tourist attraction systems. *Annals of Tourism Research*, **17**, 367–84.

Lew, A. (1987) A framework for tourist attraction research. *Annals of Tourism Research*, **14**(4), 553–75.

Questions

1 Why are visitor attractions important for tourist destinations?
2 What is the justification for public sector pump-priming funding for visitor attractions?
3 What are the future management issues facing visitor attractions?
4 What factors would you consider if you were asked to undertake a feasibility study for a new visitor attraction on a greenfield site?

10

The management of tourism

Learning objectives

This chapter builds on the previous discussion of the tourism industry, reviewing the need to manage tourism businesses. After reading it, you should be able to understand:

- the principles of management and their application to tourism businesses;
- the role of marketing as a management function;
- the role of management in establishing standards and systems of service provision;
- the significance of small tourism businesses in the tourism sector;
- the role of innovation and tourism development as a management function.

Introduction

The previous chapters have highlighted the very fragmented nature of the business that many refer to as *tourism*, being a complex amalgam of businesses that cooperate and work together to supply services and products to tourists as consumers. Each of these businesses and bodies are known as *organizations*, which are formal entities such as businesses or corporations that exist to interact, trade and exchange goods, services and knowledge to create wealth or other outputs through the use of their staff, capabilities and know-how within a tourism context. Profit is the main driver of many businesses operating in the private sector, but there are also organizations within the public sector (see Chapter 11) and voluntary sector that interact in tourism in a regulatory or voluntary sense or as interest groups (e.g. a professional organization such as ABTA), and seek to influence and affect change and represent specific interests or viewpoints. All of these organizations impact upon tourism and its direction, nature and operation – a feature that will be discussed more fully in Chapter 11. For businesses to exist and operate effectively, some form of management and organization is needed. This chapter examines and develops the theme of management with a focus on the manager as the conduit for such action.

Managing tourism businesses: key principles

The vast array of business interests that are interlinked in the delivery and production of tourism products largely operate for a profit motive, and for them to achieve this objective they need management in order to get things done. In other words, management occurs in a formal sense in organizations, and in most cases management is about harnessing the organization's resources (especially people as its most valuable asset) to create the services, outcomes or products in line with what the tourist requires as a consumer. In practical terms, in tourism it involves harnessing the power over resources (i.e. people, finance, technology and the organization) to bring some degree of order to the tasks necessary to function and achieve organizational objectives. This requires a manager (or teams of managers) to link with undertake managerial tasks, which comprise managerial worl

Most tourism businesses work towards a set of commo businesses are often organized internally into specialized functi resource management, accounts and finance), and this vertical provides a structure for employees. Companies are also organize

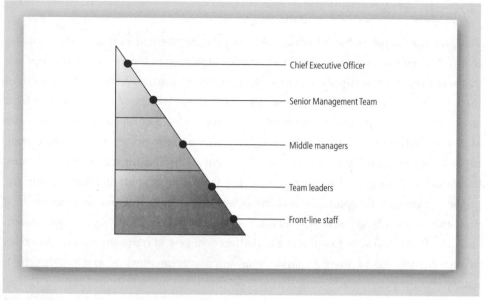

Figure 10.1   Levels of management

the hierarchy is characterized by different levels of power, authority and status. Within tourism organizations, managers are grouped by level (see Figure 10.1).

Managers can also be classified according to functional roles, including:

- *Functional Managers*, who manage specialized functions such as accounting, research, sales and personnel in large organizations.
- *Business unit, divisional or area managers*, who exercise management responsibilities at a generally lower level in an organization. Their responsibilities may cover a group of products or diverse geographical area, and combine a range of management responsibilities.
- *Project Managers*, who manage specific projects (a project is typically a short-term undertaking) and may require a team of staff to complete each one.

The purpose of management in tourism organizations

goals of managers within organizations, usually seen as profit-driven, are often iverse, and include:

- *Profitability*, which can be achieved through higher output, better service, attracting new customers, and cost minimization
- *Other goals* (e.g. coordination, liaison, raising public awareness and undertaking activities for the wider public good) that dominate the agenda in organizations in the public sector
- *Efficiency*, to reduce expenditure and inputs to a minimum to achieve more cost-effective outputs
- *Effectiveness* (achieving the desired outcome); this is not necessarily a profit-driven motive.

Yet in practical terms the main tasks of managers are based on the management process, which is how to achieve these goals. Whilst management theorists differ in the emphasis they place on different aspects of the management process, there are four commonly agreed sets of tasks; organizing, planning, leading and controlling (see Chapter 1).

The process of management is an ongoing and ever-changing one in which the wide range of managers make decisions that affect the organization and nature of the business. Chief Executive Officers make decisions that have major impacts on the organization (e.g. the decision to downsize due to a drop in demand), while more junior managers deal with routine day-to-day decision-making. In managerial decision-making the two prevailing elements of technical and human skills have to be balanced, as these are vital when interacting with and managing people both within the organization and outside it (e.g. clients, suppliers etc.). This is often underpinned by an ability to communicate effectively and confidently with others, as well as an ability to lead and motivate people. This highlights one other skill set that managers need: cognitive and conceptual skills. Cognitive skills are those that enable managers to formulate solutions to problems, and conceptual skills are those that allow them to take a broader view and consider the links with other areas of the business. These skills are apparent from studies of managers and their work.

A study by Carroll (1988) identified clusters of management tasks, which characterized managers as:

1 *Representatives* of the organization
2 *Investigators*, who research issues and problems
3 *Negotiators*, who communicate with one or more people over a transaction to reach a desired outcome, such as a contract

4 *Coordinators*, who ensure that the organization's resources are deployed to good effect to ensure flow in work tasks
5 *Evaluators*, who observe, examine and control aspects of the organization's activities
6 *Staffers*, who control human resource functions
7 *Supervisors*, who direct the everyday work of junior staff.

These clusters inherently cause competing roles for managers, and thus successful managers require a wide range of competencies.

According to Inkson and Kolb (1995: 32), a competency is:

. . . an underlying trait of an individual – for example a motive pattern, a skill, a characteristic behaviour, a value, or a set of knowledge – which enables that person to perform successfully in his or her job.

The main motivation for organizational interest in competencies is the desire to improve management through education and training. Competencies can be divided into three groups:

1 Understanding what needs to be done
2 Getting the job done
3 Taking people with you.

Quinn *et al.* (1990) examined the skills, competencies and role of managers, and concluded that the skill set of a manager often revolved around the following activities: mentoring; innovation; brokerage; as a provider; as a director; coordination; monitoring and facilitation.

The concern with competencies questions the simple notion of management as planning, organizing, leading and control; it emphasizes skills as the basis for management. However, relying only upon competencies may overlook the need for cognitive skills, which are related to personality and individual style, while conceptual skills are based on the natural abilities of individuals.

Above all, managers need to be adaptable and flexible to accommodate and lead change, particularly in fast-moving areas such as tourism. Among the common skills identified by a range of ecotourism businesses in Australia as critical to business performance were:

- Business planning, financial planning, business plan skills and research
- General marketing skills, strategic marketing skills, an understanding of price, product, place and promotion
- Operational skills, especially in terms of customers and business operations
- Personal attributes, especially in dealing with people.

(McKercher and Robbins, 1998)

This list highlights the diversity of skills and knowledge that business managers need.

Most significantly, *change* is a key feature for tourism businesses, and hence managers need to be cognisant of a wide range of factors – socio-cultural, demographic and economic issues (especially the nature of the economy), the role of legal and political changes, technological change (especially ICT), what the competition is doing, the global environment, and the role of change and uncertainty in markets. For managers, internal resistance to change may be a problem when seeking to move the business in new directions, and various techniques can be used to overcome this, including (Kotter and Schlesinger, 1979):

- Education and communication
- Participation and involvement
- Facilitation and support
- Negotiation and agreement
- Manipulation and cooptation
- Explicit and implicit coercion.

The ability to learn to manage in new situations where there are no guidelines or models to follow is, according to Handy (1989), how people grow, especially in a managerial role. In fact managerial behaviour was studied throughout the twentieth century, from the early work of Fayol, Mintzberg and others who observed and studied what managers did and why. In terms of how managers react to new challenges and tasks, research has illustrated that much managerial work is mundane, and is based on establishing ongoing reciprocal working relationships within and between businesses (i.e. networking). A number of stages in managerial responses to work are:

1 Taking hold of the job (normally takes three to six months)
2 Immersion (lasting four to eleven months)

3 Reshaping after a period of intense change (normally three to six months)
4 Consolidation (running for three to nine months)
5 Refinement.

Mintzberg argued that managers often work on a stimulus–response pattern, responding to problems, challenges and issues, and the nature of much of their work is fragmented and discontinuous, often being interrupted.

What do tourism managers manage?

Tourism is widely attributed as a service sector activity that has a high level of customer contact. Despite the wide range of tasks that managers undertake, there are three principal management functions with which tourism businesses need to be involved when dealing with people as customers: marketing, operational issues and human resource management. Although other functions are important, these three are crucial where the service output is intangible. In a tourism context, marketing differs from other products because tourism is a service industry, where the intangibility, quality of delivery and evaluation of experiences are difficult to visualize. The heterogeneity (i.e. diversity), perishability (i.e. a tour cannot be stored and resold at a different time) and intangibility of ecotourism services make marketing a challenge when combined with two other key problems:

1 The customer must travel to the product/resource-base to consume it
2 The operator has little influence over the tourism activity (holiday).

The marketing focus belies the fact that tourism consumption is based upon the provision of a service, and so marketing as a process acts to link the customer with the supplier (see the example of the holiday brochure illustrated in Chapter 8). Marketing is also vital to establishing the market research, market needs, specification and nature of service provision in consumer industries.

Marketing as a management function

Marketing is widely acknowledged as being a vital prerequisite to communicating the product or service offering of businesses or suppliers to the market (see Chapter 9). According to Kotler and Armstrong (1991), marketing is a process whereby individuals and groups obtain the type of products or goods they value. These goods are created and exchanged through a process that requires a detailed understanding of consumers and their wants and desires so that the product or service is effectively and efficiently delivered to the client or purchaser.

In particular, businesses need to understand (by using market research) which markets they wish to serve and the service attributes they wish to offer, to establish the prices to be charged and tailor the service to meet the clients needs as closely as possible, and to develop a communication programme to inform them about the service (e.g. create a brochure, advertisement or other method of communication, such as the Internet).

To meet customer needs, a company analyses its own products or services in terms of its own business expertise and how competitors' products and services may affect them. This is frequently undertaken as a SWOT analysis, which considers the Strengths and Weaknesses of, Opportunities for, and Threats to its products and services in the business environment.

For those tourism operators who may wish to expand, a number of options exist. Horner and Swarbrooke (1996: 325) indicate that these can involve:

- Marketing consortia, where a group of operators cooperate to create and develop a product
- Strategic alliances, where different businesses agree to cooperate in various ways (this varies by sector in the tourism industry, and includes such things as marketing agreements or technical cooperation)
- Acquisition, which is the purchase of equity in other operations
- Joint ventures, where operators seek to create new businesses
- Franchising, where major operators use their market presence and brand image to extend their influence further by licensing franchisees to operate businesses using their corporate logo and codes.

However, the actual implementation of marketing for tourism ultimately depends on the 'marketing mix' chosen by the company.

The marketing mix

The marketing mix is 'the mixture of controllable marketing variables that the firm [or company] uses to pursue the sought level of sales in the target market' (Kotler, cited in Holloway and Plant, 1988: 48). This means that in any tourism organization there are four main marketing variables that need to be harnessed:

1 *Product formulation*, which is the ability of a company to adapt to the needs of its customers in terms of the services it provides. Products are constantly being adapted to changes in consumer markets.
2 *Price*, which is the economic concept used to adjust the supply of a service to meet the demand, taking into account sales targets and turnover.
3 *Promotion*, which is the manner in which a company seeks to improve customers' knowledge of the services it sells so that those people who are made aware may be turned into actual purchasers. To achieve promotional aims, advertising, public relations, sales and brochure production functions are undertaken within the remit of promotion.
4 *Place*, which is the location at which prospective customers may be induced to purchase a service – the point of sale (e.g. a travel agent).

These 'four Ps' are incorporated into the marketing process in relation to the known competition and the impact of market conditions. Thus the marketing process involves the continuous evaluation of how a business operates both internally and externally to meet customer requirements.

Managing operational issues in tourism businesses

Operational issues have traditionally assumed a dominant day-to-day focus for most service organizations centred on tourism – particularly where labour-intensive operations exist (e.g. at an airport). Business operations in tourism assume a major role, especially given the highly seasonal nature of tourism, which leads to the need for seasonal staff at resorts and airports, in hotels, and for transport operators. This is a key management challenge for many businesses, and this is shown in Figure 10.2 for those businesses in North New Zealand where demand is largely concentrated in six months of the year.

In businesses where large volumes of tourists are being managed, such as attractions and airports, managers need to delegate a great deal of responsibility to front-line staff in managing the interactions with visitors, in order to ensure the smooth flow and organization of activities. This is often termed operations management, which focuses on five inter-related areas:

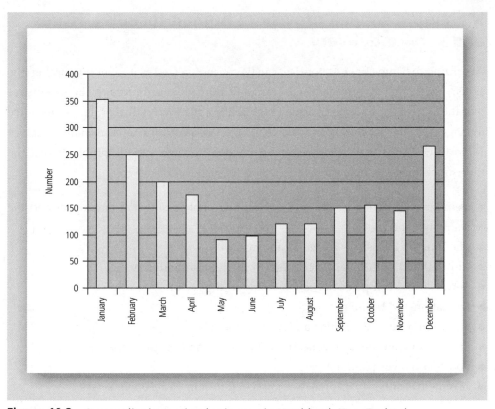

Figure 10.2   Seasonality in tourism businesses in Northland, New Zealand

1 *Capacity*, which is understanding the ability of the organization to produce something (such as a service)
2 *Standards*, which are those prevailing within the tourism sector (such as waiting times at an airport check-in or hotel reception)
3 *Scheduling*, which is the planning of work and use of the organization's physical and human resources
4 *Inventory*, which is understanding the organization's ability to meet supply and demand
5 *Control*, to ensure the operations are managed in an efficient and systematic manner, which brings the planning, preparation and readiness inherent in the four functions above into action.

Much of this is of course dependent upon having competent staff to undertake these tasks.

Managing service provision: human resource issues and service delivery

According to Baum (1993: 4), tourism can be conceptualized as a client purchasing 'the skills, service and commitment of a range of human contributors to the experience that they are about to embark upon', highlighting the importance of human resource management (HRM) issues and the challenge this poses for tourism managers (see Table 10.1). Many of these issues are embedded in some specific problems that the tourism sector face, including:

- Demographic issues related to the shrinking pool of potential employees and the resultant shortages
- The tourism industry's image as an employer
- Cultural and traditional perceptions of the tourism industry
- Rewards and compensation for working in the sector
- Education and training
- Skill shortages at the senior and technical levels
- Linking human resource concerns with service and product quality
- Poor manpower planning
- A remedial rather than proactive approach to human resource issues.

Human resource management (HRM) is concerned with planning, monitoring and control of the human resource as a management process. More complex analyses

Table 10.1 Managing human resource issues: scope and extent for businesses (modified from Baum, 1993)

1. A critical awareness of the scope and nature of the labour market
2. The design of jobs
3. Recruitment, selection, appointment and retention of staff
4. Induction, equal opportunities, training and development
5. Evaluation of staff performance
6. Salaries and incentives
7. Employment termination, grievance and dispute procedures
8. Industrial relations and employment law
9. Motivation of staff

of HRM identify the concern for the individual human resource system within any organization to be able to realize the strategic objectives of the organization (i.e. the delivery of excellent customer service to tourism consumers), as will become evident later in this chapter when the Disney model is discussed.

For medium- or large-sized tourism enterprises, human resource issues and the factors affecting their performance are usually linked to the staff and workforce; therefore, recognizing the role of recruitment and ongoing development of the staff resource to achieve strategic goals become essential. The scale of the human resource function will often reflect the size of the organization, and specific functions (e.g. training and development) may be allocated to specific individuals whereas in smaller organizations the commitment to core functions (recruitment and retention) may be all that is possible, owing to work pressures and constraints on staff time.

The major challenges for the tourism industry in the new millennium are aptly summarized by Cooper *et al.* (1998: 458):

> ... the challenges facing the tourism industry will only be met successfully by a well-educated, well-trained, bright, energetic, multilingual and entrepreneurial workforce who understand the nature of tourism and have a professional training. A high quality of professional human resources in tourism will allow enterprises to gain a competitive edge and deliver added value with their service.

People do make a difference in what is undoubtedly a people business.

More sophisticated human resource policies need to be developed and implemented in the following areas for the tourism sector to add value to its staff and change its image as an employer (Page *et al.*, 2001):

- Induction of staff
- Appraisal and staff performance evaluation
- Effective staff communication
- Rewarding initiative and excellence
- Empowering staff
- Improved industry–education collaboration.

Therefore, the quality, commitment and effectiveness of human resources can be critical in the competitiveness of businesses. Understanding how HRM issues influence the business and, more importantly, what types of service staff need to provide are significant elements for managing tourism businesses.

Service provision in tourism: a perennial management challenge

Service provision can be conceptualized as a system where elements of the product are created and assembled and delivered to the customer. Whilst parts of the service are visible to the consumer, the manner of delivery is what will entail exposure to the tourist and hence impact upon the company's reputation as a service provider. The tourist's satisfaction with the service delivered in tourism will focus upon two critical elements: the technical and functional qualities of the service. The technical quality relates to the measurable elements, such as whether an airline seat of a certain quality was provided and delivered. In contrast, the functional element relates to the impression received by a client – an overall impression that is more holistic and gauges satisfaction with what was consumed. Whilst the analysis of functional quality is less tangible, certain factors such as posture, a smile, voice, attitude, empathy and responsiveness have a major bearing. For tourism managers, levels of service in tourism will be measured by tourist satisfaction. This is a complex phenomenon, since satisfaction is linked to the consumer's emotions and level of expectation of the service being consumed. This is partly dependent upon three inter-related factors: the level of equity in the service provided, whether expectations were met, and the perception of the actual performance. This requires managers to understand in more detail the technical aspects of service provision in tourism, especially:

- What the final product is
- How it is produced
- The form and shape the service will take
- Who ultimately delivers the service.

Therefore, recognizing that customer service is central to the satisfaction levels of tourism services is significant because consumers are often buying something of which they have high expectations, based on the marketing mix (the price, product, place and promotion), which is shaped by people, physical attributes (e.g. good or bad weather) and processes of delivery. In a customer contact business, managers need to be aware of the most commonly measured elements that determine service quality. These SERVQUAL determinants are:

- Tangible elements
- Reliability
- Responsiveness
- Communication
- Credibility
- Security
- Competence
- Courtesy
- Understanding/knowing the consumer
- Access/ease of approach and contact.

These are central in managing the service encounter with tourists, and at an operational level will determine how customer expectations/needs are met. A useful illustration of how one business deals with tourists and customer service is provided by the Disney Corporation. This is often held up as a model that many tourism organizations would like to emulate, given its integrated nature and contribution to the profitability of its operations.

The Disney model of customer care

The Disney Organization is acknowledged to be one of the leaders in customer care, employing over 55 000 staff, with revenue of US$23 billion in 1999 and profits of US$2 billion. It has increased its level of repeat business from 50 to 70 per cent in the last three years – a feature many tourism businesses want to emulate in order to build a strong customer base. The concepts it uses are interesting in a customer service perspective for the tourism industry, because it uses a theatrical context – staff are referred to *as cast members*, and play their role *on stage*, which is at the point of customer contact. Staff are allowed to be themselves backstage, when they are not in front of customers, and there are a set of processes and procedures that are part of the Disney magic. The Disney formula for customer service is based on set of values that come from integrating its commercialism with a quality experience for the visitor. It is based on three elements:

1 A quality staff experience, since each individual staff member impacts on the customer experience

2 A quality customer experience, based on being customer-driven and seeking to exceed the customer needs and expectations rather than simply meeting them

3 A quality set of business practices, where knowledge, marketing, innovation and other elements are blended to ensure commercial success.

In particular, the Disney philosophy is to 'exceed customer expectations and pay attention to detail', with the visitor at the centre of all the elements that drive business activities. In Disney jargon, *Guestology* is the approach to customer service, where staff need to know their customers and understand them in terms of psychographics (see Chapter 3). This requires an understanding of 'quantitative aspects of their visitors' experience, and also of more qualitative features (e.g. feelings, attitudes and reasoning), since the visitor experience is based upon these intangible elements. On the basis of this information, Disney develops its service theme – the type of service guests want – which has four key service standards: safety, courtesy, show (to provide a seamless experience), and efficiency (to ensure smooth operations). To deliver these service standards, Disney uses a corporate brand.

A brand is a name, design or symbol (or combination of these) used to identify a service. This enables the customer to identify the product or service easily. For a company a brand can help to build customer loyalty, since it implies less risk in a purchase – something that can help with further merchandizing opportunities, as the Disney brand has achieved through its international retail outlets. Disney recognizes the need for consistency in the way the organization conveys itself via its brand to the public, as during a visit a person may interact with 60 cast members in a single day. To achieve consistency and a coherent brand image, Disney seeks to ensure that staff are competent, attentive, seamless and trained, with managers providing service support for the cast and identifying how to 'reach out' to guests.

To achieve these goals Disney has a number of processes and procedures to help in the delivery of its service, and recognizes that, in a real world, service breakdowns and interruptions may occur. Putting things right by empowering staff to alleviate the impact of such problems means that a negative event can be shaped by a positive response from staff, such as responding to problems with 'How can I help?' Service debugging, as Disney refers to it, involves seeking solutions to problems so that good communication is achieved between visitors and staff members. One of Disney's major achievements, which is often held out as a model for the tourism industry, is its ability to deal with large flows of visitors at its theme parks. It has introduced visitor management tools (see Chapter 12), including *Early Bird Programmes* to allow early entry before the main visitors, *Fast Passes* to avoid waiting, and *Tip Boards*, which advise people how long a wait is required at a specific attraction. The aim is to optimize the operation of the attraction, guest flow and queue experience so the visitor experience is enhanced.

In seeking to manage the visitor experience at Disney, sending the right message to the visitor is seen as vital, from the entry point until the point of departure. By paying careful attention to detail, Disney seeks to create a positive image. It does this by ensuring it creates the right ambience and feeling among visitors by harnessing visual and non-visual details such as design, landscaping, lighting (which can affect visitor moods), colour, signage, texture of surfaces, music and ambient noise, as well as sensory elements such as smell, touch and taste. Above all, tidiness and cleanliness in mass visitor attractions are seen as critical to the image created. This highlights how integrated the visitor experience is at an attraction, and the fact that customer service is not just about visitor contact and interaction but also about the entire environment and how service systems are designed and managed to enable satisfaction to be achieved. Above all, Disney is constantly reinventing itself, innovating and seeking to stay in front of the competition. Management research has this termed business re-engineering – seeking to reintegrate processes (e.g. tasks, labour and knowledge) to make continuous improvements to business performance. Whilst many of these Disney principles may seem quite alien to some service organizations, this example highlights a range of methods that tourism businesses can adapt and develop in understanding how to deliver services to visitors. However, one of the problems that this poses for tourism operators in many countries is their scale of operation, especially when they are based in the small business sector that has specific managerial concerns, particularly in the early set up stage.

Developing and managing tourism ventures in the small business sector

There is a tendency to assume that tourism has great potential to stimulate economic development if it is managed well. The basic argument is that the fledgling new business of today could develop and grow into a large international corporation in the future, which may indeed occur in a few cases – such as the rise of the Virgin transport conglomerate, which evolved from the Virgin Atlantic airline venture. For this reason many governments have avidly supported small business development in tourism, owing to its future employment generating potential, although they were not overtly concerned until the 1980s with ensuring that managers and owners had the skill set needed to manage such enterprises. The small business sector (known as small and medium-sized enterprises, SMEs) does play a major role in most countries, not only for its employment role but also because it is a key element of the industry.

According to Morrison (1996: 400):

> . . . a small tourism business is financed by one individual or small group and is directly managed by its owner(s), in a personalized manner and not through the medium of a formalized management structure . . . it is perceived as small, in terms of physical facilities, production/service capacity, market share and number of employees.

Morrison goes on to argue that:

> . . . traditionally the tourism industry has been dominated by the small business and this still remains true in the 1990s. Currently in Ireland . . . firms with less than fifteen employees account for around 79 per cent of all Irish tourism businesses.

Indeed, it is notable that the success often attributed to Ireland as a booming tourism destination can be directly related to activity across the tourism sectors, in which SMEs play a role.

However, in terms of small tourism firms entrepreneurship seems weakly developed, because tourism is perceived as having low entry barriers and in some cases requires little capital. The main management issues affecting tourism SMEs are highlighted by Carter (1996: 4504) who suggested that:

> . . . irrespective of the relative size of each country's small business sector, the main management characteristics of small firms remain similar regardless of nationality. Researchers have consistently noted that small firms play an important role in new product and process innovation and are characterized by their product specialization . . . [and] . . . that these firms are undercapitalized, product-led, family-owned concerns in which the management function is confined to one person or a few key individuals.

The short-term planning horizon of many tourism SMEs, their limited knowledge of the business environment and their owner-managed structure influences the way in which tasks are managed. SME managers rely upon attitudes, personal qualities (e.g. leadership skills) and experience. The difference between small and large firm management is that the preparation of ongoing business plans and the marketing function in SMEs are seen as being peripheral to the management task of running the business. Many of these characteristics were borne out in the studies by Shaw and Williams (2002), where few businesses had formal marketing strategies, skills and knowledge of the tourism business.

Many localities promote tourism business development because it has the potential to form linkages with the businesses that supply it (backward linkages) and with those it supplies (forward linkages), and so to generate economic development. An example is a new hotel sourcing local food supplies.

Research focused on the accommodation sector has shown that many new entrants to this sector have little experience of the business and have a wide range of motives for entering the market. What is interesting in the tourism sector is that the sources of venture capital for new businesses are varied, with a proportion often coming from families and contacts in small business ventures. In Cornwall, research by Shaw and Williams (2002) found that more than 50 per cent of capital came from these sources, especially for older entrepreneurs. The grounds given by many of these entrepreneurs for establishing their business included lifestyle reasons in over 80 per cent of cases (i.e. a better way of life), being new migrants to the region. However, tourism entrepreneurs need to harness managerial skills if their business idea is to work.

With many countries having a strong dependence upon small businesses for the tourism sector, it is not surprising that a number of government agencies are concerned with improving the performance and managerial skills of new businesses when they do not enter the market for profit-only motives. For example, in New Zealand 99 per cent of the country's businesses are based in the SME sector, and these employ 60 per cent of the working population. Over 85 per cent of these businesses employ less than five people, and this pattern is replicated through the tourism and hospitality sector, although the hospitality industry tends to employ more staff.

What is apparent is that new business start-ups and small business ventures in tourism have specific management requirements with a common range of obstacles to improving business performance, including:

- Inflation
- Labour costs
- Interest rates
- High rents or rates
- Debtors/poor cash flow
- Lack of external guidance on business development
- Competition from other businesses
- Labour productivity
- Lack of skilled employees
- Lack of customer demand
- Government regulations and bureaucracy
- Limited access to finance
- Large firm competition.

This highlights the scope of the management challenges that face many small tourism and hospitality businesses. Addressing these through good management skills is critical, and in the initial set-up stage of the business venture particular attention should be paid to the obvious financial issues through a feasibility study or business plan. The Scottish Enterprise-funded www.scotexchange.net website hosted by the national tourism organization, VisitScotland, has a site entitled 'Business development', which is aimed at entrepreneurs seeking to start their own business. The site examines the following points:

- How to get started
- Marketing
- Knowing your market
- Networking
- Staff-related issues
- Risks in setting up a business
- Business types.

It has related links to Scottish Enterprise advice through its network of 22 local enterprise companies and its Small Business Gateway site (www.sbgateway.com). Above all, these sites highlight much of the conventional wisdom on small business start-ups in tourism and hospitality, the importance of developing a good business plan, and the role of innovation.

Tourism and innovation: challenges for tourism managers

Innovation is a often seen as one way in which businesses may seek to gain competitive advantage, especially where innovation in the face of competition leads to growth, survival or enhanced profitability. Innovation implies change of some sort, and can be divided into a number of areas: diffusion of new ideas, products or processes; adoption by individual organizations; and levels of innovativeness. Much of the existing research on innovation emerged after Schumpeter's study (1952), which identified five principal routes to innovation (see Figure 10.3) which has a

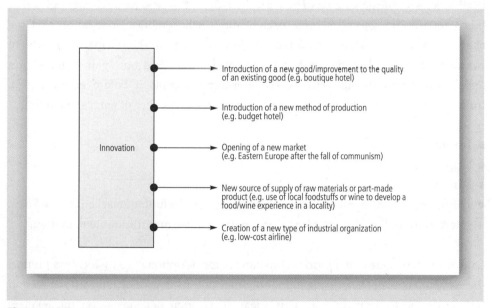

Figure 10.3 Schumpeter's types of innovation and their application to tourism

number of tourism applications included. This highlights the fact that much of the focus of innovation centres on creative thinking and inventiveness. The challenge for tourism managers is to understand the ways innovation is adopted, used by organizations and diffused to the business and commercial/non-commercial environment in order to provide solutions to problems or generate ideas that can make a difference to the way in which a business operates or functions.

How and why does innovation occur, and what is its significance in tourism?

Human actors, environmental factors such as turmoil and crisis, idea champions and external factors such as government intervention and competition can induce innovation. What is not clear from existing research is whether management is necessary to encourage innovation, or whether it will occur without the influence of management. However, managers need to understand the role of innovation and its potential to improve business processes and the client–organization interface, and to add value to the business (e.g. it may lead to a cost savings). This is important in a people industry such as tourism, which is reliant upon new ideas, experiences and destinations for the generation of new product ideas. Business research highlights that there are *pioneer adopters* in some organizations who embrace innovation and the change that it may induce, and adapt the innovation to fit the company's needs. In contrast, *innovation laggards* exist in organizations that hold out against innovation and change until the majority of the workforce accepts it before embracing it. Innovation in organizations is seen to pass through a number of stages, including:

- Invention
- Application
- Adoption
- Diffusion, where a number of sub-stages exist, including marketing the idea, interest arousal, trial implementation, continued use and full implementation.

One of the key stages for a tourism business is the adoption stage, which may reflect the receptiveness of the organization – highlighting its degree of innovativeness and willingness to experiment with new ideas. This often depends upon the level of innovation, which can range from mildly new through to being radically new (from the producer's perspective), and is also reflected in how the consumer might perceive the innovation. Two contrasting examples can be seen in the field of air travel, where a mildly innovative idea is the reduction in the number of cabin crew to reduce costs and service levels, and a very radical perspective is the removal of all in-flight service.

Innovation is critical in tourism, given its fast evolving nature. Being trend-driven, tourism has to adapt and innovate to meet consumers' needs for improved quality and new products and experiences – a feature recognized in the recent Scottish

Tourism Framework for Action (see Chapter 11). This led to a Tourism Innovation Group being formed by the tourism industry to promote such processes to make Scottish tourism more competitive (see www.scotexchange.net/new Tourism Innovation Group to see the focus of their actions and why they are engaged in such a process).

Yet small businesses often face the barriers of size and resources when trying to be innovative – especially the financial, technical and human resource bases to achieve innovation. This may also be inhibited by marketing expertise. However, where innovation occurs it can be very significant. One form of innovation that is constantly evaluated and examined by tourism managers is growth options and the need to pursue new business ideas, such as establishing new developments, and the next section examines how managers need to approach such ideas.

Tourism management in action: designing and developing a visitor attraction

One of the key features inherent in tourism is the tourist's search for something new – a new experience, and a new place to visit or new activity. Part of the innovation development process for businesses is how they evaluate the feasibility of new ideas and potential business ventures or developments. This is usually undertaken in two stages: a business plan that sets out the ideas is constructed, and then a more detailed feasibility study of the investment if external or large sums of money are involved. The formulation of a business plan generally requires the examination of a fairly standard set of issues, many of which are listed in Table 10.2 in a simplified form. This is a fairly reflective exercise for a company, entrepreneur or planner, and asks a range of questions. Many lending institutions also offer advice to new ventures regarding creating a business plan, and provide software to assist in the development of the final plan to a pre-determined structure. The business plan is the stage where many of the issues are scoped out and identified, and the proposal will identify what might be expected to occur.

However, for a much larger venture, such as the building of a new tourist attraction, or modification and expansion involving the investment of large capital sums, a feasibility study is normally undertaken. This is often contracted out to consultants who can offer specialist advice on certain aspects of the project. It requires detailed research or the compilation of existing research knowledge, and analysis of a range of issues, as shown by the example in Box 10.1.

Table 10.2 The possible structure for a simplified tourism business plan

Executive summary
- What type of business are you planning? What type of product or service will you provide?
- What do you believe are the critical success factors for this type of business?
- Why does it promise to be successful?
- What is the growth potential?

Market for the business
- Who are your potential customers and what is the market?
- How will you price your product or service?
- What market share can you expect?
- How will you promote your business?

Management
- Who will manage the business?
- What skills and characteristics will they need?
- How many employees will you need?
- What tasks will they be deployed in?
- What will their remuneration be?
- Are there potential threats to your business?

Financial elements
- What will the business cost to open?
- What will be your projected assets, liabilities, and net worth?
- What is your total estimated business income for the first financial year?
- What sources of funding will you seek/use?

Many elements of a business plan can now be prepared with the aid of business planning software available from banks and their small business venture/start-up units.

Box 10.1   A feasibility study for a new tourism attraction: the scope and range of issues

The example that follows is a real-world example that has been modified so that, for reasons of commercial confidentiality, the identity and location are not revealed. The project, which was initially released to three consulting firms as an invitation to tender, consisted of a brief to evaluate the existing business plan for a new attraction on a greenfield site, with no local competition. The brief asked for a detailed project proposal that would outline the expertise of the consultants, the timescale in which they could complete the tasks, their track record in previous projects, and the costs for undertaking the task. Any area of feasibility work in tourism requires a multidisciplinary team, and in this case quantity surveyors, a tourism planner, a tourism development expert with a detailed knowledge of the region in which the attraction was to be sited, and a managing partner were assembled to work on different aspects of the project. The brief identified certain misgivings with an existing business plan prepared previously, and questioned whether the financial assumptions and model on which the development was based were sufficiently robust. As a result, the project examined:

- The objectives of the visitor centre development
- The business requirements of the visitor centre (i.e. the requirement from the client that it had to be self-financing from visitor numbers and spending)
- Planning regulations for new developments in the region
- Existing and future tourism trends in the region, to understand if the outbound, domestic and international tourism markets would generate enough business for the new project on existing and future forecasts
- Local tourism statistics and surveys that illustrate visitor behaviour within the region and their willingness to travel to a new attraction, based on existing travel patterns
- The impact of seasonality in visitor numbers and their impact on the business model
- Visitor attraction trends in other countries and experiences of new developments
- Infrastructure constraints and opportunities to make the new development less or more accessible, such as road improvements to cut journey times
- The market segments that were likely to use the new attraction, particularly the schools market, tour groups and free independent travellers
- Methods of revenue generation, including visitor spending among domestic and international visitors as well as day trippers
- Financial assumptions and projections for the Visitor Centre, including ownership structures, visitor spending assumptions, refined assumptions based on actual experiences at other attractions, and a model of the visitor mix and projected numbers

- Construction budgets, space usage and fit out within the new visitor centre, and project programming to show the timelines for completion of each stage of the development and cost implications of different options
- The preferred model of development and likely management model that would work.

Box 10.1 shows a typical framework for many feasibility studies. The critical element, which has proved so controversial in the UK, relates to the availability of Millennium Fund grants to new visitor attraction developments. In many cases consultants have over-estimated the market for these developments, and in some cases the developments ran into financial trouble within 12–18 months of opening; some of them have already closed (see Chapter 9). This highlights the problem that the employment of consultants can pose for entrepreneurs and businesses: managers need to have a degree of understanding of the business process involved in a business plan and feasibility study. In each case, an impartial view or evaluation by a third party may help to validate or reject the outcome of the study, rather than simply reiterating the findings the client is looking for – which may lead to financial problems when the plan is implemented. In other words, the multi-skilled nature of managing a tourism business and new opportunities requires a balance of risk-taking counterweighted by financial prudence and a questioning mind to ensure that any investment is well used.

Summary

Managing tourism is a dynamic activity: change, more change and upheaval is a function of managing a fast-changing business. These businesses are subject to the vagaries of consumer tastes and market conditions, and can easily descend into crisis following catastrophic events such as foot and mouth disease (see Chapter 13), other disease outbreaks, civil disturbances, or environmental disasters such as hurricanes or floods. There is a growing recognition among large tourism organizations that they need to have contingency plans for such events.

However, this is probably less challenging than day-to-day operational issues and responding effectively in a competitive market where cost, service quality and delivery at a suitable price are now the dominant features. Indeed, some sectors of the tourism industry require major management troubleshooters to realign their businesses to the market, as is shown by the examples of three US airlines.

In July 2002, American Airlines announced losses of US$465 million between April and June 2002 (in contrast to a loss of US$105 million for the same period in 2001). The airline's airfares are at a fifteen-year low, depressing yields and performance. At the same time, United Airlines' parent company UAL announced a loss for the second quarter (April–June) of US$392 million, with a US$51 million grant aid from the federal government to reduce losses post-11 September 2001. In the same period in the previous year, the airline lost US$365 million. Lastly, US Airways announced a loss of US$248 million for the same period compared to a loss of US$24 million for the same period in 2001. In each case, management has set itself the task of reversing the fortunes through drastic reorganization of how the business operates and its cost base.

By contrast, P&O Princess Cruises announced profits of £361.4 million on a turnover of £2451 million for the financial year ended 2001. The UK-based specialist holiday group Holidaybreak plc (which has Supabreak, a short-break operator, as part of its portfolio as well as camping and adventure holiday operations) announced sales of £192.5 million, with profits of £23.8 million – an increase from £20.7 million in 2000. Lastly, Avis Europe, the car hire company announced revenue of £782.5 million for 2001 and profits of £134 million, 12.5 per cent lower than 2000 owing to the terrorist events of 11 September 2001.

These examples illustrate how important external events and quality management are in developing the business sector in which each operates. It also shows that the marketing, operations management and human resource management functions are critical to delivering their services to the tourist. Even in the face of adverse conditions businesses respond to the market conditions and adapt, innovate and respond. In the case of the US airline industry, the scope for innovation has been limited by negative publicity and the reduction in air travel. However, in other sectors of the tourism industry, innovative advertising, moving capacity such as cruise ships to new destinations and routes, and promoting domestic travel as Supabreak does, can allow managers to re-orient their business activities to fit with demand. Ultimately, management of tourism in the private sector is about marrying supply with demand, and in managing capacity so that peaked demand through seasonality is accommodated and profitability is achieved. Yet there are various agencies and organizations that work alongside the private sector businesses and act as facilitators of tourism, to ensure it is planned, managed and developed in a manner that befits each locality. For this reason, Chapter 11 turns to the role of tourism agencies and the public sector in managing tourism.

References

Baum, T. (ed) (1993) *Human Resource Issues in International Tourism*. London: Butterworth-Heinemann.

Carroll, S. (1988) Managerial work in the future. *In*: G. Hage (ed.), *Futures of Organizations*. Lexington: Lexington Books, pp. 85–109.

Carter, S. (1996) Small business marketing. *In*: M. Warner (ed.), *International Enyclopedia of Business and Management*. London: Thomson Learning.

Cooper, C., Fletcher, J., Gilbert, D. and Wanhill, S. (1998) *Tourism, Principles and Practice*, 2nd edn. London: Pitman.

Handy, C. (1989) *The Age of Unreason*. London: Business Books Ltd.

Holloway, J. C. and Plant, R. (1988) *Marketing for Tourism*. London: Pitman.

Horner, S. and Swarbrooke, J. (1996) *Marketing Tourism, Hospitality and Leisure in Europe*. London: International Thomson Business Press.

Inkson, K. and Kolb, D. (1995) *Management: A New Zealand Perspective*. Auckland: Longman Paul.

Kotler, P. (1988) *Marketing Management: Analysis, Planning and Control*, 6th edn. London: Prentice Hall.

Kotler, P. and Armstrong, G. (1991) *Principles of Marketing*, 5th edn. New Jersey: Prentice Hall.

McKercher, B. and Robbins, B. (1998) Business development issues affecting nature-based tourism operators in Australia. *Journal of Sustainable Tourism*, **6**(2), 173–88.

Mintzberg, H. (1973) *The Nature of Managerial Work*. New York: Harper & Row.

Morrison, A. (1996) Marketing the small tourism business. *In*: A. Seaton and M. Bennett (eds), *Marketing Tourism Products: Concepts, Issues, Cases*. London: International Thomson Publishing.

Page, S. J., Brunt, P. Busby, G. and Connell, J. (2001) *Tourism: A Modern Synthesis*. London: Thomson Publishing.

Quinn, R., Faerman, S., Thompson, M. and McGrath, M. (1990) *Becoming a Master Manager: A Competency Framework*. New York: Wiley.

Schumpeter, J. (1952) *Can Capitalism Survive?* New York: Harper and Row.

Shaw, G. and Williams, A. (2002) *Critical Issues in Tourism: A Geographical Perspective*, 2nd edn. Oxford: Blackwell.

Further reading

Holloway, J. C. and Robinson, C. (1995) *Marketing for Tourism*, 3rd edn. London: Longman.

Leiper, N. (1995) *Tourism Management*. Victoria: TAFE.

Questions

1 Why is innovation important to tourism? How do businesses embrace and harness the potential of innovation?

2 Why do tourism managers need to understand the role of management in tourism? How far are good managers 'people persons'?

3 Why do small businesses dominate the tourism sector? What particular management challenges does this pose?

4 Can the Disney model of customer care be widely rolled out to be adopted in tourism firms? Outline the reasons why this may or may not be the case.

11

The public sector and tourism

Learning objectives

This chapter examines the role of the public sector and the ways in which it facilitates and constrains the development, operation and management of tourism. After reading it, you should be able to understand:

- the roles and responsibilities of the public sector in tourism;
- what is meant by tourism policy, and why it is developed to guide tourism planning and development in different contexts and destinations;
- why the public sector needs to intervene in the tourism sector, and present a coherent argument to this end;
- the principles of good practice in developing public sector models of intervention that balance the needs of stakeholders, and present examples;
- why tourism planning is used as a tool, and its problems in implementation.

Introduction

Chapter 10 introduced the concept of tourism management in relation to the way private sector businesses interact, operate and perform in market economies. It highlighted the importance of management to ensure that for private sector companies profitability is achieved. However, tourism operates in a wider macro-economic environment, beyond the level of the firm, and that environment can be indirectly and directly managed, influenced and directed by government. According to Elliot (1997), there are four main questions that need to be asked in relation to the involvement of government in tourism:

1 Why are governments important to tourism, and why do governments get involved in tourism management?
2 Who are the man participants in the tourism policy system?
3 How is management carried out, and how do such managers manage?
4 What are the effects on tourism – has is led to success or failure?

This chapter explores these questions and explains how the public sector manages tourism, emphasizing the role of policy-making, the implementation through planning, and the impact on the management of tourism.

Governments and tourism

Governments become involved in tourism either through direct action to develop facilities and areas, or indirectly by nurturing organizations that foster tourism. To the political scientist tourism is an interesting phenomenon, because for tourism to thrive the ideal conditions are political stability, security, a well-defined legal framework, and the essential services and infrastructure (roads, water supplies and a suitable environment) that the state is able to provide. In addition, national governments are the main organizations that negotiate on immigration, visa requirements and landing rights. These statutory responsibilities are often delegated to different government departments, and do not take account of more active involvement in tourism. The main factor at work here is power – the ability to use influence and authority to affect decisions and change. Whilst governments are expected to perform statutory tasks, such as immigration and negotiating aviation rights for the wider public good, it is their degree of involvement with and commitment to tourism over and above these statutory functions that is important. In other words, if power is about 'who gets what, when and how in the political system' (Elliot, 1997: 10), then the political system is worthy of consideration. This is because it can explain why some countries, regions and localities are characterized by high levels of public sector management (PSM) and involvement and others are not. PSM is how the government influences tourism through actions and policies to either constrain or develop tourism. To governments, PSM is expected to effect change due to intervention that is in the 'public interest' and is based on principles of accountability, which are determined by the political and legal systems and PSM culture. In other words, PSM is the way in which governments manage tourism.

Why governments intervene in the tourism sector

At the country level, governments have an interest in tourism because it is an environmentally damaging activity if it is left uncontrolled, and because it may affect the people and economies of areas in both positive and negative ways (see Chapter 12). In other words, governments have a strong interest in tourism in terms of its benefits to the economy and society. By utilizing the concept of leverage, namely investment in facilities and infrastructure to promote and stimulate tourism, the wider benefits of tourism for the well-being of the population and government (i.e. the creation of jobs and an increase in tax income) are usually argued. This is illustrated by the World Trade Organization (1998: 29), *Guide for Local Authorities on Developing Sustainable Tourism*, which highlights the preconditions, benefits and effects of government intervention:

> Tourism requires that adequate infrastructure such as roads, water supply, electric power, waste management and telecommunications be developed. This infrastructure can also be designed to serve local communities so that they receive the benefits of infrastructure improvements. Tourism development can help pay for the cost of improved infrastructure. Tourism can provide new markets for local products ... and thereby stimulate other local economic sectors. Tourism stimulates development of new and improved retail, recreation and cultural facilities ... which locals as well as tourists can use.

The report also acknowledges that tourism can contribute to environmental improvements as tourists seek out non-polluted places, also promoting cultural and heritage protection. In fact, Middleton and Hawkins (1998: 6) identified the attraction of state-encouraged tourism in the developing world as being because of its potential to expand rapidly as an economic sector. This shows that it is a global phenomenon, has major economic (e.g. foreign currency) benefits, can promote employment growth, and create value in natural, cultural and heritage resources for visitors. In contrast to other sectors of the economy, tourism has been described as a smokeless industry (i.e. it is perceived as low polluting compared to developing heavy industry) and can contribute to the quality of life of residents and visitors. However, there are sceptics who question the positive reasons behind state intervention, since tourism can induce social and cultural change amongst the resident population, and alter the character and ambience of places as tourism development is followed by the resort life cycle and mass tourism. Furthermore, the economic benefits of tourism are not necessarily oriented to generating local wealth and employment, as in less developed countries and non-urban areas the benefits leak out and low-paid, seasonal employment is the norm rather than full employment for all. This becomes more serious when external control by multinational companies is considered, where environmental costs are borne by the locality and profits are expropriated back to the company, often located overseas.

Jeffries (2001) also pointed to wider political objectives by governments in affecting tourism development:

- In Spain in the 1960s the Franco regime sought to use tourism to legitimize its political acceptability, as well as recognizing its economic potential
- Since the 1930s, France has used the concept of social tourism (similar to the former Soviet Union's idea of recreational tourism, to improve the quality of life of workers at resorts, spas and holiday camps), especially in low-income groups, to enhance the welfare role of the state
- In the 1980s the UK government emphasized the employment potential of tourism in an era of high unemployment
- Some countries and transnational bodies, such as the EU, actively promote grants and aid to the peripheral regions to help develop the tourism infrastructure (e.g. road improvements in the Republic of Ireland and the Highlands and Islands of Scotland) and encourage the expansion of the tourism potential
- In less developed countries tourism expansion is often politically justified as an element of poverty eradication, and a number of developed countries governments (e.g. those of Australia, New Zealand, the UK and others in the EU) provide aid to assist with this objective (this is evident in the case of the Pacific Islands).

Government intervention and tourism performance

Governments also intervene in the tourism arena because it is perceived to be a complex industry, being an amalgam of different businesses and sectors, where benefits accrue if the businesses are coordinated better to achieve common goals – the development and improvement of the quality of tourism. A more controversial argument for intervention is to prevent market failure. Indeed, some commentators argue that when the public sector gets too involved in tourism, such as through major investment in business activities like visitor attractions, failure is never far away. This is because the imbalance with public sector intervention may deter private sector investment when tourism becomes overly bureaucratized, with a multiplicity of agencies involved in its management and regulation. In extreme cases, too much public sector investment may lead to a dependency culture where tourism is protected from market forces, becomes uneconomic due to public sector subsidies, is unattractive to investors, and fails to reach its full potential. However, intervention is often politically justified given the highly seasonal nature of tourism activity in some regions and countries, which means that there is frequently insufficient business to support year-round operation. In extreme cases there may not be adequate flows of tourists to support a tourist attraction. State subsidies, grants and assistance to the tourism sector in this context are justified by arguing that without support the attraction may not survive, and therefore would not provide a vital element of the region's attractiveness in the tourist season. This is highly controversial in countries where the performance of the tourism sector (in terms of visitor arrivals, productivity per business and high levels of seasonality) has been supported by public subsidies. Critics of such policy point to the obvious advantages of allowing the tourism sector to operate in a market economy with no subsidies or state intervention, in order to improve competitiveness. It is argued that such a market forces culture is very important for innovation to create new ideas, exciting developments and a dynamic tourism industry. Enterprise, development and innovation may need support and assistance at a fledgling stage, but ideas on innovation need to be generated initially. Yet if there is no incentive for such activity due to dependency, then public sector support may actually dampen vital activity if the tourism sector operates in a protective environment and does not have to compete globally. The result of increased competition may well be the loss of businesses without a viable market to support them in the short term if subsidies were removed. However, a decline in the number and range of tourism operators may actually be desirable if this removes marginal and poor quality operators with low service standards, which may depress the market for other businesses in destinations who are seeking to promote a quality product.

The perceived impact of such changes on marginal tourism regions, which have a heavy dependence on seasonal tourism for local employment, is viewed as politically unacceptable, and is only implemented where public sector funding for tourism is reduced owing to financial stringencies in central, regional or local government budgets. Yet critics of state subsidies for tourism argue that few other sectors of the economy with significant private and public sector involvement enjoy such levels of state-related support to facilitate economic activity.

Advocates of continued state support, often described as lobbying or interest groups (e.g. the Scottish Tourism Forum in Scotland, and the Tourism Industry Association in the USA) highlight the wider benefits of state involvement in tourism. They argue that improvements to the range of infrastructure (e.g. roading), attractions and business activity may also have benefits for residents of local areas. For many local councils tourism is often seen by residents in urban areas as a problem, in that it adds costs to the rates burden due to cleansing, rubbish collection, policing and marketing/ promotion costs. Yet the beneficial effects of tourist spending on the local economy (see Chapter 12) are arguably able to reduce rating levels, as tourism supports local businesses, which pay business rates, create employment and greater revenue for councils, thereby reducing the potential rates burden for local residents. Such arguments are highly controversial, and different facets of each argument are invariably highlighted by interest groups, depending upon the evidence used and the points raised, to advocate or reject public sector support. This is one reason why governments have endorsed better research methods to understand, analyse and explain how local economies work, as there is often a great deal of conjecture, supposition and value-laden argument used by interest groups and stakeholders when debating tourism. This ongoing tension sometimes explains why some local councils, which periodically change their political complexion, can be described as 'blowing hot and cold' towards tourism – exemplified in the policies and planning approaches they adopt towards tourism.

Inevitably, government involvement in tourism at any level is about the resolution of conflict, seeking to achieve a balance between actively promoting tourism and acting as guardians of the public interest in the manner, form, direction, impact and effect of tourism from a national to local level. This conflict resolution process often means balancing the protagonists (i.e. the tourism industry) and antagonists (often residents), who are both valid stakeholders in the tourism economy, in seeking to meet the needs of the visitor in a sustainable and locally appropriate manner.

A more active role for governments, and potential reason for intervention in the tourism economy or markets, is related to strategic objectives. Here, two perspectives have been identified by Jeffries (2001):

1 Strategic seasonal redistribution of tourists
2 Strategic geographical redistribution of tourism.

In the first instance, seasonal redistribution is a major global issue, given the problems of seasonality in tourism. Seasonality can lead to a highly skewed pattern of business for tourism operators outside of major urban areas, but tourism organizations responsible for tourism promotion, development and management may intervene in the market – as the case of Destination Northland (North of New Zealand, www.destinationnorthland.co.nz) suggests, where it was able to:

● Provide a new series of innovative new products for visitors in the low season, which are less weather-dependent, by emphasizing the appeal to the domestic market (e.g. sporting events, promoting sightseeing on the twin coast highway route, and wine and food tourism based on local products).
● Operate marketing campaigns via printed media and the World Wide Web to highlight the region's indigenous culture (i.e. the Maori of Tai Tokeran iwi) and the built heritage of Russell, the country's first capital, as the birthplace of New Zealand. It also recognized the appeal of the marine environment of the Bay of Islands, with the attraction for yacht-based tourists to winter-over in the region.

These examples highlight the recognition that the tourism industry in many localities is highly fragmented and lacks cohesion, political clout and the ability to influence change because the individual operators are focused on their own activities rather than the strategic development of the region. By seeking to extend the tourist season and expand the range of opportunities for low season visitation, public sector agencies argue that increased business activity and turnover will lead to greater profitability. This may also lead to employment growth and a higher profile as a tourism region.

In the second instance, the public sector directly intervenes in tourism planning and development by seeking to achieve a geographical redistribution of tourists and the volume of visits. For example, in the 1960s the French government produced a plan to develop a coastal region to the South of Montpellier, known as Languedoc-Roussillon. The initial plan was to develop a resort area with 150 000 bedspaces, which was subsequently revised and expanded in the 1970s and 1980s. This is a widely cited example of state-led tourism development in a peripheral area, and reveals the state motives for seeking to direct tourism to an undeveloped region to assist with regional development. In contrast, tourism in London (the gateway for UK tourism) saw resident views, congestion, overcrowding and high occupancy rates in hotel accommodation result in the London Tourist Board commissioning the *Tourism Accommodation in London in the 1990s* report (Touche Ross, 1988). This formed the basis for policies to limit further hotel growth in London's West End, while encouraging the development of out-of-town accommodation. The result, in the period 1988–2000, was the development of tourism accommodation in districts adjacent to the West End of London, and expansion of accommodation in London's urban fringe adjacent to Heathrow and Gatwick airports – especially budget accommodation next to the M25 junctions. This policy of constraint and directed development has taken a number of years to evolve, but even over the fourteen-year period to 2002 changes have been notable, despite the lead time for new accommodation. More explicit state intervention is evident in many of Europe's small historic towns, where the local planning authorities have adopted radical measures to constrain the saturation effects of mass tourism in, for example, Canterbury, York, Stratford-upon-Avon and Cambridge. But how do organizations in the public sector affect such change, and what processes and procedures are used to manage tourism? This begins through the development of tourism policy.

Tourism policy

According to Hall and Jenkins (1995: 2), tourism public policy can help the causes and consequences of policy decisions, since it indicates the way in which policy influences tourism through:

- The political nature of the policy-making process
- The degree of public participation in the tourism policy and planning process
- The sources of power in the tourism policy-making environment, and the choices and decisions made by civil servants towards complex policy issues
- The perceptions of stakeholders as to the effectiveness of tourism policies.

This illustrates that tourism policy-making is inherently a political activity, affected by the formal structures of government. A wide range of forces affects policymaking. According to Hall and Jenkins (1995: 5), public policy in tourism is 'whatever governments choose to do or not to do'; according to Turner (1997) it is a function of three inter-related issues:

1 The intentions of political and other key actors
2 The way in which decisions and non-decisions are made
3 The implications of these decisions.

Figure 11.1 illustrates the continuous nature of policy-making, which requires an understanding of the nature of the institutions and organizations involved in shaping policy, since policy-making is filtered through a range of different institutions and this may seem complex to the uninitiated observer. These institutions help shape policy outcomes because they are involved in negotiation and bargaining to achieve their own organization's objectives. At the same time, interest groups (producer groups such as national tourism associations), non-producer groups (e.g. environmental organizations) and single issue groups (e.g. opponents of an airport project) seek to influence the decision-making element of policy-making.

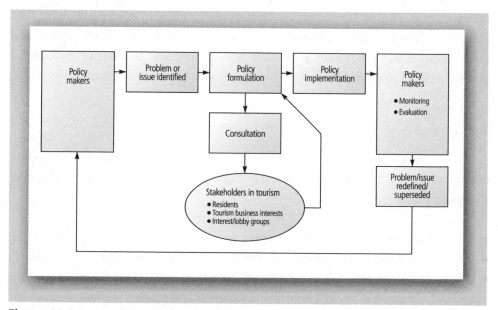

Figure 11.1   The policy-making process in tourism

Tourism policy does not exist in a vacuum, because various agencies exist to implement it. The implementation is again a resolution of conflict and attempts to meet the needs of stakeholders whilst also meeting national or local tourism development needs. Policy cannot be viewed in isolation from political decision-making, which determines the direction of policy, which is constantly evolving. For example, in the case of China, a series of policy changes post-1978, when the country first opened its doors to tourists, required major policy changes. Post-1978, policy success is often measured through one simple barometer of tourism – international visitor arrivals. In 1978 international visitor arrivals were a modest 1.8 million, these subsequently increased to 17.8 million in 1985 and 33.3 million in 1991. Five years later visitor arrivals exceeded 51 million, and in 1997 some 57.5 million arrivals were recorded. This incredible rate of growth in inbound tourism required a shift in policy from the pre-1978 Socialist idiom that tourism was a vehicle to educate visitors about the virtues of communism, to one that was accommodating a large influx of visitors who were only allowed to visit certain areas. A similar rationale characterized inbound tourism policy in the former Soviet Union and pre-1990s Albania.

In the case of China, tourism policy was effectively embodied in the Five-Year National Plans, which controlled a state command economy. From 1986–1991, state policy saw tourism as a lucrative source of foreign exchange. This evolved from the 1978–1985 period, where a general tourism policy with little state intervention created major operational problems in terms of a general shortage of supply, an inadequate non-market pricing structure and ineffective management of tourists and employees, where poor service standards resulted. By developing a National Tourism Plan, the government tourist agency (the China National Tourism Administration, or CNTA) began to establish key policy objectives to guide the future development of Chinese tourism. As Page *et al.* (2001) observed, policy changes resulted in:

- Greater coordination of tourism, with the establishment of the National Tourism Commission in 1988 and an initial focus on civil aviation followed by hotels and travel agencies
- Restoration of tourist attractions in the top fourteen tourist cities, such as the Forbidden City
- Reform in the aviation sector, particularly the Civil Aviation Authority of China, to transform the airlines and airports into independent corporations
- Improved education and training, with regional tourism bureaux governing tourism education in their region

- Greater regulation of the tourism sector by the CNTA
- The promotion of international tourism, with the CNTA's budget for overseas marketing increased from US$1.4 million in 1986 to US$3.2 million in 1991 following the decline of tourist arrivals and the impact of the Tiananmen Square incident.

Subsequent policy changes in 1992 were embodied under the new 'market economy under socialism' policy, whereby tourism could move towards a market system without unduly compromising the underlying principles of Chinese socialism. Notable changes included the introduction of competition into China's aviation sector, a greater use of tourism promotion, and recognition of the diversity of inbound tourism and niche markets and the need for state-led regulation of the tourism sector to improve quality standards. In addition, government policy towards the economy had both indirect and direct effects on tourism. In the period 1986–1996 the government used a growth pole strategy, where a key location is chosen to concentrate the investment and economic development in less developed areas to pump-prime the economy. In Yunnan in inland China, the growth pole was located at that town as a basis for economic development fostered around tourism, to assist in dispersing the current patterns of tourism development from the coastal region and key cities. This was found to help address regional economic inequality where the tourism sector had powerful backward linkages with other economic sectors (e.g. agriculture; see Chapter 12 for more discussion).

The growth pole strategy helps to spread the effects and benefits of tourism, but equally can pose planning problems where policy decisions have to be taken over the style of tourism development to be pursued (i.e. small-scale versus mass tourism). A similar strategy of growth pole development has been used and has had a tourism benefit in economically remote areas in Ireland, Scotland and Canada. In each case, the state has invested in the infrastructure and provided incentives for private sector investment in tourism.

Yet it is not just governments that influence tourism policy, but also a range of international non-governmental agencies (NGOs) such as the World Trade Organization. The WTO, based in Madrid, seeks to assist its member countries to work in a cooperative and collaborative manner to provide statistical information on tourism, and to advise on policies and practices to improve tourism planning and education and training. Other international lobby groups seek to influence the air, transport lobby and its industry groups (e.g. the IATA, ICAO, ATAG and AIC).

These bodies promote the interests of its members, who have vested interests in tourism.

An additional agency that is influential in government tourism policy is the EU. The fifteen member countries of the EU represent an important trading bloc, which is mirrored by similar blocs in other parts of the world. The EU seeks to promote tourism as a free trade activity in and between member states by trying to simplify and harmonize policies and procedures to facilitate the free movement of travellers. The

Table 11.1 The range of European Community measures affecting tourism

- Economic policies
- Enterprise policy towards tourism businesses
- Competition issues and mergers
- State aid for tourism (e.g. subsidies)
- The internal market and tourism
- Fiscal policies and tourism (e.g. taxation)
- Employment and social policy (e.g. the minimum wage)
- Enhancing Europe's potential for tourism
- Tourism and employment
- Exchange and dissemination of information
- Training, skills and the workforce
- Education and vocational training
- Qualifications, employability and lifelong learning
- Social rights, social protection, social integration and inequality
- Social dialogue
- Quality issues in tourism destinations
- Improving the quality of tourism products
- Safety in tourism installations, food safety and health
- The environment and sustainable development
- Environmental protection
- Natural and cultural heritage
- Transport
- Energy

The European Commission has produced guidelines or reports for each of these areas, all of which can be accessed at www.europa.eu.int

EU also seeks to develop measures to improve the quality of tourism in member states, although tourism policy remains the remit of individual governments. The scale and extent of the EU's impact on the wide range of issues that affect tourism are shown in Table 11.1, which highlights the diversity of EU measures affecting tourism (see www.europa.eu.int for more up-to-date information, as EU policy and developments in tourism are constantly evolving).

Among the most influential agencies that develop policy for tourism in individual countries are:

- Ministries of Tourism, which fund or part-fund National Tourism Organizations (NTOs) such as the British Tourist Authority
- NTOs
- Regional tourism organizations, which manage the implantation of national and regional policy in their respective areas
- Local authorities and other agencies, which set policies at the local area level.

This vast array of public sector agencies is complemented by *ad hoc* agencies set up within specific areas such as inner city regeneration projects (e.g. the London Docklands Development Corporation in the 1980s and 1990s). More recently, local economic development agencies have been reintroduced in England and Wales. In Scotland, Scottish Enterprise's local enterprise companies set out policies for the tourism sector and intervene, using public funds, to meet specific tourism objectives (see Chapter 9).

It is apparent that in many countries, while tourism policy may rest with the Ministry of Tourism or department responsible for tourism, a host of agencies interact to produce a multi-layered system of public sector support. Figure 11.2 illustrates this model of support in the UK, which has been described as chaotic and extremely bureaucratic. Whilst there is a growing debate that governments are no longer about direct control of tourism but about encouraging other agencies to govern the public sector and must be more accountable to stakeholders, it is creating an overly complex web of agencies that may have confused, overlapping and competing roles. For example, the UK model is characterized by:

1 One national organization, the BTA, to market the UK overseas (currently under review).

2 Four country-based NTOs, the English Tourism Council, VisitScotland (formerly the Scottish Tourist Board), the National Ireland Tourist Board and the Wales Tourism

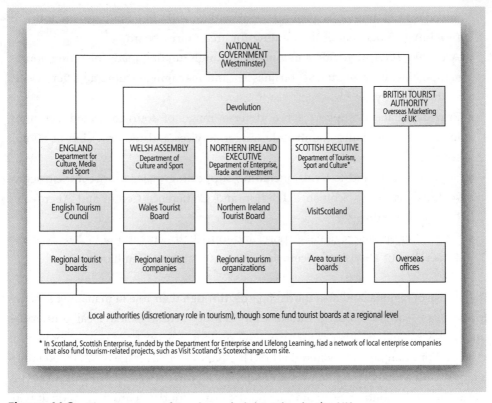

Figure 11.2 The structure of tourism administration in the UK

Board). In some cases these NTOs market each country to domestic and international tourists, which may appear to be a duplication of effort with the BTA, which markets the UK as a united destination overseas.

3 Regional tourist boards in England, Wales and Northern Ireland, with area tourist boards in Scotland. These agencies are funded by grants from the devolved governments in Wales and Scotland, and through membership subscriptions. In Scotland, a ministerial review of area tourist boards was underway in 2002 to examine their roles, activities and responsibilities.

4 Local authorities, of which there are 387 in England – 34 non-metropolitan county councils, 238 non-metropolitan district councils, 36 metropolitan councils, 46 unitary councils, 32 London boroughs, and the City of London Corporation. In Scotland, the local authorities' impact upon tourism was outlined by a report in 2002 entitled *The Role of Scottish Councils in Tourism*. This indicated that local authorities:

- Spend £14.33 million a year (in conjunction with EU funding) on tourism; providing 33 per cent of the funding for area tourist boards
- Are major service providers in tourism, through funding roads, planning, tourist signposting, licensing tourist businesses, and managing health and safety issues in their locality
- Provide financial support for a diverse range of tourism-related activities, including cycle paths, countryside ranger services and the provision of 80 golf courses
- Support events and festivals, including supporting major tourist infrastructure such as Glasgow's Scottish Exhibition and Conference Centre and Aberdeen's Exhibition Centre
- Support or operate regional airports and tourist attractions, and in 2001 received 45 per cent of all visits to Scottish Visitor Attractions (15 million visits).

In the case of regional and area tourist boards, through their role in managing services for visitors, such as Tourist Information Centres (TICs) (some local authorities undertake this role in other countries), they provide a network of contact points for visitors. For example, in Scotland the 148 TICs handled an average of 22 000 bookings a month and a total of 5 million visitor enquiries a year. Between April and July 2002, Kelso TIC in the South of Scotland (the Borders Area Tourist Board region) dealt with 26 000 visitors, indicating the scale of its activity.

Given the scope and nature of the public sector agencies in tourism, attention now turns to how these organizations plan for tourism.

How government organizations influence tourism

In the UK, the Department for Culture, Media and Sport (DCMS) is the government department responsible for tourism. Like its counterpart in many countries it is not seen as a high profile Ministry, because tourism is not accorded a portfolio that reflects its economic role in most countries. As a result, other government departments make a significant contribution both directly and indirectly to infrastructure development (e.g. the Department of Transport in terms of roads, ports and aviation). In the UK context, the DCMS has a broad responsibility for leisure, tourism and the cultural industries, including tourism, the arts, broadcasting, cultural artefacts, film, art, heritage, libraries, museums, galleries, the press, the royal estate, sport and recreation. Whilst such an integrated approach to the leisure industries can seek to achieve the ministry's objectives to improve the quality of life through cultural industries and sporting activities and by contributing to job creation, there is a danger that tourism can become subsumed and lost among so many functions.

Having outlined the organizations and bodies involved in policy-making for tourism at different levels, attention now turns to how these policies are implemented – through the planning process.

Planning and tourism

So far this chapter has highlighted the tensions that exist in the formulation of policies to guide the development of the tourism sector, as a process of negotiation between stakeholders' groups brokered by public sector agencies. At a practical level, the implementation of public sector policies requires an understanding of how agencies plan, manage and use tools in tourism destinations. The context in which agencies involved in tourism planning operate is also important, because underlying principles and ideas influence the way planning is shaped. For example, although the concept of sustainability is not the focus of this chapter, it is an important theme given its widespread use in tourism planning. In simple terms, sustainability is a common-sense approach to the use, consumption and management of the resources upon which tourism relies (see Chapter 12). In essence, the arguments developed on sustainability and embodied in the *Brundtland Report* (World Commission on the Environment and Development, 1987) suggest that resources must be used in a manner, whereby they can be enjoyed today but also conserved and managed for future generations. It questions man's historical pursuit of resource depletion in the name of progress and development, with no concern for the future. This concept, which was guided by environmentalism in the 1960s and 1970s, recognizes that there are limits to the growth of the planet, with many resources (such as oil) being finite and non-renewable. In a tourism context, this has emerged as a major debate for planners because of the global growth of tourism. Tourism equates to the consumption of environmental resources, and this poses problems for destination areas. In practical terms, it raises the challenge for planners of balancing tourism demand and supply, and of recognizing the future effects of tourism if the concept of sustainability is not considered. The public sector therefore intervenes, in tourism and planning terms, to implement tourism policy objectives and to avoid over-development from tourism, as the tourism sector pursues short-term profits. This means that without public sector intervention, the potentially beneficial effects of tourism can easily be lost if the environment and resource-base for tourism in destination areas is irreversibly damaged.

Returning to the basic premise of tourism management, then tourism planning in its practical form is about the public sector *leading* to *organize*, *plan* and *control* tourism development in relation to policies in each destination area. This requires the complex coordination of stakeholder interests (the private sector businesses, public sector agencies, residents and visitors). These tasks also have a time horizon, known as the strategic dimension, where tourism planning has a five- to ten-year timeframe during which the impact and implications of policies and plans can be monitored and evaluated. This was illustrated above in the case of London's tourism accommodation between 1988 and 2000, where policies directly shaped the future nature, form and location of accommodation development. But does tourism planning actually exist, and if so, how does it operate and how is it organized?

Does tourism planning exist?

There is an ongoing debate amongst tourism professionals regarding whether tourism planning exists as a phenomenon, since much of the planning activity for tourism is based upon public sector planning as opposed to specific tourism agency-led planning. In many cases, planning exists within regional (i.e. county councils) and local (i.e. district councils) agencies in the UK and their equivalents in other parts of the world. These bodies typically subsume tourism within economic development departments, which seek to accommodate future demands and change. As Hall (1999) argues, much of the planning for tourism is based on an *ad hoc* approach, lacking continuity, cohesion and strategic vision.

Even so, Getz (1987) has described four traditions that have evolved in planning tourism: boosterism, an economic-industry approach, a physical–spatial approach, and a community-oriented approach. This can also be extended to give a fifth approach – sustainable tourism planning, which is 'a concern for the long-term future of resources, the effects of economic development on the environment, and its ability to meet present and future needs' (Page and Thorn, 1997: 60).

Inskeep (1994) has indicated that the effective management of tourism requires certain 'organizational elements'. The most important of these in a planning context are organizational structures, which include government agencies and private sector interest groups as well as the involvement of local and regional government bodies to plan for tourism activity and tourism-related legislation and regulations. These bodies utilize the statutory planning frameworks, such as planning acts, government ordinances and directives from central government, which in turn condition the parameters for planning. For example, in late 2002 in Antigua the government announced plans to expand the number of hotel rooms from 1800 to 5000 by establishing a new vehicle to stimulate development – a private–public sector partnership – a Tourism Development Corporation. In contrast, the Mayor of London announced plans in 2002 to support a three-year Tourism Strategy for London to assist it in remaining competitive by committing: £3 million to improving tourism and £4 million for implementation and actioning the strategy. Where the planning process focuses on tourism, a process akin to that of developing policy-making is followed.

The planning process for tourism

There is normally a set of pre-defined steps that characterize the planning process for tourism, including:

1 *Study preparation*, which is where the planning authority within the local or regional government (although on small island states that do not have a complex planning structure it may be the NTO) decides to proceed with the development of a tourism plan. It is normally a statutory body that undertakes the plan, but in more complex urban environments where local and regional agencies both develop tourism plans it is important that they are integrated to ensure a unified approach to tourism. This was a problem in London in the 1990s, when the 33 London boroughs each had unified development plans but pursued different approaches to tourism. This meant that some councils promoted tourism development while others positively discouraged it, despite the efforts of the London Tourist Board, which sought to coordinate their activities in tourism. The result was a pattern of uneven development across the city.

2 *Determination of objectives*, where the objectives of the plan are identified (e.g. is the agency seeking to promote tourism to pump-prime economic development? Or is it trying to manage the problems of mass tourism and the associated effects in its locality?).

3 *Survey of all elements*, where an inventory of existing tourism resources and facilities is reviewed, requiring the collection of data on the supply and demand for tourism and the structure of the local tourist economy. It also needs to recognize which other

private and public sector interests are stakeholders in tourism within the destination.

4 *Analysis and synthesis of findings*, where the information and data collected from the previous stage are used to begin formulating the plan. This typically uses four techniques – asset evaluation, market analysis, development planning and impact analysis (see Chapter 12) – to establish the future for tourism.

5 *Policy and plan formulation*, where the data are used, sifted, sorted and organized to establish development scenarios for tourism. This invariably leads to the preparation of a draft development plan with tourism policy options. These policies must have three elements in order to be able to meet the varying needs of the tourism stakeholders – visitor satisfaction, environmental protection, and ensuring a payback for investors.

6 *Consideration of recommendations*, where the full tourism plan is sent to the organization's planning committee. A public consultation normally follows the planning committee's acceptance of the plan. The general public and interested parties are then able to read and comment on the plan. A number of public hearings may also be provided to gauge the strength of local feeling towards the plan. Once this procedure is completed, the plan is sent back to the planning authority in a revised form for approval with any changes incorporated, so the final plan can be prepared.

7 *Implementation and monitoring of the tourism plan* then follows, which includes various actions. Legislation may be required in some cases to control certain aspects of development (e.g. the density of development) that need to be implemented as part of the plan. However, the political complexity of implementing such a plan is substantial, since the political complexion of elected representatives on the statutory planning authority may change and cause the priorities to change. Where an Action Plan is produced that causes intense political debate over each issue, it may allow for some degree of choice in what is implemented and actioned within a set period of time. At the same time as the plan is being implemented it also needs to be monitored and evaluated, and is frequently criticized by commentators. The planning agency needs to assess if the objectives of the plan are being met. The operational timeframe for a tourism plan is normally five years, after which time it is reviewed.

8 *Periodic review*, which is the process of reporting back on progress after the plan has run its course. When analysing the reasons for the success or failure of the plan to achieve all its objectives, a range of reasons may be suggested. These may include a lack of resources to achieve the goals, political infighting by elected members of

the planning authority, inadequate transport and infrastructure provision, public opposition to tourism among residents, and a lack of investment by public sector businesses.

Governmental tourism strategies

To guide the multitude of public sector agencies and stakeholders involved in tourism, government departments will often embody many of the policy objectives in a strategy document. This strategy document identifies what the government wishes to achieve in broad terms in tourism, and identifies objectives and action points for other agencies, as is shown in the case study in Box 11.1.

Box 11.1   Case study: the Scottish Tourism Framework for Action 2002–2005

In 2001, the newly created Ministry of Tourism, Sport and Culture in the Scottish Executive (SE) set out to develop a number of new directions for Scottish Tourism. It closely followed the SE's first tourism strategy of February 2000 – *A New Strategy for Scottish Tourism* – with a new strategy in 2002. Interesting, the initial strategy in 2000 identified five key areas for action in Scottish Tourism to improve the performance of the industry, against a decline in overseas arrivals:

1 The effective use of information technology
2 Better marketing
3 Higher standards of quality
4 Higher standards of service
5 The development of the skills base of tourism employees.

In 2002 the new Ministry developed its new vision and priorities for Scottish tourism, embodied in *The Tourism Framework for Action 2002–2005*, setting out a vision thus:

> Scotland is a must-visit destination where visitors' needs come first, and tourism makes a vital contribution to economic growth.

This identified three specific priorities:

1 To develop a better and stronger market position for Scotland, based on clearly identified brands and products to meet customer needs
2 To improve the consumer focus to drive forward quality standards, as well as developing new products and services, ultimately to create successful business leadership
3 To enhance the status of tourism in Scotland, based on understanding the linkages between different elements of the economy and tourism that require businesses and stakeholders to work together collaboratively, particularly through partnerships and alliances to improve sales, competitive position and focus.

These objectives are embodied in Figure 11.3, which requires actions to be delivered by businesses, public sector agencies and the SE. For example, in 2002 VisitScotland launched a new brand and product portfolio to refocus VisitScotland's marketing focus for Scottish tourism.

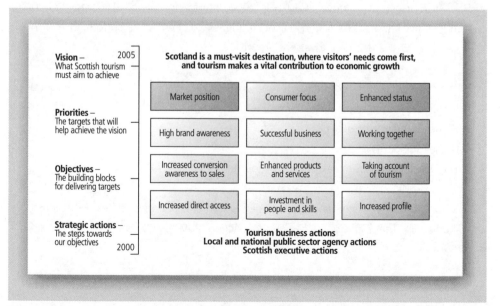

Figure 11.3 The Scottish Tourism Framework for Action, 2002–2005. Reproduced with permission from the Scottish Executive

Based on this framework, the SE identified the roles of tourism and non-tourism businesses in taking responsibility for delivering the framework for action. A detailed set of actions is identified in relation to each objective in Figure 11.3, together with the responsibility for implementation. For example, in improving Scotland's market position it outlined the following objectives:

- To achieve high brand awareness amongst target groups, with three actions spread between businesses and public sector agencies
- To increase the conversion of potential visitors from awareness to sales, with four actions split between public and private sectors
- To increase direct access opportunities for target consumers, with two actions largely aimed at the SE – to develop the infrastructure and services as well as businesses collaborating to market such improvements.

A similar matrix of objectives and actions was developed for each of the three priorities (Figure 11.3). Interestingly, the framework for action identified the multiplicity of 'relevant' public sector agencies that need to work in partnership to deliver the public sector element of the strategy, including:

- The area tourist boards, particularly in relation to leading marketing initiatives that fit with VisitScotland objectives, which as well as operating TICs deliver area tourism strategies and advise tourism businesses.
- The British Tourist Authority (BTA), working with VisitScotland to market Scotland internationally using the BTAs network of overseas offices as well as its international market intelligence/research.
- The Forestry Commission, which manages forestry resources and has a contribution to make in creating opportunities for tourism.
- Historic Scotland, which manages 330 historic visitor attractions across Scotland and markets heritage resources to the tourism market.
- The local authorities, which develop policy and deliver services within national frameworks for tourism whilst also administering planning controls and managing publicly-owned or leased tourism facilities. These agencies also work with local business associations (e.g. Chambers of Commerce) and trade associations (e.g. local voluntary tourism associations such as the Dunblane Tourism Group), part-fund the area tourist boards, and actively participate in delivering area tourism strategies.

- The Scottish Arts Council, which supports and promotes the arts and administers lottery funding for the Arts in Scotland.
- The Scottish Enterprise Network, which comprises the local enterprise companies and Highlands and Islands Enterprise Network. These are involved in formulating strategies for training and infrastructure development, and support services such as Small Business Gateway and vital coordination/networking opportunities for local tourism businesses.
- The Scottish Executive, which has legislative responsibility for the Scottish economy functions devolved from the UK government in Westminster. It is responsible for direct funding to tourism and to support agencies, including local authorities, VisitScotland, Scottish Enterprise, Historic Scotland, Scottish Natural Heritage, the Scottish Arts Council and Sportscotland.
- The Scottish Museums Council, which represents 200 members in Scotland with 320 museums.
- Scottish Natural Heritage, which provides advice on the conservation of natural heritage, and on recreation in the countryside and coastal areas.
- SportScotland, which administers the Lottery Sports Fund in Scotland and promotes sporting opportunities, and has a role to play in relation to the growing interest in sport-related (e.g. golf) and event-based tourism.
- VisitScotland, which formulates strategy for marketing Scotland, based on the 1969 Development of Tourism Act. It is also the lead organization in the promotion of tourism and in identifying research needs for Scottish tourism. It also co-funds area tourist boards (in conjunction with local authorities and its business membership) and advises government on tourism issues as well as managing tourism quality assurance schemes.

To implement the strategy and to evaluate its achievements, the following four steps were introduced in 2002:

1 The development, by the Scottish Executive and VisitScotland, of a measurement framework for the required actions, with a series of performance indicators to measure progress
2 The creation of a Steering Group, chaired by the Minister for Tourism, Sport and Culture, to oversee progress with the framework for action

3 An implementation group, chaired by VisitScotland, to monitor actions and engage the industry to advise the Steering Group

4 The hosting of events to engage the Scottish tourism industry to improve the mutual understanding of tourism and to recognize each organization's roles and responsibilities.

What is interesting about the framework is the extended coordination, communication and leadership role needed to drive Scottish tourism forward in the new millennium. It also emphasizes the range of organizations that have to be consulted in relation to tourism policy, and the potential conflicts that exist between agencies with competing objectives (e.g. conservation agencies and business development agencies). It reinforces the argument that policy-making is multi-layered and involves a large number of interest groups.

In the Scottish case, concerns regarding the industry's competitiveness, value for money, travel costs, unfavourable exchange rates and the problems of seasonality are not necessarily issues that cannot be easily addressed by a strategy. Above all, lateral thinking, industry–public sector cooperation and more visionary central government legislation aimed at tackling obstacles to improve business performance are needed to find ways to re-position Scottish tourism. With 50 per cent of overseas and 30 per cent of British visitors to Scotland visiting during the period from July to September each year, seasonality adds pressures on businesses and raises costs of production. This illustrates the need to re-position Scotland with new products and experiences to encourage a more even spread of visitation. There is also a desire to spread the geographical distribution (see Figure 5.5 on coach tourism, which highlights some of the traditional patterns that are gateway- and city-destination focused).

Public sector marketing of tourism

The majority of national tourist organizations are not producers or operators in a tourism context, but seek to influence the images that visitors and potential visitors may hold of the country or region. Most NTOs are engaged in destination promotion, usually aimed at the international market (although in large countries this may also target the domestic market). This involves the maintenance of a network of tourism offices in key international source markets, although this is more restricted among less developed countries where budgets are very limited. The most up-to-date figures on

NTO budgets are the 1997 data from the World Trade Organization, based on a self-completion survey. In 1997, European countries only spent 0.5 per cent of the gross receipts from international tourism on NTO marketing, which is considerably higher than 0.3 per cent in the USA. Yet globally it is estimated that NTOs spend US$1.5 billion on marketing, which accounts for between one-half and two-thirds of the total budgets for NTOs – illustrating the cost of seeking to influence visitors' images of a destination. This can be done by direct advertising campaigns and product launches in target markets. For example, in October 2002 the Danish Tourist Board announced plans to spend £8 million to promote short breaks from the UK, to encourage a desire to visit Scandinavia, particularly with the access now afforded by budget airlines. Similarly, Tourism Ireland (the new all Ireland promotion agency, see www.shamrock.org) announced a short breaks programme themed around the 'temptation Ireland' idea, designed to tempt visitors to visit and experience Ireland. This is a coordinated pan-Ireland approach to assist the visitor with a more united approach to Destination Ireland – The Emerald Isle.

Expenditure on marketing is just one of the influences that affects tourism volumes to a country. There is a more substantial marketing effort by the tourism industry, much of which has been led by airlines and tour operators. Indeed, given the low levels of industry membership of tourist boards, NTOs only have a limited influence in developing an industry-led campaign that seeks to send a specific message to potential visitors. Even so, in some countries (e.g. Scotland and Singapore) the efforts are very successful in harmonizing marketing messages where these are directed towards target markets and specific segments with growth potential. This provides recognition that the NTO has influence far beyond that of individual businesses and industry-sector groups such as tour operators. Indeed, the British Tourist Authority (BTA) is planning to target the American over-55s in 2003 by raising the profile and appeal of a visit to the UK with its www.maturebritain.org website, which is integrated more fully into its Travel Britain web portal. There are many other marketing initiatives that seek to promote a destination using both conventional print and new forms of media. These include using the World Wide Web to promote a destination by creating promotional messages and symbols/messages, using promotional media to provide merchandizing opportunities, and providing incentives to buy. In each case the work of NTOs in place and product marketing seeks to develop a product substitute role (i.e. come to our destination as opposed to a competitors) by using the advertising opportunities to access the destination's products and thereby provide a purchasing mechanism in some cases. The launch of an e-commerce site is now seen as a vital element of any NTO strategy for destination marketing, since it offers a mechanism to generate a sale and a convenient method of communicating with the customer. It has been evident throughout this book that e-commerce is now a vital element for all sectors of the tourism industry, in a rapidly changing business environment. It can be beneficial for NTOs to engage in e-commerce for the wider tourism sector, since tourists select particular place products (i.e. destinations) in their holiday decision-making process. Tourists normally consider a limited set of place products, often on the basis of limited knowledge of the destination and available options. Yet the holiday may be as much the place as the place is the holiday for the tourist. In contrast, the various businesses and organizations associated with tourism focus on specific aspects of the place product (e.g. an attraction or facility). Therefore, the e-commerce strategy of the NTO and ready provision of visual information and images may help to broker the tourist as purchaser with the business as a seller. It can help to promote an initial interest registered by a potential tourist after being made aware of the destination, and encourage a follow-up visit to a website. This electronic linking of the purchaser and seller often requires NTOs and the tourism industry to work collaboratively through a partnership approach.

The growing collaboration between public and private sectors in countries such as Canada and Australia has indicated how powerful these new NTO partnerships can be in marketing a dynamic industry. The Canadian Tourism Commission (a newly established organization with a remit to seek private sector partnerships) raised its funding for marketing from C$15 million in 1995 to C$100 million in 1998/1999, with the private sector contributing 50 per cent of the funds. The marketing activities of NTOs are outlined in Figure 11.4, which highlights the different options available – such as developing a visionary promotional strategy. It may also involve branding as a process, though the range and nature of activities will be dependent upon the nature of the budget. It may be controlled by its remit, established by legislation (such as the 1969 Development of Tourism Act in the UK). Figure 11.4 also reiterates the coordination and liaison roles performed by the NTOs, and how tourism businesses interact with the public sector.

Below the level of the NTO, regional or area tourist boards perform a similar function. These bodies emphasize the attributes of their local area, and many local authorities seek to promote their city or locality in a lesser way, to establish a destination as a distinctive and unique place to visit, emphasizing the unique selling proposition (USP). In Northern Ireland there are five regional tourism organizations (RTOs), each of which is themed to reflect the destination it represents and the unique

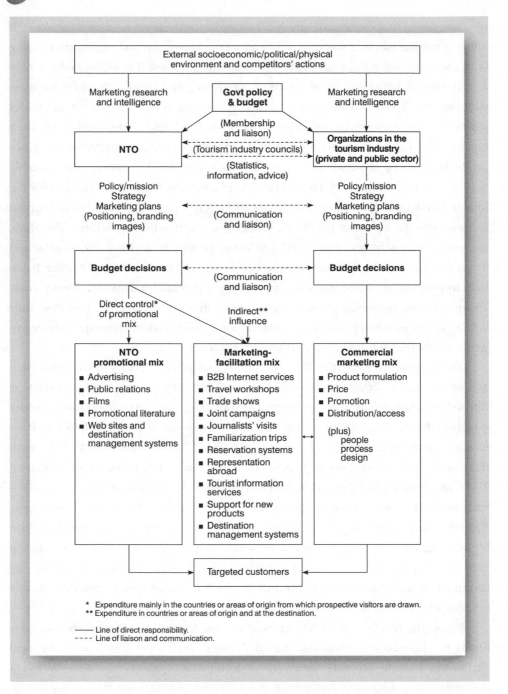

Figure 11.4 The destination marketing process for National Tourist Organizations (source: Middleton and Clarke, 2001: 338; © Butterworth-Heinemann). Reprinted by permission of Elsevier

attributes of the area: the Belfast Visitor and Convention Bureau, Derry Visitor and Convention Bureau, Causeway Coast and Glens, Kingdoms of Down and Fermanagh Lakeland Tourism. Each RTO is a company limited by guarantee, with funding from the public and private sectors in line with other parts of the UK. They are largely membership organizations, so businesses have to pay a fee to join and in return are able to draw upon the RTOs services, which include marketing, advertising, training, and research and development. The RTOs have an annual marketing budget of £2 million, with over 1600 members from private sector businesses. The RTOs' income streams are supported by the Northern Ireland Tourist Board (NITB) and local authority contributions, as well as through commercial income (e.g. the sales of goods to visitors and commissions on sales). The RTO structure was established in 1998, after a strategic review of tourism in Northern Ireland that recommended that the NITB should be more consumer-focused, work in partnership and avoid unnecessary fragmentation. This resulted in the former fifteen local authority-funded marketing consortia with limited private sector involvement being replaced with the RTO network. However, with change never far away, the NITB appointed consultants in 2002 to review this network and the wider support structures for tourism (e.g. regional and local development funding and support) since the establishment of Tourism Ireland Limited to market one Ireland.

Summary

At a global scale, there has been a growing consensus among governments that private sector tourism interests need to work more closely with the public sector to manage the marketing, planning, control and development of tourism. This is part of a withdrawal of central government from direct management of many areas of public activity, and a desire to see a greater use of public–private partnerships to govern the tourism sector. In many countries, national or devolved government still plays a role in funding NTOs and other tourism-related functions. There is recognition of the need for the tourism sector to be in charge and responsible for its own destiny. Whilst public sector-led marketing remains the norm in most countries, there is a greater awareness of the need for tourism to be a self-financing activity, with debates over the possible value of tourist taxes to fund public sector planning and management of tourism.

In some cases, the withdrawal of central government involvement in tourism and the replacement with quangos (quasi-autonomous government organizations) reflects a changing philosophy that industry-led bodies are more appropriate to deliver tourism policy and its implementation, as highlighted by the case study in Box 11.1. However, this is not being accompanied by the rationalization of tourism organizations that input into policy and planning. To the contrary, with the growth of tourism associations and interest groups there is a greater need than ever for the public sector to coordinate, liaise and interact with such bodies to monitor and evaluate the needs and issues that impact upon the performance and management of tourism. However, since policy-making is an inherently political process, the historical role of the public sector as the main agency formulating tourism policy seems set to continue. But tourism policy monitoring and evaluation still remains a neglected area for many public sector agencies, and there is a need for more critical evaluation of the assumptions behind policy.

If the public sector is to play a greater role in tourism, understanding the consequences of specific tourism policies, it requires a more explicit recognition of whether policy is successful or a failure. Indeed, there is a degree of inward-looking thinking that fails to question the need for government intervention in tourism. Policy analysis and evaluation in the public sector have remained generalized in many tourism contexts, since poorly specified objectives and goals may contribute to perceived failures in policy – and if the policy is flawed, its implementation and integration into planning mechanisms will not achieve the original issues it wants to address. The growth in the number of agencies involved in tourism inevitably delays the speed at which change in policy and planning can be affected. It is therefore no surprise that, despite criticisms about the lack of accountability with urban development corporations in the UK in the 1980s, they did remove planning obstacles for areas to be regenerated. In many cases the tourism development process was thereby streamlined to remove endless tiers of consultation, strategy development and disagreement over development goals. Whilst such a radical approach is not advocated for the public sector in tourism, there are compelling arguments for nationally determined tourism policies, strategy and planning to remove some of the layers of administration and bureaucracy. A more centralized approach (which avoids a multitude of agencies each having to review policy and planning at each level) would provide the context for area-based tourism planning and strategies, requiring cooperation at the local level to implement policy and planning. At the national level the NTO would simply market the destination, with research and market intelligence managed by an industry-led and funded agency, with regional- or area-based tourism organization driving policy and planning at the local level. Whilst this structure towards tourism may be radical, it is unlikely to be implemented for political reasons, as lobby groups and vested interests in the existing system resist change if it leads to a perceived loss of power and input to decision-making in relation to policy.

References

Elliot, J. (1997) *Tourism, Politics and Public Sector Management*. London: Routledge.

Getz, D. (1987) Tourism Planning and Research: Traditions, Models and Futures. Paper presented at the *Australian Travel Research Workshop*, Bunbury, Western Australia, November 5–6.

Inskeep, E. (1994) *National and Regional Planning*. London: Routledge/World Tourism Organization.

Middleton, V. and Clarke, J. (2001) *Marketing for Travel and Tourism*. Oxford: Butterworth-Heinemann.

Middleton, V. and Hawkins, R. (1998) *Sustainable Tourism*. Oxford: Butterworth-Heinemann.

Page, S. J. and Thorn, K. (1997) Towards sustainable tourism planning in New Zealand: public sector planning responses. *Journal of Sustainable Tourism*, **5**(1), 59–78.

Page, S. J., Brunt, P., Busby, G. and Connell, J. (2001) *Tourism: A Modern Synthesis*. London: Thomson Learning.

Scottish Executive (2002) *The Tourism Framework for Action 2002–2005*. Scottish Executive: Edinburgh (also see the web version on www.scotexchange.net).

Touche Ross (1988) *London Tourism Accommodation in the 1990s*. London: Touche Ross.

Turner, J. (1997) The policy process. In: B. Axford, G. Browning, R. Huggins *et al.* (eds), *Politics: An Introduction*. London: Routledge, pp. 409–39.

World Commission on the Environment and Development (1987) *Our Common Future* (Bründtland Commission's Report). Oxford: Oxford University Press.

World Trade Organization (1998) *Guide for Local Authorities on Developing Sustainable Tourism*. Madrid: WTO.

Further reading

Hall, C. M. (1999) *Tourism Planning: Policies, Processes and Relationships*. Harlow: Prentice Hall.

Hall, C. M. and Jenkins, J. (1995) *Tourism and Public Policy*. London: Routledge.

Jeffries, D. (2001) *Governments and Tourism*. Oxford: Butterworth-Heinemann.

Questions

1 Why does the public sector need to intervene in the tourism market? Are its reasons driven by political concerns or the pressure exerted on it by lobby groups?

2 How does tourism policy get formulated? Who are the main actors and stakeholders in policy formulation in tourism?

3 How does tourism planning occur in practice?

4 Should public support for tourism be driven by arguments surrounding the wider social benefits that accrue to destinations, or should the public sector support mechanisms for tourism be equalled financed by the public and private sectors?

12

Managing visitors and their impacts

Learning objectives

This chapter examines the practical ways in which visitors and visitor sites are managed by agencies and the tourism sector, and discusses the typical range of economic, social, cultural and environmental pressures that tourism exerts on its resource base and the ways in which management tools may be used to develop a more sustainable resource base. After reading it, you should be able to understand:

● what the problems induced by visitor activity are;
● how researchers approach the study of the economic, social, cultural and environmental impacts of tourism;
● what visitor management is, and the tools available to address visitor impacts in soft and hard ways;
● the role of tourism planning, development and management in the case of Venice, which highlights the economic, social, cultural and environmental problems induced by tourism.

Introduction

Many of the previous chapters have examined how members of the tourism industry manage and develop their businesses to produce a product or experience for a tourist. This chapter considers the consequences of these actions in terms of tourist consumption in relation to destination areas, which requires an understanding of the visitor as an agent of change in destinations due to the impacts induced directly or indirectly by their actions. Quite simply, it discusses where, why and how such impacts occur, and with what effects. Promotion and advertising by the tourism sector (i.e. tour operators, NTOs and other promotional organizations) assists in generating tourism demand as a consumptive activity, which culminates in both positive and negative effects for the places it affects. These effects often coexist, making policymaking, planning and management problematic owing to the tendency to both create beneficial and undesirable impacts simultaneously. For this reason, this chapter will focus on some of the tools and approaches used in tourism studies to understand how tourism generates impacts, how these can be managed, and the lessons that can be learned.

In any discussion of tourism's impacts, there are three principal areas of concern: its economic effects, its social and cultural effects and, of course, the environmental dimension upon which the consumption of tourism experiences are often based. Since many of these impacts are site- or place-specific, it is useful to have some understanding of the geography of tourism to identify who goes where, and when, why and what impacts occur where.

The geography of tourism: its application to impact analysis

Geography is about the study of the environment and people, and the coexistence of man with the environment at different levels, ranging from the international through the national and regional levels to the local level. More advanced studies of tourism have shown that the contribution of geography can be significant, with its interest in place and space (i.e. how activities are organized in different locations), because tourism is an inherently dynamic activity that requires movement from an origin to a destination area. Many studies of geography and tourism are highly academic, and are based on theory and concepts to understand the complexity of tourism in time and space (i.e. how it operates at different times and in different places). However, there are certain research skills that geographers use, and their application to tourism can help in understanding why tourists go on holiday to certain locations, when they go, what they do when they are there, where the impacts of such visitor activity occur, and what can be done to minimize the effects.

There are two techniques that can be used to address some of the issues surrounding visitor behaviour in order to understand the geographical patterns of tourism – particularly the nature of tourist flows, so that the scale and extent of tourism can be understood. The first technique is a simple analysis and mapping of tourism flows between origin and destination countries, to highlight the main flows. For example, at a European level, data from airport departures can be used to examine intra-regional travel (e.g. travel in and between EU member states) and can be modelled to produce Figure 12.1. This shows the top fifteen country-to-country flows of travellers within Europe, which are dominated by holiday traffic. For example, the data for 1999 show that 183.6 million intra-regional departures occurred from EU airports. Figure 12.1 shows that 13 per cent of these departures were between the UK and Spain, whilst a further 10 per cent were between Germany and Spain. A different perspective on these data can be gleaned from Figure 12.2, which identifies the top fifteen city-to-city airport flows within Europe. These city–city flows have changed little in order of magnitude over the last five years, but highlight the rise of leisure travel, business travel and the main EU capitals for intra-regional air travel. Figure 12.2 shows that the top ten city–city pairs account for 50 per cent of all intra-regional travel in the EU. What emerge as significant are the European air travel markets from the UK, Germany and other markets to Spain and the Mediterranean, as well as business travel. In addition, markets that are near to a land border and a popular destination (e.g. flows from France to Spain) have a strong propensity to use car-based travel, highlighting the seasonal effects upon the roads and airports in each respective destination area. Even at such a rudimentary level, such patterns begin to explain the seasonal rhythms of tourism, the effect of mass travel on destination areas, and the pressure this causes on infrastructure, the environment and people in the resort areas.

Recent research by Eurostat on the stability of tourism flows in the EU has shown that tourism is largely concentrated in the June–September months, based on hotel occupancy data, although this does vary by country. These variations highlight the importance of understanding the timing of tourist trips and where they are destined in order to begin to identify where impacts will occur.

The second and more sophisticated method of analysis used to understand how visitors can impact upon destinations through their activities is to study their

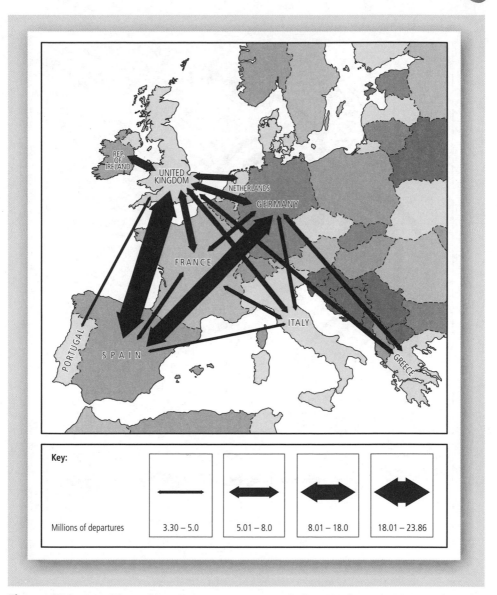

Figure 12.1 Top fifteen intra-European country pairs in 1999 (source: Eurostat, based on air departures)

activity patterns (what they do when, where, for how long, and the variations according to market segment). This can utilize the recent advances in information technology made by geographers in terms of the new Geographical Information Systems (GIS). GIS uses sophisticated computer programs, typically the industry

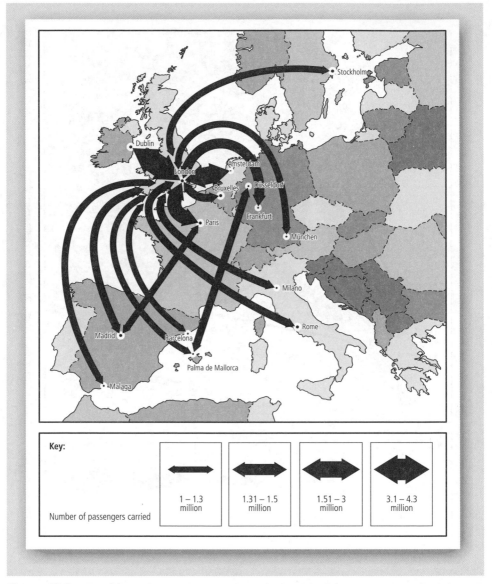

Figure 12.2 Top fifteen intra-European city pairs in 1999 (source: Eurostat, based on air departures)

standard ArcInfo and variants, to collect data on tourism with a geographical dimension. The geographical elements of the data (e.g. a tourist's travel pattern and specific activities undertaken at each point on an itinerary) can then be recorded, mapped and modelled in order to understand how overall patterns of tourist activity exist in a location or region. It is then possible to begin to identify where particular impacts are occurring, and to identify the geographical patterns of tourism business development in order to establish where the main development opportunities exist. The data are also useful in helping to identify what planning measures are needed where, when to constrain or facilitate tourism development, and the tools that might need to be used to manage different patterns of visitor behaviour. Not surprisingly, many local authority planning departments use such techniques in their daily work, but the application to tourism has been quite limited to date. GIS is a powerful yet greatly under-utilized research tool in tourism. It has an enormous potential application in assisting in managing, developing and understanding the dynamics of tourism.

The integration of different data sources in GIS has a major potential to illustrate visually the dynamics of tourism and the different impacts that exist by linking other sources of data (e.g. records of land degradation, environmental pollution and economic data). This helps in the identification and understanding of some of the impacts of tourism, and where management measures will need to be developed. Therefore with these issues in mind, attention now turns to the different impacts, how to measure them, and what management tools may be used.

Analysing the impacts of tourism

One of the major problems facing planners in assessing the impacts of tourism is the establishment of an appropriate baseline against which to measure the existing and future changes induced by tourism. This is a problem mentioned in scientific studies of Environmental Assessment (EA), which seek to combine different data sources to understand how tourism development affects the environment. EA acknowledges the practical problems of establishing baseline studies and in disaggregating the impact of tourism from other economic activities, since it is hard to isolate tourism from other forms of economic development. Mathieson and Wall (1982) highlighted the precise nature of the problem, since in many tourist destinations it is almost impossible to reconstruct the environment minus the effects induced by tourism.

While it is widely acknowledged that tourism is a major agent affecting the natural and built environment, isolating the precise causes or processes leading to specific impacts is difficult: is tourism the principle agent of change, or is it part of a wider process of development in a particular destination? As Mathieson and Wall (1982: 5) argue:

> ... tourism may also be a highly visible scapegoat for problems which existed prior to the advent of modern tourism. It certainly is easier to blame tourism than it is to address the conditions of society and the environment.

The complex interactions of tourism with the built and physical environment make it virtually impossible to measure impacts with any degree of precision. Even so, impacts may be large scale and tangible (e.g. where a destination is saturated by visitors) or small-scale and intangible.

Further factors complicating the analysis of tourism's impact include the extent to which the effect of tourism is necessarily continuous in time (i.e. how seasonal is it?), and the geography of tourism (as tourism activity tends to concentrate in certain locations such as destinations where the supply of services and facilities occurs). At this point it is important to begin to identify the specific indicators of tourism impacts chosen to represent the complex interaction of tourism and the destination, to guide the impact assessment. Whilst this involves complex methods of analysis, which may be aided by GIS and computer modelling, it is clear that impacts are more than just costs and benefits for specific destinations.

One useful starting point in analysing the impact of tourism in a practical context is to establish how to measure visitation levels as a basis for calculating visitor numbers to a destination. Yet one of the ongoing problems with visitor surveys regards their value. They are often undertaken at visitor attractions or based on accommodation occupancy rates, and the ability to yield a representative sample of visitation at the destination, and thus their reliability, is debatable. Therefore, where visitor information is collected it needs to be related to other forms of statistical information to establish the volume of tourism.

Early work by Potter (1978) provided a general framework for impact assessment. This is shown in Figure 12.3, where the impacts incorporate environmental, social and economic issues. Potter's (1978) approach has a number of steps, starting with the context of the development and proceeding through making a decision on a particular development, which is useful in a planning and management context.

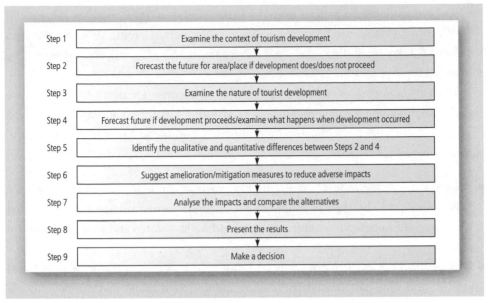

Step 1	Examine the context of tourism development
Step 2	Forecast the future for area/place if development does/does not proceed
Step 3	Examine the nature of tourist development
Step 4	Forecast future if development proceeds/examine what happens when development occurred
Step 5	Identify the qualitative and quantitative differences between Steps 2 and 4
Step 6	Suggest amelioration/mitigation measures to reduce adverse impacts
Step 7	Analyse the impacts and compare the alternatives
Step 8	Present the results
Step 9	Make a decision

Figure 12.3   Potter's impact of tourism framework (after Potter, 1978, Pearce, 1989; Page, 1995)

The economic impact of tourism

Tourism is used by many national and local governments as a mechanism to aid the development and regeneration of economies. This is because politicians and decision-makers see that it offers renewed opportunities for work, income and revenue for the local economy as places are affected by global, national and local economic restructuring. There is a prevailing perception among national and local governments that economic benefits accrue to tourism destinations, which then creates employment opportunities and stimulates the development process in resorts and localities. This is shown in Figure 9.1, which depicts the economic development process and how tourism is often used to pump-prime regeneration initiatives in declining areas (e.g. the inner city). Proponents of tourism development often argue that investment in tourist and recreational facilities provides a positive contribution to the local economy. One very controversial illustration of this can be seen in the debate regarding the impact of casino development in localities. This is very topical, given the proposed reform of legislation governing the development of casinos in the UK, as the taxes levied from gambling generate positive economic benefits for localities in terms of visitor spending and employment. For example, in Auckland, New Zealand, a casino constructed in the 1990s acts as the City's main drawcard. The scale of the impact on the local economy can be gauged from the 12 000 visitors a day it receives, but around 80 per cent of visitors are residents or New Zealanders. Gaming revenue averages NZ$595 000 a day (including goods and service tax at 12.5 per cent), and the operating company employs around 2400 people.

Tourism is not necessarily a stable source of income for destinations, because tourists are not noted for their high levels of customer loyalty to tourism destinations. Page and Hall (2002) have identified a number of features to support this argument, based on urban tourism destinations:

- Tourism is a fickle industry, being highly seasonal, and this has implications for investment and the type of employment created. Tourism employment is often characterized as being low skilled, poorly paid, of low status and lacking long-term stability.
- The demand for tourism can easily be influenced by external factors (e.g. political unrest, and unusual climatic and environmental conditions) that are beyond the control of destination areas.
- The motivation for tourist travel to urban destinations is complex and variable, and is constantly changing in the competitive marketplace.
- In economic terms, tourism is price- and income-elastic, which means that it is easily influenced by small changes to the price of the product and the disposable income of consumers.
- Many cities are becoming alike – a feature described as *serial reproduction*. This means that once an idea for urban economic development is successful in one location, the concept diffuses to other places. The example of waterfront revitalization is a case in point; many such projects are similar in structure and character across the world.

Pearce (1989: 192) argued that 'the objective and detailed evaluation of the economic impact of tourism can be a long and complicated task'. This is because there is little agreement on what constitutes the tourism industry, although it is normally classified in relation to:

- Accommodation
- Transport
- Attractions
- The travel organizers' sector (e.g. travel agents)
- The destination organization sector.

Hospitality and ancillary services are also important. Understanding the economic impact of these disparate sectors of the economy requires a method of analysis that allows isolation of the flow of income in the local tourism economy. This is notoriously difficult, because it involves attributing the proportion of tourist expenditure on goods and services in relation to the total pattern of expenditure by all users of the destination (e.g. residents, workers and visitors). Usually, the different forms of tourist expenditure and how they affect the local economy are identified. Typically these include (Page, 1995):

- The nature of the destination area, and its products, facilities and physical characteristics
- The volume and scale of tourist expenditure
- The state of the economic development and economy in the destination
- The size and nature of the local economy (is it dependant on services, manufacturing or is it a mixed economy?)
- The extent to which tourist expenditure circulates around the local economy and is not spent on 'imported' goods and services
- The degree to which the local economy has addressed the problem of seasonality and extended the destination appeal to all year round.

On the basis of these factors, it is possible to assess whether the economic impact will be beneficial or detrimental (Page, 1995). In this respect, it is possible to identify some of the commonly cited economic benefits of tourism:

- Generation of income for the local economy
- Creation of new employment opportunities
- Improvements to the structure and balance of economic activities within the locality
- Entrepreneurial activity is encouraged.

In contrast, there are also costs commonly associated with tourism, and these include:

- The potential for economic over-dependence on one particular form of activity
- Inflationary costs in the local economy as new consumers enter the area, and potential increases in real estate prices as the tourism development cycle commences and tourism competes with other land uses

- Depending on the size and nature of the local economy, a growing dependence on imported rather than locally produced goods, services and labour as the development of facilities and infrastructure proceeds
- Seasonality in the consumption and production of tourism infrastructure and services leading to limited returns on investment
- Leakage of tourism expenditure from the local economy
- Additional costs for city authorities.

Constructing the economic impact of tourism

In seeking to understand the extent of the consequences of tourism on the economies of countries and destinations, a range of analytical methods have been developed by economists. These usually involve collecting data to model the expenditure from tourism and its impact, as information gathered in visitor surveys can be used to identify (Page, 1995):

- *Direct expenditure* by tourists on goods and services consumed (e.g. hotels, restaurants and tourist transport services), although this is not a definitive account of expenditure owing to the leakage of tourist spending to areas and corporations outside the local economy.
- *Indirect expenditure* by visitors, which is often estimated by identifying how many tourism enterprises use the income derived from tourists' spending. This spending is then used by enterprises to pay for services, taxes and employees, and then recirculates in the urban economy. In other words, tourist expenditure stimulates an economic process that passes through a series of stages (or rounds).
- *The induced impact*, by calculating the impact of expenditure from those employed in tourism and its effect on the local economy.

These three impacts are then used to estimate the nature of tourist spending, as illustrated in Figure 12.4. This highlights the inter-relationships that exist between tourism, tourist spending and other sectors of the economy. It also introduces the concept of leakage, in which expenditure is lost from the local system to other areas. For planners and managers, maximizing local economic linkages (e.g. buying local produce and employing local people) can enhance the benefits of tourism to a locality. Where the local economy is very vulnerable and is dependent upon a large number of imports (e.g. labour, goods and services), leakage will be high; hence reducing the

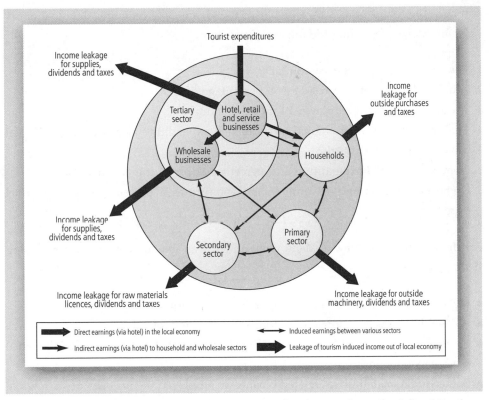

Tourist expenditures

Income leakage
for supplies,
dividends and taxes

Income
leakage for
outside purchases
and taxes

Tertiary
sector

Hotel, retail
and service
businesses

Wholesale
businesses

Households

Income leakage
for supplies,
dividends and taxes

Secondary
sector

Primary
sector

Income leakage for raw materials
licences, dividends and taxes

Income leakage for outside
machinery, dividends and taxes

Direct earnings (via hotel) in the local economy

Induced earnings between various sectors

Indirect earnings (via hotel) to household and wholesale sectors

Leakage of tourism induced income out of local economy

Figure 12.4 The economic impact of tourist spending in an urban area (after Murphy, 1985; Page, 1995)

openness of the tourism economy will help to improve the impact locally. Many rural areas are characteristically open economies and there are high levels of leakage in tourism, whereas in urban areas leakage is reduced as the economy is more closed.

In many less developed countries and island nations that depend upon tourism the leakage is also high owing to external control of tourism by multinational companies and a reluctance of these businesses to use local products. Instead, high volume imports reduce the beneficial local effects of tourism. Economists use various tools to measure tourism demand in local economies, referred to as Multiplier Analysis, where a formula expresses changes that tourism spending can generate.

More recently, governments have tried to understand how tourism affects the national economy. In conjunction with the WTO and OECD, some countries have developed Tourism Satellite Accounts (TSA) to measure the economic impact of tourism more precisely. Taking New Zealand as an example, in 1999 the government launched the results of its TSA, which used a wide range of economic data to identify six main themes regarding the impact of tourism:

1 The direct impact of tourism on GDP
2 Tourism expenditure expressed as a percentage of GDP
3 The level of tourism employment in the economy
4 The proportion of international travel related expenditure as a percentage of total travel-related expenditure
5 Domestic personal expenditure as a percentage of total travel expenditure
6 Domestic business and government expenditure as a percentage of total travel expenditure.

For the first time, the New Zealand government was able to identify precisely, using 1995 data, that:

- NZ$4.3 billion was generated by international visitors
- NZ$4.8 billion was generated by domestic tourism demand
- 58 000 full-time equivalent jobs were directly created by tourism, and a further 6000 were generated indirectly
- Some 16 000 small tourism-related businesses employed the majority of staff, while the major employers in size were airports and the airline sector (e.g. Air New Zealand).

This modelling of the tourism economy is increasingly gaining credence in many governments, since reliable information on the economic impact of tourism is useful in the following fields:

- Policy-making
- Planning and macro-management of the economy
- Allocating public sector resources towards tourism projects
- Internal government processes to secure additional resources for the Ministry of Tourism and the NTO.

In the New Zealand example, the TSA also helped to raise the profile of the tourism sector because the magnitude of the economic impacts were far in excess of existing estimates of tourism's effects on the national economy. Yet while it is now becoming easier to gauge the economic effect of tourism as researchers use more refined methods of analysing its impact, the economic effect is much less visible and tangible than the social and cultural impacts that tourism induces.

Social and cultural impacts of tourism

Tourism can emerge as a source of conflict between hosts and visitors in destinations where its development leads to perceived and actual impacts. There has been a wealth of studies of the social and cultural impacts by anthropologists and sociologists, embodied in the influential studies by Valene Smith (1977, 1992). The attitudes of residents towards tourism represent an important way in which this stakeholder group contributes to policy and public support for, or opposition towards, tourism. At a simplistic level, resident attitudes may be one barometer of an area's ability to absorb tourists. However, the analysis of tourism's social and cultural impacts is related to the way in which it affects or induces change in a number of elements (see Figure 12.5).

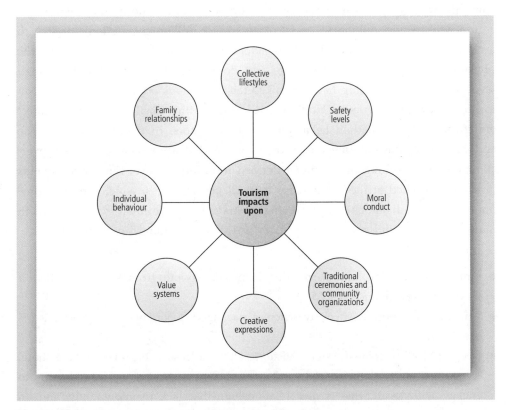

Figure 12.5   The social and cultural impacts of tourism

Any analysis of host–guest impacts is a function of the interaction between these two groups, and will be dependent upon:

- The nature and extent of social, economic and cultural differences between tourists and hosts
- The ratio of visitors to residents
- The distribution and visibility of tourist developments
- The speed and intensity of development
- The extent of foreign and employment.

(Douglas and Douglas, 1996: 51)

In the context of the Pacific Islands, Douglas and Douglas (1996) highlighted the differing ethnic origins of residents, and the history of colonialization and tourism development, which provide a backcloth to any analysis of tourism's socio-cultural impacts. Also, the scale of development varies enormously across the region, with over 6 million visitors to Hawaii (1.2 million population) through to less than 1000 per annum on Tuvalu (resident population of 9000). In each case the physical presence of tourism is huge and dominates the island. Similarly, high levels of foreign ownership have provoked the indigenous population's antagonism towards tourism in certain islands, where some multinational corporations expect employees to adopt certain behaviour towards visitors. In many of these fragile and ancient cultures indigenous people's art and culture have also been over-commodified, resulting in the much derided term 'airport art'. Similar arguments have been levelled at the demand for cultural performances, which create income but result in indigenous peoples being portrayed as a 'human zoo'. Indeed, in many of these island contexts it leads to host–guest relationships that are:

- Limited in duration, and so require distinct behaviour from residents where a service or performance is sold
- Transitory in nature, especially where a packaged experience or performance is provided
- Geographically isolated, since visitors stay in resort enclaves where hotel companies meet all their needs and only encourage temporary staged visits to engage with locals; this creates relationships that lack in spontaneity, and an unequal and unbalanced experience.

Pearce (1989) cited a range of other social and cultural impacts resulting from tourism, including:

- The impact of migration from rural areas to urbanized tourism resort areas to secure employment in service industries due to the higher income levels; this can often modify the population structure in destinations, putting pressure on services
- Changes in occupational structure, as the demand for low-skilled, female and seasonal labour expands
- Changes in social values, with greater levels of community turnover
- The impact of gentrification in inner city districts where urban regeneration with a strong tourism element transforms the local housing market, and leads to the movement of residents to accommodate development
- Increased levels of crime when special events and hallmark events such as the Olympics are held
- Potentially negative effects related to the increase in prostitution and gambling to meet visitor needs – in some destinations (such as Sydney, Bangkok and Amsterdam) distinct sex zones have emerged, changing the social structure of the area
- A decline in the use of native language, because the universal method of conversation in tourism is in European languages (English and French).

But how do we understand the way these changes affect resident attitudes?

Probably the most widely cited study that sought to explain how tourists react to, respond to and interact with tourism is Doxey's Index of Tourist Irritation. This is based on Doxey's (1975) study, which observed resident responses in the Caribbean and Canada in order to identify a series of stages that they passed through. The stages identified were:

- Euphoria, following the initial development of tourism
- Apathy, as tourism developed further and became part of the local way of life
- Annoyance, as tourism began to interfere with everyday life and caused a level of disturbance
- Antagonism, where residents became tourist averse and tensions, conflict and anti-tourism feeling became widespread.

More detailed research by Ap and Crompton (1993) questioned the validity of such an approach, arguing that this was too simplistic. Instead, they pointed to the diversity of views in any community at any point in time – especially the significance of varying views from different stakeholders (i.e. the business and resident views) – which make the Doxey model problematic, as minority and majority views will always exist. Indeed, a community will not necessarily progress through a simple set of phases, but may well reflect the seasonal impact of tourism and the overall analysis of tourism's general impact on the residents' quality of life. Nevertheless, a wide range of studies have been published that seek to encapsulate resident's attitudes to tourism, but comparatively few studies have been longitudinal – to try and understand attitude change through time. One notable exception was Getz's (1993) longitudinal study of resident attitudes in Scotland. Without such a framework, it is not feasible to assess how attitudes have changed as tourism development progresses. As a result, many *ad hoc* resident attitude studies are not sufficiently detailed or methodologically sophisticated enough and are unable to adopt a longitudinal approach to help understand how social values, community feelings and everyday life are affected by tourism.

The environmental impact of tourism

Throughout this book the link between tourism and the environment has been emphasized as one that has been assuming greater significance, particularly with the rise of the sustainability debate. Yet this relationship between tourism and the environment has evolved over a much larger time period, namely the last 50 years. Dowling (1992: 33) states that:

> In the 1950s it was viewed as being one of coexistence . . . However, with the advent of mass tourism in the 1960s, increasing pressure was put on natural areas for tourism developments. Together with the growing environmental awareness and concerns of the early 1970s the relationship was perceived to be in conflict. During the next decade this view was endorsed by many others . . . at the same time a new suggestion was emerging that the relationship could be beneficial to both tourism and the environment.

Fostering a beneficial relationship between tourism and the environment requires public sector intervention to plan and manage each element, whilst highlighting the benefits for the tourism industry. For example, the UK government-led study on

Tourism and the Environment (English Tourist Board/Employment Department, 1991) examined and established the scale and nature of environmental problems induced by mass tourism at major tourist sites, and produced guidelines on how such problems were to be addressed. The study pointed to the need to maintain the resource base for tourism activities. As part of the study, common problems resulting from tourism were identified, including wear and tear on the urban fabric, overcrowding, and social and cultural impacts between the visitors and local communities.

Indeed, some authors have portrayed tourism–environment impacts as running along a continuum where the effects may be positive in inner city environments that benefit from tourism-led regeneration, ranging to more negative impacts as in other tourism environments (e.g. coastal areas, rural areas, upland and mountain environments). Depicting this dependent relationship between tourism and the environment, Mathieson and Wall (1982: 97) argued that:

> In the absence of an attractive environment, there would be little tourism. Ranging from the basic attractions of sun, sea and sand to the undoubted appeal of historic sites and structures, the environment is the foundation of tourism.

This is nowhere more evident than in the South Pacific, where stereotypical images of palm trees, beaches, lagoons and sun create an impression of an idyllic tourist landscape. Yet many of the Pacific Islands encapsulate the environmental problems created by tourism, and these are illustrated in Box 12.1.

Box 12.1   Case study: the environmental impact of tourism on the Pacific Islands

Many Pacific Islands are fragile ecosystems where the impacts of tourism are highly visible, particularly given the tendency for tourism development to concentrate on coastal areas. As Hall (1996: 68) observed:

> . . . because of the highly dynamic nature of the coastal environment and the significance of mangroves and the limited coral sand supply for island beaches in particular, any development which interferes with the natural system may have severe consequences for the long-term stability of the environment.

As a result, inappropriate tourism development on coastal areas causes:

● Erosion, where vegetation clearance exposes the beach to sea storms, and building activity on beaches makes sand deposits loose and more vulnerable
● The salination of fresh ground water sources, which are usually in limited supply
● Sewage outfall into shallow waters, which causes nutrients to build up and algal growth that adversely affects the coral reefs.

Furthermore, the modification of mangrove swamps on lowland areas to create harbours and marinas, and for land reclamation, leads to loss of ecological diversity and the rich environment for wildlife. It also removes a barrier to sediment build up. As a result, tourism's environmental impacts on Pacific Islands include:

● Environmental degradation and pollution
● The destruction of habitats and ecosystems
● The loss of coastal and marine resources
● Coastal pollution
● Impacts on ground water.

As island ecosystems are characterized by limited space and species, impacts are very evident – especially where the geographical isolation of an island state is suddenly affected by the rapid development of tourism. Some attempts to address these concerns have been seen with the development of ecotourism. In the South Pacific, Hall (1996) indicated that ecotourism could be construed in two ways:

1 As 'green' or nature-based tourism, with a niche market, as part of special interest tourism (e.g. scuba diving)
2 As any form of tourism development that is considered to be environmentally responsible.

Both of these should pay regard to the sustainable use of very fragile resources. In many island microstates in the Pacific the significance of environmental issues in tourism is apparent, as a number of common themes characterize its development and the pressures on the resource base:

● Scale, where impacts can easily be damaging to fragile resources
● The high levels of dependency on external international tourism interests that do not have a long-term stake in the local environment
● An absence of indigenous sources of capital to develop tourism, removing many opportunities for sustainable tourism development that is community owned and locally managed
● The predominance of colonial patterns of control in the tourism sector limiting the permeation of new ideas such as environmentalism
● An economic system characterized by outward migration, a dependence upon remittances back to families, aid to assist economic survival, and bureaucracy (known as the MIRAB model)
● Increasing competition among island microstates for tourists in the Pacific and resulting compromises in tourism planning and development to attract visitors.

There is also a growing dependence upon tourism, which is politically promoted as a solution to problems of underdevelopment. Yet the main problem is the consumption of a finite resource – the environment needed to meet tourism aspirations in island microstates in the Pacific.

The environmental impacts in the Pacific islands can be combined with the list of the more general problems that Mathieson and Wall (1982) identified in resort areas, which include:

● Architectural pollution owing to the effect of inappropriate hotel development on the traditional landscape
● Ribbon development and urban sprawl in the absence of planning and development restrictions (as is the case in many Spanish resorts in the Mediterranean)
● The resort infrastructure becoming overloaded and breaking down in periods of peak usage
● Tourists becoming segregated from local residents

- The possibility of good quality agricultural land being lost to tourist development
- Traffic congestion resort areas
- Pollution of the local ecosystem from sewage and litter
- Too many visitors in the peak season.

So how has the tourism industry responded to criticisms over its impact on the environment?

The tourism industry response

A substantial lobby has emerged amongst environmental groups to question the seemingly unstoppable march of tourism as a consumer of environmental resources. The hotel industry has responded with environmental initiatives such as the International Hotels Environment Initiative, which promotes recycling, codes of conduct, best practice among members, accreditation schemes and improved standards of energy efficiency (see Chapter 7). In some hotels waste minimization strategies have resulted from environmental audits of the tourism and hospitality operations. This may include purchasing more eco-friendly products, waste reduction (e.g. not laundering guests' towels every day), re-use of resources and packaging, and a 'green' policy towards operational issues. In the Balearic Islands, an ecotax was introduced 2002 to fund environmental improvements to address decades of tourist development. However, this has had a negative impact on one market – the Germany package holiday market. In Germany the ecotax has been called *Limonadenstener* – a lemonade tax – because hotel owners have been giving guests drink vouchers in lieu of the tax. It has also been dubbed a *Kurtax* (a cure tax), which has raised ecological issues among visitors. This approach to attempting to remedy the impacts of mass tourism development is at least beginning to move the sector towards a greater understanding of its effect on the environment. So how does the tourism industry manage the impacts of visitors? This is normally undertaken through the use of visitor management techniques.

Visitor management

The tourism sector has to address an ongoing problem: it needs to permit access to sites and yet to protect the resource base upon which tourism is based. This requires

Table 12.1 Examples of visitor management techniques in tourism (modified and developed from Hall and McArthur, 1998)

Technique	Examples
Regulating access by area	Excluding visitors from sacred sites such as Aboriginal lands
Regulating access by transport	Park and Ride Schemes to prevent in-town use of cars, or car-free environments and pedestrianization schemes as part of Town Centre Management programmes
Regulating visitor numbers and group size	The use of group size restrictions in Antarctica
Regulating types of visitors permitted	Discouraging certain groups through marketing and products on offer
Regulating visitor behaviour	Zoning of visitor activities in marine parks in Western Australia to allocate certain activities to certain areas
Regulating equipment	Prohibiting off-road driving except in permitted areas (e.g. in Forest Enterprise's four-wheel drive track in the new Loch Lomond National Park)
The use of entry or user fees	Charging visitors to Kenya's National Parks and Reserves so that some of the fee is used for conservation
Modifications to sites	Constructing hardened paths to direct visitors
Market research	To identify reasons for visitation, to understand how to develop tools to modify visitor behaviour
Promotional marketing campaigns	The provision of alternative destinations in the Lake District, UK, to relieve pressure on congested sites
Provision of interpretation programmes	Provision of guided tours or guides to avoid congestion at key sites

a wide range of management tools to balance the needs of the visitor, the place (i.e. resource base), the host community and other tourism stakeholders (e.g. the industry) in providing a quality tourism experience. As a result, the area known as visitor management has emerged in a tourism context, developing, modifying and adapting many of the principles and practices used in the outdoor recreation and leisure areas. There are two types of measures that are usually used: *hard measures*, which are place extensive and place permanent restrictions on visitor activity; and *soft measures*, which

Table 12.2 Qualitative assessment of visitor management techniques (source: Hall and McArthur, 1998:123; © The Stationery Office, reproduced by permission of The Stationery Office, Norwich)

Visitor management techniques	Ability to address heritage management paradox		Other aspects of performance		
	Conservation of heritage	Improve quality of visitor experience	Create support for heritage management	Proactiveness	Reliance by management
Regulating access	◆◆◆	◆	◇	◇	◇
Regulating visitation	◆◆	◆◆	◇	◇	◇◇
Regulating behaviour	◆◆	◆	◇	◇	◇
Regulating equipment	◆◆	◆◆	◇	◇◇	◇◇
Entry or user fees	◆◆	◆	◇	◇◇	◇◇◇
Modifying the site	◆◆	◆◆	◇◇	◇	◇◇◇
Market research	◆◆	◆◆	◇	◇◇◇	◇
Visitor monitoring and research	◆◆	◆◆◆	◇	◇◇◇	◇
Promotional marketing	◆◆◆	◆◆	◇◇◇	◇◇◇	◇
Strategic information marketing	◆◆◆	◆◆◆	◇◇◇	◇◇	◇◇
Interpretation	◆◆◆	◆◆◆	◇◇◇	◇◇◇	◇◇
Education	◆◆◆	◆◆	◇◇	◇◇◇	◇
Profile of heritage management	◆◆◆	◆◆	◇◇◇	◇◇	◇
Alternative providers – tourism industry	◆◆	◆◆◆	◇◇	◇◇◇	◇
Alternative providers – volunteers	◆◆◆	◆◆◆	◇◇◇	◇◇◇	◇◇
Favoured treatment for accredited bodies bringing visitors to a site	◆◆◆	◆◆◆	◇◇◇	◇◇◇	◇

Performance in relation to heritage management paradox: ◆, Limited; ◆◆, Reasonable; ◆◆◆, Good.
Performance in relation to other criteria: ◇, Limited; ◇◇, Reasonable; ◇◇◇, Good.

Table 12.3 Applications of visitor management models (source: Hall and McArthur, 1998: 136; © The Stationery Office, reproduced by permission of The Stationery Office, Norwich)

Visitor management models	Applications across the world
The Recreation Opportunity Spectrum (ROS)	• In Australia ROS has been developed for Knarben Gorge, Fraser Island National Park • In an innovative study ROS was applied to the urban parklands around Newcastle, Australia • ROS has been an underlying principle behind the development of management strategies for national parks in New Zealand and the USA
Carrying Capacity Model	• Yosemite Valley, Yosemite National Park, USA – implemented by the United States Parks Service • Boundary Waters Canoe Area, USA – investigated but not fully implemented by the United States Parks Service • Angkor World Heritage Site, Siem Reap Province, Cambodia – the Angkor Conservation Office implemented an annual and daily capacity, as well as a capacity for any one moment in time • Green Island, Queensland, and the Queensland Department of Environment and Natural Heritage, Australia – implemented an annual and daily capacity, as well as a capacity for any one moment in time • In the early 1990s, the New Zealand sub-Antarctic islands had a limit of 500 visits per year • Waitomo Caves in New Zealand have a carrying capacity set at 200 persons at any one moment in time • Bermuda in the USA has set a capacity of 120 000 cruise-ship passengers during the peak visitation period • Lord Howe Island in the Tasman Sea has a limit of 800 visitors at any time
Visitor Activity Management Program (VAMP)	• Cross-country (nordic) skiing in Ottawa, Canada – partially implemented by the Canadian National Parks Service • Mingan Archipelago National Park Reserve, Canada – implemented by the Canadian National Parks Service to help establish the new park • Point Pelee National Park, Canada – implemented by the Canadian National Parks Service with an interpretation focus • Kejimkijik National Park, Canada – partially implemented by the Canadian National Parks Service
Visitor Impact Management Model (VIMM)	• Florida Keys National Marine Sanctuary, Florida, USA – pilot implemented by the US Travel and Tourism Administration and the US Environmental Protection Agency

Table 12.3 (*Continued*)

Visitor management models	Applications across the world
Visitor Impact Management Model (VIMM) (*Continued*)	• Netherlands – pilot explored for expansion by the World Tourism Organization • Buck Island Reef National Monument, Virgin Islands, USA – implemented but discontinued by United States National Park Service • Youghiogheny River, Western Maryland, USA – implemented but discontinued by Maryland Department of Natural Resources • Price Edward Island, Canada – pilot implemented by Parks Canada and the World Tourism Organization • Los Tuxtlas, Veracruz, Mexico – pilot implemented by the World Tourism Organization • Jenolan Caves, New South Wales, Australia – fully implemented and monitored by the Jenolan Caves Management Trust • Villa Gesell, Buenos Aires Province, Argentina – pilot implemented by the Buenos Aires Province Tourism Authority and the World Tourism Organization • Peninsula Valdes, Northern Patagonia, Argentina – pilot implemented by the World Tourism Organization
The Limits of Acceptable Change (LAC)	• Bob Marshall Wilderness Complex, Montana, USA – tested and implemented by the United States Forest Service. • Selway-Bitteroot Wilderness, Idaho, USA – tested by the United States Forest Service • Cranberry Wilderness Area, West Virginia, USA – tested by the USDA Forest Service and West Virginia University • The Wet Tropics World Heritage Area, Queensland, Australia – prepared for but never fully implemented by the Wet Tropics Management Authority • The Nymboida River, New South Wales, Australia – prepared for but never fully implemented by the New South Wales Department of Water Resources • Wallace Island Crown Reserve, New South Wales, Australia – developed but never implemented by the Wallis Island Reserve Trust and New South Wales Department of Water and Land Conservation
Tourism Optimization Management Model (TOMM)	• Kangaroo Island, South Australia, Australia – implementation in progress by the South Australian Tourism Commission, Department of Environment and Natural Resources and Tourism Kangaroo Island

Table 12.4 Qualitative assessment of visitor management models (source: Hall and McArthur, 1998: 137; © The Stationery Office, reproduced by permission of The Stationery Office, Norwich)

Visitor management models	Key characteristics of visitor management models	Level of sophisti- cation	Range of contributing stakeholders	Actual application by heritage managers
The Recreation Opportunity Spectrum (ROS)	● Determines the threshold level of activity beyond which will result in the deterioration of the resource base ● Its main dimensions are biophysical, socio-cultural, psychological and managerial ● Used for planning, site design and development, and administration	✓✓	✓✓	✓✓✓
Carrying Capacity Model	● Creates a diversity of experiences by identifying a spectrum of settings, activities and opportunities that a region may contain ● Helps to review and reposition the type of visitor experiences most appropriate to a heritage site	✓	✓✓	✓✓
Visitor Activity Management Program (VAMP)	● Planning system that integrates visitor needs with resources to produce specific visitor opportunities ● Designed to resolve conflicts and tensions between visitors, heritage and heritage managers ● Requires heritage managers to identify, provide for, and market to designated visitor groups	✓✓✓	✓✓✓	✓

Table 12.4 (*Continued*)

Visitor management models	Key characteristics of visitor management models	Level of sophisti-cation	Range of contributing stakeholders	Actual application by heritage managers
Visitor Impact Management Model (VIMM)	• Focuses on reducing or controlling the impacts that threaten the quality of heritage and visitor experience • Uses explicit statements of management objectives and research and monitoring to determine heritage and social conditions, then generates a range of management strategies to deal with the impacts	✓✓	✓✓	✓✓
The Limits of Acceptable Change (LAC)	• Focuses on the management of visitor impacts by identifying, first, desirable conditions for visitor activity to occur, then how much change is acceptable • A monitoring programme determines whether desirable conditions are within acceptable standards • A decision-making system determines management actions required to achieve the desired conditions	✓✓✓✓	✓✓✓	✓✓

Table 12.4 (*Continued*)

Visitor management models	Key characteristics of visitor management models	Level of sophisti-cation	Range of contributing stakeholders	Actual application by heritage managers
Tourism Optimization Management Model (TOMM)	● Instead of limiting activity, it focuses on achieving optimum performance by addressing the sustainability of the heritage, viability of the tourism industry and empowerment of stakeholders ● Covers environmental and experiential elements, as well as characteristics of the tourist market, economic conditions of the tourism industry and socio-cultural conditions of the local community ● Contains three main parts; context analysis, a monitoring programme and management response system	✓✓✓	✓✓✓	✓

✓, Low; ✓✓, Moderate; ✓✓✓, High; ✓✓✓✓, Very high.

involve improved marketing, interpretation, planning and visitor co-ordination. These are summarized in Table 12.1.

Hall and McArthur (1998: 123) reviewed the value of these management tools, in a heritage tourism context, to achieve the twin goals of conserving the resource (heritage) and contributing to improving the quality of the visitor experience. Table 12.2 is a qualitative assessment of each approach they identified, which suggests that hard measures to regulate visitor activity are the dominant mode of control. It also illustrates the need for managers and planners to consider ways of integrating these approaches to manage tourism. One approach is to develop visitor management models that seek to assess the capacity of a site or location and the types of management needed to ensure a maximum visitor experience without affecting the sustainable use of the resource and its long-term appeal. A number of technical models have been developed and applied in visitor management contexts across the world, as Table 12.3 shows.

Each approach is reviewed in terms of its key characteristics, and its ability to meet the varying needs of different stakeholders and be applied in practical contexts. As Table 12.4 suggests, these models (which are widely used and understood in the recreation and tourism management literature – see Pigram and Jenkins, 1999, for more detail) adopt different management approaches that are useful in illustrating the diversity of tools available to managers. The case study of Venice in Box 12.2 illustrates the practical problems posed by visitor management.

Box 12.2   Case study: managing the tourist impact in Venice

(by Stephen J. Page and C. Michael Hall)

Venice is acknowledged as one of the world's leading cultural and art cities, with its acclaimed fifteenth century renaissance art. Venice is located on a series of islands in a lagoon, and is the capital of the Vento region of Italy. In terms of the impact of tourism the historic city of Venice has experienced continued population loss, which dropped from 175 000 in 1951 to 78 000 in 1992 and 65 000 in 2001. It receives 47 000 commuters daily. The condition of many of Venice's aged buildings is also under threat. Venice is suffering from:

- A sinking ground level
- A rising sea level
- Pollution of the lagoon in which it is located
- Atmospheric pollution
- Congestion on the main canals from motorized traffic
- Over-saturation at key locations for tourists
- increased frequency of flooding – in the 1970s and 1980s there were 50 high tides a year; in 1996 there were 101, and in 2000 some 80.

This illustrates the range and extent of environmental concerns amidst a booming visitor industry.

As a tourist destination, visitor arrivals have developed greatly. In 1952, 50 000 tourists spent 1.2 million bednights in the historic city of Venice. By 1987 these figures had risen to 1.13 million tourist arrivals and 2.49 million bednights, and by 1992 to 1.21 million arrivals and 2.68 million bednights. The average length of stay was 2.21 nights in 1992. These visitor numbers are swelled by a large day-visitor market from other parts of Italy, especially the Adriatic beach resorts and Alpine areas. In 1992 the day-tripper market was estimated to be 6 million visitors, providing a total market in excess of 7 million visitors a year.

Russo's (2002) study of tourism in Venice highlighted the motivations for visiting cultural attractions and described the impacts of tourism as the latter stages of the resort life cycle – nearing stagnation and decline. The result was that Venice was saturated at key times in the year (such as Easter), and that the police have had to close the Ponde del Liberta since the optimum flow of 21 000 tourists a day has been exceeded (60 000 at Easter and 100 000 in the summer). This poses increased competition between residents and visitors in the use of space within the historic city. Generally up to 34 per cent of the public space in the historic square is used by visitors and 49 per cent by residents; however, during special events the use by visitors increases to 56 per cent and this adds to congestion in the city, competition for facilities and a declining visitor and resident experience.

Since 1987, on selected spring weekends the land route from the mainland to Venice has been closed to visitors as an extreme form of crisis management. Montanari and Muscara (1995) developed a nine-fold classification of tourists based on differences in their spatial behaviour (i.e. where and what they visit in the city), perception and spending power, which can be summarized thus:

1 First-time visitors on an organized tour
2 Rich tourists
3 Lovers of Venice
4 Backpacker campers
5 Worldly-wise tourists
6 Return tourists
7 Resident artists
8 Beach tourists
9 Visitors with a purpose.

This reflects the unique tourism environment and the diversity of motives for visiting the city.

Yet Russo (2002) argues that the city does not manage visits prudently. The time spent on queuing at well-known attractions leads to lost opportunities at lesser-known cultural attractions, owing to poor marketing and communication with the visitor. This is complicated by the existence of ten agencies responsible for museums in the city. Venice is dominated by excursionists (83.1 per cent) in comparison to tourists (16.9 per cent), with a very even pattern of distribution throughout the year: Between January and March 14 per cent of visitors arrive, 30 per cent come in April–June, 32 per cent in July–September, and 24 per cent in October–December. Russo (2002) noted that the average duration of a visit was eight hours, with many tour operators promoting day trips rather than overnight stays. The destination's accessibility has also been increased with the recent advent of low-cost airlines in Europe. Venice's tourist market comprises 26.3 per cent of arrivals from within Italy, 36 per cent from Europe, 17.7 per cent from the USA, 11.1 per cent from Japan and 8.9 per cent from other countries/regions.

The social impact of the existing patterns of demand led van der Borg et al. (1996) to calculate the visitor/resident (host) ratio for Venice and a number of other European heritage cities. In Venice's historical centre there was a ratio of 89.4 : 1, while for the wider Venice municipality this dropped to 27.6 : 1. This level of visitor pressure reflects the scale of the problem facing the city.

Venice's capacity for tourism

To assess the capacity of the historic centre of Venice, Canestrelli and Costa (1991) undertook a complex mathematical modelling exercise that examined the parameters to be considered in any future visitor management plan. This established what is called the 'carrying capacity' – that is, how many visitors the historic city can accommodate. They calculated that the optimal carrying capacity for the historic city of Venice would be to admit 9780 tourists who use hotel accommodation, 1460 tourists staying in non-hotel accommodation, and 10 857 day trippers on a daily basis. Even if the day trippers who visit Venice were evenly spread, this would still amount to 11 233 trippers a day. In fact it is estimated that an average of 37 500 day trippers a day visit Venice in August. Canestrelli and Costa (1991) argued that a ceiling of 25 000 visitors a day is the maximum tourist capacity for Venice.

There are important implications for the environment and its long-term preservation if the tourist capacity is being exceeded. Once the capacity is exceeded, the quality of the visitor experience is eroded and the physical fabric may be damaged, and there is extra strain placed on the infrastructure.

Yet the large volume of visitors descending on Venice each year not only exceeds the desirable limits of tourism for the city, but also poses a range of social and economic problems for planners. As van der Borg *et al.* (1996: 52) observed:

> . . . the negative external effects connected with the overloading of the carrying capacity are rapidly increasing, frustrating the centre's economy and society . . . excursionism [day tripping] is becoming increasingly important, while residential tourism is losing relevance for the local tourism market . . . [and] . . . the local benefits are diminishing. Tourism is becoming increasingly ineffective for Venice.

Thus the negative impact of tourism on the historic centre of Venice is now resulting in a self-enforcing decline as excursionists (who contribute less to a local tourism economy than staying visitors) supplant the staying market as it becomes less attractive to stay in the city. Up until 2000, changing the attitude of the city's tourism policymakers was difficult: the pro-tourism lobby heavily influenced it. A number of positive measures have been enacted since 2000 to address the saturation of the historic city by day visitors, including denying access to the city via the main coach terminal by unauthorized tour coaches.

In 2001 a new mayor was elected, and a number of emergency measures are now being considered to safeguard the future of tourism:

- The introduction of a tourist tax to recover some of the external costs of tourism
- A strict control on motorized traffic in the canals to reduce the wash effects on gondolas and buildings
- A multi-million pound mobile flood barrier, despite protests from ecologists, to reduce the regular flooding.

Another serious issue that impacts upon the quality of the tourist experience is the effluent problem in the city owing to the absence of sewers, which results in algal growth and a notable stench in the summer season.

Environmental processes that affect both the local and tourist population must also be recognized – such as flooding. St Mark's Square, an icon for visitors, floods 40–60 times a year compared to 4–6 times a year at the beginning of the twentieth century.

A balance of tourism has to be achieved using measures of environmental protection and management. Positive steps are needed to provide a more rational basis for the future development and promotion of tourism in the new millennium. Glasson *et al.* (1995: 116) summarized the problem of seeking to manage visitors and their environmental impact in Venice:

> . . . every city must be kept as accessible as possible for some specific categories of users, such as inhabitants, visitors to offices and firms located in the city, and commuters studying or working in the city. At the same time, the art city needs to be kept as inaccessible as possible to some other user categories (the excursionist/day trippers in particular).

It is clear that while the tangible economic benefits of tourism accrue to the city, the social and environmental costs are very substantial. Montanari and Muscari (1995) argued that Venice water transport plays a major role in tourism within the city, and could be used to manage visitors, while the city needs to plan to separate the access, circulation and exit of the resident/commuting population and the tourists. Russo (2002) expanded this debate, and argued that the better matching of tourism demand (i.e. visitors) with the available supply of attractions through improved marketing and information would bring some economic benefits to the city. It would also assist in geographically spreading the impact of visitors. However, a much more visitor-focused management strategy is also needed, with policies and actions to increase the attraction potential in some areas and place access restrictions in others.

Table 12.5 illustrates a range of visitor management measures. These combine 'soft' and 'hard' controls. Russo's (2002) advocacy of greater taxation/tariffs to 'disincentivize' excursions is likely to be implemented. Russo rightly advocates tourism management as a starting point to plan the future for tourism in the city, and to raise the industry from saturation and stagnation.

Table 12.5 The problems, causes, measures and future actions needed to manage tourists in Venice (source: Russo, 2002: 178; ©Elsevier, reprinted from *Annals of Tourism Research*, vol. 29, A. Russo 'The 'vicious circle' of tourism development in heritage cities', 165–82, 2002 with permission of Elsevier)

Causation	Context	Hard interventions	Soft interventions
1. Increase of tourist demand → enlargement of tourism region, shorter visits	Difficult expansion of tourism supply, irreproducible heritage (*small centres, islands*)	Zoning, regional planning, enlargement of accommodation capacity in the city centre	Entrance ticket, incentives based on adv. booking, discrimination policies, tariffs, creation of a supra-local 'tourism authority'
2. Shorter visits → increasing congestion costs, asymmetric information	Many cultural resources, difficult mobility (*medium-sized art cities*)	Zoning, access regulation, closing of portions of city centre, infrastructure policy, decentralization of cultural supply	Information and discrimination policies, promotion, creation of 'alternative routes'
3. Asymmetric information → decline in the quality of tourism supply (primary and complementary)	Limited competition, low controls, scarce homogeneity of cultural institutions (*mature destinations, transition countries*)	Licensing regulations, law enforcement, police controls in central areas, interpretation and welcome centres	Integral management of the cultural system, incentive to start ups, quality labels, virtual access to cultural products, tourism e-commerce
4. Decline in quality → incentive to commuting and disincentive to cultural visits	Sensitiveness to reputation, international attention, prevalence of tour-operated holidays, presence of alternatives in the hinterland (*mature metropolitan destinations, high accessibility*)	Regional–national planning	Reputation policies, promotion, diversification of tourism supply, fidelization, marketing, rejuvenation of products

This case study is significant in that it highlights the prevailing problems that affect many historic cities, and both the political and policy issues that have to be addressed to manage the impacts so that tourism does not destroy its vital resource – the environment.

With the global spread of tourism, the growth in the demand for domestic and international travel is creating an insatiable demand for leisure spending in the new millennium. As new outbound markets such as China and India develop, it will also create a huge increase in the rate of tourism growth in certain regions such as Asia-Pacific. The consequences of such growth, if allowed to develop in an unplanned, unconstrained and unmanaged manner, are clear: a continued negative impact on the environment, people and ecosystems, which will be irreversibly damaged by tourism consumption. Since tourism is a powerful force in many economies, some degree of planned intervention by the public sector, as well as the increasing number of public–private sector partnerships, will be essential in terms of implementing visitor management plans and tools. The example of Venice clearly shows that the excesses of tourism, if unchecked, can quickly destroy the visitor experience, the resource base and the potential for sustainable tourism.

Summary

The impacts of tourism will continue to pose ethical dilemmas for planners and managers. On the one hand governments are seeking to develop more socially inclusive societies, where principles such as 'tourism for all' argue against management measures to limit access to those with the purchasing power. Running counter to such ideological arguments is the recognition that visitor management needs to limit rather than expand access to many tourist sites and resources. The introduction of charging people to enter religious sites such as Canterbury Cathedral is one example that raised many moral issues – in the face of problems caused by unlimited access. The dilemma introduced by pricing as a management tool is that political arguments regarding allowing all members of society to engage in tourism and leisure trips become redundant. Instead a caveat has to be added – participation for all in a defined range of activities and events. Tourism only becomes accessible if people have the disposable income.

Globally, the application of sophisticated management tools used in niche markets such as ecotourism is beginning to permeate other destinations and sites. As Page and Dowling (2002) have noted, soft measures in ecotourism management designed to influence visitor behaviour, in order to mitigate impacts, seek to change user attitudes and behaviour, and even out the distribution of visits between heavily and lightly used sites. An intermediate category of visitor management seeks to lower use levels, by balancing decisions on whether to concentrate or disperse visitors. Lastly, hard measures seek to ration use by controlling tourist numbers – often by the requirement for advance reservations, by different pricing strategies and queuing.

These tools and techniques will begin to gather momentum at many tourist sites and destinations, with the most radical measure – taxing tourists – being seriously considered by destinations under extreme pressure. This tool is really a manager's last resort to control tourism. In an ideal world, Page and Dowling (2002) identify the value of environmental planning for ecotourism that destinations can extend and apply in other locations. Here the principles of identifying discreet planning zones with well defined conservation values, which also accommodation tourist activities and development, require a detailed classification of visitor activity in relation to the need for protection and compatibility with the resource base. This involves identifying types of zones for tourism where ecotourism or environmental issues are critical, such as:

- Sanctuary zones, with special preservation provisions
- Nature conservation zones, where protection and conservation are balanced
- Outdoor recreation zones – natural areas where a wide range of outdoor activities is accommodated
- Tourism development zones, with clusters of tourist activities and attractions/ infrastructure
- Other land uses, to accommodate social and economic activity.

This approach allows tourism management to combine the reduction of environmental impacts with enhancing the visitor experience.

These principles can be modified and refined for application in resorts and urban tourism destinations to achieve a more sustainable, coordinated and rational approach to tourism. In sum, the activities and freedom of tourists will have to be curtailed in the future as resorts, destinations and sites realize that it is imperative to use visitor management tools to implement a sustainable use of resources, and thus maintain a viable and dynamic tourism industry. This will require more innovative thinking, planning and partnerships between stakeholders, and good communication to explain to visitors the rationale and need for such measures. The resolution of conflict, balancing tourism, non-tourism and other interests, will require planners and tourism managers to cooperate in the best interests of the locality in an increasingly competitive marketplace.

References

Economic impacts

Page, S. J. (1995) *Urban Tourism*. London: Routledge.

Page, S. J. and Hall, C. M. (2002) *Managing Urban Tourism*. Harlow: Prentice Hall.

Environmental impacts

Canestrelli, E. and Costa, P. (1991) Tourist carrying capacity: a fuzzy approach. *Annals of Tourism Research*, **18**(2), 295–311.

Dowling, R. (1992) Tourism and environmental integration: the journey from idealism to realism. *In*: C. Cooper and A. Lockwood (eds), *Progress in Tourism, Recreation and Hospitality Management*, Vol. 4, pp. 33–44. Chichester: John Wiley and Sons.

English Tourist Board/Employment Department (1991) *Tourism and the Environment: Maintaining the Balance*. London: English Tourist Board.

Glasson, J., Godfrey, K., Goodey, B. *et al.* (1995) *Towards Visitor Impact Management: Visitor Impacts, Carrying Capacity and Management Responses in Europe's Historic Towns and Cities*. Aldershot: Avebury.

Hall, C. M. (1996) Environmental impact of tourism in the Pacific. *In*: C. M. Hall and S. J. Page (eds), *Tourism in the Pacific: Issues and Cases*, pp. 65–80. London: International Thomson Business Press.

Hall, C. M. and McArthur, S. (1998) *Integrated Heritage Management*. London: The Stationery Office.

Montanari, A. and Muscara (1995). Evaluating tourist flows in historic cities: the case of Venice. *Tijdschrift voor Economische en Sociale Geografie*, **86**(1), 80–87.

Page, S. J. and Dowling, R. (2002) *Ecotourism*. Harlow: Prentice Hall.

Russo, A. (2002) The 'vicious circle' of tourism development in heritage cities. *Annals of Tourism Research*, **29**(1), 165–82.

Van der Borg, J., Costa, P. and Gotti, G. (1996). Tourism in European heritage cities. *Annals of Tourism Research*, **23**(2), 306–21.

Impact analysis

Mathieson, A. and Wall, G. (1982) *Tourism: Economic, Physical and Social Impacts*. Harlow: Longman.

Murphy, P. (1985) *Tourism: A Community Approach*. London: Methuen.

Pearce, D. G. (1989) *Tourism Development*. Harlow: Longman.

Pigram, J. and Jenkins, J. (1999) *Outdoor Recreation Management*. London: Routledge.

Potter, A. (1978) The methodology of impact analysis. *Town and Country Planning*, **46**(9), 400–404.

Social and cultural impacts

Ap, J. and Crompton, J. (1993). Residents' strategies for responding to tourism impacts. *Journal of Travel Research*, **32**(1), 47–50.

Douglas, N. and Douglas, N. (1996) The social and cultural impact of tourism in the Pacific. *In*: C. M. Hall and S. J. Page (eds), *Tourism in the Pacific: Issues and Cases*, pp. 49–64. London: International Thomson Business Press.

Doxey, G. V. (1975) A causation theory of visitor–resident irritants: methodology and research inferences. *In*: *Proceedings of the Travel Research Association 6th Annual Conference*, San Diego, pp. 195–98. Travel Research Association.

Getz, D. (1993) Impacts of tourism on residents' leisure: concepts, and a longitudinal case study of Spey Valley, Scotland. *Journal of Tourism Studies*, **4**(2), 33–44.

Smith, V. (ed.) (1977) *Hosts and Guests: The Anthropology of Tourism*. Philadelphia: University of Pennsylvania Press.

Smith, V. L. (ed.) (1992) *Hosts and Guests: An Anthropology of Tourism*, 2nd edn. Philadelphia: University of Pennsylvannia Press.

Further reading

Schyvens, R. (2002) *Tourism for Development: Empowering Communities*. Harlow: Prentice Hall.

Questions

1 Why does tourism create impacts?

2 How can tourism impacts be managed?

3 In what situations does a tourism manager decide to use 'hard' and 'soft' visitor manager approaches?

4 What would you do, as the Mayor of Venice, to address the problems and potential of tourism?

Chapter

13

The future of tourism: post-tourism?

Learning objectives

This chapter discusses the range of management problems that the tourism industry will have to address in the new millennium. After reading it, you should be able to understand:

- why the tourism industry needs to be proactive in managing its impacts;
- how tourism has developed to a point where it may be uncontrollable (the 'snowball concept');
- what the main drivers of change in the tourism sector will be in the next decade;
- the significance of crises and disasters in tourism for tourism managers.

Introduction

Throughout the book there has been only limited discussion of the way in which the global growth of tourism will change, develop and require new forms of planning and management to control its effects. One of the most pressing questions for planners, decision-makers and businesses is: will tourism stop growing, and will it stop spreading across the globe?

The spread of tourism

Early chapters examined the way in which tourism has evolved from classical times through to the post-war period. One of the enduring themes in the history of travel is the search and pursuit, by individuals, the ruling elite and, latterly, the increasing numbers of leisure travellers, for unique, special and unspoilt locations to visit. The problem, however, has been the reluctance of such places to control tourism to retain these vital unique elements. The result can be described by means of the resort life-cycle concept. In this, the growing demand (popularity) and supply by the tourism sector initially creates a vibrant and dynamic business activity that begins to expand and develop. At this point, planning and policy issues need to be explicitly stated and the future of tourism considered, so that sustainable development is implicit in the future rationale for the destination.

This seemingly logical and phased approach to tourism destination management assumes that tourism will continue to grow, and that the destination can manage and accommodate the effects. Yet the evidence from the post-war period, in terms of tourism development, is that the growth in visitor arrivals has been far from orderly, phased and consistent. This is illustrated by the case of Spain in the 1960s. Mass tourism established itself with few mechanisms in place to control development and growth, and indeed public sector backing for tourism in Spain utilized the foreign exchange and political benefits of international tourism, with little concern for long-term sustainability or environmental protection. Ironically, though not surprisingly, the introduction of a tourist tax in Spanish resorts addresses such concerns in the new millennium, but has had negative impacts on some mass markets (e.g. Germany), where the image of a tourist tax to address environmental degradation has contributed to a decline in visitor arrivals.

It is apparent in the recent growth of tourism that newly discovered destinations, marketed and promoted by tour operators, have witnessed phenomenal growth over and above the annual growth rates of global tourism. This has been compounded in some cases by the opening of new outbound markets, such as South Korea in the 1990s and China in the new millennium.

So *will tourism stop growing*? Some mature destinations that have passed through all the stages of the resort life cycle have probably reached the end of their growth period. The UK coastal resorts in East Kent provide an example. Margate, Ramsgate and Broadstairs reached their heyday in the 1950s and 1960s, before low-cost overseas package holidays became more appealing to domestic tourists. Despite substantial interventions from the public sector (e.g. the local authorities and county council) and funding from the EU, the area has not been able to rejuvenate the resorts successfully, owing to the social and economic deprivation post-tourism.

In contrast, where destinations have been created, re-imaged and re-modelled to generate a new economic sector based on tourism and the cultural industries (such as Glasgow, Bradford, and East London's Docklands area), visitor growth has been significant. Yet it is the coastal resorts created in the 1980s and 1990s across the Mediterranean and Asia-Pacific (e.g. Pattaya in Thailand) that have experienced growth in excess of 10 per cent per annum. Given the time lag involved in a new tourism supply coming on-stream, this has often posed major impacts on local infrastructure, the environment and residents. Likewise, developing countries facing problems of lack of clean water, scarce water supplies for agriculture and a fragile environment have seen inappropriate forms of tourism developed following public policy decisions. One example is the development of golf tourism in South East Asia and Goa, Southern India; golfing greens here require large quantities of water and fertilizers to maintain the greens, resulting in pesticides leaking into the water table, which pollutes the ground water and compromises its drinking quality. So how can this phenomenon of tourism growth be explained?

The snowball and amoeba concepts in tourism

The resort life cycle was used above to explain the linear growth of tourism through a series of stages of development, ending in either stagnation or rejuvenation to stimulate the development process once again. This linear growth is best described as a snowball that begins to gather momentum as it rolls down a hill (Figure 13.1). The agents of change that have the idea of stimulating tourism development as a small snowball (i.e. the public and private sector) do not envisage the rapid transition to mass tourism. Initial visions of tourism are rapidly compromised, despite the best

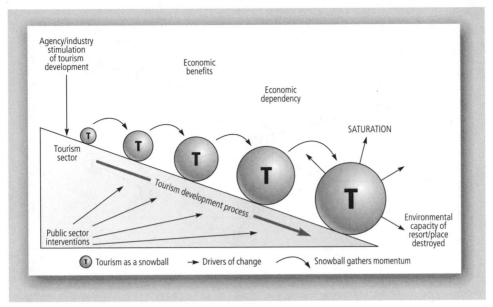

Figure 13.1   Tourism growth and development – snowball concept

intentions of the public sector to control it. The pressure exerted by entrepreneurs, tour operators and other stakeholders takes precedence in the early stages of development. In time these interest groups impact upon policy, and the growing economic dependence upon tourism in the resort adds to further pressure. This is reflected in the snowball gathering momentum, becoming almost unstoppable and out of control. At this stage public sector interventions become less effective and are only able to work around the edge of the problem to try and control the uncontrollable phenomenon, which takes on a prominent role in the resort or locality. Although local antagonism grows, tourism cannot be restricted owing to the inevitable political fallout because of employment issues. Yet as the development process continues, it has the potential to saturate and destroy the destination and its resource base. This means that the destination cannot sustain tourism any longer in that form; it becomes unattractive, over-developed and environmentally compromised (i.e. visual and physical pollution prevail), and images of saturation lead tour operators to using it as a low-cost, mass resort while high-spending visitors seek more attractive locations.

Although this is a gross simplification of the public and private sector roles in tourism development, the basic principles have been replicated across the world. Locations have embraced tourism without really appreciating how complex and

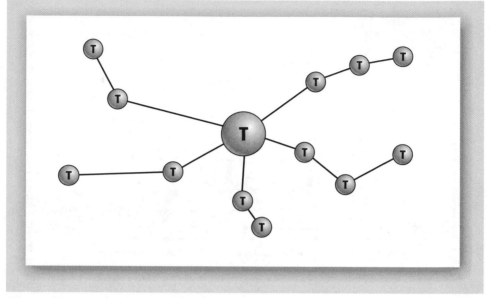

Figure 13.2   The 'amoeba' concept of tourism

powerful it can be – or become – once vested interests begin to drive it forward to reap potentially short-term profits.

Another explanation of the way in which tourism grows and expands might be described as the amoeba effect. The amoeba, as a single-cell life form, has the ability to reproduce itself. Once the initial amoeba is introduced to a locality and finds a welcoming home, it begins to replicate. Tourism is not dissimilar – once an area embraces it as a mechanism to help stimulate economic activity, the process has begun (see Figure 13.2). The ability of tourism to replicate itself and then adapt and change to meet customer needs in certain cases means that, like the amoeba, it keeps producing new entrepreneurs as innovation and change lead to more development. Taking the example of London's tourism accommodation stock, constraints in Central London led to development elsewhere as tourism, like the amoeba, looked for a new niche where it could survive and prosper.

Tourism as a development process makes control, planning and management difficult because the ground rules keep changing as tourism assumes new forms and nurtures new visitors. It is only at the point when the resort or destination reaches total saturation and is destroyed as an attractive location that it moves to a new home and the process begins again. Yet there are positive examples, where public sector interventions to manage tourism seek to prevent further growth, especially at sensitive environmental sites.

So to re-examine the question: will tourism continue to grow? Considering the snowball and amoeba analogies, then there will almost certainly be growth at a global scale. At a national and regional/local level, growth will largely be dependent upon the attractiveness of the locality in providing a conducive location for tourism to root itself and begin developing. The example of tourism and regeneration in Chapter 9 explained how this might occur. The challenge for public and private sector stakeholders is to try to control, direct and, if necessary, constrain tourism to meet local social, environmental, economic and political objectives while ensuring that it does not escalate too quickly and get out of control. Given this assessment of tourism, it is interesting to review briefly the ways in which researchers, analysts and policy-makers consider the future of tourism in different contexts.

Understanding the future of tourism

The highly variable nature of tourism – and particularly its vulnerability to change owing to fashion, trends and shock events such as the terrorist attacks of 11 September 2001 – requires public and private sector interests to try and understand these fluctuations. In particular, it is important to understand how tourism activity, especially trends, is likely to affect countries, localities and places in the short term (up to five years) and long term (up to ten years). To try and envisage how tourism will perform, analysts attempt to forecast the future of tourism. Forecasting in tourism is far from an exact science, owing to the effect of so many unknown factors (e.g. exchange rates, fuel prices, the cost of travel, political stability in the origin and destination areas, and the impact of inflation); however, it is still helpful for planners trying to measure the order of magnitude of potential change that may occur in tourism. This is important in a commercial context to try and match future supply with likely demand (e.g. will an airline need to invest in additional capacity to meet demand?) in order to maximize revenue and profits through the optimum efficiency in resource or asset use. This has been summarized by Archer (1987: 77), in a management context, as:

> . . . no manager can avoid the need for some form of forecasting: a manager must plan for the future in order to minimize the risk of failure or, more optimistically, to maximize the possibilities of success. In order to plan, he must use forecasts.

Forecasts will always be made, whether by guesswork, teamwork or the use of complex models, and the accuracy of the forecasts will affect the quality of the management decision.

In essence, forecasting is about the assessment of future change in the demand for tourism – estimating future traffic, and considering a range of possible scenarios to gauge likely changes in the scale of demand. This invariably involves looking at past tourism trends and using statistics to model future demand, using a variety of models, formulae and developments in the sub-field of economics known as econometrics. In constructing these models, analysts normally build in key tourism variables – such as the number of tourist trips, tourist expenditure, market shares of tourism, and tourism's share of the Gross Domestic Product. The resulting models look at the factors that are likely to have a bearing on demand, to develop the forecasts. For example, the international study by Edwards and Graham (1997) examined the top 30 origin countries and 190 leading tourism destinations, which predicted growth in tourism between 2000 and 2010 of 4.4 per cent per annum, to give up to 964 million trips by 2010 – 75 per cent comprising short- to medium-haul travel, and the remaining long-haul. These forecasts pre-date the events of 11 September 2001, but were more conservative than those undertaken by WTO, illustrating the diversity of predictions. Therefore, when examining any tourism forecast it is important to look at the assumptions and data sources used by the analyst, and what the analyst is intending to produce. However, regardless of forecasts, there will always be pressures for tourism to change.

The pressures for tourism to change

At a global scale, and particularly in the industrialized Western countries, there is evidence that the self-destructive nature of tourism causes some visitors to question where they travel. A greater consciousness of the effects of tourism is now permeating both the consumer and the more environmentally responsible tour operators. This is a slow and gradual process of change, and there is always likely to be a role for the mass-packaged, low-cost, high-volume, sun, sea and sand holidays. However, at the upper end of the market a greater demand for environmentally-sensitive and conservation-oriented niche products may begin to permeate the activities of the tourism sector, as airlines, tour operators and accommodation providers introduce environmental policies to recognize consumer tastes. In explaining the wide range of pressures upon tourism to change, the factors involved can be divided into those that are external to tourism and beyond its control (e.g. exchange rates) and those that are within its grasp.

An ageing travelling public

In many of the Western industrialized countries, tourism markets are becoming characterized by an ageing population. This has been termed the *senior market*, which internationally, exceeds 100 million arrivals (or one in six of all international trips). It is particularly notable in the USA, Europe and Japan, which are major contributors to outbound travel globally. In many European countries, the over-55s now comprise 25 per cent of the total population – although the likelihood of travel statistically reduces with increased age. Senior markets are less seasonal, have high disposable incomes in many cases, and require more attention to their needs. This is reflected in the growth of specialist tour operators such as Saga in the UK and Elderhost in the USA. What is evident is the continued growth in this market and the potential for tourism businesses to adapt to meet the consumers' needs. For example, the revival of coach tourism for long holidays in many parts of Europe reflects one niche product that is particularly favoured by the grey market, since it is perceived as safe and convenient, and meets the travellers' needs.

New social trends

New social trends have emerged over the last decade in developed outbound markets. For example, women are playing a more dominant role in the labour market than twenty years ago, are marrying later and are deferring having children. This leads to more disposable income, and thus there is a lucrative expanding niche market for these 20–40-year-olds.

New outbound markets

In global terms, the rise of the Chinese outbound market and the increase in outbound middle-class travellers in Asia have yet to be fully understood in terms of their impact on tourism trends. Many tourism commentators are watching to see how these markets may create new outbound opportunities, the perceived needs of the market, and their likely global travel patterns, given the international family and kinship ties with all parts of the world. What is certain is that the scale of such markets is huge, and they have the potential to change the nature of international travel patterns dramatically. China has been described as the 'sleeping giant' who is about to awaken. This reflects the importance of political changes, such as allowing outbound and inbound travel, which are notable in shaping future tourism trends.

Crises and disasters in tourism

One of the principal external factors that can affect tourism, and is highly unpredictable for organizations and countries, is a crisis or disaster (man-made and natural). The challenge of coping with such events poses many issues for an organization's ability to adapt to change, and this was illustrated in the foot and mouth crisis in the UK in 2001 (see Box 13.1).

Box 13.1 Foot and mouth in the UK – its impact on tourism

The impact of foot and mouth disease on the UK's tourism industry highlighted its vital role, particularly in the rural economy, with losses of £140 million to £500 million a week in 2001. The English Tourism Council estimates put total losses at £5 billion, resulting from restrictions to rural access and negative images leading overseas visitors to cancel holidays and trips to the UK. Some estimates place the economic impact at between £1 billion and £3.5 billion in lost overseas income for the UK tourism sector.

At the local level this posed many strains on small businesses, as public policy failed to respond quickly to safeguard and develop strategies to assist tourism businesses in rural areas. The closing of the countryside, especially land in public ownership, restrained the rural tourism sector, and compensation payments for agricultural businesses were not considered for rural tourism operators. In April 2001 alone, 80 per cent of businesses in the outdoor recreation sector saw drops in turnover of up to 40 per cent. In the same month, 1000 jobs in rural tourism were lost in Cumbria, directly because of foot and mouth. The crisis highlighted the poor political status of tourism businesses compared to agriculture at a national level, despite a government White Paper on tourism in 2000 that described tourism as a 'key rural industry'. The crisis also raised the question of how businesses and their managers respond to such challenges.

Crises in tourism, and the business response: a management challenge?

Although such crises may be short-term in nature, the exposure of the tourism sector is significant where apparently stable business activities can be transformed into chaos. However, such crises may also have the potential to stimulate innovation (see Chapter 10). Ultimately, the concept of crisis and chaos illustrates that tourism can be highly volatile, and indicates how adaptable organizations need to be. In a management context, Faulkner and Russell (1999) identified the typical modes of operation for entrepreneurs in tourism who instituted chaos and change, and for those who were planners and regulators of change. This has important implications for how tourism ventures are managed. Chaos makers were characterized by being:

- Individualistic
- Flexible
- Innovative
- Experimental
- Intuitive
- Risk-takers.

Regulators were characterized by being:

- Risk-averse
- Rational
- Control-led
- Planners
- Rigid in their outlook
- Concerned with reaching consensus on decision-making.

Therefore, the profitability of tourism organizations is increasingly being linked to the ability to:

- Innovate
- Manage and adapt to change
- Manage, recruit and retain high-quality human resources
- Develop competitive business ventures by understanding the economic, social, political and managerial challenges of operating tourism enterprises

- React to public policy, and influence its formulation and implementation
- Think creatively and globally, with an ability to apply international best practice in a local context
- Understand how tourism trends affect day-to-day business operations.

In order to react to and embrace change, many tourism organizations need to be able to understand and implement technology.

Technology and tourism

Technology is connecting tourism businesses and clients together globally. In tourism environments, the harnessing of technology to achieve entertainment and enhance fun has been widely embraced in the theme park sector. In the USA, the theme park industry generates US$11 billion a year, while globally there are more than 119 large theme parks, each attracting over a million visits a year. Indeed, from a management perspective the creation of man-made tourism environments such as theme parks may fill a niche in the market for accommodating mass tourism without compromising the local environment. Theme parks allow for large numbers to be accommodated, using technology, fantasy, escapism, and a safe, monitored and highly managed experience (as in the Disney model; see Chapter 10). This is certainly a trend that will continue, as continuous improvements and innovation helps these tourism environments to adapt to new consumer tastes and trends.

At an individual business level, information technology is the main driver of change, requiring better management for tourism operations to harness their potential. It provides up-to-date, managed client data, and the scope to search for and select a wide range of products and experiences. Information technology enables forward-looking businesses to respond to the demand for more up-to-date information and tailor-made products. The World Wide Web also allows customers to undertake this process themselves, thus challenging the supply chain and its traditional role in selling tourism products. The rapid growth in the late 1990s in online booking may have stabilized, but it continues to make inroads into traditional travel-agent business. Information technology is now widely adopted in the tourism sector, and innovation is likely to see further developments that will allow tourism products to reach a wider audience. Above all it is making society, and the consumer, more demanding and conscious of getting value for money.

New business trends

Change is rapid in the tourism sector – today's trends are redundant tomorrow. It has gathered momentum since the 1980s as technology has increased the scale, extent and rate of communication across the tourism sector. Information technology has made many tourism businesses scrutinize their operations to assess whether they are operating in an efficient and profitable manner. Greater industry concentration through mergers and acquisitions will certainly continue, premised by perceived economies of scale and efficiency gains. This also reflects competition strategy in the tourism sector, with larger players seeking to dominate certain sectors (e.g. retailing, aviation and tour operation) or adapt integrated operations to raise profitability (e.g. TUI in Europe). This creates a new operating environment in which evolving trends can create recognition of the need to participate in certain products to compete. The announcement in August 2002 that British Midland was replacing its standard airline service from its East Midlands hub with services operated by its bmibaby budget airline was recognition of the need to reduce costs and reorient its business towards an expanding sector of the market.

In an information technology context, recent software launched by RWA – the 'sell it' software package – is also allowing more tour operators to compete for the online market by allowing clients to search by destination, departure point and holiday type. It uses the same technology as MyTravel-owned travel agents in Germany. These tools allow businesses to develop new business strategies and to tailor the products to the client. Canadian research on post-11 September 2001 travel noted that these new trends have seen traveller behaviour changes, including demands for increased evidence of security, more road-based trips, shorter trips and cruises, and a growth in the demand for safer destinations. There have also been more discounted travel offers to stimulate demand.

Furthermore, new business processes, called hypercompetition, are now seen in the fast-growing tourism sector. D'Aveni (1998) characterized hypercompetition in this sector of the tourism industry in terms of:

- Rapid product innovation
- Aggressive competition
- Shorter product life cycles
- Businesses experimenting with meeting customers' needs
- The rising importance of business alliances

- The destruction of norms and rules of national oligopolies, such as the state-owned airlines that still dominate South American and South East Asian aviation.

D'Aveni (1998) identified four processes that are contributing to hypercompetition:

1 The customer demand for better quality at lower prices
2 Rapid technological change, enhanced through the use of information technology
3 The expansion of very aggressive companies who are willing to enter markets for a number of years with a loss-leader product (e.g. low-cost airlines), with a view to destroying the competition so that they will harness the market in the long-term
4 The progressive removal of government barriers towards competition throughout the world.

Hypercompetition changes how competitors enter the marketplace and how they disrupt the existing business:

- By redefining the product market by offering more at a lower price
- By modifying the industry's purpose and focus by bundling and splitting industries
- By disrupting the supply chain by redefining the knowledge and know-how needed to deliver the product to the customer
- By harnessing global resources from alliances and partners to compete with non-aligned business as competition becomes more global.

But given such changes, will tourism be limited by governments in the future – and if so, how?

Limiting tourism: the beginning of the end?

With global concerns for environmental impacts generated by the pollution that tourism causes, environmental management has emerged as a new buzzword for the tourism sector. This has also been embodied in a much larger debate on the ethical issues involved in what forms of tourism government will allow to develop, and how. For example, legal and moral issues surrounding the exploitation caused by sex tourism in many countries have produced a great deal of debate on how tourism fuels such activity. NGOs such as the WTO and End Child Prostitution and Trafficking

(ECPAT) have pursued a campaign since 1996 to eradicate this unacceptable element of tourism. One notable development has been the introduction by the tourism industry of voluntary codes of conduct (see www.world-tourism.org for the WTO view on these codes). This is seen as one attempt by the industry to try and reform some of its bad practices and impacts.

Similar debates are also emerging concerning the impact of air travel and transport on global warming, as illustrated by the 2002 World Summit in South Africa. Global warming highlights the interdependencies that exist between different ecosystems, and man's damaging effects through tourism. If tourism continues to make a major contribution to such environmental problems, then it will become a self-destroying activity. With the awareness of world poverty, tourism as a consumer activity is simply accentuating the socio-economic extremes between the haves and have-nots in society at local, national and international levels, especially in less developed countries with fragile environments.

Proponents of peace have argued that tourism can aid understanding between cultures and societies. Yet Westernized travellers visiting less developed areas simply highlight the poverty and income gap, further fuelling discontent and envy, and, in some cases, crime and political upheaval. Human nature is such that the real impact of tourism and the wealth and consumption of visitors in places with low levels of development can be psychologically and culturally damaging. At the same time, the economic benefits it may bring highlight the tourism conundrum – its internal tension and tendency to be both positive and negative. In this context, policies and public sector management will be required to manage these relationships more forcefully to limit potentially damaging effects.

But should tourism be allowed to spread to all parts of the planet in an uncontrolled or even planned manner?

There is evidence that tourism's growing influence is set to impact on every corner of the globe. Even pristine wilderness areas and very fragile environments such as Antarctica are not immune from the visitor phenomenon. Attempts to license and manage visitors to such pristine environments and charging premium prices have not limited impacts, but rather have simply accentuated the demand for visits. For example, the first recorded overflight of Antarctica was by the Chilean National Airline (Linea Aerea Nacional) in 1957, and the first commercial ship visited in 1958. By 1998, tourism had expanded to 15 000 ship-borne visits per annum concentrated in the November–February period. Some forecasts suggest that this could grow to 20 000 by 2010. There are various policies to limit the development of commercial tourism in Antarctica, such as the 1991 Madrid Protocol, the 1994 Antarctic Treaty Consultative Meeting in Kyoto, and a voluntary code of practice among the Association of Antarctic Tour Operators (formed in 1991). Yet it is patently obvious that tourism has developed: it exists as a business activity, if only in the form of scenic flights and ship-borne visits by Western visitors who are typically prosperous, well educated and professional. This highlights both the amoeba principle and the evolution of the snowball concept. In this case, attempts by those with vested interests (e.g. tour operators) and conservation agencies to limit visits are slowly being eroded, although arguably limitation is in their interest, as restricting supply keeps the prices high.

The tourism industry's pursuit of the next business opportunity has led to even those countries that limited visitors, such as Bhutan, allowing more visitors, in order to gain additional foreign currency. It would appear that tourism knows no bounds, and planning and self-management by industry codes of conduct have only had a superficial effect on visitor damage in sensitive environments. Rather than being phrased in restrictive ways, these need to be phrased positively (e.g. 'Do not dump your rubbish here' might be replaced with 'Please take your litter home to help minimize your impact on the environment'). To the critic, however, this is the industry policing itself – which usually only kicks in when serious problems begin to emerge. For example, in New Zealand such a debate emerged following the aftermath of numerous adventure tourism accidents. The policy debate focused on whether the state should intervene and regulate operators, or whether the industry should be self-regulating through a wider use of codes of conduct. The latter prevailed in a climate of minimal state intervention, as major accidents were covered by a no-fault accident compensation legislation, although there is evidence that legal challenges are now questioning whether this will continue. However, it is time for commentators and researchers to make a stand and pose the following questions in order to engage in a greater debate about tourism:

1 Is there a real need now to make certain parts of the world 'tourism-free'?
2 Should certain pristine areas be kept pristine and free of the vagaries of tourism?
3 Should Antarctica be retained as a natural wilderness?
4 Should nature have some respite from continuous pressures from tourism?

The notions implied in these questions seem to be common sense, as well as making a stance on environmental preservation, but they remain controversial. This is because the very implementation of such a position would limit the personal freedom of the affluent tourist and, more importantly, prevent business from exploiting the tourism potential of an area. However, surely with the introduction of virtual reality these environments can be experienced in more novel ways than in a manner that destroys the resource base? In visionary destinations, tourism revenue has been used to protect and conserve nature and heritage, but these examples are not the norm. One of the problems that has been posed by tourism development in China is the tension caused in areas of environmental potential where there is a demand for economic revenue from large-scale tourism when the area is better suited to small-scale, locally-owned ecotourism developments. Given the scale of demand for domestic and international travel, tourism can only really be described as an uncontrollable process once the basic elements of economic development become established and drive the ideological development of the sector; therefore, where tourism gets out of control it becomes a destructive force.

There is just not enough public debate or academic discussion regarding the justification for halting tourism, or even making a stance and saying – no tourism here, please. This has major political overtones, but in public policy contexts alternative economic development options will be required if tourism is not the solution. It is not necessary to be anti-tourism, but rather to understand realistically what a future committed to tourism means for people, the locality and environment, and to consider the measures to control it.

Summary

Although there is a growing sophistication among travellers, understanding of the link between travel, environmental damage, personal consumption and development remains limited. If tourism is not subjected to greater control in many destinations, self-destruction will lead to post-tourism or to destinations suffering 'tourism trauma', where they are deluged by demand and stretched to a point where they cannot cope effectively with visitors or the demands placed on the resource base. Such a scenario exists in many destinations, which look forward to the shoulder season to allow the area to recover from 'tourist shock' and the local population once again to feel that they are not marginalized and pushed out by the influx of visitors. This is very apparent in many small historic cities in Europe. Post-tourism and tourism trauma should be developed as a new element of the resort life cycle. At this stage, the loss of attractiveness and the damage induced has led to over-development, and the tourist seeks new pastures once the destination is past its 'sell-by' date. Tourism is a free market activity, where price, affordability and appeal remain the determinants of consumer demand. If the destination loses its appeal, it may have an economic crisis to address. As examples in this book have shown, many destinations have never recovered from their tourism heydays and the redundancy that is now apparent in many former coastal resorts is a permanent reminder of what happens when the resort cycle hits decline. Therefore, striking the right balance between development, sustainable use, and destination or tourist appeal is a dynamic element that needs constant review, given the ability of tourism to change rapidly. This is why an understanding of tourism, how to manage it and how to take action quickly when things go wrong are fundamental to a healthy, prosperous and enriching tourism environment for all stakeholders.

The new millennium will clearly be a very testing time for tourism. The challenge for the tourism sector, policy makers and governments is to ask a number of very fundamental questions:

1 Why do we want tourism?
2 What does it mean for our locality or country?
3 How will it impact upon our society?
4 How will it be managed to make a win–win situation for all stakeholders?

In countries with a substantial indigenous population with ancient rights over tourism resources, this also poses a further dimension to the public policy-making process on the future of tourism in a locality or destination. In Australia, New Zealand, the Pacific Islands and many parts of Asia, the indigenous people are an integral part of the cultural tourism product. Sensitivity to and accommodation of their needs is also assuming a higher priority for many governments that have belatedly recognized how integral these groups of people are to the tourism industry. If integrated and managed in a sensitive manner, such cultural diversity can actually provide destinations with a competitive edge by offering a unique and memorable element in the tourist experience. If managed badly, it can destroy any tourism development potential.

Ultimately, many destinations and businesses will seek to develop a 'sustainable tourism industry' – it is good for the marketing of the destination and for businesses, and may appeal to the environmentally conscious traveller. For very sensitive environments the best form of tourism may be no tourism, unless the benefits are reinvested in protection and preservation – such as in some of Africa's game reserves. Arguably the best way to manage mass tourism is to let it concentrate in purpose-built man-made developments, many of which have already degraded the environment and are now taking measures to improve their impact and image. From a planning perspective it keeps the destructive effects of tourism in one place, but it does limit the economic benefits to the wider population. Some countries are seeking to appeal to a specific type of market and are not looking for large numbers of tourists, but all too often the efforts of industry supersede such plans because ultimately tourism remains a free market activity with few major constraints on incremental growth. Limits are the exception rather than the rule.

There is no doubt that tourism is a dynamic industry. However, the use of the latest buzzwords and jargon to appeal to tourists can only be judged by actions: Can tourism really be developed in a way in which profits and demand are balanced by the long-term needs of the environment and people it affects? That is the challenge for tourism.

References

Archer, B. (1987) Demand forecasting and estimation, In J. R. B. Ritchie and C. R. Goeldner (eds) *Travel, Tourism and Hospitality Research*. New York: Wiley, pp. 77–85.

D'Aveni, R. (1988) Hypercompetition closes in. *Financial Times*, 4 February (Global Business Section).

Edwards, A. and Graham, A. (1997) *International Tourism Forecasts to 2010*, London: Travel and Tourism Intelligence.

Faulkner, B. and Russell, R. (1997) Chaos and complexity in tourism: in search of a new perspective. *Pacific Tourism Review*, 1(2), 93–102.

Questions

1 What are crises in tourism, and how should individual businesses respond to them?

2 What is the future growth potential of tourism in relation to the earth's resource base?

3 What are the principal management problems facing tourism managers in the new millennium?

4 How would you develop an action plan for managing tourism in a destination area you know or have recently visited? Would you need to take radical action to limit or prohibit tourists?

Index

North America, 15, 17, 62, 67, 68, 69, 83,
    84, 88, 107, 123, 125, 176, 177, 193,
    198, 215
  Great Lakes, 107
Northern Ireland, 179, 289, 301
Northern Ireland Tourist Board (NITB),
    303
North Pacific, 44
North Sea, 126
Norway, 83, 87, 123
Nuclear tourism, 65

Oceania (*see also entries for individual
    countries*), 43, 45
Oktoberfest (Germany), 169
Olympic games, 27, 85, 321
OMNIMAX, 244
One World Global Alliance, 159, 160
'Open skies' policy (*see* Airlines –
    deregulation)
Organization for Economic Co-operation
    and Development (OECD), 17, 317
Orient Express, 90, 121
Outbound travel/tourism, 43, 65, 66–70,
    88, 192, 193, 199, 351–2

Pacific (*see also* North Pacific), 19
Pacific Islands, 82, 125, 279, 320, 323–5
  Environmental impacts of tourism,
    323–6
  Tuvalu, 320
Package holidays/tours, 26, 36, 41, 42,
    43, 47, 57, 66, 69, 80, 82, 93, 94, 99,
    109, 112, 115, 122, 181, 185, 186, 187,
    189, 190, 191, 192, 194, 199, 201, 202,
    204, 207–9, 216, 346
  EU Directive on Package Travel, 202,
    205
Paid holidays, 40, 61
Paris Convention (1919), 148
Partnerships, 91, 103, 122, 128, 129, 244,
    296, 297, 301, 303
  public-private, 220, 293, 301, 303, 340
Pearce's Leisure Ladder, 59
Perceptions, 53, 65, 100, 258

Philippines, 216
Planning acts, 40, 271, 293
Planning for tourism, 12, 40, 91, 110, 128,
    179, 189, 282, 283, 286, 290, 291–5, 303,
    304, 307, 311, 318, 325, 341, 348, 361
  boosterism approach, 292
  community-oriented approach, 292
  economic industry approach, 292
  existence of, 292–3
  integration, 293
  physical-spatial approach, 292
  process, 293–5
  sustainable approach, 292
Plog's psychographic traveller types, 58,
    62
Poland, 193
Political stability/unrest, 27, 44, 144, 277,
    314, 349
Pollution (*see also* Impacts and
    environmental issues), 107, 109, 279,
    324–6
Ports, 105, 120, 128
Portugal/Portuguese, 83, 115, 121, 167
Potter's impact of tourism framework, 313
Pricing strategies/structures, 42, 76–7,
    107, 108, 152, 190, 194, 197, 199, 200,
    202, 231, 285, 357
Private sector, 34, 81, 91–2, 102, 103, 129,
    136, 137, 220, 221, 241, 249, 273, 277,
    280, 281, 286, 292, 294, 295, 297, 301,
    303, 346–7, 349
Privatization, 77, 103, 135, 137, 138, 140,
    145, 146, 150
Product Life Cycle (PLC), 236–8, 244, 355
Psychographic segmentation, 58, 62–3,
    262
Psychology/psychologists, 50, 52, 57, 70,
    213
Public consultation, 92, 140, 294, 295
Public sector, 32, 81, 91, 114, 129, 136,
    137, 179, 220, 221, 238, 241, 244, 246,
    249, 274, 276–304, 318, 322, 340, 345,
    346–7, 349, 357
  government intervention, 278–9
  marketing of tourism, 299–303